Research Series on the Chinese Dream and China's Development Path

Drawing on a large body of empirical studies done over the last two decades, this Series provides its readers with in-depth analyses of the past and present and forecasts for the future course of China's development. It contains the latest research results made by members of the Chinese Academy of Social Sciences. This series is an invaluable companion to every researcher who is trying to gain a deeper understanding of the development model, path and experience unique to China. Thanks to the adoption of Socialism with Chinese characteristics, and the implementation of comprehensive reform and opening-up, China has made tremendous achievements in areas such as political reform, economic development, and social construction, and is making great strides towards the realization of the Chinese dream of national rejuvenation. In addition to presenting a detailed account of many of these achievements, the authors also discuss what lessons other countries can learn from China's experience.

More information about this series at http://www.springer.com/series/13571

Cuiping Zhu
Editor

Annual Report on the Development of the Indian Ocean Region (2018)

Indo-Pacific: Concept Definition and Strategic Implementation

SSAP

Springer

Editor
Cuiping Zhu
Research Institute for Indian Ocean
Economies
Yunnan University of Finance
and Economics
Kunming, Yunnan, China

ISSN 2363-6866 ISSN 2363-6874 (electronic)
Research Series on the Chinese Dream and China's Development Path
ISBN 978-981-13-7692-4 ISBN 978-981-13-7693-1 (eBook)
https://doi.org/10.1007/978-981-13-7693-1

Jointly published with Social Sciences Academic Press, Beijing, China
The print edition is not for sale in China Mainland. Customers from China Mainland please order the print book from: Social Sciences Academic Press.

This Springer imprint is published by the registered company Springer Nature Singapore Pte Ltd.
The registered company address is: 152 Beach Road, #21-01/04 Gateway East, Singapore 189721, Singapore

Series Preface

Since China's reform and opening began in 1978, the country has come a long way on the path of socialism with Chinese characteristics, under the leadership of the Communist Party of China. Over thirty years of reform, efforts and sustained spectacular economic growth have turned China into the world's second-largest economy and wrought many profound changes in the Chinese society. These historically significant developments have been garnering increasing attention from scholars, governments, and the general public alike around the world since the 1990s, when the newest wave of China studies began to gather steam. Some of the hottest topics have included the so-called China miracle, Chinese phenomenon, Chinese experience, Chinese path, and the Chinese model. Homegrown researchers have soon followed suit. Already hugely productive, this vibrant field is putting out a large number of books each year, with Social Sciences Academic Press alone having published hundreds of titles on a wide range of subjects.

Because most of these books have been written and published in Chinese; however, readership has been limited outside China—even among many who study Chinese—for whom English is still the lingua franca. This language barrier has been an impediment to efforts by academia, business communities, and policy-makers in other countries to form a thorough understanding of contemporary China, of what is distinct about China's past and present may mean not only for her future but also for the future of the world. The need to remove such an impediment is both real and urgent, and the *Research Series on the Chinese Dream and China's Development Path* is my answer to the call.

This series features some of the most notable achievements from the last 20 years by scholars in China in a variety of research topics related to reform and opening. They include both theoretical explorations and empirical studies and cover economy, society, politics, law, culture, and ecology—the six areas in which reform and opening policies have had the deepest impact and farthest reaching consequences for the country. The authors for the series have also tried to articulate their visions of the "Chinese Dream" and how the country can realize it in these fields and beyond.

All of the editors and authors for the *Research Series on the Chinese Dream and China's Development Path* are both longtime students of reform and opening and recognized authorities in their respective academic fields. Their credentials and expertise lend credibility to these books, each of which has been subjected to a rigorous peer review process for inclusion in the series. As part of the Reform and Development Program under the State Administration of Press, Publication, Radio, Film and Television of the People's Republic of China, the series is published by Springer, a Germany-based academic publisher of international repute, and distributed overseas. I am confident that it will help fill a lacuna in studies of China in the era of reform and opening.

Xie Shouguang

Contents

Part I
General Report

The Strategic Game in Indo-Pacific Region and Its Impact on China's Security

Cuiping Zhu

Abstract Recently, the term of "Indo-Pacific" has often been mentioned by US, Japan, Australia as well as India. The Trump administration's strategy for advancing a free and open Indo-Pacific, which aims to place multiple big powers or middle powers in the Great Chessboard of "Indo-Pacific" to cope with the rise of China and form a balance among major powers under the American hegemony. It can be said that the "Indo-Pacific" strategy is a continuation of "Asia-Pacific Rebalancing" and a new containment against China in the Indo-Pacific Region. It seems that China is excluded from the strategic system, but in fact it is not only involved, but also the main target of the "Indo-Pacific" strategic conception. The core region of this strategy includes the West Pacific and Bay of Bengal in the East Indian Ocean. The main intention of the US is to make India, Japan and Australia as the strategic strongholds, especially by taking the strategic advantage of India in the East Indian Ocean to exert pressure on the Western Pacific and squeeze China's strategic space. In this strategic dynamics, China will not only inevitably be facing some pressures brought by the "hegemonic threat" in this region, but will also suffer a negative impact on China's promotion of economic integration here, as well as the security order in the region. Although the "Indo-Pacific" strategy is at the conception stage, or more of a "strategic deterrent", and there is still a lot of uncertainty in whether it can be implemented in the future, but the strategic game caused by the US's regarding China as a competitor will continue. Based on this, China should regard the Pacific and Indian Ocean areas as a whole from the perspective of geo-economics and make plan in combination with the "Belt and Road". China can take the advantages of its geo-economic advantages to explore positive factors in the "Indo-Pacific" geo-economy, accelerate the integration of the economies of the Indian Ocean and the Pacific regions and resolve the "security dilemma" in geopolitics with geo-economy

Zhu Cuiping, professor, Deputy director, Research Institute for Indian Ocean Economies(RIIO), Yunnan University of Finance and Economics; Her research fields include Indian Ocean strategy, South Asia issues and Sino-Indian relations.

C. Zhu (✉)
Research Institute for Indian Ocean Economies (RIIO), Yunnan University of Finance and Economics, Kunming, China

C. Zhu (ed.), *Annual Report on the Development of the Indian Ocean Region (2018)*, Research Series on the Chinese Dream and China's Development Path, https://doi.org/10.1007/978-981-13-7693-1_1

as a breakthrough. China can create and utilize opportunities for cooperation with the countries in this region and appropriately expand the maritime rights and strategic space to serve the construction of "Belt and Road", especially the 21st Maritime Silk Road.

Keywords "Indo-Pacific" · Hegemonic threat · Belt and Road Initiative · Security order

The concept of "Indo-Pacific" has existed for a long time as a marine geography or geographic space concept. In the 1920s, Karl Ernst Haushofer, a German geopolitical scholar, put forward the concept of "Indo-Pacific Region/Space", making it a concept having geopolitical significance. In the 1960s, the term "Indo-Pacific" has been used successively by Australian scholars in regional security research. Australia, as a middle power, is located at the crossroads of the Indian Ocean and the Pacific Ocean. Once two oceans are regarded as a strategic entirety, Australia, the unique geographical advantage, can no doubt bring natural geopolitical advantages and its value to the global strategy of the US is self-evident. Since 2005, the term "Indo-Pacific" has frequently appeared in academic discussions and government documents in Australia. In particular, the *Australian National Defense White Paper* released in May 2013 proposed the "Indo-Pacific Strategy Arc", symbolizing that this concept has been fully recognized by the strategic community. The "Stable Peripheral Area" mentioned in the white paper is defined as the Indo-Pacific region, and the white paper regards Indo-Pacific region as one of the four strategic interests of Australia. However, Australia prefers that this region shall be developed in an inclusive way.[1] Meanwhile, Japan is quite in favor of the concept of "Indo-Pacific". In 2007, Abe, during his first term as Prime Minister of Japan, proposed the initiative of establishing the "G4" to counter against China, including the US, Japan, India and Australia. After re-elected as Prime Minister in 2012, Abe continued to hype the so-called "Democratic Security Diamond" strategy composed by the US, Japan, India and Australia, and played up the strategy of "free and open Indo-Pacific" that connects Asia-Pacific, the India Ocean and Pacific Ocean. But the hype failed to have much effect. Compared with Japan and Australia, India's attitude towards the concept of "Indo-Pacific" is more complicated. In the long run, the mainstream ideology in India is to try to establish an exclusive order in the Indian Ocean, but this shall start from preventing China from participating in the Indian Ocean affairs, disregarding whether it has corresponding ability. The "Indo-Pacific" strategy with the US, Japan, India and Australia as the core is conducive to transforming India's unique geographical advantages in the Indian Ocean into geo-advantages, which also coincides with India's "Act East" policy and the strategic appeal to prevent China from entering the Indian Ocean.

Although Japan, India and Australia have actively rendered the strategic conception of "Indo-Pacific" to different degrees, without the attention and fueling of the US, the strategy is hard to have real effect. Compared with the Obama' administration, the Trump' administration not only regards China as the primary strategic

[1] Taylor (2014).

concern of the Indo-Pacific region, but also clearly points out that China is a strategic competitor of the US. It may be just the "old wine in old bottles"[2] for the Unites States to hype the concept of the "Indo-Pacific" again, more out of "strategic flickering",[3] which is "like a bubble, gone with a poke."[4] This paper believes that even though the "Indo-Pacific" in the Trump administration is more of a conception hype, it is necessary to pay attention to the negative impact of this strategic thinking on the security situation of China and its neighboring areas. Based on the fact that the US is almost the leader in the "Indo-Pacific" strategy, and the important influence of the US-Indian interaction on the strategic direction of the "Indo-Pacific" strategy, this paper will focus on the main considerations and limitations of the US "Indo-Pacific" strategy, the US, India, Japan and Australia, in particular, the impact of the strategy and security interactions between the US, India, Japan and Australia, especially between the US and India on China and China's strategic measures to maintain the security in the Indo-Pacific region.

1 Change of the Connotation of the "Indo-Pacific" Concept and Its Characteristics

In regard to "Indo-Pacific", many domestic scholars have researched from multiple perspectives.[5] Although there are differences in the construction of "Indo-Pacific" concept and the recognition of the importance of this concept between the US, Japan, India and Australia, changes of this concept have five main characteristics from the definition of the concept by existing research, the hype from the academic circle and government of the US, Japan, India and Australia.

First, difference in the definition of the geographical scope of the "Indo-Pacific" concept. As to the definition of "Indo-Pacific" in the academic circle, there are differences in broad and narrow senses in extension, and in concept, conception and strategy in connotation. In a broad sense, Indo-Pacific consists of the area from the entire Indian Ocean to South Asia, Southeast Asia and Pacific in the east (Rumley et al. 2012). From the perspective of geopolitical integration, it contains the vast area of the Indian Ocean and the Western Pacific. Beijing and New Delhi will play important roles in this region (Raja Mohan 2013). The concept discussed currently by governments and strategic circles of the US, India, Japan, and Australia, mainly refers to the vast sea area and its coastal shelves from the western Pacific to the western Indian Ocean, or to be exact from 140° east longitude to 60° east longitude, to

---

[2]Zhao (2017).

[3]Li Anfang: *From "Asia-Pacific" to "Indo-Pacific", Which Four Sticker Does the United States Lack of for Its "Strategic Flickering?* http://www.shobserver.com/news/detail?id=71243.

[4]Jin (2017).

[5]For related studies, see: Rong (2017, pp. 48–61), Xia (2015a, pp. 32–51), Wei (2013, pp. 140–160), Cao (2014), Lin (2018a), Zhu (2014a, pp. 40–65); Zhu (2016), Zhang (2013), Wu (2014), Zhao (2013), Xu (2017), Chen (2015), Wang (2016a, pp. 49–60).

southern Indian Ocean in the south and coastal countries in the north.[6] Some scholars believe that the core of the "Indo-Pacific" concept is that the US on the east coast of the Pacific, India to the north of the Indian Ocean and Australia between the Indian Ocean and the Pacific play important strategic roles in the this region.[7] In the hot discussion on the concept of "Indo-Pacific" during the Obama administration, some scholars even believe that the world has entered the "India-Pacific" century (Medcalf 2012). As a geographical concept, this paper argues that, "Indo-Pacific" refers to the vast regions of the Pacific Ocean and the Indian Ocean in general; as a geo-concept, it refers specifically to the vast waters of the Western Pacific and the entire Indian Ocean region; as a strategy that Trump administration takes to balance China's rise, it refers to the Western Pacific and East Indian Ocean regions. The strategic focus is the South China Sea in the Western Pacific and the Bay of Bengal in the Northeast Indian Ocean. Moreover, as a strategic concept, "Indo-Pacific" emphasizes the constraints of the strategic stronghold of Japan, Australia and India, especially the role of India.

Second, there is flexibility in the connotation of the "Indo-Pacific" concept. As a concept with a clear geopolitical connotation, it rarely shows clear links and rough basic consensus. The ambiguity of the concept provides the possibility for the concept creator and definer to maintain power, display power, and gain power.[8] That is to say, as a concept with geostrategic significance, there is flexibility in defining the connotation, which not only reserves the imagination space for power game and strategic extension. The disputes of the academic circle on whether the intensification of "Indo-Pacific" has only stayed at the level of concept or risen to the strategic level during the Trump era mainly come from the hype of "Indo-Pacific" during the Obama administration. It is worth mentioning that in 2010, Obama, senior officials of the US Department of State and the Department of Defense repeatedly used the concept of "Indo-Pacific" in their speeches. The main contents involved were: strengthening cooperation with the Indian Navy and making the Indian Navy the manager of the India Ocean-Pacific Ocean Passage (including the South China Sea, the Straits of Malacca and the broader Pacific Ocean); strengthening the US-India policy stance coordination on East Asian maritime security issues; and making Australia's northwestern coastline a power projection point facing West Pacific Ocean and East Indian Ocean of the US in the Indo-Pacific region.[9] In January 2012, the US re-emphasized the significance of the Indian Ocean to the US global strategy in its defense strategy report of *Maintaining US Global Leadership: Priorities of Defense in the 21st Century*: "The economic and security interests of the US are closely related to the development of West Pacific and East Asia to the Indian Ocean and South Asia. This has brought increasingly serious challenges, as well as a lot of opportunities to the US."[10] The US emphasizes the importance of "Indo-Pacific" strategy to its global strategy. Although there's certain exaggeration, there's credible "real" threat,

---

[6]Mcdaniel (2012), Quoted from Wei (2013, p. 141).

[7]Jin (2013).

[8]Lin (2018b).

[9]Chen (2012a).

[10]American Department of Defense (2012).

including the reaching of the agreement on military base sharing between the US and India, which can at least be regarded as a significant achievement of the "Indo-Pacific" strategy during the Obama administration.

Third, the strategic intent for the construction of "Indo-Pacific" concept is relatively clear. Since 2010, the four countries of the US, Japan, India and Australia have not only hyped the concept of "Indo-Pacific", but also placed the strategic conception and cooperation proposals under the framework of "Indo-Pacific" in bilateral and trilateral dialogues. Therefore, it's unquestionable that this strategy is created against China. The Obama administration rendered the "Indo-Pacific" strategy to promote its "Asia-Pacific Rebalancing" strategy as the "Indo-Pacific" strategy is actually one of the important components of the "Asia-Pacific Rebalancing" strategy.[11] Compared with the relatively mild "contact + contain" of the "Returning to Asia-Pacific" strategy during the Obama administration, the Trump administration has identified China as a strategic competitor and intends to upgrade the "Indo-Pacific strategy", indicating that the US will focus more on India's "strategic function" in balancing China's rising influence and India's role in creating a new power landscape in this region and reshaping regional security order under hegemonic support. And the US intends to construct the Indo-Pacific security network led by the US through the US-India-Japan-Australian alliance system. Even it has not been formed or is only the "re-popularization" of concept again, it has chance to be popular repeatedly. In fact, the US has already made some deployment. Moreover, the Trump administration has not concealed its strategic intention to counterbalance China by making use of India and with the India, Japan and Australia as strategic strongholds when it hyped the concept of "Indo-Pacific". India is an important part of its strategic deployment of the "Indo-Pacific", which attributes to the significance of the Indian Ocean to India and the increasingly important strategic position of India and the India Ocean in the global strategy of the US. Meanwhile, the US, as the leader, not only intends to leverage Japan, India and Australia, but also will regard Singapore, Vietnam and Indonesia as important assistants. While balancing China, it will further build a credible "China threat" to stir up the security situation in the region, then achieve its economic goals of selling arms and the strategic goals of consolidating hegemony.

Fourth, hotness of "Indo-Pacific" concept once again attributes to the US promotion. Although the concept has been mentioned or used by India, Japan and Australia on different occasions and in different ways, it's the influence of American that makes the "Indo-Pacific" a "hot word". That is to say, the real popularity of the concept originated from the promotion and hype of senior American officials on different occasions in 2010, making it a "new geopolitical concept". It not only became a hot word used by the media of the four countries, but also has frequently appeared in the speeches and academic research of the elites and political circles. In 2010, Hillary Clinton, the US Secretary of State, delivered an address of *The US Presence in the Asia-Pacific Region* in Hawaii, emphasizing "that the US was readjusting the strategic deployment in the Indo-Pacific region and strengthening the cooperation with the Indian Navy in the Pacific region". At the same time, the article

[11] Xia (2015a, p. 35).

in the *Diplomatic Journal* pointed out that the "Asia-Pacific region has become a key driver of global politics. The region extends from the Indian subcontinent to the west coast of the US, covering the Pacific Ocean and the Indian Ocean, and is increasingly linked owing to the transportation and strategic factors". Later, many senior US officials, including the military commander-in-chief in Pacific Samuel Locklear and Vice President Joe Biden have emphasized the strategic importance of "Indo-Pacific" to the US on different occasions. This is not only because China became the world's second largest economy surpassing Japan in 2010, but also that the rise of emerging market countries represented by China and India, and the huge potential of trade, investment and energy supply in this region, as well as the strategic consideration of the US in maintaining its hegemonic position in the world and the influence in the Indo-Pacific region.[12]

The new round of "Indo-Pacific" strategy proposed by the Trump administration seems to be "old wine in new bottles". From the perspective of strategic intent, it can also be regarded as a continuation of the "Indo-Pacific" concept in the Obama administration or the extension of "Asia-Pacific Rebalancing". What different is that, in terms of the connotation of conceptual construction and the strategic interaction of various actors, compared with the importance of marine security and anti-terrorism to the cooperation of four countries in the Obama administration, the target of the "Indo-Pacific" strategy for the four countries, especially the US is more clear, and the offensive posture is also very obvious in the Trump administration. The attitude is not only tougher but even more hostile. The strategic goals and intents of the new "Indo-Pacific" strategy are clearer. In addition to the economic interests, it pays more attention to the balance role of India and does not hide its intentions against China at all. In early November 2017, US President Trump announced that the "Indo-Pacific Strategy" will become the Asia-Pacific strategy of the new US government during his trip in East Asia. Later, the Trump administration has successively launched three strategic documents, including: *National Security Strategy*, *National Defense Strategy*, and *Nuclear Posture Review*. These reports have specified the US strategies and policies from the perspectives of overall national security, national defense and nuclear, and provided guidance and support for the implementation of the "Indo-Pacific Strategy."[13] On December 18, 2017, the US government issued the *US National Security Strategy Report*. It pointed out that China's "aggression" against the US economy and "unfair trade" between China and the US has already threatened the economic security of the US. At the same time, China and Russia are scrambling the geopolitical advantage of the US and trying to change the international order in a direction that benefits them.[14] Therefore, the US clearly positioned China as a strategic competitor and regarded China as "revisionist force" and "economic

---

[12]Zhu (2014a).

[13]*Trump Has Issued Three Hit Reports and Stepped up the Implementation of the "Indo-Pacific" Strategy*, *China Youth Daily*, February 24, 2018, http://news.ifeng.com/a/20180224/56231054_0.shtml.

[14]The full text of the *US National Security Strategy Report* both in English and Chinese, http://www.sohu.com/a/213628403_120790.

aggressor" in the report. It intends to compulsorily overturn the ongoing international rules that are not in the interest of the US and further reshape the benefit distribution rules and order that benefit the US in order to regain the priority through the alliance system built under the "Indo-Pacific" strategy. It can be said that the concept of "Indo-Pacific" is a kind of "strategic deterrence" constructed by US, India, Japan and Australia under the leadership of the US with a goal to counterbalance the rise of China. It is not only conducive to building up allies and cultivating a multilevel strategic alliance and a strategic partnership network led by the US to prevent the appearance of a country that can compete with US power. It treated the Indian Ocean and the Pacific Ocean as a unified strategic unit, which is good to rebuild a balanced Asia-Pacific power landscape dominated by US hegemony.

Fifth, the Indo-Pacific strategy emphasizes the role of India. Besides trumpeting to change 50% of the warships in the Pacific Ocean and the Atlantic Ocean to 60% in the Pacific Ocean and 40% in the Atlantic Ocean, the "Asia-Pacific Rebalancing" strategy's another strategic measure is to emphasize and value the role of India. As Hillary said, "The US will bet on the future of India and believe that India's opening up to the world will contribute to the prosperity of India and the whole South Asia, and such prosperity will extend to central Asia and a wider region outside Asia Pacific."[15] During the Obama administration, the US and India have got obvious achievements in deepening defense and security cooperation, including: *US-India Joint Strategic Vision for the Asia-Pacific and Indian Ocean Region* jointly issued by the two countries in January 2015; *The Logistics Support Agreement* officially signed by the US and India in Washington in June 2016, which allows the two countries to share military bases for logistics operations. For Washington, a major concern is strengthened China-India cooperation, which will speed up the decline of its hegemony. Therefore, compared with the "contact + contain" policy to China, the US regards India, whose strength is rising and its geographical advantage is prominent, as its important strategic partner to contain China in the Asia-Pacific region. It hopes to contain China by wooing and utilizing India and finally get the effect of "The wolf has a winning game when the shepherds quarrel".[16] After Trump entered office, besides emphasizing the principles of "US priority" and "US interests first", he also realized that deepening defense and security cooperation with India can bring tangible benefits to the US. After all, the US is the world's largest arms exporter, and India is the world's largest importer. According to a report released by the Stockholm International Peace Research Institute in Sweden, global arms deals have risen to the highest level since the Cold War in the last five years (2012–2016). India has become the world's largest buyer with arms imports accounting for 13% of the global total.[17] In recent years, the arms exports of the US to India have been rising year by year.

---

[15]Hillary R. Clinton, "Remarks on India and the United States: Vision for the 21st Century", http://www.scoop.co.nz/stories/WO1107/S00450/remarks-on-india-and-the-united-statesvision-for-the-21st-c.htm.

[16]Zhu (2013, p. 8).

[17]India Has Become the Largest Arms Buyer, http://news.163.com/17/0318/14/CFQL7SGV00014AED.html.

The US has been exporting high-end weapons to India, to continuously squeeze Russia's share in India's weaponry market. In other words, the "Indo-Pacific" strategy of the US can not only be used to check and balance China, but also escalate the arms race by creating security threats, thereby achieving the goal of selling more arms to the Indo-Pacific region and gaining more benefits. Meanwhile, developing defense and security cooperation under the "Indo-Pacific" concept can not only get economic interests, but also meet the common strategic appeal of coping with the rise of China. After Trump took office, the close relationship between the US and Indian continued, and India has been still identified as the "major defense partner" of the US. Therefore, no matter the hype of "Indo-Pacific" concept in 2010 in the Obama administration, or the rendering of this concept by Trump administration, its core goal is to highlight the role of India and use India's power to check and balance China, as well as gaining economic interests.

From the above analysis, we can see "Indo-Pacific" is not only the construction of a concept, but more of the construction of "strategic deterrent". Moreover, the geopolitical goal of the strategic deterrent is also very clear. From this perspective, the "Indo-Pacific", a geographical and spatial concept, has developed into a strategic area. Not only the US but also the strategic stronghold countries of India, Japan and Australia all agree with the geographical importance of "Indo-Pacific". As a constructed geopolitical concept, it has the dual connotation of strategy and security. Moreover, the US has made the hegemony maintenance its own responsibility and treated China as a potential threat to US hegemony and a strategic competitor. The "Indo-Pacific" concept can never "go with the wind" in any case, and the threats and negative effects caused by the strategy cannot be ignored. If this concept has been continuously hyped, it will inevitably pose a huge challenge to China's peripheral security by creating various "insecurities", which will also inevitably aggravate the geopolitical tensions in this region and undermine the marine security order and the regional security landscape, impeding the advance of the "Belt and Road" towards the Indian Ocean.

Therefore, we need not to overestimate the influence of the "Indo-Pacific strategy" led by the US, but we also need to take precautions and pay due attention to the complicated impact of the strategy on the Taiwan Strait, the South China Sea and the East China Sea, the devastating impact on the construction of the 21st Century Maritime Silk Road in South Asia and Southeast Asia and the challenges to China's peripheral security. As the leader and the main promoter of the "Indo-Pacific" concept, the US has combined the Indian Ocean and the Pacific Ocean as a unified strategic unit to maintain its hegemony.

2 The Intention and Important Consideration of the US "Indo-Pacific" Strategic Conception

The geo-strategy of the US has always been in a dynamic adjustment. Although the current "Indo-Pacific" strategy is still in the concept stage, more of a "strategic deterrent". There is still very big uncertainty about whether or not it can be implemented in future. However, the Sino-US strategic game caused by the US's regarding China as strategic competitor will continue. As Brzezinski said, "It is absolutely necessary not to have a power which can rule the Eurasian continent and thus challenge the US."[18] Although the US still has absolute control over the Indian Ocean and the Pacific Ocean, the relative decline of the economic power and hegemony make the strategic community of the US full of anxiety that the rising China will challenge its world hegemony. The strategic goals of the two successive administrations of the US are exactly the same. If the "Indo-Pacific" concept during the Obama administration is more on a whim; the "Indo-Pacific" strategy of the Trump administration is the inheritance and development of the "Asia-Pacific Rebalancing" strategy. It's also a new check and balance strategy that the US has adopted to balance China's influence by making planning for the Indian Ocean and the Pacific Ocean region as a whole. As the "leader", although the US is not the only promoter of the "Indo-Pacific" strategy, it is undoubtedly the leading country that determines the future trend of the strategy.

The "Indo-Pacific" strategic conception geographically refers to the vast seas of the Indian Ocean and the Pacific Ocean, but the core areas that the US focuses on are the Western Pacific Ocean and the East Indian Ocean. Centering on this core area, the main intentions of the US strategic conception include: **First, establish strategic strongholds in India Ocean and the Pacific Ocean**. The US, Japan, India and Australia have the willingness and common needs to strengthen defense and security cooperation in the Indian Ocean-Pacific region. The main strategic intention of the US is to select three strategic strongholds in the East (India), the West (Japan) and the South (Australia), to balance the rising regional influence of China from three directions, finally preventing the appearing of another country that can compete with the US; **Second, play the role of India**. The US hopes that India will play the role of a "quasi-ally" and takes the India's strategic advantage in the East Indian Ocean to exert pressure on the western Pacific, especially by putting more military forces into the Bay of Bengal to squeeze China's strategic space and put pressure on the South China Sea issue to check and balance the rise of China. At the same time, the US hopes that India will take more responsibility in the security of the Indo-Pacific region, especially in the Indian Ocean, and encourages India to become a "net security provider". This is not only in line with India's goal of pursuing a "leader power", but also meets India's desire to be recognized as a big country, and more in line with India's strategic intention to leverage China's rising influence in the Indian Ocean region. What's more, India's attitude seems to be changing quietly. The cautious attitude for India to deepen strategic cooperation with the US, Japan and

[18] Brzezinski (1998).

Australia has already been abandoned, which means the strategic consensus and the interdependence between the US and India in the Indo-Pacific region is strengthening; **Third, construct and render the "China threat theory"**. Through the construction, speculation and rendering of the "China threat theory", the insecurity cognition of the surrounding countries, especially the claimant of the interests in South China Sea, such as Vietnam, the Philippines, Malaysia, will be constantly escalated, forcing these countries depend more on the US in terms of security. It also provides the US with excuses and opportunities for direct and indirect involvement in the South China Sea issues; Further, by deepening the military and security interactions with traditional allies such as Singapore and Vietnam, regional conflicts are created to achieve the hegemonic goal of the so-called "international free navigation" of the US in the South China Sea. Moreover, the US is likely to use the current contradictions and differences in Sino-Indian relations to encourage India to create obstacles for China's economic and security cooperation with South and Southeast Asian countries and hinder the construction of the Maritime Silk Road. Obviously, there are two key factors in the US strategic conception of "Indo-Pacific".

The first factor is China. China is the main target of the US's "Indo-Pacific" strategy. As mentioned above, the rise of regional influence of China resulting from the constant increasing of economic power in recent years made the US feel anxious and uncomfortable. Especially, in May and October 2013, Chinese President Xi Jinping proposed the Belt and Road Initiative of "Land Silk Road" and "21st Century Maritime Silk Road" respectively in Kazakhstan and Indonesia. The countries and regions along the Belt and Road Initiative are the geographical regions with the most complicated geopolitical relations, the biggest historical and cultural differences, the most serious religious and ethnic group conflicts, the most turbulent state and regional situations, and the most entangled relationship between major powers. Although the main intent of the Initiative is to expand new space for China's reform and opening up and peaceful development, rather than launching a new "Cold War" against the US at the regional and global levels.[19] The Belt and Road Initiative has deteriorated the strategic differences and trust deficit between China and the US. The US strategic circle generally believes that the Initiative has obvious geopolitical intentions and regards it as an initiative for China to expand its geographical influence, and even to a certain extent constitutes a challenge to the US hegemony. Through the study of the US media, academic circles, think tanks, and so on, Ma Jianying found that although there are some rational and objective voices in the US, there is a great doubt about China's intentions in general. They think the Belt and Road Initiative is the strategic tool for China to expand international influence, which will bring forth extensive competition between China and the US and threaten the interests and leadership of the US in Eurasia.[20] After Trump took office, the US's new security and defense strategies have clearly identified that the priority of the current US national security is strategic competition between countries, not terrorism. This means that the international relations in the eyes of US government have returned to the traditional

[19] Li and Li (2015).

[20] Ma (2015).

power politics, and the status of non-traditional security issues has declined.[21] The US, which has always guided diplomacy with realistic theory, not only acts in a hegemonic logic that guarantees its absolute security, but also bluntly and illogically considers its strategy against China by putting China in the context of offensive realism, no matter how China emphasizes it will rise peacefully. The US is trying to use the strategic alliance with India, Japan, and Australia to turn from defensive deterrence to offensive one. Through creating credible threats and enhancing the credibility of deterrence, it hopes to achieve effective check and balance against China under its strategic containment objective. To a certain extent, the "Indo-Pacific" strategy of the US will aggravate China's insecurity, not only causing an escalation of Sino-US strategic mutual suspicion, but also inevitably exacerbating the strategic competition of powers centering on sea supremacy in the Indo-Pacific region, adding unsafe and uncertain factors to world landscape.

The second factor is India, the key dependence of the US's "Indo-Pacific" strategy. First, the traditional strategic deployment of the US is to deploy the maritime forces mainly in the Atlantic and Pacific regions. As the US shifts its strategic focus to Asia-Pacific or Indo-Pacific, the position of Indian Ocean is rising rapidly in the ocean strategy of the US. As the US does not have the absolute maritime hegemony in the Indian Ocean as it does in the Atlantic and Pacific oceans, it objectively needs to seek external security cooperation to maintain its rising interests in the Indian Ocean. As the largest intra-regional country in the Indian Ocean region, India has naturally become the objective of the US seeking security cooperation in this region[22]; **Second**, both the US and India have the common strategic demand of balancing China. Although the US military base in Diego Garcia is the biggest challenge for India to pursue the hegemony in South Asia and even the Indian Ocean, it is rare for Indian political and academic circles to talk about the "US threat." India is naturally vigilant on China's developing relations with countries around India and reaching Indian Ocean. It regards China as the biggest threat to its rise. The US also believes that China's rise will threaten its hegemony. Therefore, balancing China and China's growing influence is the common strategic appeal of the two countries. In 1998, India conducted a nuclear test on the ground of the "China threat", which seriously affected the development of Sino-Indian relations. In order to balance the rise of China, the US and India constantly deepen military and security cooperation and greatly enhance the cooperation in the fields of civil nuclear energy, technology transfer, weapons and military. In fact, US investment in the economic field of India has also risen sharply. What's more, India is in the process of establishing itself as a world power and regards itself as a potential and important global power. The US just caters to India's needs in this regard. In order to woo India, the US fully satisfies India's dream of becoming a "world leader". The Obama administration encouraged India to play the role of a global leader, which invisibly made India, which was originally confident, more confident, and even overestimated its ability to some extent. In

[21]Song Wei: The US New Security Strategy Has Intensified the Arms Race in East Asia, http://news.163.com/18/0212/07/DAE8LFFM0018AOR.html.

[22]Zhang (2015).

contrast, China does not pay special attention to India or the relationship with India, let alone deliberately catering to India. Although China has repeatedly invited India to join the Belt and Road Initiative and share the benefits of cooperation, India, as an over-proud country, is possible to give up the opportunity to gain economic benefits from Sino-Indian cooperation for the sake of "face". The "Belt and Road" not only made India fall into the dilemma of choice, but also made the Sino-Indian relations slid into the "prisoner's dilemma", which invisibly promoted the close ties between the US and India; Third, the US regards India as the dependent objective in its "Indo-Pacific" strategy. It not only intends to use the US-India security cooperation to serve the strategic objective of coping with "China threat" in the Indo-Pacific region, but also replace Russia as India's main weapon supplier and gain huge economic benefits through deepening the US-India defense cooperation. This is why the biggest achievement of US-India cooperation has been in the field of defense and security. It can be said that the US and India are two important powers in the geopolitical game in the Indo-Pacific region. The geopolitical and security significance of the defense cooperation will transcend the bilateral levels, and will have profound impacts on regional security architecture, power balance and hot issues.[23] Therefore, the key to the "Indo-Pacific" strategy is whether the quasi-ally relationship between the US and India can be formed and its strategic direction after formation.

3 Limitations on the Implementation of the "Indo-Pacific" Strategy

Given the characteristics that Japan and Australia almost totally dependent on and rely on the US in security, whether the "Indo-Pacific" strategy can succeed depends on the following two indispensable factors: First, to what extent does the US help India to enhance its capacity to balance the rise of China and the strategic costs of the geopolitical game; Second, in the context of the mutual demand and different strategic appeals of the US and India, with decreasing marginal strategic benefits of US-India defense cooperation, whether the strategic benefits brought by India-US quasi-ally relations to India are greater than the cost of India's abandonment of gaining advantages from both the US and China. Of course, it cannot be ignored that the interaction between China and the US and the dynamic changes in the strategic game between the two countries in the Indo-Pacific region are also important factors influencing to what extent the "Indo-Pacific" strategy can be implemented and how it will work in the future.

Every country has the desire to expand, but all countries have their own limits and base lines with their original territory as the starting point.[24] As Robert Kaplan put forward, "We all know that any countries, even the US which fancies it's a country

[23]Lou (2017).

[24]Zhang Wenmu: *National Strategic Capabilities and Geographical Game*, http://baijiahao.baidu.com/s?id=1596600717819060726&wfr=spider&for=pc.

of freedom and democracy, if uses power indiscriminately, they will not necessarily form a virtuous circle. The good you do, comes back to you.[25] Therefore, the US's "Indo-Pacific" strategy has the following limitations.

First, there is uncertainty in the direction of bilateral and multilateral relations under the strategic game of powers, which is the friction of the "Indo-Pacific" strategy. There are both commonalities and differences in the conception and goals of the "Indo-Pacific" strategy for the US, India, Japan, and Australia. The reason why the four countries actively make strategic planning by centering on the "Indo-Pacific" strategy more comes from their struggle for maritime power rather than concerns about regional security. Security is only a "reasonable excuse" for power struggling. In the process, it is inevitable that the powers will seek "power existence" in the name of "security governance." Whether the "Indo-Pacific" strategy can be implemented depends not only on the mutual influence of the relationship among the four countries, but also on the US-India interaction and the mutual functioning of state behaviors. What's more, it's closely related to the dynamic development of the China-India, China-US and US-India relationships. In particular, there's very big uncertainty whether the US-Indian relationship can be as passionate as the past, and whether defense and security cooperation can continue to deepen. Meanwhile, the geostrategic dynamics of South Asia, the terrorism situation, and Pakistani factor in the US-Indian relationship, are all under dynamic changes, resulting in the apparent fragmentation characteristics of security governance in the Indian Ocean region, and are also important variables for the instability of bilateral and multilateral relations. After all, "the India Ocean needs more strategic stability than any other oceans. This is the place that is most likely to use nuclear weapons among seven sea areas. Of the powers with nuclear weapons, the US, Britain, France, Russia, China, India, Pakistan and Israel station navy here".[26]

In recent years, India and the US have maintained close ties, which are not only the result of their mutual strategic needs, but also closely related to the competition and the deep-rooted multi-layered contradictions between China and India. What India needs to consider is whether it should maintain closer ties with the US at the expense of the "non-alliance" political legacy and the "strategic autonomy" that it has always been adhered to and play a role like Japan in West Pacific, even it wants to abandon the huge profit from economic cooperation with China. Even doing so can enhance India's regional and world influence, as a "net security provider" of the Indian Ocean, India not only needs to buy more arms from the US, but also pay more for the security of the region. However, the hegemony of the US in the Indian Ocean doesn't shake at all. Therefore, under the premise that the status quo of Sino-US relations does not change greatly, India's attitude are of great significance for the direction of the "Indo-Pacific" strategy.

Second, the interdependence between the four countries is loose because they pursue their respective interests under the "Indo-Pacific" strategy, which restricts the implementation of the "Indo-Pacific" strategy. There is no perma-

---

[25] Kaplan (2013a, p. 30).

[26] Kaplan (2013b).

nent friend, only permanent interests. On the one hand, the connotation of the "Indo-Pacific" strategic conception includes geopolitics and transnational security issues, as well as economic interests. On the other hand, the driving factors for the four countries to create the "Indo-Pacific Strategic Arc" are not to promote common regional conception, but to solve their internal and external policy issues respectively.[27] **First of all**, they actively promote the "Indo-Pacific strategy". Although the strategic objectives of the four countries for security considerations have certain convergence, the strategy serves economic interests all along, and the internal driving force for a country to pursue power is still economic interests. Although the US, Japan and Australia are strategic alliances, India and the US are quasi-alliance, both India and the US regard China as a strategic competitor, and Japan and Australia have formed "inertia" or "path dependence" on the military presence of the US to varying degrees. However, this cannot cover up the fact that the US is incompetent to maintain its hegemony due to the decline of the relative strength. Under such circumstances, the US wants to establish a strategic alliance system and strategic partnership network under the leadership of hegemony, but lacks the power or does not want to bear more "investment costs" for the alliance, and hopes that partners, especially allies, can share more cost for the marine security cooperation. This to a certain extent will shake the dependence and trust of other allies to the US. **Second**, India and Australia, as countries in "Indo-Pacific" region, not only want to leverage the US and Japan to obtain security gains, but also take the opportunity to scramble and strengthen their respective discourse right in the Indo-Pacific region. This has certain derangement with the strategic goals of the US, which also leads to major strategic differences between India and Australia. In particular, India has always wanted to have the dominance of the Indian Ocean to enhance its influence in the "Ocean of India" and strengthen its leader position in the region and to be identified as the "net security provider" of the Indian Ocean. The US's help of India to build the identity of a power and a leader is in line with India's goal and desire to be a world power, but this obviously does not match with India's own strength. From the geopolitical point of view, the US deliberately promoted India's position in the region and even the world, and regarded India as the dependent factor in its "Indo-Pacific" strategy. What the US values is not purely India's strength and ability, but it wants India to play the role of "spoiler" like Japan in the Western Pacific in the East Indian Ocean to compensate for the "incapability" due to the relative decline of US hegemony. The role of India depends not only on its position in the US global strategy, but also on its own strength and how much it expects to benefit from US-India cooperation. The strategic choices of India will still be influenced by the game landscape of powers and the interaction between China, the US and India, which makes India's cognition and judgment on China be in dynamic changes. This is the logical starting point for the analysis of Sino-Indian relations in the context of the "Indo-Pacific" strategy. **Third**, every country will pursue its own national interests and as much power as possible from the perspective of self-interest. When the intentions of other countries not confirmed, there will always be a "security dilemma", which leads to strategic

[27]Xiao (2014).

mutual suspicion. The extent of such mutual suspicion depends on the cognition and interaction. All the four countries have their considerations. They try to get more profit from cooperation, which makes the strategic alliance of the four countries unstable and lacks cohesiveness and finally constrains the implementation of the "Indo-Pacific" strategy.

Third, there is a "collective action dilemma" in the strategic interaction and cooperation among the four countries, which is the resistance of the "Indo-Pacific" strategy. In general, a country worries that the distribution of possible benefits may be more favorable to other countries, which is the first expression that the international politics restricts cooperation. Moreover, a country worries it may be more dependent on other countries for the cooperation and the exchange of goods and services, which is the second expression that international politics restricts cooperation.[28] Nowadays, these are the resistance to international co-operations. Meanwhile, uncertain conditions and uncertain practices emerge one after another in international politics. Even among the alliance countries, there is collective irrationality caused by individual rationality. After all, the driving factor for the rational individual to pursue the "collective action" is not to promote the common goal, but the consideration of their own interests, resulting in difficulties for collective actions. As Olson said, "unless there is a small number of people in a group, or unless there is compulsion or certain special means to make individuals act for their common interests, because rational and self-interested individuals will not take action to realize their common or group interests." In other words, even if all individuals in a large group are rational and self-interested, and as a group, they can take action to achieve their common interests or goals, they will not voluntarily take action to achieve common or group interests.[29] Especially in the Indian Ocean region, there are many stakeholders having different attitudes and priorities in regional security governance. The differences in governance concepts and ways among various stakeholders are also important constraints. Especially in practice, the policy priorities of some countries are how to deal with the threat of land terrorism, not maritime terrorism.[30] Even there is a unified strategic goal, there will be a "collective action dilemma" caused by collective irrationality due to the individual's rational pursuit of self-interest, thus affecting the strategic interaction and cooperation between the alliance countries.

Fourth, there are variability and uncertainty for India to consider the "Indo-Pacific" strategy. India is the key dependent object of the US's "Indo-Pacific" strategy. The strategic choice of India and the military and security interaction between India and the US are the key to the implementation of the "Indo-Pacific" strategy and how effective it is. On the one hand, the strategy can better highlight India's geopolitical advantages, and help India to promote the "Act East" policy by leveraging the strength of the US, Japan and Australia. In addition, the strategy will help expand India's influence from the Indian Ocean to the Pacific Ocean, which is in line with India's strategic pursuit to enhance regional and even world influence; On

---

[28]Waltz (2008, p. 112).

[29]Mansell (2003).

[30]Liu (2017).

the other hand, by leveraging the "Indo-Pacific" strategy, India can solidify and even further strengthen its strategic stronghold in the Andaman Islands around the Bay of Bengal, which will help transform geographical advantages into strategic advantages and form a maritime deterrent force against powers out of the region. For India, it is regarded as an important balancing force by the US in the "Indo-Pacific" strategy, and the strategy is regarded as a strategic opportunity by India. This will help deepen India-US relations and win the recognition of its identity as a power by west countries led by US. Moreover, under the current situation that India's own strength does not match with its dream of a power, the "Indo-Pacific" strategy is an opportunity for India to seek a special status in the international system. This is conducive for India to benefit from the interactions with the US, Japan, Australia and Southeast Asia countries, and increases its jetton in the game with China to balance the growing influence of China in the Indian Ocean and restrict the extension of Marine Silk Road to the Indian Ocean.

However, India's strategic consideration has both variabilities and uncertainties. **First**, India's concerns about strategic autonomy and its own interests. From a strategic perspective, India's strategic considerations will inevitably be influenced by the tradition of strategic autonomy. In fact, India also worries about the deepening of the relations with the US. The development of India-US relations is controversial in India, for fear that over close relations with the US may make India lose its autonomy. Therefore, the strategic choices of India will inevitably be affected by the "non-alliance" political legacy. As David Brewster, an Australian scholar, said, "Although there are quite a number of good reasons for India-US co-operations, the development of relations between the two countries is sometimes difficult. If some people in Washington hope that India will become a key ally and play a role in the Indian Ocean region like Japan in Pacific region, they are likely to be disappointed. For India, the purpose of developing relations with the US is more for convenience. India's concerns about strategic autonomy and some past unpleasant contact experiences also restrict the development of their bilateral relations."[31] In the future, India may still "unswervingly" pursue the "non-alliance" policy, but this is likely not to affect India's further inclining towards the US, just like India's inclining towards the Soviet Union without hesitation during the Cold War. In essence, international politics and geopolitics are ruthless. They are based on realistic interests rather than moral or ideology.[32] Moreover, India has always been "swinging" in its foreign strategic choices. Of course, if India is willing to act as a strategic chesspiece of the US and a strategic stronghold of the "Indo-Pacific" strategy, its spoiling role should not be underestimated. **Second**, there is limited space for defense cooperation between India and the US. Defense cooperation is the main content for the development of India-US strategic relations. Under the situation that the benefits of security cooperation is not certain, the depth and breadth of India-US defense cooperation is not only affected by the demisable interest and compromise space from the US to India, but also by India's economic growth potential and existing strength, as well as by the

[31]Brewster (2016).

[32]Wang (2016b, p. 109).

South Asian strategy of the US, particularly the Pakistani factors. In recent years, with the deepening of defense cooperation between India and the US, the defense expenditure of India has also risen sharply. Not only defense expenditure occupies a high proportion in India's central government expenditure, but the gap between the budget requirements of the Ministry of Defense and its annual budget is also widening, from the 125 billion rupees in fiscal year of 2009–2010 to 800 billion rupees in fiscal year of 2014–2015. India's predicament of a high defense spending deficit demands prompt solutions.[33] This not only increases the pressure of economic growth and exacerbates India's financial burden, but the imports of a large amount of weapons and equipment restrict the development of India's local technological and production capacity; **Third**, India is sure to fall into the security dilemma if it tries to rely on the US to balance the rise of China. In recent years, India chooses to rely on the US in politics and security largely out of the consideration of balancing China, not the maximization of India's power in the Indian Ocean. In general, if one is free to choose, the country will flock to the weaker side, because the stronger side threatens it. If the alliance they join has enough defense and deterrence to deter the enemy's attack, they will gain more respect and security.[34] In fact, the military presence of the US in Diego Garcia has always been a huge threat to India. India is unable to change, but to shelve the issue, but this does not mean that India does not worry or has no psychological barriers, and willingly take orders from the US without considering the price paid for it. On the one hand, India intends to cope with the threats brought to China through the defense and security cooperation with the US, Japan and Australia. On the other hand, it worries that the over-close relations with the US will not only shake the foundation of "strategic autonomy" but also restrict India's hegemony in South Asia and its discourse right in the Indian Ocean, ultimately harming its interests. This is also one of the main reasons for India's relatively cautious attitude in face of the hype of "Indo-Pacific" concept during the Obama administration. Therefore, whether the Indian and the US can continue to deepen strategic cooperation depends on the evolution of the situation in the Indo-Pacific region and the gains and losses of the two countries.

Nevertheless, whether the hype of the "Indo-Pacific" strategy by the US, Japan, India and Australia is sustainable and the final outcome depends on the tendency of the strategic landscape, the US-India interaction, and China's strategic response under the context of competition of powers. Currently, influenced by balance of interests, geostrategic considerations and current Sino-Indian relations, India intends to increase its jetton in the competition with China through the cooperation with Japan and Australia, especially with the US. It is an indisputable fact that India attempts to strategically restrict the increasing influences of China in the South Asian subcontinent and the Indian Ocean. India is a key factor in dispelling the negative impact of the "Indo-Pacific" strategy led by the US on China. Although in the foreseeable future, it is unlikely to count on India to help China, but various negative influence

---

[33] Indian Blue Book: The annual growth rate of India's defense budget has remained at 10% in recent years, http://world.people.com.cn/n1/2017/0510/c1002-29266597.html.

[34] Waltz (2008, p. 134).

cause by India's regarding China as its main rival can't be ignored, including leading Sino-Indian relations to confrontation, India's creating obstacles to the co-operations between China and the countries in the South Asian subcontinent and spoiling the peripheral security of China and impede the smooth progress of the Belt and Road Initiative in South Asia and even the Indian Ocean by collaborating with powers like the US and Japan.

4 Challenges and Threats of the "Indo-Pacific" Strategy to China

Either the US's control of the key junction of the Indo-Pacific region, or India's desire to play a leading role in the Indian Ocean as a regional power, or even to play an active role in the Pacific Ocean, or Australia's enhancing of regional influence due to its unique geopolitical value, all have triggered the change in landscape of powers in the Asia-Pacific region and boosted world and regional powers to compete for the influence in Indo-Pacific region. If the purpose for strategic extension of powers is unclear or threats are constructed only to counter threats, geopolitical conflicts and structural confrontation may be caused.[35] In other words, No matter "Indo-Pacific" strategy is currently a concept or a strategy, the most important thing is that its strategic deterrence will surely have a non-ignorable impact on the game of powers, the strategic choice of small countries, and the cognition and judgment of powers' strategic intention by small countries. In recent years, the US has been regarding China as a major threat to its hegemony. Although there is still a lot of uncertainty in whether the "Indo-Pacific" strategy can be implemented or to what extent it can be implemented in the future, strategic game caused by the US's regarding China as a competitor will not only expose China to the strategic pressure brought by the "hegemonic threat" from this region, but will also have a "tearing" impact on China's promotion of economic integration here, as well as the "isolating" impact on the common security concept between China and neighboring countries

First, in the context of the "Indo-Pacific" strategy, China will be exposed to the strategic pressure brought by the "hegemonic threat" from this region. Henry Kissinger wrote in the book *World Order* that "order always requires a delicate balance among restraint, power and legitimacy. The order of Asia must combine equilibrium with the concept of partnership. Maintaining equilibrium through pure military means will further lead to confrontation, while creating a partnership only by exerting psychological pressure will trigger other countries' concern on hegemony. If the balance cannot be achieved, a big disaster will be caused sooner or later."[36] As Ludwig Dehio said, "The international system is under very serious test when it just comes out: it was threatened by the hegemony ghost, which will reappear

[35] Zhu (2013, p. 1).

[36] Kissinger (2015).

frequently in the following centuries."[37] The concept of "Indo-Pacific" is a strategic threat or even a credible strategic deterrent constructed by the US in response to its perceived threat from China, exposing the peaceful rise of China to the threat of hegemony. Specifically, the US makes plannings by regarding the Indian Ocean and the Pacific Ocean as a strategic whole, and takes the advantage of strategic stronghold countries, especially Japan and India, to balance China's geopolitical influence in the Indo-Pacific region. This will not only provide an "excuse" for the direct and indirect involvement of the US in the South China Sea issue to exacerbate the turmoil in the South China Sea, but also affect the relationship between China and its neighboring countries by creating a "security dilemma". It will also interfere and destroy the advance of the Belt and Road, especially the 21st Century Maritime Silk Road, and finally hinder the construction of the community with a common future between China and neighboring countries.

With the changes of the world's economic landscape, the US hopes to continue to maintain its hegemonic status on the one hand, and on the other, it gradually feels incapable of bearing the responsibility of the "World Police" for the global security by itself. As the hegemony has gradually weakened, the US raised its "security defense" strategy to an unprecedented high level to cope with possible threat, especially from China.[38] This is because China's economic and military strengths have been rising rapidly, and therefore is supposed to be the "real and potential threat" that most likely to challenge the US hegemony. Mearsheimer, a representative of offensive realism, wrote in the book *The Tragedy of Power Politics* that if the Chinese economy continues to grow, China will dominate Asia like the US dominates the Western Hemisphere. But the US will strive to go all out to prevent China from gaining regional hegemony. Most of China's neighbors, including India, Japan, Singapore, South Korea, Russia and Vietnam, will cooperate with the US to contain China's power. The outcome will be fierce competition for security, or probably a war."[39] Robert Kaplan, a well-known American scholar in the strategic field, also believes that "the US, as the regional hegemon of the Western Hemisphere, will try to prevent China from becoming the regional hegemon of most of the Eastern Hemisphere, which may become an epoch-making drama."[40] During the visit to Asia in November 2017, Trump, President of the US, officially proposed the concept of "open and free Indo-Pacific" for the first time and the negotiation for the Maritime Cooperation Mechanism in the Western Pacific between the US, Japan, India and Australia was launched, marking new changes to the Asia Pacific strategy of the new administration. The influence of the "Indo-Pacific" strategy is highlighted by the fact that the US has imposed constraints on China on the South China Sea issue through strategic guidance to its strategic stronghold countries - India, Australia, Japan and strategic interactions with these countries, therefore increasing the difficulty for China to

---

[37] Dehio (2016), Quoted from Han and Huang (2017).

[38] Zhu (2014a, p. 52).

[39] Mearsheimer (2015).

[40] Kaplan (2013a, p. 227).

safeguard rights in the South China Sea.[41] Either the new version of the "free route plan" or the "Indo-Pacific" strategy under discussion can make the situation in the South China Sea tense once again or even acute.[42] The South China Sea has always been the focus of the Sino-US strategic game, and the turmoil in the South China Sea is mainly the result of direct or indirect involvement by the US. Just as Speakman called the Caribbean "the Mediterranean of the US" to show its importance, we can also call the South China Sea "Asia's Mediterranean", which will be the core of political geography in the coming decades.[43] With respect to the South China Sea issue, the main reason that the US can form strategic interactions with stronghold countries and thus exert influence on the issue is that these stronghold countries have important strategic interests and internal driving forces in the South China Sea, so they turn into important pillars for the US to impose influence on the South China Sea issue through "Indo-Pacific" strategy.[44]

Thus, in the *National Security Strategy Report 2017* issued by the US government, China is identified as a "strategic competitor" and a country with a "revisionist" intention. To cope with the "China threat" and maintain the world hegemony, the US, which has a foreign policy guided by realism especially offensive realism, always spares no efforts to render the "China threat theory" and build the perception of "insecurity" from the "China threat" to all the surrounding countries of China. The US is trying to place a number of powers or middle powers in a landscape of competitive interaction and strategic checks and balances to deliberately construct an international power system that is conducive to the US hegemony strategy, forming the situation of balance of multiple powers under one super power. Accordingly, the US's attempt to form a large crescent-shaped balance circle against China in regional strategy will increase strategic suspicion between China and the US and stimulate naval arms race in the region.[45] The US encourages India, Japan and other countries to play a greater role in the Indo-Pacific region. Especially under the current situation that the development of the Sino-Indian relations is hindered due to border disputes, Tibet issues, and the construction of the China-Pakistan Economic Corridor, if India could play the role of spoiler in the Indian Ocean like Japan in the Western Pacific, the US can benefit from the strategic competition between China and Japan and China and India. What's more, the US supports the construction of maritime security capabilities of the major claimants in the South China Sea, provokes the relations between China and surrounding countries and intensifies the arms race in the Indo-Pacific region. These "anti-threat" means not only increase China's insecurity and pose a threat to China's security, but also add complexity and variables to the South China Sea issue by constructing the perception and cognition of small countries to the threats of powers. After all, the development of international relations between China and the Philippines, Vietnam, Malaysia and other coun-

[41] Wang (2016a, pp. 49–50).

[42] Zhu (2018).

[43] Kaplan (2013a, p. 221).

[44] Wang (2016a, p. 54).

[45] Xia (2015b).

tries is the key to resolving the dispute in the South China Sea. In the context of "Indo-Pacific" strategic background, the game of powers and the South China Sea issue are intertwined, which will certainly pose challenges and threats to China's peripheral security. This "threat of the hegemonic ghost" will gradually penetrate into the economic field from the political and security fields in the future. Under such a situation, the US's "Indo-Pacific" strategy will exert enormous pressure on China. The strategic space for China's peaceful development will be compressed, and the peaceful rise will face challenges and threats from the hegemony.

Second, the "Indo-Pacific" strategy has a "tearing" impact on China's promotion of regional economic integration and poses a threat to China's economic security. Although the hype of the "Indo-Pacific" concept by the four countries is based on the geopolitics of the Indo-Pacific region, it's also the result of the geo-economic changes in the region and shift of the world's economic focus from the Atlantic to Indo-Pacific region. With the shift of economic focus, the whole world will look towards the Indo-Pacific region. The international political and economic order centering on the West will inevitably develop towards the east-west equilibrium. The world is moving toward an international order with relatively balanced power and no hegemony.[46] For the US, the trend of economic integration in the Indo-Pacific region means that the geostrategic position of this region will continue to rise in the world, however, the strategic and economic landscape is likely to develop towards the direction that is in favor of China, instead of the US. This is one of the main considerations that the US actively promotes the "Indo-Pacific" strategy. For China, the rise of Asia needs firstly to promote the economic integration between the Indian Ocean and the Pacific Ocean, which are connected by the Straits of Malacca. At present, APEC continues to languish, the prospect of the Trans-Pacific Partnership (TPP) is complicated and confusing. China's active promotion of the Belt and Road Initiative is conducive to the formation of the institutionalization process of sub-regional and regional economic cooperation such as Bangladesh-China-India-Myanmar Economic Corridor, the China-Pakistan Economic Corridor, the Indo-China Peninsula Economic Corridor and China, China and ASEAN "10+1", Regional Comprehensive Economic Partnership (RCEP). This will not only help release the demand and growth potential of trade and investment of countries and create a win-win or even multi-win economic landscape, but also provide a platform for resolving various negative factors in bilateral and regional security. After all, the main goal of geopolitics is to serve the geo-economy and further expand the circulation of capital and goods in this region. In this sense, the Indian Ocean region and the Pacific region have been strategically linked.[47]

At present, the economic integration of the Indo-Pacific region shows a good development momentum. In the context of the international system, the rise of a country and the prosperity of a region are fundamentally based on the economic strength, which comes from a mechanism of cooperation and win-win, and a peaceful and stable international environment. From the perspective of economic integration,

---

[46]Zhang (2012).

[47]Zhu (2014a, pp. 61–62).

the Western Pacific and the East Indian Ocean have great economic potential, which is also the key to economic integration in the Indo-Pacific region.[48] From the current situation, although the US has withdrawn from the TPP, Japan has taken over the flagpole and revised the mechanism into the *Comprehensive and Progressive Trans-Pacific Relations Agreement* (CPTPP). If this mechanism is proved to be beneficial to the US, the possibility that the US will consider re-takeover in the future can not be ruled out. Meanwhile, it is possible that the US will expand the strategic presence of trade and investment in the Indo-Pacific region by means similar to TPP to reconstruct the Indo-Pacific rules and the cooperation mechanisms that are conducive to the absolute discourse right of the US and in line with its national interests at the time of promoting domestic economic growth.

According to the hegemony theory, when the strength of the superpower declines, the external competition may force it to abandon free trade and turn to trade protection. In this case, the process of world trade liberalization will also be plagued to a certain extent, and, the US-China trade friction is also more affected by political factors.[49] In fact, a maritime power is certainly an economic power that is open to the outside world. The birth and development of a maritime power is based on the development and prosperity of maritime trade. Profiting from exchange of needed goods and stimulating and satisfying demand in commodity exchange to promote production is the economic standpoint pursued by maritime powers based on maritime trade, as well as a model of wealth growth driven by exchange and demand.[50] In recent years, the anti-globalization trend of the Western countries led by the US and the frequent trade protectionism measures against countries including China will inevitably exacerbate the differences in interests and divisions in co-operations between countries and have had a "tearing" effect on the economic integration process in this region. Finally, this will result in frictions in economic integration at various levels and based on different rules and different regions that China has actively promoted and certain achievements have been obtained, and added uncertainty factor to the economic cooperation between China and surrounding countries.

Third, the "Indo-Pacific" strategy will trigger the security turmoil around the Bay of Bengal, and may have a "splitting" impact on the common security concept of China and surrounding countries and threaten the security order of China and surrounding countries by constructing and upgrading the "insecurity" perceptions of countries around the bay. The core areas of the "Indo-Pacific" strategy are the Northeast Indian Ocean and the Western Pacific Ocean. In the Indo-Pacific region, the Bay of Bengal is close to the entrance of the Straits of Malacca, the main junction connecting the Western Pacific and the East Indian Ocean. The Andaman and Nicobar Islands in the Bay of Bengal has an island chain with a length of 720 km, running from north to south through Andaman Sea. The island chain is close to the western end of the Straits of Malacca. The two islands give India a natural advantage and strategic confidence in projecting maritime forces to the Straits of

[48]Zhu (2014a, p. 64).

[49]Zhou (2013).

[50]Chen (2012b).

Malacca and places further. Located in the northeast Indian Ocean, the Bay of Bengal is an important geographical connection point in Asia and the largest gulf in the world. India's control over the Andaman Sea and Nicobar Islands has strengthened its strategic position in the region along the Bay of Bengal, which is considered the "natural sphere of influence" of India and the core area of India's "Act East" policy. The Indian Navy has always focused on developing security relations with countries along the Bay of Bengal, including joint patrols, bilateral military exercises, holding biennial "Milan" naval exercises in the Andaman Islands, and providing maritime security in fighting against piracy, smuggling, terrorism and separatism and refugees. India has made great efforts to prove that it is the leader and a net provider of security products in the area of Indian Ocean. Meanwhile, the countries along the Bay of Bengal are also rich in energy and mineral resources, which is also a major factor for the growing importance of the bay. It means the strategic competition centering on energy development will become increasingly fierce in the future. Myanmar has become an important energy exporter, Thailand is becoming the biggest energy import market of Myanmar, maritime boundary dispute between Bangladesh and Myanmar, the competition of energy mining among India, Thailand and other countries in the region and the US, France, Japan, Russia and other countries out the region, and the construction of China-Myanmar oil and gas pipelines, as well as the competition and potential conflicts caused by new oil and gas resources have become sources of the severe security problems and non-negligible geopolitical competition in the Bay of Bengal.

Countries along the Bay of Bengal including India, Sri Lanka, Bangladesh, Myanmar, Thailand, Malaysia and Indonesia are key areas in China's peripheral relations. Among the seven countries along the Bay of Bengal, India, Myanmar and Vietnam are China's land neighbors, and Malaysia and Indonesia are maritime neighbors, of which Indonesia is an important link of the 21st Century Maritime Silk Road. The countries along the Bay of Bengal are the "core areas" of 64 countries along the Belt and Road. These "core area" countries are located to the southwest of China, being the "first stop" to promote the Belt and Road. At the same time, the region along the coast of the Bay of Bengal is also the "target zone" for the fabrication and publicity of "China threat theory" by the US and India. The region has both traditional security issues and non-traditional security challenges. In addition, conflicts including ethnic groups, religions, territories, resources, oceans, terrorist attacks, and Islamic extremist forces rise one after another. Meanwhile, transnational crimes, such as smuggling, drug trafficking, corruption, and cyber hackers, also exist in the region. China needs to proactively establish a regional mechanism to address the security threats and challenges in the Bay of Bengal, while actively participating in and shaping the security landscape of the region to cope with the structural security contradictions between China and India, and to some extent alleviate the cognition and doubts of countries in the region on China threats.

With the ever growing strategic and economic interests of China in the Bay of Bengal, including the construction of the China-Myanmar oil pipeline, China will inevitably increase naval force to protect the safety of ports and passages. New Delhi and Washington have been worried about the security cooperation between China and countries in the Bay of Bengal. The asymmetry of power structure in this region, especially India's rising influence, is an important interference factor for China's strategy and diplomacy with surrounding countries. The hype and heating up of the "Indo-Pacific" concept by the US, India, Japan, and Australia will not only further construct and upgrade the so-called "China threat" and strengthen the "hegemonic threat" of the US in this region, but also may break up the status that the Bay of Bengal has never been valued or even marginalized. In this case, it may trigger security concerns and the perceptions of subjective safety and objective security of countries such as Indonesia, Malaysia, Thailand, Myanmar, making the security situation in this region more volatile.[51] Apart from the India, Indonesia and Malaysia also hope to play important roles in this sea area, but India's strategic intention of extending the sphere of maritime power to the Straits of Malacca has increased the strategic conflicts between India and Indonesia, Malaysia and Australia. All of these will inevitably trigger frictions between countries and countries' raising their respective security demands for feeling unsecure, making these countries more dependent on the US for security. In the Bay of Bengal, Sri Lanka and Bangladesh also have obvious geographical advantages, which are the goals for powers to scramble. From the perspective of interest landscape protection, the competition of economic interests among powers tends to trigger political confrontation between relevant countries, constructing negative imaginary enemy on the basis of nationalism, and triggering security dilemmas in imagination.[52] The "Power Balance Strategy" of small countries is not only an important factor leading to potential uncertainty and security risks, but also has an impact on the perception of threats of countries along the Bay of Bengal and their cognition of "insecurity". It will make relevant countries uphold a collective security concept of "all for one, one for all" and worsen the geo-security environment in this region, thus impacting such security concepts as "co-building security", "cooperation security" and "sharing security" and splitting the existing regional security landscape. This will inevitably lead to turmoil in the security situation around the Bay of Bengal and exacerbate the "insecurity" perceptions of surrounding small countries on powers. This actually constitutes a challenge to China's surrounding security, and is also unfavorable for China's building of strategic strongholds for security cooperation with neighboring countries.

If the place around South China Sea is currently a key target of the US's "Indo-Pacific" strategy, the Bay of Bengal may become an important breakthrough point for the US to balance China with the help of India in the future. In 2007, India established Andaman–Nicobar headquarters in the Bay of Bengal, which not only accelerated the development of the Andaman Sea Base in the Bay of Bengal—the strategic outpost for India's "Act East" policy, but also strengthened the integration and connectivity between countries in the bay and surrounding countries. It even pays more attention to the Bangladesh-India-Myanmar Economic Cooperation (BIMSTEC) established in 1997, and plans to complete the establishment of a free trade zone in 2017. The

[51] Objective security means that there is no exact threat from the material aspect. Subjective security refers to psychologically defining the feeling that there is no threat.

[52] Jiang and Li (2017).

strategic deployment of New Delhi in the Bay of Bengal will greatly influence the geopolitical and security landscape of the gulf region. In July 2012, the Indian Navy launched the "Hawk Eye" base located at the southernmost tip of the Andaman Nicobar Islands. The base is regarded as an important one for India to project its military power to the Indian Ocean and the South China Sea. This base is an important maritime strategic asset of India, not only because it is situated at the junction of the Straits of Malacca and the Ten Degree Channel, more importantly, it provides the Indian Navy with a frontier position for military operations.

At the same time, the *Logistics Exchange Memorandum of Agreement* reached by India and the US is a milestone in the development of India-US military relations, laying a foundation for India's military activities in the "Indo-Pacific" region, and highlighting India's attempts and ambitions to be a leading ocean power in the Indo-Pacific region through the cooperation with the US.[53] Since 1992, the navies of the US and Indian have regularly held Exercise Malabar in the Bay of Bengal or offshore of Japan. In July 2017, India, the US and Japan held the 21st Exercise Malabar in the Bay of Bengal. The development of Exercise Malabar from small to big and from bilateral to trilateral reflects the evolution of the "Indo-Pacific" geostrategic landscape and the new trend of strategic competition between powers. The exercise has become an important platform for India, the US and Japan to coordinate maritime security cooperation.[54] Hence, the Bay of Bengal is the core area for the maritime security cooperation among the US, India, Japan and Australia, the critical area for India's "Act East" policy, as well as an important area for India and the US to hedge China's influence in Southeast Asia and squeeze China's strategic space in the South China Sea, therefore, threats and challenges of the area to the peripheral security of China cannot be ignored.

5 Reflections on China's Security Strategy for India Ocean and Pacific Ocean

In recent years, economic downturn, geopolitical turmoil, terrorist crisis and civilized friction emerge one after another and the current international order and system are facing new challenges. Some Western scholars even exclaimed that we are entering a "disordered world." During the "gray stage" when the old international order is gradually broken and the new order has not yet been established, the world is entering a period of strategic turmoil or an era of "strategic competition" full of anxiety. The cooperation among the US, Japan, India and Australia under the strategic conception of "Indo-Pacific" also indicates increased geostrategic competition in this region. The external expression of strategic competition is turbulence and even conflict while the internal expression is mutual suspicion. The strategic competition can be coped

[53] Yang (2017).

[54] Rong (2017, pp. 48–50).

with through an arms race or the creation of credible threats.[55] As Henry Kissinger put forward in *The Global Strategy of the US*, conflicts in the Atlantic or Western Hemisphere resulted from economic factors, in Asia from strategic competition, while in the Middle East fundamentally from ideology and religion.[56] The fact that China has become the world's second largest economy and the rising military power in recent years suggests that China is rising rapidly. The rising China has made the US feel anxious, Japan feel distressed, and India feel jealous. The US's hegemony in the Indian Ocean is difficult to shake in the foreseeable future; India wants to secure its unique dominant position in the South Asian subcontinent and strives for absolute influence on Indian Ocean affairs; China shall safeguard the passage of the Indian Ocean and seek economic interests in the Indian Ocean region. These goals are very clear currently, and the strategic structural contradictions caused by the competition among China, India and the US in the Indian Ocean are also inevitable. Therefore, the most important is how to control the conflict and maintain a situation of "fighting but never breaking up".[57]

First, look for opportunities to reshape the geopolitical landscape that is beneficial to China in the turmoil due to the geopolitical game of powers and the deconstruction and reconstruction of the Indian Ocean order. The geographic position determines the significance of China. China's territory and civilization extends from the center of Euroasia Continent to the warm waters along the Pacific coast.[58] At present, the core area of Sino-US strategic game in the western Pacific includes the Taiwan Strait, the East China Sea and the South China Sea. If the scope of Sino-US strategic competition extends to the entire Indo-Pacific region in the context of the "Indo-Pacific" strategic conception in the future, China will be confronted with both pressure and tension, as well as opportunities and challenges at the same time. This means that while the regions where China and the US compete and defend are expanding, the room for mutual compromise and cooperation will extend as well. In the future, it's the general trend that the US will "take a back seat" on the issues of Taiwan, the East China Sea and the South China Sea. But the US will use various possible strategic advantages to create obstacles to China, so as to maintain its maritime hegemony and permanent existence in the Western Pacific. The constant deepening bilateral and multilateral defense and security cooperation among the US, Japan, India and Australia in the Indo-Pacific region has deep geopolitical and strategic implications, and also reflect the new trend of strategic interaction and geo-competition of major world powers in the this region. In particular, the strategic priorities and strategic resources allocation of the US navy is shifting from counter-terrorism and security cooperation to effectively responding to challenges from "strategic competitors". Although It is variable and uncertain that the US is willing or able to provide more public goods for the security of the Indo-Pacific region to ensure the safety of the sea passages in the region, it is sure

---

[55] Zhu (2014b).

[56] Kissinger (2009).

[57] Zhu (2017).

[58] Kaplan (2013a, p. 123).

that the advance of the "Indo-Pacific" strategic conception will exert influence on the situation in the South China Sea and the security situation in the Bay of Bengal. What's more, the US's hegemonic protection strategy and India's exclusive strategic intentions towards the Indian Ocean will exacerbate the "security dilemma" of the powers in the strategic interaction and geopolitical competition in the Indo-Pacific region.

Nowadays, the world is facing various kinds of security issues, including fierce strategic competition among powers, regional hot spots like DPRK nuclear issue, the Afghan issue, the Syrian issue, and non-traditional security issues like the terrorism and transnational crimes. This means that China is confronted with both enormous security challenges and cooperation needs with other powers, and even may have some strategic opportunities contained in the balance of powers, complex security architecture and structural changes. Given that the "safety dilemma" and many unstable factors prevail in the surrounding areas of China, the institutionalization of power through multilateral mechanisms in the region can not only achieve strategic objectives with synergy, but also gain legitimacy, recognition and follow-up, which are in line with the essence of the new security concept advocated by China.[59] Moreover, the perceptions, judgments and strategic choices of the US, India, Australia and Southeast Asian countries of the Indo-Pacific strategy as well as their impact on China's main and secondary strategic direction are in dynamic changes. China should take advantage of the trend to look for cooperation opportunities in a complex security environment, and strive to find strategic opportunities in the process of deconstruction and reconstruction of regional ocean order. China shall consider rebuilding the security landscape for surrounding areas by combining the security order in both India Ocean and Pacific Ocean with the advance of the Belt and Road, and use the opportunities in the strategic turmoil in the East Indian Ocean to ease the strategic pressure in the Western Pacific. As Wang Jisi puts forward, "China has already possessed certain strength, so it can actively make plannings among the world's major powers and regional powers, and strive to establish a 'balance of power favoring stability and development'. With geographical Asia (not just East Asia) as the support of its geo-strategy, China shall play a bigger game in the Eurasian continent and even the world.[60]

Second, China shall attach importance to the investment distribution in Southeast Asia and South Asia, deepen bilateral and multilateral cooperation mechanisms to accelerate regional economic integration, and reconstruct the geo-economic landscape in the Indo-Pacific region. Almost all the surrounding countries are implementing fence-sitting tactics, intending to rely on the US for security, China for economics, and the third-party power for more benefits or jetton in negotiations with powers. In the future, this will be common for surrounding countries, so we must not only be psychologically prepared, but also need countermeasures or strategic considerations. As the only superpower in the world, the biggest goal of the US in geopolitics is to secure its hegemonic position in the world

[59]Song (2012).

[60]Wang (2016b, pp. 109–110).

and maintain a world order centering on the US. To achieve this goal, it must first ensure its dominance in the Asia-Pacific region. Moreover, as the "leader" of the alliance, the US not only focuses on both geopolitical and security fields in strategic conception, but gives consideration to economic interests. Therefore, the US will definitely pay attention to the investment distribution in Southeast Asia and South Asia in the future. China should take advantage of the trend to actively combine China's economic security in the Indian Ocean and the Pacific Ocean with the advance of the Belt and Road Initiative. After all, economic interdependence does not necessarily improve political relations between countries, but is the ballast stone of political relations. Compared with the influence of economic interdependence, political interdependence is more likely a "myth" that masks regional conflicts and potential problems to some extent. While, economic interdependence is more stable and more conducive to promoting regional and World Peace. President Xi Jinping pointed out in the report of the 19th National Congress that "We will pursue coordinated land and marine development, and step up efforts to build China into a strong maritime country. We should pursue the Belt and Road Initiative as a priority, give equal emphasis to "bringing in" and "going global. we hope to make new ground in opening China further through links running eastward and westward, across land and over sea."[61] In fact, the scope of the Belt and Road covers the Asia, Europe and Africa and the India Oceans and Pacific Oceans. As a major power in the "Indo-Pacific" region, China plays an indispensable role in the change of regional structure from the perspective of economy and security. China shall take the opportunity to think about and build its security strategies in the India Ocean and Pacific Ocean, consolidate and develop relations with Pakistan, Myanmar, Sri Lanka, Bangladesh, Thailand, Indonesia and other countries in Indo-Pacific region by leveraging the geo-economic advantages, and seize the opportunity to expand China's maritime rights and strategic space to mitigate the threat of strategic competition to China. With the Belt and Road, especially the "21st Century Maritime Silk Road", as an opportunity, China also shall promote maritime security cooperation with relevant countries in the Indo-Pacific region, to serve China's road to a maritime power and build a regional security order of peace, development, cooperation and mutual benefit. This is not only the responsibility of China as a responsible power, but also a great contribution to the security in the Indo-Pacific region and world peace.

Third, China needs to constantly explore the way to get along with India in the context strategic game among China, the US and India and the "security dilemma". The strategic competition of powers under the "Indo-Pacific" strategy, especially the Sino-US strategic game, will lead to a new "security dilemma" to economic cooperation in the Indo-Pacific region. China shall pay attention to the threats and challenges to China's peripheral security and the implementation of the Belt and Road Initiative from the change of the US's geo-strategy in the Indo-Pacific region. If the goal of increasing trust and removing doubts cannot be achieved due to

---

[61] *The Report of the 19th National Congress of the Communist Party of China puts forward: Adhere to the Coordination of Land And Sea to Accelerate the Construction of a Maritime Power*, People's Daily, October 18, 2017, http://www.cme.gov.cn/info/1527.jspx.

"security dilemma", sub-regional cooperation can only be in a secondary position in decision-making, and non-cooperation will still be a rational choice for all countries. The existence of the "security dilemma", to a large extent, weakens the weak trust relations between member states, resulting in the abortion of cooperation projects and difficulty in achieving the construction goals.

Of the relations among China, the US and India, the US is the most important factor for both China and India. India's policy to China or China's policy to India will inevitably be affected by the US. India, in particular, is more sensitive to the development of Sino-US relations, worrying that the emergence of G2 in the world will seriously affect India's strategic environment. This is also a major reason why India seeks to incline to the US. India claims that it will not form an alliance with the US according to India's diplomatic tradition, but this does not mean that India will not use the power of the US to balance China and thus increase jetton for negotiation with China. However, India will also more often emphasize "equal distance diplomacy" with both China and the US. On the one hand, India strengthens cooperation with the US in the field of civilian nuclear energy, deepens technology transfer and cooperation, and weaponry and military cooperation. On the other hand, it also emphasizes the unchangeable neighborhood, and great impacts on the region and the world from the cooperation between the two largest developing countries. In any case, the US and India have continuously deepened military and security cooperation, virtually making the political mutual trust between China and India more fragile. Although India does not want other countries to enhance their influence on South Asia and the Indian Ocean within India's "sphere of influence", there is no doubt that it will not refuse to benefit from strategic cooperation with major powers including China and the US. With the rapid rise of China's strength, especially the continuous improvement of the Belt and Road, psychological imbalance and anxiety of India further increase. In the future, India will continue to rely on the US to balance China's growing influence in South Asia and the Indian Ocean. The strategic game among the three countries and the consequent complex interactions will not only exist for a long time, but also show an upward trend. Therefore, we shall not only value the Sino-US relations, but also need to explore ways to get along with India. Moreover, the key is to choose a way which is acceptable by India. After all, it's unavoidable for the two largest developing countries, the two populous countries, and the two major civilizations to collide and communicate. In addition, China and India share common needs in opposing US hegemony and advancing the world's development toward multi-polarization. This will make it easy for China and India to reach consensus and have strategic demands for mutual cooperation on regional and global governance issues as well as some major international issues. Meanwhile, under competitive and complementary relations in the economic field, China and India have a huge demand for mutual cooperation, which also plays an important role in stabilizing Sino-Indian relations and exploring the way for China and India to get along with.

Nevertheless, not a few underdeveloped countries in the Indo-Pacific region still face many problems including security, poverty, disease, etc., and economic development is the basis for solving all problems. As President Xi Jinping said in the opening ceremony of the Boao Forum for Asia Annual Conference 2018, "the Belt and Road may be China's idea, but its opportunities and outcomes are going to benefit the world. China has no geopolitical calculations, seeks no exclusionary blocs and imposes no business deals on others."[62] "The world is undergoing great development, great change, great adjustment, with peaceful development as the theme of the times." "With the idea of peace, development, cooperation and win-win, and the foreign policy of promoting common development, China endeavors to construct a new international relationship characterized by mutual respect, fairness, cooperation and win-win."[63] Based on this, China should take India Ocean and Pacific Ocean as a whole and make plannings in combination with the Belt and Road from the perspective of geo-economy. By taking advantage of China's geo-economic advantages, China should actively explore the positive factors in the "Indo-Pacific" geo-economy and accelerate the economic integration of the Indian Ocean and the Pacific region and address "security dilemma" in geopolitics with geo-economy as the breakthrough point. Meanwhile, China shall create and utilize cooperation opportunities in regional security as appropriate, and expand China's maritime rights and strategic space to serve the construction of the Belt and Road, especially the "21st Century Maritime Silk Road". If China can promote others countries to build a community of economic cooperation, mutual benefit and win-win, and build a community with common future for China and surrounding countries based on "common security" and "cooperation security", China is hopeful of resisting the threats and pressures from the "Indo-Pacific" strategy, and realize peaceful rise in the turbulent world's strategic landscape.

References

American Department of Defense. 2012. *Sustaining U.S. Global Leadership: Priorities for 21st Century Defense*, 2.

Brewster, David. 2016. *The Ocean of India: The Truth of India Seeking Regional Leadership*, translated by Youkang Du and Yue Mao, 2016 ed., 232. Social Science Literature Publishing House [Australia].

Brzezinski, Zbigeon. 1998. The great chessboard: The United States' preliminary position and its geo-strategy, translated by the China Institute of International Studies, 1998 ed., 4. Shanghai People's Publishing House [United States].

Cao, Yuyang. 2014. The Maritime Security Deployment and Impact of US "Indo-Pacific" Strategy. *Modern International Relations* 8: 27–35.

Chen, Yali. 2012a. The "Rebalancing" Strategy of the United States: A Realistic Assessment and China's Response. *World Economics and Politics* 11: 68–69.

---

[62] Xi Jinping delivered a keynote speech at the Boao Forum (full text), https://m.zhangle.com/views/information/newspaper.htm?repetId=100100796860&titleTag=1&from=timeline&isappinstalled=0.

[63] Xi Jinping proposed to adhere to the path of peaceful development and promote the building of a community of human destiny, http://cpc.people.com.cn/19th/n1/2017/1018/c414305-29594530.html.

Chen, Tong. 2012b. Returning to Geographical Characteristics, Exploring the Essence of Sea Power. *World Economy and Politics* 2: 60–61.
Chen, Bangyu. 2015. The Similarities and Differences of the Strategic Conception of the US-Australia-India and China's Response. *Socialist Studies* 6: 147–154.
Dehio, Ludwig. 2016. *The Vulnerable Balance: The Power Struggle of Four Centuries in Europe*, translated by Yinhong Shi, 2016 ed., 24, People's Publishing House [German].
Han, Zhaoying, and Zhaolong Huang. 2017. The Problem of Check and Balance: Rethinking the Absence of the United States Check and Balance after the Cold War. *Pacific Journal* 11: 1.
Jiang, Peng, and Shujian Li. 2017. The Illusory Incompatibility and Imaginable Security Dilemma—The Mutual Assistance Construction of Hostile Identity in the Process of Power Transfer. *International Safety* 1: 55.
Jin, Canrong. 2013. The United States Motivation Behind the Concept of "Indo-Pacific". *Xinhuanet*, 11 Jan 2013, http://news.xinhuanet.com/globe/2013-01/11/c_132095969.htm.
Jin, Canrong. 2017. The Concept of "Indo-Pacific" Is Like a Bubble, Gone with the Sun. *Global Times*, 22 Nov 2017.
Kaplan, Robert D. 2013a. *The Upcoming Geopolitical War*, translated by Pu Han, 2013 ed. Guangdong People's Publishing House [United States].
Kaplan, Robert D. 2013b. *Monsoon: The Indian Ocean and the Future of US Power*, translated by Zhaoli Wu and Yue Mao, 2013 ed., 8. Beijing: Social Science Literature Publishing House [United States].
Kissinger, Henry. 2009. *The Global Strategy of the United States*, translated by Liping Hu and Jianping Ling, 2009 ed., 9. Hainan Publishing House [United States].
Kissinger, Henry. 2015. *World Order*, translated by Liping Hu et al., 2015 ed., 303–304 CITIC Publishing Group [United States].
Li, Xiao, and Junjiu Li. 2015 The Belt and Road Initiative and the Reconstruction of China's Geopolitical and Economic Strategies. *World Economics and Politics* 10: 53–54.
Lin, Minwang. 2018a. The Construction of "Indian" and the Tension of Asian Geopolitics. *Diplomatic Review* 1: 16–35.
Lin, Minwang. 2018b. The Construction of "Indo-Pacific" and the Tension of Asian Geopolitics. *Diplomatic Review* 1: 18.
Liu, Siwei. 2017 Development and Reconstruction of the Indian Ocean Security Governance System. *International Safety Research* 5: 92.
Lou, Chunhao. 2017. *A New Posture Review of US-India Defense Cooperation. International Studies* 1: 106.
Ma, Jianying. 2015. Cognition and Response of the United States to the Belt and Road Initiative. *World Economics and Politics* 10: 104.
Mansell, O. 2003. *The Logic of Collective Action*, translated by Yuqi Chen, 2003 ed., 2. Shanghai People's Publishing House [United States].
Mcdaniel, D. 2012. *India, China and the United States in the Indo-Pacific Region: Coalition, Co-existence or Clash?*, 2.
Mearsheimer. 2015. *The Tragedy of Power Politics*, translated by Yiwei Wang and Xiaosong Tang, 2015 ed., 391. Shanghai People's Publishing House.
Medcalf, Rory. 2012. Unselfish Giants? Understanding China and India as Security Providers. *Australian Journal of International Affairs* 66 (1): 1–13.
Raja Mohan, C. 2013. SAMUDRA MANTHAN-Sino-Indian Rivary in the Indo-Pacific, 212. Oxford University Press.
Rong, Ying. 2017. A New Trend of Strategic Interaction between the Powers in Indo-Pacific Region from the "Malabar" Military Exercise. *Peace and Development* 5.
Rumley, Dennis, Timothy Doyle, and Sanjay Chaturvedi. 2012. Securing the Indian Ocean? Competing Regional Security Constructions. *Journal of the Indian Ocean Region* 8 (1): 1–20.
Song, Dexing. 2012. Strategic Realism—A Choice for China's Grand Strategy. *World Economy and Politics* 9: 17.

Taylor, Melissa Conley. 2014. Differences between Australia and India on the Understanding of "Indo-Pacific". *Indian Ocean Economies Research* 1: 138.
Waltz, Kennedy. 2008. *International Political Theory*, translated by Xinqiang, 2008 ed. Shanghai Century Publishing House [United States].
Wang, Xiaowen. 2016a. The Impact of the US "Indo-Pacific" Strategy on the South China Sea Issue: Focusing on the "Indo-Pacific" Strategic Supporting Countries. *Southeast Asian Studies* 5.
Wang, Jisi. 2016b. *Strategy of Powers: Exploration and Reflection on International Strategy*, 2016 ed. CITIC Publishing Group.
Wei, Zongyou. 2013. Strategic Adjustment of the US in India and the Influence of Geostrategy. *World Economics and Politics* 10.
Wu, Zhaoli. 2014. The Origin of Indo-Pacific and Multi-country Strategic Game. *Journal of the Pacific* 1: 29–40.
Xia, Liping. 2015a. The US "Indo-Pacific" Strategy from the Perspective of Geopolitics and Geo-Economics. *American Studies* 2.
Xia, Liping. 2015b. The US "Indo-Pacific Strategy" from the Dual Perspective of Geopolitics and Geo-Economics. *American Studies* 2: 50.
Xiao, Yang. 2014. The Strategic Space Expansion of a "Medium Power"—Australian Security Reconstruction under the Vision of "Indo-Pacific" Strategy. *Pacific Journal* 1: 43.
Xu, Juan. 2017. The US-India-Japan Maritime Security Cooperation in the Context of "Indo-Pacific" Strategy. *South Asian Studies* 2: 95–112.
Yang, Siling. 2017. The India Ocean and the US-Japan Interaction for Ocean Security: An Offensive Realism Perspective. *International Safety Research* 5: 74.
Zhang, Jianxin. 2012. The Post-Western International System and the Rise of the East. *World Economics and Politics* 5: 4.
Zhang, Li. 2013. The Impact of the "Indo-Pacific" Conception on the Multilateral Landscape of the Asia-Pacific Region. *South Asian Research Quarterly* 4: 1–7.
Zhang, Jiegen. 2015. The Analysis of Current US-India Security Cooperation and Prospect. *Research on Indian Ocean Economies* 1: 42.
Zhao, Qinghai. 2013. The Concept of "Indo-Pacific" and Its Implications for China. *Modern International Relations* 7: 14–22.
Zhao, Minghao. 2017. The United States "Indo-Pacific" Strategy: Old Wine in Old Bottles? *Beijing News*, 20 Nov 2017.
Zhou, Zhe. 2013. A Probe into the Political Motivation of Economic Conflicts between Powers—Based on a Comparative Analysis of US-Japan, US-China Trade Friction. *Political Economy Review*.
Zhu, Cuiping. 2013. Perceiving Threats, Constructing Threats and the US-India Ocean Strategy Extension. *South Asian Studies* 2.
Zhu, Cuiping. 2014a. Strategic Competition and Multilateral Relations in the Indo-Pacific Region. In *Indian Ocean Regional Development Report*, 2014 ed. Social Science Literature Publishing House.
Zhu, Cuiping. 2014b. The Security Situation in the Indian Ocean and the Dilemma of Cooperation between China and India. *South Asian Studies* 3: 1.
Zhu, Qingxiu. 2016. Can Japan's "Indo-Pacific" Strategy Succeed? *Northeast Asia Forum* 3: 103–113.
Zhu, Cuiping. 2017. The South Asian Direction of the Belt and Road Initiative: Geopolitical Landscape, India's Difficulties and Breakthrough Paths. *South Asian Studies* 2: 11.
Zhu, Feng. 2018. The Contest Between the Powers of the South China Sea Under the Shadow of the "Indo-Pacific Strategy", *World Knowledge* 1: 18.

The Prospect of the "Indo-Pacific" Concept and China's Countermeasures

Hailin Ye

Abstract The report has reviewed the development and evolution process of the concept of "Indo-Pacific", outlined the attitude of the United States, Japan, India and Australia towards the Trump version of the "Indo-Pacific" concept, analyzed the strategic intention of the parties concerned to push "Indo-Pacific" from concept to actual operation and on this basis, discussed the future trends and policy prospects of the interaction among the United States, Japan, India and Australia under the "Indo-Pacific" concept. The report believes that although Trump's "Indo-Pacific" concept shows the strategic intent of the United States to prevent the rise of its strategic rivals, reinforces its collaboration with major allies in the Pacific, satisfies India's vanity as a world power and can contain China to some extent, however, due to the lack of implementation means, inadequate geopolitical conditions and the difficulty to coordinate the strategic demands of all parties concerned, it is hard for "Indo-Pacific" strategy led by the US to achieve the goal of reconstructing global strategic pattern and preventing by the US of the rise of strategic rivals.

Keywords Indo-Pacific · US-Japan-India-Australia · Strategic intention · Strategic capability

The US President Donald Trump issued a new version of *The National Security Strategy of the United States of America* in December 2017. This basic document representing the official position of the United States on national security and international strategy is not only a historic and public manifestation of the United States' determination to take China as its strategic rival and try to contain the rise of China, but also, for the first time, puts forward and interprets the Indian-Pacific Ocean as

---

Ye Hailin is the director of the Editorial Dept. of *South Asian Studies* published by National Institute of International Strategy, CASS, director of South Asia Research Centre, National Institute of International Strategy, CASS, director of International Strategy Institute, Research Institute for Indian Ocean Economies, Yunnan University of Finance and Economics.

H. Ye (✉)
National Institute of International Strategy, CASS, Beijing, China

Yunnan University of Finance and Economics, Kunming, China

C. Zhu (ed.), *Annual Report on the Development of the Indian Ocean Region (2018)*, Research Series on the Chinese Dream and China's Development Path, https://doi.org/10.1007/978-981-13-7693-1_2

a geostrategic whole, which reveals the strategic intention of the United States to achieve strategic linkage in the Indian Ocean and Pacific Ocean, strengthen and expand its own alliance system and contain China. Before and after the introduction of the Report, the United States has had several interactions with its key Pacific allies Japan and Australia and its potential Indian Ocean ally India, forming certain momentum in the fields of diplomacy and security.

Linking the Indian Ocean and the Pacific Ocean into a geostrategic whole is not initiated by the United States. However, since the United States is the only superpower in the world, Trump's repackaging and high-profile introduction of the "Indo-Pacific" strategy has greatly enhanced the discourse power of the "Indo-Pacific" concept and become a hot issue of concern in the circle of international relations for some time, meanwhile, China's academic and policy research circles have also made preliminary targeted research results on Trump's new version of the "Indo-Pacific" concept on the basis of previous studies.[1] This report will analyze the implementation prospect of the "Indo-Pacific" concept with the matching degree of strategic intentions and strategic capabilities of the United States, Japan, India and Australia as a starting point, and provide suggestions for China's possible countermeasures.

1 The Introduction and Evolution of the "Indo-Pacific" Concept

It was Japan that first drew on the concept of "Indo-Pacific" from the expressions of scholars and think-tanks and used and elaborated it at the official level. In August 2007, the then Prime Minister of Japan Shinzo Abe visited New Delhi. In a speech to the Indian Parliament, Abe stated Japan's understanding of the concept of "Indo-Pacific" for the first time, Abe said, "the intersection of the Indian Ocean and the Pacific Ocean has shaped a new 'wider Asia', I feel that it is imperative for democratic states at both sides of the two oceans to deepen friendship among the people at any level." During his visit to India, Abe not only used the "Indo-Pacific" concept for the first time, but also made it clear that Japan, India, the United States and Australia were the main partners under the "Indo-Pacific" concept. Abe claimed, "as Japan and India come together, a 'wider' Asia will evolve into a vast network across the Pacific

[1] From 2013 to early 2018, nearly 100 papers on the concept of "Indo-Pacific" have been published in the field of international relations in China, especially since the beginning of 2017, with the enhancement of the interaction among the United States, Japan, Australia and India under the concept of "Indo-Pacific", the scholars of international relations in China have attached greater importance to the study of "Indo-Pacific". Among the most representative achievements in recent years are Wei (2013), Wu (2014), Zhao (2013), Xia (2015), Zhang (2013, 2017), Song (2016), etc., these papers focus on the four countries of the United States, Japan, India and Australia and the concept of "Indo-Pacific" as a whole for research. Since Trump introduced the new version of the "Indo-Pacific" concept at the end of 2017, many scholars have made targeted research and provided valuable countermeasures, such as Zhang and Wang (2018), Lin (2018), Xu (2018), Wu (2018), Zhou and Wang (2018), Li (2018), etc.

Ocean, including the United States and Australia."[2] The four-party mechanism of "US, Japan, India and Australia" which has got official approval and is trying to be promoted just started here.

Although the speech of the Japanese prime minister in India's parliament received generally positive response from the Indian government to the media, however, Abe's speech did not lead to a significant increase in the level of cooperation between Japan and India under the "Indo-Pacific" concept, and two other key strategic partners in Abe's vision, the US and Australia, have also been less responsive. During the Obama administration from 2008 to 2016, especially when Hillary Clinton served as Secretary of State, the United States has repeatedly stressed the importance of strategic cooperation between the United States and India and given India a high degree of diplomatic attention, in 2011, Hillary Clinton used the "Indo-Pacific" concept for the first time, claiming that "the Indian Ocean and the Pacific Ocean are increasingly connected for shipping and strategic reasons."[3] But for one thing, the actual results are not significant, the level of cooperation between the United States and India has risen slowly, and the huge potential of cooperation in geopolitics and geoeconomics strongly advocated by the two sides has not been demonstrated at the practical level; second, the diplomatic focus of the Obama administration in his second term is not in the India Ocean, and the position and role of India in the US's high-profile strategy of "Pivot to Asia" are not so clear; third, with the outbreak of the Arab Spring, the focus of American diplomacy when John Kerry served as Secretary of State actually shifted back to the Middle East. The most important reason is that the United States had showed obvious inertia in the diplomacy during the late Obama administration, for its strategic initiative declined and strategic determination was not that firm, and as a world hegemon, the United States has continued to lose interest in its own alliance system.

Under such circumstances, whether multilateral cooperation among the United States, Japan, India and Australia or bilateral cooperation between the United States and India, the relationship architecture necessary for "Indo-Pacific" to evolve from concept to mature strategy with practicality has not been put into practice. Over the years, "Indo-Pacific" has been constantly talked about, but very few people have taken it seriously. This awkward situation did not change quickly and noticeably until Trump came to power.

On June 2, 2017, the Australian Prime Minister Turnbull delivered a speech at the Shangri-La Dialogue (SLD) held in Singapore, talking about "China Threat" and the importance of Indo-Pacific cooperation. Turnbull said, "in response to increasing uncertainty and instability, we need to play a greater role in defending and shaping the future of the region (Indo-Pacific), which, as the most dynamic region, is a key region to shape and control the world economically, strategically and culturally." Turnbull

[2]"Confluence of the Two Seas" Speech by H. E. Mr. Shinzo Abe, Prime Minister of Japan at the Parliament of the Republic of India. http://www.mofa.go.jp/region/asia-paci/pmv0708/speech-2.html.

[3]Hillary Clinton: America's Pacific Century, *Foreign Policy*. http://foreignpolicy.com/2011/10/11/americas-pacific-century/.

touted the United States' global leadership, claiming that "peace and stability in the Asia-Pacific region are achieved by the consistent global leadership of the United States." Turnbull added that "the alliance with the United States reflects a profound alignment of interests and values." Australia demanded that the Indo-Pacific region "has free navigation and that the rights of small states can be unimpeded, that the national land, maritime and airspace boundaries that are shared can be respected and protected, and that differences among nations should be resolved through dialogue on the basis of respecting for agreements already reached and existing mechanisms. In this world, big fish should not eat small ones, nor should intimidate them."[4]

Turnbull took a lot of time talking about China, saying: "China's growing power is sparking a heated debate, and China will play a bigger role in shaping the order of the region. It is natural that Beijing wants to gain strategic influence commensurate with its economic volume. We want to see China demonstrate the leadership it aspires to, but it should be done in a way that reinforces the order of the region on which we are also working. Some countries worry that China will implement Monroe Doctrine in this hemisphere to control the region and marginalize the roles and contributions of other countries, especially the United States. Some argue that China will isolate those who oppose it or are not in its interests while offering generous economic returns to those who are in tune with it. Such negative thought is bad for our future. China has benefited most from peace and harmony in the region, if peace and harmony are threatened, China will suffer the most. Rapidly rising powers, such as modern China and ancient Athens, can cause anxiety. President Xi Jinping himself has pointed out the need to replace fear with confidence so as not to fall into the Thucydides trap and the ensuring conflicts.[5]

Turnbull's remarks drew widespread media and academic attention, not because the shift of Australia's attitude towards China could have serious political, economic and security consequences for the Asia-Pacific region. In fact, Australia's ability to check and balance China is the weakest in the four-party mechanism of the United States, Japan, India and Australia. The focus on Turnbull's speech was because, to a large extent, Australia's attitude represented America's position. In April 2017, when Turnbull visited the United States and met with the new President Trump, the two sides reached an important consensus on pushing "Indo-Pacific" from concept to strategy. Just days after Turnbull's speech, U.S. Secretary of State Rex Tillerson and Secretary of Defense James N. Mattis held the 27th US-Australia "2 + 2" ministerial consultation with Australia's Foreign Minister Julie Bishop and Secretary of Defense Marcel Payne in Sydney, at which the two sides decided to further strengthen the US-Australia alliance to implement Trump's India-Pacific security strategy. At a press conference, Bishop said, "Australia and the United States stress that the two countries will continue to deepen their mutual commitments to ensure the security, stability and prosperity of the India-Pacific region and to consolidate the regional mechanisms

[4]Keynote address at the 16th IISS Asia Security Summit, Shangri-La Dialogue.https://www.malcolmturnbull.com.au/media/keynote-address-at-the-16th-iiss-asia-security-summit-shangri-la-dialogue.

[5]Ibid.

represented by East Asia Summit, APEC and ASEAN Defense Ministers' Meeting Plus".[6] It is the first time that the two countries highlighted the concept of Indo-Pacific in the "2 + 2" consultation. Just as the "Iron Curtain" speech of former British Prime Minister Winston Churchill lifted the curtain of Cold War, the speech made by the Australian Prime Minister at the Shangri-La Dialogue also means that the game among the major powers in the Pacific Ocean Area is evolving from the "Asia-Pacific" concept to the "Indo-Pacific" concept. A new era has begun.

After the United States and Australia jointly promoted the concept of "Indo-Pacific", the interaction among the four sides of the United States, Japan, India and Australia under the concept of "Indo-Pacific" increased significantly, and the concept of "Indo-Pacific" was gaining momentum. In September 2017, Mattis visited India, the first visit by a cabinet member since the Trump administration came to power. A Pentagon spokesman said Mattis "will stress that the United States views India as an important and influential partner, and there is a wide range of common interests between the two sides, not only in South Asia." A month later, Tillerson visited India. "The United States and India discussed a number of issues such as strengthening the US-India partnership and India's leadership in peace and security matters in the India-Pacific region, as well as India's unique position in the US government's South Asia strategy,"[7] he said. Within just one month, two heavyweight U.S. cabinet members visited India, which not only demonstrated the importance attached by the new administration of the United States to India, but also paved the way for the cooperation of the US-Japan-India-Australia four-party mechanism under the concept of "Indo-Pacific".

With the increasingly close security and strategic ties between the United States and India, the interaction between the major Pacific allies of the United States and India in the field of security has also become more frequent and deeper. September 15, 2017, Australia's Defense Minister Kevin Andrews visited India and announced the approval of the Australian navy to participate in a joint naval exercise by the United States, Japan, India and Australia. The Australian government had experienced a long hesitation about whether to participate in the Malabar exercise. In May 2017, after Turnbull's returning from a visit to the United States, Canberra was determined not to worry about the possibility that the move may cause anxiety in China and affect the Sino-Australia relations, and formally requested to participate in the joint navel exercise of the United States, Japan and India.

Interestingly, Australia's request for participation did not receive a positive response from India at first. It is clear that New Delhi, while strengthening cooperation with the United States and Japan, is unwilling to unduly stimulate China and damage its relations with China. A Chinese Foreign Ministry spokesman positively affirmed India's move, commenting that "we would like to see normal dialogue and

---

[6]Top White House officials visit Sydney for terrorism talks. www.xinhuanet.com/english/2017-06/05/c_136341297.htm.

[7]Rex Tillerson's visit to India highlights emerging Indo-US ties. https://economictimes.indiatimes.com/news/defence/rex-tillersons-visit-to-india-highlights-emerging-indo-us-ties/articleshow/61256055.cms.

exchanges between the parties in the military field. Of course, I also hope that when all parties carry out relevant activities, they will fully take into account the security concerns of the countries in the region, and that relevant exchanges and cooperation should be able to play a constructive role in safeguarding regional peace and stability."[8] However, just a few months later, due to the occurrence of Doklam crisis, India's position has changed dramatically. In September 2017, India and Australia formally reached an agreement. As the most intuitive manifestation of the four-party mechanism of the United States, Japan, India and Australia in the field of military security, the Malabar exercise could finally cover all the key members of the "Indo-Pacific" alliance envisioned by Abe that year and now strongly pushed by Trump.

On November 11, 2017, officials of the United States, Japan, India and Australia held talks when attending the 31st ASEAN Summit and officials' meetings (SOM) on East Asia cooperation in Manila, Philippines. After 10 years of gestation, the United States, Japan, India and Australia have broken through the previous bilateral or trilateral coordination model, and the four-nation mechanism has officially launched. The Manila meeting was a landmark event held by the four parties under the Indo-Pacific concept, and the four countries agreed that "a free, open and inclusive Indo-Pacific region is in line with the long-term interest of the region and of all countries in the world. Officials attending the meeting also discussed how to address common challenges affecting the region, such as terrorism and nuclear proliferation, and exchanged views on strengthening ties".[9] So far, the carrying out of strategic cooperation among the United States, Japan, India and Australia under the "Indo-Pacific" concept has completed ex-ante preparatory work.

At the end of 2017, Trump signed a new version of *National Security Strategy Report of the United States*, repackaging the concept of "Indo-Pacific" and introducing it as the basic concept of the US regional security strategy in the new era. The Report puts "Indo-Pacific" as a separate region and places it on the top of the strategic regions that the United States needs to deal with. The United States "supports and welcomes the strong leading role of Japan as a key ally", and affirms the value of Australia as its long-term ally, "Australia has been on our side in every major conflict since the World War I and continued to strengthen our economic and security arrangements to safeguard our common interests and defend democratic values throughout the region".[10] The United States also said that it "welcomes the rise of India as a world power and a strong strategic and defense partner, and will work to promote the cooperation among the United States, Japan, India and Australia".[11] The Report played up China's "threat" to the Indo-Pacific region, saying, "China claims that its ambitions will benefit many, however, China's dominance will undermine the

---

[8]Foreign Ministry Spokesperson Hua Chunying's Regular Press Conference on May 31, 2017. http://www.fmprc.gov.cn/web/fyrbt_673021/t1466605.shtml.

[9]India, Australia, Japan, US discuss cooperation in Indo-Pacific region. http://www.tribuneindia.com/news/nation/india-australia-japan-us-discuss-cooperation-in-indo-pacific-region/496499.html.

[10]http://nssarchive.us/wp-content/uploads/2017/12/2017.pdf.

[11]http://nssarchive.us/wp-content/uploads/2017/12/2017.pdf.

sovereignty of many countries in the region. The countries in the region called on the United States to continue its leadership and respond jointly to maintain regional order that respects sovereignty and independence".[12]

After the formal establishment of the four-nation mechanism and the release of Trump's new version of *National Security Strategy Report*, the stance of the United States, Japan, India and Australia on the concept of "Indo-Pacific" and the attitude towards China have become more aligned. At the Raisina Dialogue held on January 19, 2018, India's Chief of Naval Staff, Sunil Lanba, publicly criticized China's maritime activities in the Indian Ocean, misinterpreting the construction of maritime infrastructure by China and the countries along the Indian Ocean as military projects of the Chinese navy, the Chinese navy "has a base in Djibouti and a port in Hambantota, Sri Lanka", India's comments were widely echoed by the participants from the United States, Japan and Australia.[13]

2 The Strategic Intention and Implementation Means of the Four Countries to Promote the Concept of "Indo-Pacific"

The US, Japan, India and Australia jointly promoting the concept of "Indo-Pacific" has obvious geopolitical considerations, that is, containing the rise of the common strategic rival supposed by the four countries—China through the realization of strategic linkages in the Indian and Pacific regions. On the premise of the same or similar overall strategic objectives, there are still some differences in intentions, strategies and means of implementation among the four countries, which need to be paid attention to.

The US is not the inventor of the "Indo-Pacific" concept, but the key promoter to change the decade-long downturn of the "Indo-Pacific" concept. Without the high-profile declaration of the Trump administration, "Indo-Pacific" is still a self-comforting concept created by a few politicians and scholars in Japan and India. The US plays a decisive role in the development and evolution of "Indo-Pacific" concept. Although the strategic path of the US' Indo-Pacific concept is still under planning for now, it must be acknowledged that Trump's concept of Indo-Pacific already has the basis to develop into a containment and confrontation strategy. First of all, it has obvious directionality, that is, to carry out curved containment on China from the perspective of geostrategy, the strategic motive is very clear. Trump has taken a hard line with China on issues such as South China Sea, Taiwan and Korean Peninsula since taking office, and attempted to challenge China's bottom line and tested China's strategic determination by signing *Taiwan Travel Act*. Among Trump's policy tools

[12]http://nssarchive.us/wp-content/uploads/2017/12/2017.pdf.

[13]China a disruptive power: Quadrilateral nations navy chiefs. https://economictimes.indiatimes.com/news/defence/china-a-disruptive-power-quadrilateral-nations-navy-chiefs/articleshow/62565183.cms.

against China, there are trade balance and intellectual property rights at the economic and trade level, the nuclear issue in the Korean Peninsula, the Taiwan Issue and the South China Sea dispute at the geopolitical field, and the concept “Indo-Pacific” with the strategic linkages in the two oceans at the global strategic level. Secondly, the major means is to build a military alliance for coordinated deterrence against China. Trump has a clear tendency to unilateralism in terms of economic policy, prefers to force strategic rivals to compromise through blackmail that directly affects bilateral relations, and has no interest in regional multilateral arrangements that need to bear the costs. The possibility of the US to return to TPP (Trans-Pacific Partnership) under the “Indo-Pacific” concept of course exists, yet Trump’s extreme egoism in economic policy will greatly undermine the effectiveness of the U.S. economic cooperation programs in any direction—if the US could introduce multilateral economic cooperation programs in Trump era.

Japan is the core ally of the US in the strategic layout of the Asia-Pacific region, and the Abe government has imitated America at every step. Moreover, Abe himself is the founder of the “Indo-Pacific” concept politically and diplomatically and Japan is naturally more active in pushing “Indo-Pacific” from concept to realization. But even so, Japan’s expectations and intentions for India are different from that of the United States. On the issue of security, the “Indo-Pacific” concerned by Japan is still mainly on the South China Sea issue. Japan expects to draw as many countries as possible into the South China Sea dispute and launch a confrontation with China to prevent China from seizing command of the sea in the South China Sea, while at the same time consuming China’s diplomatic and military resources in order for Japan to gain an advantage in the East China Sea when gaming with China. Economically, the Abe government attaches great importance to the concept of “Indo-Pacific”, and Japan hopes to expand its economic interests in a vast area from Southeast Asia to South Asia based on this concept. In Southeast Asia, Japan has teamed up with India to compete with China by virtue of its economic influence and India’s cultural influence; in South Asia, Japan has made use of its industrial layout in Southeast Asia and ASEAN-India Free Trade Agreement to enter the Indian market and avoid India’s tariff protection. Of the four major players under the Indo-Pacific concept, Japan has the strongest economic motivation. Japan even envisions magnifying the “Indo-Pacific” and joining hands with India to promote the “Asian-African Growth Corridor” extending from Southeast Asia to the African continent. The assumption is at least broader than the “Belt and Road” driven by China in terms of coverage. Of course, this assumption is largely utopian in nature. Don’t say Japan plus India, even plus the US, there is no way to create a collaborative program that goes beyond symbolism in such a vast area.

By far, Australia has been the most active and swift to take a stand on the concept of “Indo-Pacific”. Since coming to power, the Turnbull government has changed the balanced foreign policy of the previous government and has been at the forefront of containing China. It is no exaggeration to describe Turnbull’s speech at the Shangri-La Dialogue as the first horn of the western countries led by the US to contain China under the concept of “Indo-Pacific”. However, it is precisely to say Australia has the vaguest specific appeal to the concept of “Indo-Pacific” and the biggest room for policy adjustment. Unlike Japan and India, Australia has no direct security conflicts or territorial disputes with China, and unlike the US, Australia has benefited enormously from its economic relations with China. Participation in containing China under the concept of "Indo-Pacific" would only expose Australia to unnecessary security risks and specific economic losses. Turnbull's policy is largely based on the values of Australia's western attributes, not on precise calculation of Australia's national interest. That means that Turnbull's policy is reversible and, if there is a change of government in Australia, the possibility of a change in foreign policy is much greater than that of the other three major players under the concept of "Indo-Pacific". And even if Australia does not adjust its policy, it will not have particularly serious impact on China, both because Australia's direct link with China is relatively weak and because Australia is only a medium-sized power, it does not have the ability to project power to areas where China has a stake. In a sense, Australia's embracing of "Indo-Pacific" is just an attitude that can hardly produce meaningful results.

Relative to the US, Japan and Australia, India's embracing of the "Indo-Pacific" concept has the best performance price ratio. The main intentions of India to participate in the "Indo-Pacific" interaction are as follows: first, to enhance its international status, demonstrate its great power posture and consolidate its dominant position in the South Asian Subcontinent. India has dreamed of being a powerful country since the Nehru era. After the Modi government came to power, New Delhi's appeal for international status has become stronger and stronger, with both a desire to be recognized as a world power on an equal footing with other major powers and a requirement for other powers to respect its exclusive dominance in the South Asian Subcontinent. Trump's new version of the "Indo-Pacific" concept not only formally inherits the diplomatic stance of previous U.S. administrations towards India, but also gives India some real benefits. The US's affirmation and support for India have strengthened India's attitude of strengthening its presence and displaying its image as a great power on the international stage. Unlike China, India has always been very high-profile in its own development, however, what New Delhi is trying to achieve is its rise within the international system, it has no will or possibility to challenge the global hegemony of the United States. Therefore, actively cooperating with the US' concept of "Indo-Pacific" will not impair India's international status, instead, it helps India create the image of a great power in front of other countries, especially small and medium-sized countries in South Asia. Secondly, to improve the game situation with China, increase the weight of India-China relations in China's foreign policy, and improve its checks and balances on China. India itself is well aware of the huge gap in overall strength between China and India. The reason why India has dared to challenge China repeatedly in recent years on issues involving China's core or at least vital interests is not because India is confident that it already has the power to stand up to China, but because India sees the current global strategic situation as favoring India over China. India can use situational advantage to hedge against China's strength advantage. Actively participating in the four-party mechanism and strengthening the expression of the concept of "Indo-Pacific" can increase the deterrence and checks & balances on China. On the one hand, India believes that China will be subject to the momentum of the US-Japan-India-Australia four-party mechanism and is more cautious about India; on the other hand, India can get the technical and equipment support it needs from the US and Japan to increase its tactical advantage over China in some areas. Finally, increase its participation in the international market to reap real economic benefits. Modi's economic development strategy of "Made in India" has raised the importance of overseas markets to India's economic development. In recent years, India has attached great importance to the development of overseas markets including Southeast Asia and taken it as a crucial growth point for economic development. India has also put forward a series of regional economic cooperation plans aimed at strengthening its geo-economic influence. From the Bay of Bengal to a vast area of the South Pacific, India has historically maintained very close cultural and economic ties with them. Guided by the "Act East" policy and relying on the advantageous path already established by the US, Japan and Australia, India can save the cost of market development, assist Indian enterprises in overseas layout and operation and provide overseas support for India's economic growth.

Based on the above strategic differences, the policy focus of the US, Japan, India and Australia to promote the concept of "Indo-Pacific" is different, for there are division of labor and coordination, as well as mutual constraints. The US strengthens the effect of "Indo-Pacific" mainly by deterrence through military means, while Japan, on the other hand, emphasizes the economic color of "Indo-Pacific" and focuses on seeking the dominant power of regional economic order through close economic ties with relevant countries, thus hedging the rise of China's economy that has put severe psychological pressure on Japan. India, for its part, is the biggest real beneficiary of the "Indo-Pacific" concept, yet is unwilling to pay any costs for it. In India's view, the US, Japan and Australia, in order to contain China, should have supported India and helped India economically and militarily. India itself does not need to develop a dedicated "Indo-Pacific" engagement strategy, it would be enough as long as it expresses its support when the US, Japan and Australia promote relevant strategies. India's participation in promoting the concept of "Indo-Pacific" as a recipient and responder not only conforms to the nature of the relationship between India and the US, Japan and Australia, but also reflects the power gap between India and the other three parties, especially the US and Japan. More importantly, this strategy will enable India to maintain a certain degree of strategic autonomy on the premise of participating in the "Indo-Pacific" concept, to reserve the possibility of coordinating with China and even striving for China's "surrendering part of the interests", so as to maximize India's interests. Of course, in the long run, this strategy will not help India's strategic cooperation with the alliance system led by the US, nor will it deepen the strategic mutual trust between the two sides. This, however, is not important for the nascent concept of "Indo-Pacific", at least for the time being.

3 The Impact of "Indo-Pacific" on China and the Strategic Risks that China Needs to Avoid

There is no doubt that the strengthening of strategic cooperation among the US, Japan, India and Australia under the concept of "Indo-Pacific" will further complicate China's surrounding environment, and in China's foreign strategy, the relevant considerations between the major powers and the neighboring diplomacy will be more complicated. The difficulty of maintaining strategic coordination between China's primary strategic direction and secondary strategic direction has increased, resulting in the rise of external constraints on China's rise. However, for China, the key to the problem is not to determine the negative nature of the impact of the "Indo-Pacific" concept on China, but rather to establish appropriate coping strategies on the basis of accurately assessing the extent of such negative impact and correctly analyzing the degree of impact and threat.

Under the concept of "Indo-Pacific", the negative effects on China caused by the strategic linkage among the US, Japan, India and Australia are mainly reflected in the following aspects:

First, the security environment around China has deteriorated and strategic pressure has increased. For a long time, the US-Japan alliance has been the primary strategic direction of China and the main source of pressure at sea.[14] Whether it's the South China Sea dispute, the Taiwan Strait issue or the Diaoyu Islands issue in the East China Sea, a closely coordinated US-Japan alliance is the primary threat to China's national security and national interests. China's so-called security dilemma of the "four-sea linkage" in the South China Sea, the Taiwan Strait, the East China Sea and the Korean Peninsula is exactly the result of the United States' strategy of suppressing China through the US-Japan alliance. The pressure from the US-Japan alliance cannot be resolved, and the hostile policy of the Turnbull government towards China has added the Australian factor to the pressure on China at sea. The "confrontation" between the two navies in the South China Sea in April 2018 shows Australia's eagerness to show its efforts following its participation in the four-party mechanism. Although Australia's weighting has limited impact on China, yet India, as a major Indian Ocean power, once formally participates in the US-Japan-India-Australia mechanism, it's not just a matter of adding an adversary to China, a more serious possible consequence is the addition of a strategic direction that could lead to the adverse situation of double containment.

Second, the relative factors of China's major-power diplomacy and its neighboring diplomacy are more complicated, and strategic coordination becomes more difficult. Since the 16th CPC National Congress, major-power diplomacy, neighbor diplomacy and diplomacy of developing countries have been the three basic directions of China's diplomatic work. Although the 19th CPC National Congress has

[14]For more on the strategic direction of China's rise, please refer to my article "The Rise of China and the Response to the Challenges from Secondary Strategic Direction - Taking the Sino-India Relationship After the Dong Lang Incident as an Example", *World Economics and Politics*, Issue No. 4, 2018.

changed relevant statements since the 16th CPC National Congress that "major powers are the key, neighboring countries are the priority and developing countries are the foundation", and replaced it with related statements such as "actively developing global partnership, expanding the convergence of interests with all countries, promoting coordination and cooperation among major countries, constructing a framework for major-country relations featuring overall stability and balanced development, deepening the relationship with neighboring countries in accordance with the concept of amity, sincerity, mutual benefit and inclusiveness and the diplomatic policy of being a good neighbor and partner with neighboring countries, adhering to the correct view of justice and interests and the concept of honesty, amity and sincerity to strengthen solidarity and cooperation with developing countries, as well as strengthening exchanges and cooperation with political parties and organizations of other countries and promoting external exchanges of the NPC, the CPPCC, the armed forces, local authorities and mass organizations, etc.,[15] however, the classification of China's diplomatic objects has not changed, and China still divides its diplomacy into three main categories by object: major powers, neighboring countries and developing countries. Of which, how to coordinate the interests, goals and strategies of major-power diplomacy and neighboring diplomacy has always been a key challenge in China's diplomacy. Whether taking major powers as the priority or taking neighboring countries as the priority,[16] the related problems have always been flickering in China's diplomacy. On the Korean Peninsula issue, whether the priority goal is to maintain peace and stability on the peninsula in the context of neighboring relations, or to pursue the denuclearization of the peninsula in the context of major power relations? How should China respond if it cannot have both? The recurrence of such problems reflects the difficulty for China to conduct relational consideration in major power diplomacy and neighboring diplomacy. With the embodiment of the four-party mechanism of the US, Japan, India and Australia, the boundary between China's major power diplomacy and neighboring diplomacy has become more blurred. Is India a major power or a neighboring country? Is it necessary to consider the US factor in the policy towards India? Specifically, under the US-Japan-India-Australia mechanism, if India wants to retain Doklam crisis on the border issue, will China's considerations change?

Third, it is more difficult for China to maintain strategic coordination in primary and secondary strategic directions, and the possibility of restraining each other has increased. India has long been a secondary direction in the rise of China, posing little threat to China, and its relations with China are also under control. Once India participates in the four-party linkage, both the strength of seeking the game against China and the correlation effect of specific strategies will increase. The strategic risk faced by China when responding to India's challenges in the secondary direction will also increase, China will have to be more concerned about the regional and

[15] http://www.xinhuanet.com/politics/19cpcnc/2017-10/27/c_1121867529.htm.

[16] For relevant studies, please refer to my article "Selection of Strategic Objectives, Strategic Priorities and the Possibility of Strategic Overdraft", *Journal of Strategy and Decision Making*, Issue No. 3, 2017.

even international effects of the strategies towards India, for which could lead to the situation of "holding back from taking action against one party for fear of injuring other parties". On the one hand, if China takes a tough strategy against India, it may be countered by the US in the primary strategic direction; on the other hand, if China tries to stabilize Sino-India relations to avoid putting too much effort into the secondary strategic direction, for this will reduce the ability and raise the difficulty of China to cope with the primary strategic direction, it may on the contrary make India believe that the current situation is favorable for it to strengthen the strategic and tactical blackmail against China by relying on the four-party mechanism and repeatedly attempt brinkmanship, as a result, China will not only find it difficult to balance the primary and secondary strategic directions, but may also fall into the dilemma of ineffective means in the secondary strategic direction.

The possibility and potential risk of China's being restricted by two lines as a result of the concept of "Indo-Pacific" must be highly valued and carefully dealt with by China. It is necessary to see that strategic risk exists objectively, but the degree of risk must be analyzed calmly. At least for the time being and for some time to come, the four-party mechanism of the US, Japan, India and Australia is still very far from the Asian version of NATO envisioned by the Indian scholar Nalapat in 2006, for its strategic connotation is not clear, the strategic coordination is far from reaching the level of military and political alliance, the power of the member states is seriously unbalanced, the intentions are not matched with the capabilities, moreover, it's restricted by other directions and other factors, with obvious shortfalls and difficulty in meeting the strategic expectations of the members of the four-party mechanism.

I. The new version of "Indo-Pacific" concept has no clear content and specific means. Although the US, Japan, India and Australia have carried out a great deal of propaganda on the concept of "Indo-Pacific" and released a lot of strategic signals, so far, the four sides still lack credible means and clear goals as for how to build the concept of "Indo-Pacific" into an overall strategic concept. Theoretically, the Indo-Pacific linkage would put China in a situation where it would be trapped on both sides. In practice, however, achieving this requires the parties concerned to carry out precise strategic coordination and make mutually supportive strategic arrangements and tactical actions, at least not just to be content with multilateral or small multilateral joint military exercises, or momentum-building diplomatic and PR activities. To achieve strategic coordination, the first thing to be done is finding an effective entry point for the Indo-Pacific linkage, and the current maritime security issues can not really offset China's actions.
II. The capabilities of some participating countries do not match with their intentions and they lack the strength to achieve their strategic goals. Promoting its status as a major power and increasing checks and balances on China are India's important strategic intention to participate in the "Indo-Pacific" framework. However, the realization of the former requires India not only to demonstrate its ability to deter neighboring countries, but also to create and develop public

goods based on inclusiveness or even unilateral preferences for these countries in order to build their dependence on India. India is unable to achieve this goal at the moment, instead, it is counting on other members of the four-party mechanism to aid it. Economically, three of the four sides need to support India, yet India cannot offer returns. On the security front, India's protracted conflict with Pakistan over the line of control shows that New Delhi is not capable of challenging two major rivals at the same time as it claims. More importantly, India can indeed delay or even temporarily thwart some of China's cooperation programs in the South Asian subcontinent, but it cannot provide compensation or substitution for the third party factors affected therefrom, so the effect of such checks and balances can only be temporary. To sum up, for now, the US, Japan and Australia cannot expect India to truly become the second front in containing China.

III. Differences in the status of the members within the four-party framework make it hard to maintain stable collaboration. Among the four parties, the US is overwhelmingly dominant, with Japan, Australia and India all as its followers. However, the status of the three followers is not so equal. Japan and Australia are long-term allies of the United States, and the US-Japan alliance is the cornerstone of the United States' Pacific security strategy. The relationship between India and the US is by no means comparable to that of Japan and Australia with the US. The unbalanced relationship pattern is bound to have adverse effects on the action ability and efficiency of the four-party mechanism. This is why India should still attach great importance to the bilateral interaction with the US, with Japan and with Australia, and the trilateral interaction with Japan and Australia and with Australia and the US even after participating in the four-party mechanism of the US, Japan, India and Australia. The complexity of the level of collaboration itself indicates the difficulty of collaboration. The Pacific collaboration among the US, Japan and Australia has no obstacles and is dominant, while the collaboration between the three parties and India in the Indian Ocean is still subordinate, and the strategic trust required to produce results, at least at India's part, is not available for the time being.

IV. Other diplomatic directions have checks and balances on the US, Japan, India and Australia, and it is difficult for all parties to make up their minds to concentrate their efforts. The US has to deal with the game with Russia in the Middle East and Europe, while India has always attached great importance to its cooperation with Russia. The "2 + 2" Dialogue between India and Australia was held on January 12, 2018, followed by the fourth round of Japan-India-Australia Dialogue at Deputy Foreign Minister Level. The day before the two meetings, the 15th China-Russia-India diplomatic meeting was also held in New Delhi. In 2017, India both responded positively to the new version of "Indo-Pacific" and became a full member of Shanghai Cooperation Organization (SCO). It can be seen that even as India is increasingly embracing the "Indo-Pacific" framework, it is afraid or unwilling to change its longstanding tradition of balanced diplomacy. Restraint in other directions is always there. While Japan and Australia, on the other hand, have a complex mindset on economic relations with China and are reluctant to fully follow America's lead in launching a full-scale trade confrontation with China.

To sum up, due to the limitations of the strength, strategic intention, the implication of other directions of the members of the four-party mechanism, the US, Japan, India and Australia still need a fairly long run-in under the "Indo-Pacific" framework. It is uncertain to ultimately realize the designer's strategic intention and achieve strategic results. China should believe that it has the means and the ability to play games with them, minimize the disadvantages and even break the strategic plots of the US, Japan, India and Australia.

Superficially, since India and the other three countries—the US, Japan and Australia are not strategic alliances and are in a relatively independent strategic direction. China is most likely to divide the four-party mechanism by winning over India. However, China must note that there are significant strategic risks that cannot be ignored in winning over or strategically placating India so that it does not participate or actively participate in the four-party mechanism. China needs to realize that, in terms of the current Sino-India relations and the global strategic situation, China does not have the policy space to win over and placate India, for if doing so, China may be blackmailed by India. In the trilateral interaction among China, the US and India, almost all of India's needs can be met by the US, and the US does not have to pay a price for it. Yet demands made by India on China, however, cannot be satisfied if China does not make interest concessions or even strategic compromises. China has few resources available to prevent the US and India from approaching each other. Therefore, on the basis of acknowledging the reality, China should consider how to formulate effective policies and strategies against India and against the concept of "Indo-Pacific" when the US and India's approaching from each other cannot be stopped.

First of all, China should maintain its strategic determination, observe the concrete actions of the four-party mechanism of the US, India, Japan and Australia to promote strategic coordination under the concept of "Indo-Pacific". There is no rush for preventive diplomacy, especially for the so-called division and disintegration. For a strategy that is not actually deployed and executed and has no practical effect, a more appropriate intervention means is strategic deterrence, rather than differentiation that needs to pay a higher cost, so as to avoid the blackmail mentality of the game opponent. In the course of playing the game with an opponent, the strategic shortsightedness of stabilizing the situation by voluntarily surrendering the interests should be strictly avoided.

Secondly, China should, based on its own, hedge the "Indo-Pacific" concept through cooperation with Southeast Asian countries. China should actively participate in the local economic construction in Southeast Asia by relying on the early harvest of the "Belt and Road" initiative to consolidate the friendly relations with Southeast Asian countries. As long as Southeast Asian countries do not respond positively to the concept of "Indo-Pacific", the Indian Ocean and the Pacific Ocean will always be two independent strategic directions, and there is little chance of being integrated by the US into one strategic region to form a chorus to contain China.

Thirdly, China should vigorously strengthen cooperation with small and medium-sized countries in South Asia, reject India's claim that India has exclusive influence in the Indian Ocean region, force India to recognize the reality of China's entry into the Indian Ocean through competition, and ultimately achieve Sino-India cooperation on the basis of mutual respect.

Finally, China should mainly use economic means to counter the "Indo-Pacific" strategy, supplemented by necessary military preparations. At the diplomatic level, China does not need to pay too much attention to the signals released by the four-party mechanism, so as to avoid being blackmailed by the four-party mechanism at low cost or even zero cost.

References

Li, Li. 2018. "India's Look East Strategy and Indo-Pacific Diplomacy". *Contemporary International Relations* (1).

Lin, Mingwang. 2018. "The Construction of Indo-Pacific and the Tension of Asian Geopolitics". *Foreign Affairs Review* (1).

Song, Wei. 2016. "On Australia's Concept of Indo-Pacific System and Its Choice of Strategic Path". *Journal of Shanghai Jiaotong University* (Philosophy and Social Science Edition) (2).

Wei, Zongyou. 2013. "The Impact of the "Indo-Pacific" Concept on the Multilateral Pattern of the Asia-Pacific Region". *World Economics and Politics* (10).

Wu, Zhaoli. 2014. "The Origin of "Indo-Pacific" and Multinational Strategic Game". *Pacific Journal* (1).

Wu, Huaizhong. 2018. "The Abe Administration's Indo-Pacific Strategy and China's Countermeasures". *Contemporary International Relations* (1), 2018.

Xia, Liping. 2015. "The 'Indo-Pacific Strategy' of the United States from the Dual Perspective of Geopolitics and Geo-economics". *American Studies* (2).

Xu, Jinjin. 2018. "The Trump Administration's 'Indo-Pacific Strategy'", *American Studies* (1).

Zhang, Li. 2013. "On Australia's Concept of Indo-Pacific System and Its Choice of Strategic Path". *South Asian Studies Quarterly* (4).

Zhang, Dongshun. 2017. "The Current Strategic Adjustment of Japan in the US Indo-Pacific Strategy". *Journal of Strategy and Decision Making* (2).

Zhang, Genhai, and Ying Wang. 2018. "The Orientation Analysis of the US-India-Japan-Australia Combination on the Security of the South China Sea from the Perspective of 'Indo-Pacific Strategic Arc'". *South Asian Studies* (1).

Zhao, Qinghai. 2013. "The Strategic Adjustment of the United States in the Indo-Pacific Region and Its Geostrategic Implications". *Contemporary International Relations* (7).

Zhou, Fangyin, and Wan Wang. 2018. "The Indo-Pacific Strategy From the Perspective of Australia and China's Countermeasures". *Contemporary International Relations* (1).

Part II
Special Report

The US' Indo-Pacific Initiative and Its Impact on China

Jiadong Zhang

Abstract Since President Trump took office, the term of "Indo-Pacific" has evolved from a mere geographical and geopolitical concept to a policy initiative. The Indo-Pacific Initiative calls for a closer economic, cultural and strategic links between the Asia-Pacific region and the Indian Ocean region. It is claimed that this new initiative, based on the rapid progress of regional integration in the Indo-Pacific area, reflects the overall aspirations of the countries in the area. In fact, it is intended by the US and its western partners to counterbalance the 21st Century Maritime Silk Road initiative put forward by the Chinese government. Behind this new initiative is the Cold War mentality, which has proved to be against the overall trend of current world development. The impact of the Indo-Pacific Initiative on China is multi-faceted. As a positive effect, the new initiative helps to confirm that China's presence in the Indian Ocean region is lawful and legitimate. As such, China, while disproving the Cold War mentality of containment, can take this chance to enhance its presence in the Indian Ocean region by engaging more actively in the regional affairs under the framework of the Indo-Pacific Initiative.

Keywords The Indo-Pacific · The US · The PRC

1 Introduction

In November 2017, the US President Trump paid a 12-day visit to five Asian countries. Trump's debut in Asia marks the longest visit by a US president in the past 25 years. Some information sources disclose that President Trump himself is very satisfied with this trip, remarking that his visit is a "great success" which has generated "incredible" achievements. Trump's journey to Asia has also caused a lot of controversy, as the president, during his visit, officially proposed the Indo-Pacific Initiative, which significantly differs from the previous Asia-Pacific concept. In the same journey, Trump also started the Group of Four Nations, which is widely rec-

J. Zhang (✉)
Fudan University, Shanghai, China

C. Zhu (ed.), *Annual Report on the Development of the Indian Ocean Region (2018)*, Research Series on the Chinese Dream and China's Development Path, https://doi.org/10.1007/978-981-13-7693-1_3

ognized as a new signpost of American foreign policy. Taking Trump's visit to Asia as a case study, this article tries to probe into the evolution of the US foreign policy with a focus on the Indo-Pacific Initiative.

2 Origin of the Indo-Pacific Initiative

The term of "Indo-Pacific" was originally a geographic concept. For ages, there was little discussion about this concept, nor was there any specific policy formulated for this geographic territory. However, since the beginning of the 21st century, this concept has drawn increasing attention, particularly with the rise of China and India. The US government did not take much interest in the "Indo-Pacific" concept until President Obama's administration. Even at that time, the concept showed no substantial difference from the term Asia-Pacific. As a matter of fact, the two terms were often used interchangeably. Things changed, when it came to Trump. The president, by following Japan, Australia and some other countries, formally proposed the Indo-Pacific Initiative as part of his foreign policy. It is said that Trump proposed this initiative for no other reason but to distinguish himself from his predecessor in terms of foreign policy. Whatever, the proposal of the "Indo-Pacific" initiative has indeed entailed the formulation of series of policies and strategies. Briefly, the term of Indo-Pacific has undergone three stages of evolution as a geographical concept, a geopolitical concept, and a specific policy initiative. Besides, more and more people would prefer to understand it as a specific containment "strategy" in the US' foreign policy.

2.1 Indo-Pacific as a Geographical Concept

The term of Indo-Pacific first came into being as a geographical concept with no geopolitical or strategic implication at all. In the 19th century, the Indian Ocean and the Pacific Ocean were deemed as one region for ethnographical reasons. Since the beginning of the 20th century, the term of Indo-Pacific region has appeared in academic writings in many countries.[1] Between the 1920s and the 1930s, German geopolitical scholar Karl Ernst Haushofer used the concept of "Indo-Pacific region/space" in his book entitled *Geopolitics of the Pacific Ocean*.[2] According to Rory Medcalf, a scholar with the Lowy Institute in Australia, the term of Indo-Pacific has long been an academic concept in Australia. In the 1950s and 1970s, the Australian Institute of International Affairs and the Australian National University (ANU) held several meetings on the decolonization issues, where this concept was mentioned from time

[1]Medcalf (2012).

[2]Haushofer (2002).

to time.[3] However, at that time, the term of Indo-Pacific was usually referred to in its geographical dimension, with other dimensions untouched for ages.

Even in its geographic sense, the term of Indo-Pacific arouses controversy regarding what areas shall be covered with this term. The Indo-Pacific Governance Research Centre at the University of Adelaide believed that Indo-Pacific refers to "the region ranging from the West Indian Ocean along the east coast of Africa to the Western Pacific". The India government would argue that Indo-Pacific should include the region from the Pacific Ocean to the entire Indian, which is a big Indian Ocean concept. Some American agencies, especially the Pacific Command, generally held that Indo-Pacific, similar to the jurisdiction of the Pacific Command, covers the region from the West Coast of the US to the west coast of India. Overall, the Indo-Pacific was a vague geographical concept in the early days.

2.2 *Indo-Pacific as a Geopolitical Concept*

Due to geographical factors, Australians were among the first to discover the geopolitical significance of the term of Indo-Pacific. Situated on the rim of the Asia-Pacific region, Australia is also on the crisscross of western and eastern civilizations. It always aspires to improve its marginalized status in international affairs. As early as in the 1960s and 1970s, Australian scholars put forward the Indo-Pacific concept for the reason of international security, arguing that maintaining a (strategic) balance between the Indian Ocean and the Pacific would help to guarantee Australia's national security.[4] However, this argument has not received sufficient attention for ages. Since the beginning of the 21st century, scholars from India, Japan, and Australia prefer to use the concept of the Indo-Pacific or Indo-Pacific region in their military and diplomatic writings.

This is particularly prominent in Australia. In 2005, Michael Richardson from the Institute of Southeast Asian Studies argued that the East Asia Summit (EAS) including India, Australia and New Zealand should mark the formation of a more unified India-pacific region. Other frequent users of this concept include Defense Minister Smith, also the former foreign minister, Peter Varghese, Secretary General of the Ministry of Foreign Affairs and Trade, Ric Smith, the former Defense Secretary General.[5] Rory Medcalf from the Australian Loy Institute of International Policy believes that the world has now entered the Indo-Pacific century.[6] Dennis Rumley argues that the Asia-Pacific era came to an end in 2011, giving way to the Indo-Pacific era.[7]

---

[3]Tyler and Shearman (2013).

[4]Wei (2013, p. 141).

[5]Zhao (2013).

[6]Medcalf (2012).

[7]Rumley (2013).

India's interest in the concept of Indo-Pacific is similar to that of Australia. As early as in 2007, Indian scholar Gurpreet Khurana began to use this concept on official occasions.[8] Gurpreet S. Khurana, a strategic scholar at the National Maritime Foundation of India, published an article entitled *Security of Sea Lines: Prospects for India-Japan Cooperation* in the *Journal of Strategic Review*, which was sponsored by the Institute of Defense Research and Analysis (IDSA). It was in this article that Khurana first proposed the "Indo-Pacific" as a strategic term, using it to refer to the waters from the East African and West Asian coasts to the East Asian coast. Other Indian scholars, such as Shyam Saran and C. Raja Mohan, also used this concept frequently. Raja Mohan even believe that the arrival of the Indo-Pacific era is inevitable.[9]

The Japanese academic community has long been concerned about the Indo-Pacific concept. In 2013, Japan Institute of International Studies released a report entitled *Security Order in Asia*, in which it is stated that a new "Indo-Pacific Security Complex" is emerging on the basis of the traditional security mechanism in Northeast Asia and Southeast Asia. Based on this analysis, the report recommended the following strategic policy: "First, priority should be given to developing relations with the 'marine alliance countries' in the Indo-Pacific region as well as the maritime countries located in key straits and sea areas, and appropriate ideology and strategic interests should be attended to. Secondly, it is imperative to cope properly with maritime territorial disputes in the region, while preserving the freedom of navigation and 'law-based' order in the Indo-Pacific waters. Thirdly, in-depth cooperation among local countries shall be conducted in terms of the exploitation and utilization of marine minerals, fishery resources and energy. Finally, the 'emerging ocean states' in the South Pacific and the Indian Ocean should build military and paramilitary marine forces sustained by certain systems, technologies and facilities".[10]

Compared to the passionate scholars from Asia, American scholars have kept relatively reserved towards this concept. It is accepted among only a limited group of American scholars such as Michael Oslin from the American Enterprise Institute, and Walter Lohmann from the Heritage Foundation. However, in November 2011, the Loy Institute for International Policy, the Heritage Foundation and the Indian Observer Research Foundation jointly published a research report entitled *Shared Goals and Converging Interests: A Plan for the US-Australia-India Cooperation in the Indo-Pacific*, where it is recommended that the US, Australia and India shall establish a trilateral dialogue to promote the establishment of an order which can contribute to the economic and political stability and security, free trade, and democratic governance

---

[8]Gurpreet Khurana, "Security of Sea Lines: Prospects for India-Japan Cooperation", https://idsa.in/strategicanalysis/SecurityofSeaLinesProspectsforIndiaJapanCooperation_gskhurana_0107, access at 2018-04-11.

[9]Mohan (2011).

[10]Quoted from: Wang Dingjie, "Decoding Abe's "Free and Open India-Pacific" Strategy", http://wemedia.ifeng.com/45539544/wemedia.shtml.

in the Indo-Pacific region.[11] This signifies that the "Indo-Pacific" concept has been generally recognized and accepted by academics from the US, Australia and India.

At this phase, although the understanding of the Indo-Pacific concept might vary among scholars from different countries, there were at least two things in common. One is that most scholars expressed in the concept their worries about the potential impacts brought by the rise of China; the other is that scholars agreed that the vast sea area from Japan to the Arabian Sea constitutes a region of strategic interest. These common grounds serve as an academic basis for further discussion of the Indo-Pacific concept in specific policy fields.

2.3 Indo-Pacific as a Specific Policy Initiative

As a specific policy initiative, the concept of Indo-Pacific also has a long history. During the Cold War, the US initiated two treaty organizations of the Central Treaty Organization and the Southeast Asia Treaty Organization, and tried to link the two together to form a large-scale Indo-Pacific alliance including the US, with the former Soviet Union, China and some other socialist countries as the target. However, such strategic attempt was destroyed by the anti-colonial movement and the subsequent revolutionary movement.

Japanese Prime Minister Shinzo Abe may be the first head of state to simultaneously mention the Indian Ocean and the Pacific Ocean in official texts.[12] As early as in 2006, Abe proposed the "Japan-US-Australia-India" strategic cooperation mechanism, regarding the Pacific Ocean and the Indian Ocean as a strategic entity. In August 2007, Abe visited India and delivered a speech on "Convergence of the Two Seas (Oceans)" at the Parliament of India, arguing that "the Pacific Ocean and the Indian Ocean are becoming a sea of freedom and prosperity, bringing dynamic links. It has already made it clear for a broader Asia that breaks the geographical boundaries to come into being." "Through the alliance with Japan and India, including the US and Australia, this 'broader Asia' can develop into a vast network covering the Pacific Ocean".[13] The above initiative was not carried out because Abe's term was drawing to a close. In September 2012, Abe returned to power and Japan also restarted a new round of Indo-Pacific strategy. In December 2012, Abe issued an article, where he proposed the concept of "Asia's Democratic Security Diamond", which once again links the four countries together. The so-called "diamond-shaped alliance" consists of Australia, India, Japan and Hawaii of the US for the sake of

---

[11]"Shared Goals, Converging Interests: A Plan for U.S.-Australia-India Cooperation in the Indo-Pacific", https://www.lowyinstitute.org/publications/shared-goals-converging-interests-plan-us-australia-india-cooperation-indo-pacific, accessed at 2018-04-03.

[12]Mr. Shinzo Abe, Prime Minister of Japan at the Parliament of the Republic of India, "Confluence of the Two Seas", http://www.mofa.go.jp/region/asia-paci/pmv0708/speech-2.html, August 22, 2007, access at Nov. 17, 2017.

[13]Shinzo Abe, "Confluence of the Two Seas", Speech at the Parliament of the Republic of India, http://www.mofa.go.jp/region/asia-paci/pmv0708/speech-2.html, access at April 04, 2018.

defending the open seas spanning from the Indian Ocean to the western Pacific. He said that "the peace, stability and navigation freedom in the Pacific Ocean are inseparable from those of the Indian Ocean… As the oldest marine democracy in Asia, Japan needs to play a bigger role in defending the shared interests in the above two regions."[14] On January 18, 2013, Abe issued another article, arguing that "now the US stands between the Indian Ocean and the Pacific Ocean. If we turn our focus to there gradually, we will bring the unprecedented significance to the Japan-US alliance." The Japan-US alliance "must strive to expand this network across the two oceans. The close cooperation with US and our partner countries will be of unprecedented significance for Japan." In late February, during his visit to the US, Abe delivered a famous speech entitled *The Return of Japan* at the American Center of Strategic and International Studies (CSIS). He pointed out that "the Asia-Pacific region or the Indo-Pacific region is currently prospering".[15]

Not only does Japan propose the initiative, but also it constantly strengthens its relations with relevant countries. At the bilateral level, Japan continues to strengthen its relationship and cooperation with the US, Australia and India. With Japan's loosening of the three principles on arms export, the lifting of the ban on collective self-defense right, and the adoption of the "New Security Law," Japan has played an increasingly active role and will play a greater role in the future. At the same time, Japan has actively strengthened its security cooperation with Australia and upgraded the bilateral ties from the "indispensable partnership in the region" in 2007 to the "all-round strategic, security and economic partnership" in 2008. Furthermore, in 2014, the Japan-Australia relations were once again promoted to a "new special strategic partnership", which promotes the indirect alliance relations between the two countries under the US leadership to the quasi-alliance relations. On the other hand, Japan is actively strengthening its cooperation with India. In 2006, Japan and India upgraded their relations from "21st Century Global Partnership" to "Strategic and Global Partnership", and then to "Special Strategic Global Partnership" in 2014. At the trilateral level, Japan has actively promoted the trilateral strategic dialogue and cooperation among Japan, the US and Australia and among Japan, the US and India.[16] In 2017, Japan joined in the US-India Malabar naval exercise, foregrounding its military nature of the trilateral cooperation among the US, India and Japan.

As early as President Obama's administration, some US politicians began to accentuate this Indo-Pacific initiative. Hillary was the first American senior official to use the Indo-Pacific concept. In October 2010, the US State Secretary Hillary Clinton said in a speech in Hawaii, "we are expanding our cooperation with the Indian Navy in the Pacific because we know the importance of the Indo-Pacific Basin to the global trade and commerce".[17] One year later, Hillary Clinton wrote in the article

[14] Abe, "Asian Democratic Security Quadrilateral", https://www.project-syndicate.org/commentary/a-strategic-alliance-for-japan-and-india-by-shinzo-abe/chinese?barrier=accessreg.

[15] Refer to: Wang Dingjie, "Decoding Abe's "Free and Open India-Pacific" Strategy", http://wemedia.ifeng.com/45539544/wemedia.shtml.

[16] Refer to: Qu (2016).

[17] Clinton (2010).

America's Pacific Century, "We are expanding our alliance relations with Australia from the Pacific partnership to the Indian Ocean partnership".[18] In July 2011, Hillary encouraged India to change its "Look East Policy" into the "Act East Policy", overtly using India to counterbalance China.[19] In November 2011, Hillary published an article *America's Asian Century* in the *Foreign Policy* magazine, in which she pointed out that "Asia Pacific covering from the Indian subcontinent to the western coast of the US has become a key engine of the global politics. This region spans two oceans—the Pacific Ocean and the Indian Ocean, which are increasingly tied through shipping and strategy."[20] In April 2013, in testimony to the US Congress, the commander of the US Pacific Command, Admiral Samuel Locklear elaborated on the growing importance of the "India-Asia-Pacific region" in the US global strategy. In July 2013, when the US Vice President Biden visited India and Singapore, he declared that the US regards the "Indo-Pacific" as an integral part of the future of Asia.[21] This indicates that during the period of Obama administration, the US strategic community already tried to construct a strategic link between the Indian Ocean and the Pacific. Furthermore, statistics based on the White House documents also show that the "Asia-Pacific" has been mentioned for 537 times and the "Indo-Pacific" for six times in the Obama administration's diplomatic strategy.[22]

Australia was the first country to write the Indo-Pacific into its governmental documents. Australia published the white paper *Australia in the Asian Century* in October 2012 and the *National Security Strategy* in January 2013, and released its national defense white paper in May 2013. In such papers, the "Indo-Pacific" concept was mentioned many times. Some Southeast Asian countries have made similar expressions. In May 2013, Indonesian Foreign Minister Marty Natalegawa delivered a keynote speech entitled *Indonesia's Views on the Indo-Pacific* at the American Center for Strategic and International Studies (CSIS), in which he pointed out that regional countries should commit themselves to building trust, resolving disputes peacefully, promoting a common security and striving for the Indo-Pacific treaty on friendship and cooperation.[23]

Indian officials have been interested in this concept for long. In February 2012, Indian Foreign Secretary Ranjan Mathai made a speech entitled *Building on Convergences: Deepening the India-US Strategic Partnership* at the Center for Strategic and International Studies (CSIS), arguing that "the India-US partnership is very important for building a stable, prosperous and safe Asia-Pacific region—or in the

[18]Clinton (2011).

[19]Later, Indian Prime Minister Modi officially changed the policy of LOOK EAST to the policy of ACT EAST.

[20]Hillary Rodham Clinton, "Security and Opportunity for the Twenty-first Century", https://www.foreignaffairs.com/articles/2007-11-01/security-and-opportunity-twenty-first-century, access at 2018-04-04.

[21]There were still many US officials discussing the significance of the Indian Ocean region and the Indo-Pacific concept on various occasions. For details, please refer to: Wei (2013, pp. 141–143).

[22]Wei Hongxia, "The Evolution of the "Indo-Pacific" Concept", http://www.xinhuanet.com/globe/2017-12/02/c_136788048.html.

[23]Refer to: Zhao (2013).

so-called Indo-Pacific region".[24] In December 2012, Indian Prime Minister Singh gave a speech at the India-ASEAN Summit in Delhi, noting that "a stable, safe and prosperous Indo-Pacific region is of vital importance for our own development and prosperity".[25]

2.4 *Indo-Pacific as a "Strategy"*

Generally speaking, during the Obama administration, the Indo-Pacific was mainly a geographical concept despite some political undertones. After President Trump took office, the use of the Indo-Pacific concept became much more frequent. Long before Trump visited Asia at the end of 2017, senior US officials had already conducted high-profile diplomatic activities around the Indo-Pacific issue. The US Secretary of State, the Secretary of Defense, and the National Security Adviser all have used this concept on different occasions.

On June 3, 2017, the US Secretary of Defense Jim Mattis used this concept in a speech.[26] On October 18, 2017, the former US Secretary of State Tillerson made a speech at the American Center of Strategic and International Studies (CSIS), where he first proposed the concept of "free and open Indo-Pacific", revealing the regional security structure headed by the four countries of the US, India, Japan and Australia in the future.[27] At that time, the Indo-Pacific already had a strategic prototype for the US. Former US National Security Assistant H. R. McMaster has also used the Indo-Pacific concept many times.[28] McMaster believes that the Indo-Pacific is a "useful construct". "Look at geographical and trade route, you'll find that the route goes from east to west and runs through the Indo-Pacific region".[29]

On the eve of Trump's visit to Asia in 2017, the White House stated that one of Trump's three goals was to promote the construction of a free and open India-Pacific region.[30] Patrick M. Cronin, Senior Director of Asia Pacific Security Program, Center of New American Security, Washington Think Tank, wrote in the magazine *The Diplomat* on November 11, 2017 that Trump's visit to the five Asian countries would mark the start of the US "post-pivot to Asia" strategy.

In fact, during his recent visit to Asia, President Trump used the Indo-Pacific concept in his speeches for so many times as to almost ignoring the existence of

---

[24]Ranjan Mathai, "Building on Convergences: Deepening India-U.S. Strategic Partnership", https://www.indianembassy.org/archives_details.php?nid=1713, access at 2018-04-06.

[25]PM's Opening Statement at Plenary Session of India-Asean Commemorative Summit, December 20, 2012, New Delhi.

[26]Mattis (2017).

[27]Tillerson (2017).

[28]Tracy Wilkinson, Shashank Bengali and Brian Bennett, "Trump crosses Asia touting a 'free and open Indo-Pacific,' a shift in rhetoric if not actual strategy", http://www.latimes.com/nation/la-fg-trump-indo-pacific-20171108-story.html, access at 2017-11-17.

[29]PTI (2017).

[30]The White House (2017).

the Asia-Pacific. In Tokyo, Trump called his visit "the first visit to the Indo-Pacific region." In Vietnam, Trump said that he was visiting the "heart of the Indo-Pacific region". In addition, Trump also remarked, "We will seek new opportunities for cooperation with new partners and allies, and strive to establish the Indian-Pacific region in the principle of freedom, justice and reciprocity."[31]

At the invitation of the US, the four countries of the US, Japan, India and Austrian conducted Director-General's consultation on the "Indian Ocean-Pacific" issues in Manila on November 13, 2017, which marked the restart of the four-sided talks. It seems that although the Indo-Pacific is still not a strategy, it is already a specific initiative with specific strategic denotation and connotation. Whether you like it or not, the "Indo-Pacific region is becoming the next center of the global geo-economy and geo-politics".[32]

3 Status Quo of the Indo-Pacific Strategy

The Indo-Pacific strategy was first proposed in the US, which, to certain degree, indicated that the US' self-positioning in the international community was ready to undergo fundamental shift from the past. Since World War II, the US has been working hard to defend and uphold the existent international order. With the changed structure of the world order, particularly with the recent rise of China and India, the US tendency towards revisionism grows remarkable, as in the eyes of President Trump, the world has become a "firm world of sovereign states".[33]

3.1 Background for the Indo-Pacific Strategy

The US first held a negative attitude towards the Indo-Pacific concept, then began to accentuate the Indo-Pacific initiative, and now attempts to develop it in a strategic direction. The reasons are not hard to find:

The first reason lies in the rise of the Asia-Pacific region as a whole. Its was against this historic background that the Indo-Pacific Initiative was proposed. In the Asia-Pacific region are 3 of the world's biggest economies, 7 of the world's 8 fastest growing markets, and 7 of the world's 10 heavily armed forces, with its economic aggregate accounting for 60% of the world total. In 2015, Asia replaced North America and Europe to become the world's largest economic region. For example, 9 of the world's top 10 ports are located in South and East Asia. The former US Assistant Secretary of Defense Chas Freeman is convinced that "the Indo-

[31] "Trump gives glimpse of 'Indo-Pacific' strategy to counter China", https://www.ft.com/content/e6d17fd6-c623-11e7-a1d2-6786f39ef675, access at 2017-11-17.

[32] Wei (2013, p. 155).

[33] Parameswaran (2017).

Pacific region is the new economic center in the world, and the balance of power here is also changing… The Indo-Pacific region is currently a fulcrum of the global geopolitics".[34] Vikram Nehru also holds that "the Indo-Pacific region covering East Asia and South Asia has the potential to become an engine of the world economy, of which the peaceful rise should become the core goal of US foreign policy".[35]

In addition to that, the economic pattern of the Asia-Pacific region has undergone major changes. Starting from the economic vassal of the US and Europe, the Asia-Pacific region has gradually turned into a self-contained economic entity, where regional economic integration has become increasingly prominent. In this circumstance, the Asia-Pacific region has "an emerging Asian strategic system including the Pacific Ocean and the Indian Ocean, partly due to the geographical expansion of the national interests and activities of China and India, and partly due to the continued strategic role and existence of the US in the two regions".[36]

Secondly, the Indo-Pacific initiative is a natural result of the US strategic adjustment. The US has long been pursuing a bigger vision. In the Bush administration, the US Asia-Pacific policy revolved around Central Asia and South Asia. When Japanese Prime Minister Shinzo Abe proposed the Indo-Pacific concept in August 2006, he did not receive the support of the US. The foundation of Indo-Pacific is the G4, but the normalization of Japanese diplomacy is not completely in line with the strategic goal of the US hegemony. Therefore, while supporting this alliance in checking China, the US had reservation about Japan's proposal. In May 2007, the US, Japan, India and Australia held the first Director-General's dialogue on security on the ASEAN Regional Forum, an event widely considered to be the prototype of the "four-nation alliance" (also nicknamed Asian NATO). However, Shinzo Abe was out of office in September 2007, so was Australian Prime Minister Howard in November 2007 (Kevin Rudd took over the premiership). Indian Prime Minister Manmohan Singh was frequently questioned by the left-wing parties and opposed by the veterans of the Congress Party at home. The G4 has long been at a standstill.

Before formulating the Asia-Pacific strategy, President Obama seriously discussed the issue of South Asia, especially the issue of India. The substantive content of the Asia-Pacific rebalancing strategy proposed by President Obama is similar to that of the Asia-Pacific strategy. Joseph Yun, Acting Assistant Secretary of State for the East Asian Bureau of the US Department of State, remarked, "The US views the Indian Ocean and East Asia in a coherent and holistic manner." "Our action is based on the perception that the new Indo-Pacific world is becoming a reality".[37] After 2012, some the US officials even came up with the idea of the Indo-Pacific Economic Corridor.

Thirdly, among the various reasons behind the Indo-Pacific initiative, China's rise is the biggest stimulating factor. Strategically, the US seeks a balance among Asian

---

[34]"India could be world's third largest economy by 2030: StanChart", The Economic Times, June 1, 2011, http://articles.economictimes.indiatimes.com/2011-06-01/news/29608483_1_china-s-gdp-third-largest-economy-india-s-gdp.

[35]Nehru (2013).

[36]Medcalf et al. (2011).

[37]Yun (2013).

countries. This balance has a two-fold meaning. First and foremost, there should not be a dominant country in Asia, nor should a strategic integration under the leadership of any country. Furthermore, any form of Asian integration is unwelcome to the US, especially in the field of political security. In this context, both Japan and India have to seek a dominant position in their sub-region, while acknowledging the multi-polar pattern of Asia. Based on this structure, they try to pursue the position as a world power. The US, Japan and India all have deep concern about China's rapid development over the past three decades. In their eyes, the rise of China has broken the strategic balance of Asia, while the rise of the continental Asia means that a potential new Asian pattern is conceived with China at the center. Particularly, China has proposed the Belt and Road Initiative, an initiative which simultaneously contains the Indo-Pacific oceans and the Eurasia continent. With this initiative, common grounds among countries in the area shall be strategically enlarged and exploited.

With the rise of China, the bilateral balance between China and Japan, and that between China and India are broken, and the Asia-Pacific countries are obviously losing their ability to contain China except for the US, while the traditional US-Japan and US-Australian alliances are not sufficient to contain the influence and impact of China. In the context of the relative decline of the US itself, it is necessary to invite India to work as a new geographical factor to counterbalance China. India is not included in the traditional sense of the Asia-Pacific concept. In order to have India included and to optimize the strategy of the US and India, some countries proposed the Indo-Pacific Initiative.

Therefore, the Indo-Pacific initiative of Trump administration is not for the purpose of construction but for deconstruction. To offset the Chinese Dream and the One Belt and One Road Initiative, Trump stated that the Indo-Pacific involves "many dreams and many roads." To prevent a "China-led Asia", President Trump emphasized sovereignty, security, freedom and economic reciprocity of the Indo-Pacific initiative as opposed to dependence and domination in his speech at the APEC. The US intends to resolve China's regional leadership by promoting the Indo-Pacific multi-polarization.

Fourthly, the new US presidency is conducive to the Indo-Pacific strategy. So far, no specific objectives or approaches have been formulated for the Indo-Pacific Initiative so that it is not a strategy in strict sense. The geographical scope of the Indo-Pacific is almost identical to the concept of Asia-Pacific in President Obama's administration. In some sense, the so-called Indo-Pacific strategy is actually a replica of the Asia-Pacific rebalancing strategy. President Trump has always been ready to take over the strategic concept suggested by Japan, compared to his reluctance to carry on the idea of his predecessor, a US political tradition perhaps. However, Trump does agree to Obama on the role of India. During President Obama' administration, American politicians have already begun to discuss whether India should be included in the Asia-Pacific rebalancing scheme. Today, with of the proposition of the Indo-Pacific Initiative, the discussion stage has finished, and India is officially regarded as an important part of the US' Asia-Pacific or Indo-Pacific scheme.

3.2 Aspects of the Indo-Pacific Initiative

The Indo-Pacific Initiative comprises series of aspects, military, political, and economic, with some important aspects having not yet taken shape. Currently, the most visible are military cooperation and political cooperation.

When President Trump proposed the Indo-Pacific Initiative at the end of 2017, nothing was clear as to how to implement the initiative. On April 2, 2018, the US Assistant Secretary of State for Asia-Pacific Affairs, Alex Wong, in explaining the "Indo-Pacific Strategy" in the State Department briefing, emphasized "freedom and openness". "Freedom" has a two-folded meaning. At the international level, they "hope that countries in the Indo-Pacific region will not be stressed and deterred by powerful countries, and they can choose their own way as a sovereign state". At the national level, they "hope that the countries in the Indo-Pacific region become increasingly free in terms of political rights, basic rights and interests, transparency and anti-corruption". "Openness" also has a two-folded meaning. It first means "open sea passages and air passages". It simultaneously means infrastructure construction, "hoping to help regional countries with infrastructure construction in an appropriate way, thus truly promoting the integration and participation in infrastructure construction of GDP instead of weighing them down." The core of "freedom and openness" is to ensure that India plays an increasingly important role in the Indo-Pacific region. Wong acknowledged that Indo-Pacific Strategy has inherited traditional free and open policies of the US in the Asia-Pacific region, but it also embodied some differences. First, in the Indo-Pacific Strategy, India is supposed to plays an important role in the Pacific, East Asia and Southeast Asia. Secondly, India would also play an increasingly important role in safeguarding the interests of the US and the Indo-Pacific region.[38] In other words, changes are made regarding the role of India in the Indo-Pacific region and the Asia-Pacific region.

Political cooperation is the most important aspect of the Indo-Pacific Initiative, mainly reflected in the Quad initiative. As early as in August 2006, Japanese Prime Minister Shinzo Abe referred to the Indian Ocean and the Pacific as a strategic entity. This strategic entity is led by the coalition of the four like-minded and free-trade-oriented democracies, namely the US, Japan, India and Australia. Abe believes that the four countries should strengthen security cooperation and promote diplomatic and economic coordination. On March 2, 2016, the US Pacific Command Commander Harris remarked in New Delhi that India, Japan, Australia, the US, and many other like-minded countries should be "ambitious" and should seek to collaborate anywhere on the high seas and related airspace. Former Australian Defense Minister Kevin Andrews recently stressed that the "four-sided process" may greatly contribute to the situation in the Indian Ocean-Pacific region.[39] In April 2017, Japanese Foreign

[38]"The Trump administration has mentioned the Indo-Pacific strategy once again, emphasizing "freedom and openness" and warning China", April 4, 2018, http://news.mingjingnews.com/2018/04/blog-post_592.html.

[39]"The United States and Australia desired to piece together the "four-nation maritime alliance" to contain China", http://news.ifeng.com/a/20160307/47731852_0.shtml.

Minister Kishida Katsuo said in Tokyo that the dialogue among the US, Japan, India and Australia is of great importance.[40] In November 2017, the four countries held the first deputy director general-level dialogue, but failed to issue any joint statement.

Military cooperation also stands at the heart of the Indo-Pacific Initiative, though it is simultaneously the most difficult to realize. The US is the closest political, as well as military, ally of Japan and Australia, while the latter two have long maintained a quasi-alliance relationship. The military cooperation among the US, Japan and Australia has risen to the level of joint command, joint operations and intelligence integration. This is the political and military basis for the US to propose the Indo-Pacific Initiative. However, the relationship of the three countries with India is obviously premature for any alliance, especially in the military field. At present, the military cooperation of the Indian-Pacific countries mainly lie in the unilateral and bilateral levels, with no cooperation mechanism formed among the four countries. The US Senate and House of Representatives passed a defense budget of up to $700 billion in the fiscal year of 2018, more than 10% up from the previous year. This helps to reflect the extent to which the US attaches importance to the military capacity building.

The concept of "Indo-Pacific" is embodied in Japanese military strategy. It was reported in Japanese media on December 7, 2017 that the Japanese government had studied the *National Security Guarantee Strategy*, and planned to have it revised the next year as a Japanese foreign and security strategy document. It was also reported that the government would revise the *Defense Plan Outline* and *Medium-Term Defense Plan* (referred to as "Mid-term Defense") under the guidance of the new strategy in the second half of the next year. In so doing, Japan not only hopes to deal with the North Korean nuclear issue, but also desires to dominate the regional affairs and expand Japan's defense capability and policy space through the Japan-US alliance. In the future, the "Indo-Pacific Strategy" may be incorporated into Japan's new strategy for containing China. Accordingly, Japan's military spending will rise to a new record.

Australia is also actively strengthening its military capabilities. In May 2017, Australian Prime Minister Turnbull said that Australia would invest 89 billion Australian dollars (about 460 billion yuan) in the next few decades to implement the naval shipbuilding program. From September 4 to November 26, 2017, the Australian Navy held a military exercise codenamed "Indo-Pacific Struggle-2017" in the Indian Ocean and the Pacific Ocean. The flagship of Australian Navy comprised the Canberra-class amphibious assault ship "Adelaide", four frigates and one supply ship. The Australian Army and Air Force also sent their troops to participate in the oceangoing exercise, including more than 1200 military personnel. It was the largest-scale offshore deployment of the Australian Army since the 1980s. During the military exercise, the Australian fleet visited various Asian countries, including Japan, South Korea, the Philippines, Brunei, Thailand, Malaysia, Singapore, Cam-

[40]"Japan's Foreign Minister Kishida Katsuo said in Tokyo that the dialogue among the United States, Japan, India and Australia is of great importance," http://news.fx678.com/C/20170420/201704201737171562.shtml.

bodia and Indonesia.[41] On January 18, 2018, Australian Prime Minister Turnbull visited Japan. One of his agenda was to discuss the legitimacy of the military presence of one country in the other, so as to facilitate "future joint military exercises and military materials transportation." If this goal is achieved, Australia will become the second country permitted to temporarily station in Japan after the US (except for UN peacekeepers). Turnbull stressed that "Japan-Australia relations are based on the common interests. What we are doing now is to carry out the free and open 'Indo-Pacific strategy' called by you".[42]

Economic cooperation is relatively absent in the Indo-Pacific strategy. On the contrary, President Trump selected to withdraw from the TPP, giving up its endeavor for the Indo-Pacific free trade zone. This may sound strange, but is consistent with of US' own logic. What the US needs is the so-called high-standard trade, investment and financial activities that are rule-based rather than being subject to any dangerous obligations.[43] Compared with the US, Japan is more active in the economical field. In February 2018, Japan's White Paper on Overseas Development Assistance (ODA) stated that Japan was to promote a broader "free and open India-Pacific strategy" through economic assistance and technical cooperation, including "high-quality infrastructure".[44] However, the US, upholding the new trade policy with the slogan of "reciprocity", haggles over economic interests with the other three countries. This especially dissatisfies India, being prepared to vigorously develop its manufacturing industry.

On the whole, the Indo-Pacific strategy has not yet been implemented substantially, with the absence of economic cooperation. Though it is repeatedly articulated by the US and its partners, compared with President Obama's Asia-Pacific rebalancing strategy, it suffers the lack of economic sustainment, thus being reduced to a crappy strategic initiative. However, the Indo-Pacific strategy is actually coherent with President Obama's strategic adjustment. In the past, the US security system in the Asia-Pacific area relied heavily on the military alliance with Australia, Japan and South Korea. Now, beyond the existent alliance system, the US attaches greater importance to the long-term partnerships with such countries as Singapore, and to a much deeper defense cooperation with such countries as India, Indonesia, Malaysia and Vietnam.

---

[41] "Australian Navy "Indo-Taiwan Struggle-2017" oceangoing voyage exercise started: sailing route is used to "surround" China?" http://www.sohu.com/a/190185262_441013.

[42] "What we are doing now is the Indo-Pacific strategy which you are talk about!" http://military.china.com/important/11132797/20180123/31996579.html; April 08, 2018.

[43] Cronin (2017).

[44] "Japan's new ODA white paper: advance the Indo-Pacific strategy", http://www.guancha.cn/global-news/2018_02_19_447416.shtml.

3.3 *Goals of the Indo-Pacific Initiative*

The main goal of the US' Indo-Pacific Initiative is to reshape its national security strategy by promoting a new regionalism across regions. This cross-regional new regionalism corresponds to the decline of the US' global power and is intended to reduce the global strategic burden of the US. Moreover, it helps the US to find allies in a wider scope, differentiate the camp of emerging countries, and cope with strategic challenges from such emerging countries as China. In this sense, the abandonment of TPP and the proposal of the Indo-Pacific Initiative both serve the same goal. It should be noted that the Indo-Pacific concept of the US, India and Japan is also a response to the rising economic and trade interactions between the Pacific Ocean and the Indian Ocean. Specifically, the US' Indo-Pacific Initiative is based on the following motivations.

First and foremost, the Indo-Pacific Initiative can be used to supplement the bilateral system with the multilateral system so as to gain more strategic freedom. During the Obama administration, the US began to encourage its allies to take the lead on some issues, while the US itself acted as a "behind-the-scenes leader" or a coordinator. For example, in the fight against Libya's Qaddafi regime, the US acted as a "behind-the-scenes leader" by providing logistical and intelligence support, whereas France and other countries stood at the forefront.

The US promoted the Indo-Pacific Initiative, taking advantage of Asian countries' concerns about China. Its strategic vision is echoed by some Asian countries. For instance, some top officials of the Japanese Ministry of Foreign Affairs once stated that they cannot ignore the "key reasons" for China's provision of development assistance. As a matter of fact, China's route development through the "Pearl Chain Strategy" is encircling India, with ports successively built in Sri Lanka and Djibouti. In addition, China is also expanding its offshore base. Based on security considerations, Japan demands to stop China's actions.[45] On the other hand, the US aims to control and alienate major Asian countries. By promoting the Indo-Pacific Initiative, the US hopes to divert the attention of Australia, India and other countries to China-related issues such as the South China Sea, so as to share the strategic burden of the US. This will also help intensify the strategic competition between China and other Asian countries such as Japan and India, increase the strategic dependence of India and Japan on the US, and enhance US control over India and Japan. From a long-term perspective, the US is trying to establish a broader alliance and quasi-alliance system with an ultimate aim to create a new hybrid version of NATO to facilitate its hegemonic relocation.

Secondly, the Indo-Pacific Initiative is intended to establish a land-and-ocean balanced strategy by interfering with land affairs from the sea. The Asia-Pacific concept was widely recognized in the past as a concept of land-and-ocean integration. It aimed to promote the integration and cooperation among countries concerned. By comparison, the Indo-Pacific Initiative consists of ocean-surrounding countries or

---

[45] "Japan's new ODA white paper: advance the Indo-Pacific strategy", http://www.guancha.cn/global-news/2018_02_19_447416.shtml.

countries with marine characteristics. Maritime countries such as Singapore and Indonesia have publicly expressed their support for the Indo-Pacific Initiative. As a result, the land-sea integration in the Asia-Pacific concept gives way to the land-sea competition in the Indo-Pacific Initiative. In other words, the current Indo-Pacific concept does inherit something from the previous Asia-Pacific concept, but it tends to be a "marine Asia-Pacific" with a narrowed scope of interest.

As the US has recognized the fact of its relative decline, it abandons many of its global hegemonic goals, with less interest in dominating the affairs of the whole Asia-Pacific region. The US feels hard to lead an increasingly integrated Asia. To protect its leadership under the new power structure, the US adopts a divide-and-control approach, which turns its hegemonic strategy into the offshore rebalance strategy. The US has changed from a hegemonic power during the Cold War to something like the maritime Britain in the 18th–19th century.

Thirdly, the Indo-Pacific Initiative is intended to contain China in a relatively comprehensive way. Originally, the Indo-Pacific concept was not proposed for any form of containment, despite its military nature similar to that of containment during the Cold War. However, the current Indo-Pacific Initiative comprises comprehensive strategies for containment, politically (democratic values), diplomatically (cliques for private gains), and militarily (military exercises, arms sales and so on). It distinguishes itself from its previous existence in the following aspects. First, this is not a comprehensive alliance. For example, the current Indo-Pacific Initiative does not include economic cooperation. Rather, the US is in intense economic competition with Japan and India. Secondly, this is not intended for an explicit purpose. Although member countries are fully aware that the core task of the initiative is to cope with China, they deliberately refrain from calling it explicitly an anti-China strategy. Thirdly, instead of the various forms of repatriation, containment, and super containment previously organized by the US, the Indo-Pacific Initiative is to set a few steeplechases, rather than a breakwater, in the direction of China's "expanding", so as to slow down China's steps of going global. Briefly, the Indo-Pacific Initiative is based on the alliance system of the US with Japan and Australia, but it simultaneously includes non-aligned India. All in all, the strategic goal of the Indo-Pacific Initiative is not to contain China through merely military forces, but it establishes a cooperation system among "like-minded countries" that helps to hedge the rise of China. In the meantime, the US is delicate enough not to brew a new form of confrontation between a China camp and a US camp, due to its limited capability and willingness.

Fourthly, the Indo-Pacific Initiative is for the US to engage India and to control India ultimately. The biggest difference between the Indo-Pacific Initiative and the US's traditional Asian policy lies in the fact that India's strategic position is upgraded on the same level as Japan. This is a very positive reward for India's long-term pursuit of raising its international status. It is also a strategy for the US to hook in India on its own side. In the eyes of small and medium-sized countries such as Sri Lanka, the Indo-Pacific strategy is for "squeezing China out, introducing the US in, and enabling India to rise." In fact, the strategic goals of the US are more than that. For the US, it is for engaging India to counterbalance China. On the other hand, counterbalancing

China also serves as an effective means to hook in India. These double goals are simultaneously intended by the US policy makers.

As the US' recent international performance fluctuated dramatically, demonstrating different goals and logics, countries such as India fails to improve their trust in the US. Instead, their mutual trust continues to decline. Furthermore, India tends to become closer to Japan, with mutual trust being accumulated. In such circumstances, the competition of China against India and Japan would become the most dominant one in Asia, one possibly out of the US' control.

Fifthly, the Indo-Pacific Initiative is for creating tensions between Asian countries while facilitating the US' military expansion and arms exportation to this area. The most competitive commodity of the US exportation is its military equipments. For President Trump, it is one of the most effective ways to reduce trade deficits and increase employment at home. In the meantime, Trump is fully aware that arms exportation is affected by regional security situation. Only by creating a regional tension and promoting a wide-ranging regional sense of danger can the US persuade other countries to import more weapons from the US. Before taking office, President Trump once called for the withdrawal of troops from the Middle East and Afghanistan so as to reduce US financial pressure. After taking office, he did not withdraw the any troops at all. Instead, Trump's administration strengthened the US military presence in Afghanistan and the Middle East. The goal is to maintain regional tensions and power balance. As long as the conflicts continue, there would be opportunities for the US' arms exportation to this region. In the Asia-Pacific region, the US attempts to exert pressure on China through Asia-Pacific rebalancing and Indo-Pacific Initiative. In the meantime, it tries to persuade other countries to import more arms and weapons on the excuse of the China's military threat. The US tried to counterbalance China's rise while increasing its revenue from military exportation. On February 5, 2018, the US State Department official in charge of arms sales and Acting Assistant Secretary of State for Political and Military Affairs Tina Kadano arrived in Singapore to attend the Singapore Air Show. After making a verbal attack on China, Kadano revealed his true intention—the US has better weapons, and the US will "do everything it can" to provide American weapons to Southeast Asian countries, such as the F-35 fighter.[46] It seems that the US is endeavoring to turn the growing Asia into the destination of the US' arms export.

4 Limitations of the Indo-Pacific Initiative

The Indo-Pacific Initiative manifests the Cold War mentality, regarding ideology as a dividing line of different camps. However, the Cold War is over. The relationship between China and the US is fundamentally different from the one between the US and the Soviet Union. Although these countries hope to check China by resorting

[46]"Where will the Indo-Pacific strategy go?", China Youth Daily, February 22, 2018, http://www.xinhuanet.com/mil/2018-02/22/c_129814427.html.

to the US, they do not necessarily accept the US Cold War mentality. As such, the Indo-Pacific Initiative brings the US challenges as well as opportunities.

First, the US may find it difficult to decide on its strategic priorities. After the Cold War, two theories on war are concluded in the US. One concerns the Korean Peninsula and the other concerns the Middle East. The US seemed unprepared for India for a long time. Presently, President Trump has to cope with the North Korean nuclear crisis and the Middle East issue, which would inevitably involve the US' relationship with its major allies and Russia. For Trump, the most important task is perhaps to improve the US' economic and trade ties with its trading partners, as partial fulfillment of his campaign promises. Trump has repeatedly complained that "the US has had a deficit with Japan for many years." "Our trade with Japan is neither fair nor open".[47] The trade between the US and South Korea "is clearly unsuccessful and is not good for the US".[48] Compared to these issues, the Indo-Pacific initiative is less important. In fact, it has proved difficult to implement the Indo-Pacific strategy and fulfill its goals as quickly as expected. President Trump may find it difficult to keep a positive image and to increase public support at home with the Indo-Pacific initiative. It is also unlikely that the US would inject much energy and resources into this slow-to work strategic initiative.

In fact, the US, Japan, India and Australia have different understandings of the Indo-Pacific concept, considering their different strategic goals. The US holds that Indo-Pacific ranges from the west coast of the US to the west coast of India and is mainly used to counterbalance China. Australia holds that the Indo-Pacific region is "a strategic arc connecting the Indian Ocean and the Pacific Ocean and passing through Southeast Asia". Australia would regard it as one of its four strategic interests, with the emphasis on the stability and security of the region. India hopes that the Indo-Pacific map can get bigger, including the North Pacific and the entire Indian Ocean. In this way, India can enter the Pacific Ocean through the Indo-Pacific concept to consolidate its strategic position in the western Indian Ocean.

Secondly, the US may find itself in a grid of asymmetric diplomatic relationships. At present, the US is undergoing an obvious retrogression from multilateralism to bilateralism. At the beginning of his term, President Trump announced the US' withdrawal from the Trans-Pacific Partnership Agreement (TPP), all of a sudden. He attempts to replace the multilateral trade agreements with bilateral trade negotiations for the sake of economic advantages of the US, forcing its trade partners to make concessions. In a speech at APEC, President Trump showed his dissatisfaction with the World Trade Organization and the multilateral trading mechanism, vowing that the US would no longer tolerate any form of trade abuse and threatening to launch

---

[47]"Remarks by President Trump to U.S. and Japanese Business Leaders | Tokyo, Japan", U.S. Ambassador's Residence, Tokyo, Japan, Nov. 6, 2017. https://www.whitehouse.gov/the-press-office/2017/11/06/remarks-president-trump-us-and-japanese-business-leaders-tokyo-japan, access at 2017-11-17.

[48]"Remarks by President Trump and President Moon of the Republic of Korea in Joint Press Conference | Seoul, Republic of Korea", Blue House, Seoul, Republic of Korea, Nov. 7, 2017. https://www.whitehouse.gov/the-press-office/2017/11/07/remarks-president-trump-and-president-moon-republic-korea-joint-press.

a unilateral trade sanction against China. These attacks on China cause concerns to the allies and partners, because the attacked Chinese practice also applies to other countries. In this context, the Indo-Pacific plan requires the US to first establish a framework of cooperation among the US, Japan, India and Australia, and then, on this basis, to integrate the strategic forces in the Indo-Pacific region. This is another kind of multilateralism strategy. While weakening the multilateral trade mechanism, the US stressed the multilateral security mechanism. As is indicated above, there is an asymmetrical development in the economic relationship and the military relationship among countries in the Indo-Pacific region, which would eventually affect the efficiency and effectiveness of the US-dominated multilateral security mechanism in the region.

Thirdly, the Indo-Pacific Initiative suffers a diversity of goals among member countries. The Indo-Pacific Initiative is undoubtedly proposed with China as the main target. However, the initiative is not limited to the security field, it also includes the adjustment of economic and trade relations. In terms of economic and trade relations, there are serious differences and sometimes conflicting interests between the US and other member countries. President Trump announced that "economic security is a national security", the key to the national strength of the US. If other countries are not able to reciprocate with the US, they will be punished by the US, a principle of "the US first" policy. On November 10, 2017, when attending the APEC Leaders Conference at DaNang Vietnam, Trump reiterated the "the US first" policy. Trump has a tough tone on trade with its allies, while keeping a low profile over such issues as democracy and human rights. This sounds ironic, considering the so-labeled "Four Democracies" of the US, Japan, India and Australia. It is obvious that the ultimate goal of the Trump administration is to protect the US' own security and its own economic interests rather than the security of other countries or the international community. In so doing, President Trump undermined the new initiative immediately after he proposed and promoted it.[49] Since World War II, the US has never behaved in this way regarding its regional strategy. After all, it involves such a large population in this area.

In this context, one ally of the US in the region has begun to work on a regional order without the US' presence. After the US withdrew from Trans-Pacific Partnership (TPP), Japan began to dominate the mechanism, working as the banner-bearer. The TPP-based Comprehensive Progress Agreement for Trans-Pacific Partnership (CPTPP) was adopted in March 2018.[50] In addition, the trust of European countries in the US decreases sharply. In May 2017, German Chancellor Angela Merkel remarked at a campaign in Munich that Europe must take control of its own destiny and could not rely entirely on its allies.[51]

---

[49]Doshi (2017).

[50]On April 12, 2018, US President Trump tried to re-enter the TPP that he had given up. This shows that the United States sometimes moves forward by following the pace of its Asia-Pacific allies. It's unimaginable in the past.

[51]"German Chancellor Merkel said: "Europe can't rely on The United States and Britain but can only rely on itself", https://baijiahao.baidu.com/s?id=1568722077241107&wfr=spider&for=pc, April 11, 2018.

Fourthly, it could be difficult for the US to isolate China through the Indo-Pacific Initiative, considering the fluidity of international and regional relationships. China, as an integral part of the world, has engaged itself with the US, Japan, Australia and India respectively. Over the past few years, China has become the US' largest trading partner in place of Canada, Japan's largest trading partner in place of the US, and India's largest trading partner in place of the United Arab Emirates. The trade relation between China and each of the four countries in the Indo-Pacific region has become more important. In the meantime, the humanistic ties between China and each of these four countries have become much closer. The interdependence between China and each of the four countries must have a pivotal role to play in their strategic decision towards each other. Put it another way, these interweaving and interactive bilateral relationships will, to large extent, prevent either side from participating in a cold- war-style strategic camp.

In view of this, Australia proposed a two-ocean strategic program. Now that there is doubt about the Indo-Pacific initiative, Australia hopes to be a bridge, rather than a bridgehead, for the US and China relationship. China has been Australia's largest trading partner for many years. The trade volume between China and Australia is about twice that between the US and Australia. There is a very complicated relationship between Australia and India, with a serious lack of strategic mutual trust and understanding, comparing to the links between Australia and the US and that between Australia and Japan.[52]

Japan and the US also feel that they are "sharing the same bed while making different dreams." Trump's Indo-Pacific strategy is aimed at establishing a free and open trade zone in the Indo-Pacific, based on "the US-first" principle, with priorities on promoting trade relations and reducing bilateral trade deficits between the US and other member countries. Trump's idea is essentially different from Abe's "original intent." Japan emphasizes an "Indo-Pacific zone of peace and prosperity", rather than the four-nation mechanism. On January 18, 2018, Japanese Prime Minister Shinzo Abe and the visiting Australian Prime Minister Turnbull held a press conference, when the Australian Prime Minister stressed the Indo-Pacific strategy. In echoing the Australian Prime Minister, Abe stressed the bilateral cooperation between Japan and Australia rather than the Indo-Pacific strategy.[53] Japan is convinced that China will surpass the US by 2030 as the world's largest economy, whose volume may exceed the US and Japan combined. Therefore, Japan tries to be resilient, not betting on entirely for the US.

India is positive about Indo-Pacific Initiative, but it is not without reservations. On the one hand, India needs the political and military support from the US. On the other hand, India also cares about its relations with Russia and China, unwilling to entirely move to the US side. More importantly, India has been worried about the sustainability of US foreign policy. An Indian government official once said that "Trump's speech is far from consistency and I have no idea to which extent he can

[52]Editorial Board, East Asia Forum (2018).

[53]"What we are doing now is the Indo-Pacific strategy which you are talk about!" http://military.china.com/important/11132797/20180123/31996579.html, April 08, 2018.

be believed." More importantly, India has its own interests and concerns. Unwilling to act as an instrument for the US to counterbalance China, India puts its economic development top on its national agenda. Neutrality and non-alignment remain to be an important part of Indian diplomatic policy. Nor is the "free and open Indo-Pacific" proposed by the US in line with India's goal of being "leadership" in the Indian Ocean region. India, while upholding the openness and freedom in the Indo-Pacific region, is actually most concerned about its own position in the region. When Prime Minister Shinzo Abe paid a visit to India in September 2017, the Prime Minister of India stated, "I believe that the relationship between Japan and India will be the most potential bilateral relations in the world. I have made up my mind to promote the joint leadership of India and Japan in the Indian Ocean and the Pacific Ocean regions and to take the road to peace and prosperity".[54]

In fact, many countries, while being concerned about the strategic pressure from China, need China to counterbalance the US. Scholars from Southeast Asian countries have stated that a powerful China is good for the US policymakers to make more rational and much healthier foreign decisions. Even Japan, India, and Australia have strategic needs of China to counterbalance the US pressure and to offset the pressure from the US. This is why Chinese president Xi Jinping won more applauses than Trump at the APEC summit meeting.[55]

5 Impacts of the Indo-Pacific Strategy on China

The Sino-US relationship is at the core of the Asian security structure,[56] with the Indo-Pacific strategy being organized around the axis of Sino-US relations. This so-called "free and open Indo-Pacific" initiative is actually neither free nor open. On the contrary, it may lead to the split of Asia and the high-intensity zero-sum game.[57] Against the backdrop of the rise of China and Asian countries, the US tried to alienate Asian countries through its own alliance system and the so-called ideological dividing line. By provoking disputes among Asian countries, the US tries to achieve the so-called "balance of power" among these countries and to realize its ultimate hegemonic goal of controlling Asia. President Obama's Asia-Pacific rebalancing was aimed at China, but it did not challenge China on major issues such as One-China

[54]"What is the prospect of Trump's "Indo-Pacific Strategy"? Which countries are involved?" http://war.163.com/17/1116/16/D3CKIL2R000181KT.html.

[55]President Xi Jinping spoke after Trump. It's said that Trump spoke only on one microphone. After Trump left, the organizer immediately added the three microphones to President Xi. Oliver Holmes in Da Nang and Tom Phillips in Beijing, "Trump attacks countries 'cheating' America at Apec summit", Nov. 10, 2017, https://www.theguardian.com/us-news/2017/nov/10/trump-attacks-countries-cheating-america-at-apec-summit, access at Nov. 17, 2017.

[56]Rory Medcalf, C Raja Mohan, "Responding to Indo-Pacific rivalry: Australia, India and middle power coalitions", https://www.lowyinstitute.org/publications/responding-indo-pacific-rivalry-australia-india-and-middle-power-coalitions, access at 2018-04-10.

[57]Swaine (2018).

policy. The bilateral cooperation continued in global areas such as climate change, counter-proliferation and anti-terrorism.[58] Under the Indo-Pacific framework, the US policy toward China has changed from cooperation plus competition to competition plus cooperation, which will have the following impacts on China.

5.1 Counterbalancing the Impact of the China Rise

Since the beginning of the 21st century, with the rapid rise of China, the US, Japan, India and Australia began to consider how to "contain" China. President Clinton started to place his strategic emphasis on China in the last two years of his administration. President George Bush changed his original policy in the first half of his presidency, repositioning China as a main strategic rival after the 9.11 terrorist attacks. After President Obama took office, he stressed the cooperative relations with China while rebalancing Asia and Asia-Pacific region so as to counterbalance China strategically. Kissinger once remarked at a US Senate hearing that China is trying to shift the focus of the world through the Belt and Road Initiative. The US needs to maintain a balance of power, while not causing major catastrophic conflicts.[59] However, China has developed so significantly and so rapidly that the original strategies of the US may not be effective any more. It is estimated that China's GDP may surpass the US by 2030, more than the combination of the US and Japan. Under the traditional Asia-Pacific framework, it would be difficult for the US-Japan alliance to contain China. In this circumstance, the inclusion of India as a new force through the Indo-Pacific Initiative will help the US and Japan to rebuild their strategic balance in a larger geospatial space. "Compared to the exclusive East Asia, China's influence is more diluted under the Indo-Pacific concept".[60]

The Indo-Pacific initiative is obviously different from the previous Asia-Pacific rebalancing strategy in coping with China. Some US politicians, out of utilitarianism, have occasionally mentioned the cooperation between China and the US. They in fact keep on deeming China as a threat. This is partly reflected in Former US Secretary of State Rex Tillerson's speech at the Center for Strategic and International Studies (CSIS) in October 2017, the Report on the National Security Strategy (NSS) released by the US in December 2017, and the report on the US National Defense Strategy (NDS) in January 2018. During Obama's administration, the US political leaders generally referred to China as a "non-enemy and non-friend".[61] When it comes to Trump's administration, a form of alliance of maritime nations began to emerge, which is aimed to isolate China.

---

[58] See Footnote 57.

[59] Kissinger (2018).

[60] Refer to: Zhao (2013).

[61] "The commander of the US military: China is neither an enemy nor a friends and we shall pay close attention to the movement of the People's Liberation Army", http://world.huanqiu.com/exclusive/2013-04/3819307.html.

5.2 *Counterbalancing the Impact of China's Belt and Road Initiative*

The Indo-Pacific Initiative is ideologically tinted, signifying that the US and its partners are resorting to the Cold War mentality. In his speech, Rex Tillerson described China as "a country often damaging the rules-based international order, and India as a country acting in a framework that protects the sovereignty of other nations".[62] In this speech, Tillerson portrayed the so-called authoritarian China as a rule-breaker and challenger of the international order, and the so-called democratic India as a rule-observant and guardian of the international order. This dichotomy obviously ignores the international reality, a typical representation of the Cold War mentality with ideology as a dividing line. Some US officials, especially former Secretary of State Tillerson, even referred to the Belt and Road initiative as "predatory economics", accusing China of trying to control other countries by economic means. He advised that the US should provide an "alternative financial mechanism" to help those countries fight against China's Belt and Road. Tillerson stated, "Many Indo-Pacific countries have limited options for infrastructure investment". The US should seek to "expand a transparent and high-standard regional credit mechanism—that will really help such countries to get out of fast-rising debts".[63]

During President Trump's visit to Japan, the US and Japan reached a number of agreements to hedge the impact of the Belt and Road initiative. First, the US Overseas Private Investment Corporation (OPIC) concluded the agreement with the Japan Bank for International Cooperation (JBIC) and the Nippon Export and Investment Insurance (NEXI) to provide "high quality US-Japan infrastructure investment alternatives" in the Indo-Pacific region. The U.S. Overseas Private Investment Corporation stated that its cooperation with Japan would emphasize a shared "obligation to addressing the development challenges of infrastructure, energy and other key sectors in Asia, Indo-Pacific, the Middle East and Africa." The agreement will encourage US and Japanese financial institutions to collaborate and coordinate on "politically-targeted projects" in the above-mentioned regions. Secondly, the US and Japan launched the "Japan-US Strategic Energy Partnership, which is aimed to promote the adequate and reliable energy availability in Southeast Asia, South Asia and sub-Saharan regions". The US Trade and Development Agency (USTDA) and Japan's Ministry of Economy, Trade and Industry (METI) signed an agreement to "help provide high-quality energy infrastructure solutions for the Indo-Pacific region." According to the USTDA, the agreement will "support and promote international best practices in areas such as the third world's public infrastructure".[64] In November 2016, India and Japan proposed the Asia-Africa Growth Corridor. The Nikkei Chinese Network reported in September 2017 that the Japanese Ministry of Foreign Affairs' ODA budget application for 2018 rose by more than 10% from the

[62]Tillerson (2017).

[63]See Footnote 62.

[64]Tiezzi (2017).

434.3 billion yen in 2017. Most of the budget will be used for the "Free and Open Indian Ocean and Pacific Strategy" and "High-quality Infrastructure Investment" policies proposed by Japanese Prime Minister Shinzo Abe. The key areas covered by such policies are completely coincident with the "21st Century Maritime Silk Road" in the "Belt and Road" initiative proposed by China.[65]

Many Chinese scholars are concerned that the "Indo-Pacific" strategy would prevent the westward advancement of China's "Belt and Road" Initiative.[66] This worry stands to reason, as Australia and India are included in both the US' "Indo-Pacific" framework and China's "Belt and Road" Initiative. The two countries would possibly side with the US to resist the development of China's "Belt and Road" Initiative.

5.3 Legitimizing China's Maritime Silk Road Initiative

From a geographic concept, through a policy initiative, and finally to a containment strategy, the term of Indo-Pacific has manifested both continuity and transformation during the course of evolution. Although many countries have talked about the Indo-Pacific, their understanding is not necessarily the same. The Australian Indo-Pacific concept is based on two basic facts. One is that China and India, the two emerging powers, will inject more interests in the Pacific Ocean and the Indian Ocean, leading to heavier military presence and more intense competition. The other is that, the Indian Ocean, serving as the "energy superhighway" will link the Middle East, the energy producer, with the East Asia, the energy consumer. In so doing, it will also connect many countries along the coast. Compared with the traditional Asia-Pacific concept, the Indo-Pacific initiative can provide India and Australia with an "imaginative strategic central position", embodying their strategic importance and continuing to tie the US to this region.[67]

As such, the Indo-Pacific strategy highlights the already existing economic and strategic links between the Indian Ocean and the Pacific Ocean. With the proposal of the Indo-Pacific, some hope to exclude China from the Indian Ocean region and to block China from the East Asian coast. However, India recognizes the integration of the two oceans, which paves the way for China have an identity in the Indian Ocean. Put it another way, China's presence in the Indian Ocean region finally becomes legal and legitimized, benefiting from the proposal of the Indo-Pacific strategy.

---

[65] "Japan's new ODA white paper: advance the Indo-Pacific strategy", http://www.guancha.cn/global-news/2018_02_19_447416.shtml.

[66] Wei Hongxia, "The Evolution of the "Indo-Pacific" Concept", http://www.xinhuanet.com/globe/2017-12/02/c_136788048.html.

[67] Nick et al. (2012).

6 Recommending Countermeasures for China

The Indo-Pacific Initiative has generated both positive negative impacts on China. Positively, the initiative is a response to the rise of Asian countries and the growing trend of regional economic integration. It is largely inspired by China's Belt and Road Initiative, with China's Maritime Silk Road project sometimes being nicknamed the Chinese version of the Indo-Pacific Initiative. Both initiatives would contribute to the increase of investment into the infrastructure construction in the region. In view of that, China shall be welcome. Negatively, the Indo-Pacific Initiative is intended to establish a "small circle" of selective partners. Instead of promoting the regional integration, it may lead to the deterioration of inter-state relations and the worsening of security situations in the region. Therefore, China shall not completely reject the Indo-Pacific Initiative, but to adopt different attitudes towards different aspects of the initiative. Generally, under the framework of the US dominated Indo-Pacific Initiative, China shall fight to improve aspects of the mechanism, while keeping cooperative and accommodating in other aspects of the mechanism.

6.1 Cooperating with the Indo-Pacific Initiative in Certain Aspects

The Indo-Pacific Initiative and the Quad (G4) are both exclusive small groups. The Indo-Pacific Initiative does reflect the aspiration of relevant countries to invest in and improve infrastructure in the region. Although some countries in the region have tried to use this Indo-Pacific Initiative to counterbalance the impact of China's Belt and Road Initiative, the infrastructure construction as public goods can indeed help raise funds for the infrastructure construction in the region. It is safe to say that the Indo-Pacific Initiative and China's Belt and Road Initiative are working towards the same direction. After all, countries like the US do not mean to build a strategic camp to confront China in an overtly hostile way. Japan and India even keep opener up to China than the US and Australia, with the latter two countries from an Anglo-Saxon League.

Furthermore, under the framework of the Indo-Pacific Initiative and the Quad (G4) mechanism, the status of Indonesia, South Korea is not clear enough. They are forced to vibrate between China and the US. When the Indo-Pacific Initiative was proposed, the US once pressed South Korean to join the initiative. However, South Korea adjusted its position several times and finally adopted a very cautious attitude.[68] On January 23, 2018, US Defense Secretary Matisse visited Indonesia, stating that the US hopes that Indonesia will play a "key fulcrum" role in safeguarding the security on South China Sea and on the Pacific. In response, the Indonesian Defense

[68]"South Korea's attitude towards the "Indo-Pacific Strategy" of the United States is worthy of thinking more", November 21, 2017, www.cyol.com; (Beijing), http://news.163.com/17/1121/19/D3PR5FA1000187VI.html.

Minister made a "soft nail", "The situation in the South China Sea has cooled down, and we are committed to maintaining this favorable momentum and safeguarding the regional common interests."[69] Obviously, some Asian countries may hope to establish a system that can balance China's power, but they are not to accept the Cold War pattern so as to put Asia in a state of confrontation. In the meantime, such countries have strategic concerns about the US. Most countries are no longer happy to see a unilateralist US, They do not want to take the side of either China or the US,[70] as they believe that China can also cooperate with member states of the Indo-Pacific Initiative. Based on this analysis, China should continue to promote multilateral cooperation in the region, and to engage as many countries in the region as possible, including Japan, India and even Australia, so as to resolve the strategic containment by the US.

6.2 *Accommodating the Indo-Pacific Initiative with the Maritime Silk Road*

The Maritime Silk Road initiative is intended to integrate the Pacific-Indian Ocean and the Mediterranean Sea, while the onshore Silk Road Economic Belt is actually a New Asia-Europe Integration Initiative. China's vision is more ambitious and more comprehensive than the US' Indo-Pacific Initiative. The former is much more accommodating, including many aspects of the Indo-Pacific Initiative in a manner.

Member countries of the Indo-Pacific Initiative are very concerned about China's attitude. Aimed at containing China, the G4 initiative has not attracted so much attention. On the contrary, China's response to the G4 has become a major concern of its member countries. In 2007, at the repeated request of the Japanese government, the four countries held the first round of strategic dialogue in Manila. However, the other three member countries were not so enthusiastic about such a strategic dialogue. They even did not agree on a fixed date for the next round of dialogue. In particular, Australia and India do not want the strategic alliance of the four countries to be understood as an "encirclement circle" against China. They adopt a very cautious attitude. Australian diplomats, in an interview with Kyodo News, revealed that "the policy of excessive containment of China does harm to Australia's national interests." In Japan, there have been conflicting views on the G4. In his speech at the Japan Press Club, former Japanese ambassador to China Anami Korehiro pointed out that the establishment of the four-nation strategic alliance "is by no means a brilliant foreign policy". Such a diplomatic gesture can only create concerns of China.[71] With the continuous accumulation of its overall national strength over the past decade, the

[69]"Where will the Indo-Pacific strategy go?", February 22, 2018, China Youth Daily, http://www.xinhuanet.com/mil/2018-02/22/c_129814427.html.

[70]Editorial Board, East Asia Forum (2018).

[71]"Australia and India's worries results in China's doubts. Japan's creation of the 'four-nation strategic alliance' has been frustrated," http://news.sohu.com/20070805/n251419238.shtml.

Chinese government has adjusted its foreign policy. In the meantime, the cooperation of the G4 countries in counterbalancing China becomes strengthened, with concerns about China's response going deeper. It is against this backdrop that the Indo-Pacific Initiative decided to have China included.

China shall make greater efforts to promote extensive and in-depth cooperation with the Indo-Pacific member states in the economic, trade and humanities aspects. China is strong in those aspects, and this cooperation can serve as an effective means for China to accommodate the Indo-Pacific Initiative. Be it the Asia-Pacific or the Indo-Pacific, countries, especially the developing countries, in this area are most concerned about their own economic and social development. In the future, China's economic volume will continue to expand, and the economic and trade ties with neighboring countries could become much closer. Under such circumstances, China must adhere to the reform and opening up so as to provide more economic opportunities for other countries. At the opening ceremony of the 2018 Annual Meeting of the Boao Forum for Asia in Hainan on April 10, 2018, Chinese President Xi Jinping pointed out that China would make the access to Chinese market much easier, create a more attractive investment environment, strengthen IPR protection, and expand imports so as to create a new environment for foreign trade.[72] On the other hand, China shall try to establish a regional economic cooperation mechanism, through which to reduce economic risks and to prepare for further political and security cooperation.

6.3 Fighting Against the Cold War Mentality of the Indo-Pacific Initiative

The Indo-Pacific Initiative contains obvious Cold War mentality, incompatible with the demands of the world for peace, stability and development and inconsistent with the basic characteristics of current international situation. China is the main target of the US "Indo-Pacific strategy", but China is different from Japan in World War II and the Soviet Union during the Cold War. In those years, the main goal of Japan was to establish the Greater East Asia Commonwealth Circle by invading, occupying, and colonizing other countries. As a result, it faced fierce resistance. The former Soviet Union was to manipulate other countries, sometimes resorting to invasion, a common enemy of many countries. However, China has undergone tremendous development in a socialist system, having established close economic and cultural links with most economies in the Indo-Pacific region. China's strategic goal is also different from previous great powers. China is not interested in regional hegemony. Rather it intends to expand its international political influence by participating in international affairs, using economic and cultural means. In so doing, it hopes to

[72]"Keynote Speech by Xi Jinping at the Opening Ceremony of the 2018 Annual Meeting of the Boao Forum for Asia", April 10, 2018; http://cpc.people.com.cn/n1/2018/0410/c64094-29917187.html.

enhance its security flexibility and reduce its vulnerability in the energy supply and economic chain. Not all member countries of the Indo-Pacific initiative feel hostile to China, and many keep a relationship of both competition and cooperation with China. It is the same case with the US. The US cooperates with and competes against China simultaneously. These intertwined relationships exist in various fields. Thus, it sounds impossible for the US to ally all the member countries to contain China, politically and militarily. The Indo-Pacific initiative is more like a club. To humiliate China, the US once upheld the slogan of freedom and democracy, which the Trump administration has failed to perform at home. More importantly, although some Asian countries are concerned about the rise of China, they do hope that there exist some disputes between China and the US regarding their ideology and interests, and that the US can pursue a more consistent and much healthier foreign policies. In other words, they would like to see the two powers to be counterbalanced by each other, for the sake of a stable Asia.

The discontinuity of the US' foreign policy has aroused concerns among many countries in the region. On the opposite, China has benefited a lot from the vibration of the US' foreign policy. Asian countries are generally concerned about Trump's attempts to confront countries in this region and its indifference to the potential risks. They are fully aware that the ultimate goal of the US is to protect the US's own economic security rather than the security of other countries. Regarding its regional strategy, the US has never behaved as such since World War II. After all, it involves such a large population. Countries concerned feel obliged to reconsider the reliability of the US, while focusing on the building of their own strength to ensure regional and national security. China is not alone in this regard.

7 Conclusion

With the proposal of the Indo-Pacific Initiative, the US began formally to adjust its hegemonic strategy. During the Cold War, the core task of the US hegemonic strategy was to maintain its superiority over the Soviet bloc and its leadership in the Western camp. After the Cold War, there were indeed opportunities for the US to devise a global hegemonic strategy. It failed to do so because a global hegemonic strategy could have cost too much. At the beginning of the 21st century, the Afghan war, the Iraq war and the financial crisis had a remarkable influence on the US foreign policy. After all these events, the US began to shift the focus of its hegemonic strategy to the offshore rebalancing, trying to dominate global affairs by maintaining strategic balance between major geopolitical regions. Now that the US has abandoned this low-cost hegemonic strategy, it has managed to organize the Asia-Pacific strategic rebalancing framework. In other words, the US is convinced that it can no longer maintain its hegemony at a lower cost. Behind the proposition of the Indo-Pacific Initiative, there is a new understanding of the world power structure, which cannot afford to neglect China's strategic position. All in all, the Indo-Pacific Initiative is primarily for the US to maintain its global hegemony, but it also helps to optimize the world power structure and quicken the improvement of international order in a more balanced direction.

References

Nick Bisley, La Trobe University, and Andrew Phillips, UQ. 2012. "The Indo-Pacific: What Does it Actually Mean?", 6 October 2012. http://www.eastasiaforum.org/2012/10/06/the-indo-pacific-what-does-it-actually-mean/. Access at 12 Apr 2018.

Clinton, Hillary. 2010. "American's Engagement in the Asia-Pacific", 28 October 2010. http://www.state.gov/secretary/rm/2010/10/150141.html.

Clinton, Hillary. 2011. "American's Pacific Century". *Foreign Policy*, November, pp. 62–63.

Cronin, Patrick M. 2017. "Trump's Post-Pivot Strategy: Trump's Indo-Pacific Dream Focuses on Reciprocity, as well as Economic and Military Security", 11 November 2017.

Doshi, Rush. 2017. "Trump's 'Indo-Pacific Dream' Stumbles—But China Alone Won't Fill the Void", 15 November 2017. https://warontherocks.com/2017/11/trumps-indo-pacific-dream-stumbles-china-alone-wont-fill-void/.

Editorial Board, East Asia Forum. 2018. "Sorting Out Strategic Confusion in the Indo-Pacific", 28 January 2018. http://www.eastasiaforum.org/2018/01/29/sorting-out-strategic-confusion-in-the-indo-pacific/.

Haushofer, Ernst. 2002. *Geopolitics of the Pacific Ocean* (p. 141). Lampeter: Edwin Mellor.

Kissinger, Henry A. 2018. "Opening statement", Before the Senate Armed Services Committee, 25 January 2018.

Mattis, Jim. 2017. "Remarks by Secretary Mattis at Shangri-La Dialogue", 3 June 2017. https://www.defense.gov/News/Transcripts/Transcript-View/Article/1201780/remarks-by-secretary-mattis-at-shangri-la-dialogue/. Access at 17 Nov 2017.

Medcalf, R., R. Heinrichs, and J. Jones. 2011. *Crisis and Confidence: Major Powers and Maritime Security in Indo-Pacific Asia*, 56. Sydney: Lowy. https://www.lowyinstitute.org/publications/crisis-and-confidence-major-powers-and-maritime-security-indo-pacific-asia. Access at 5 Apr 2018.

Medcalf, R. 2012. "Unselfish giants? Understanding China and India as Security Providers". *Australian Journal of International Affairs* 66 (1): 13.

Medcalf, Rory. 2012. "A Term Whose Time Has Come: The Indo-Pacific", 4 December, 2012 https://thediplomat.com/2012/12/a-term-whose-time-has-come-the-indo-pacific/. Access at 17 Nov 2017.

Mohan, C. Raja. 2011. "India and Australia: Maritime Partners in the Indo-Pacific". *The Asialink Essays* 3 (7): 1–4.

Nehru, Vikram. 2013. "The Rebalance to Asia: Why South Asia Matters". In: *Testimony Before the House Committee on Foreign Affairs Subcommittee on Asia and the Pacific*, 13 March 2013.

PTI. 2017. "Donald Trump's China Visit: US Defends 'Indo-Pacific' Concept", 8 November 2017. https://economictimes.indiatimes.com/articleshow/61564716.cms?utm_source=contentofinterest&utm_medium=text&utm_campaign=cppst. Access at 17 Nov 2017.

Parameswaran, Prashanth. 2017. "Trump's Indo-Pacific Strategy Challenge: A Look Ahead at the Administration's Early Regional Vision and the Challenges Before It", 27 October 2017.

Qu, Caiyun. 2016. "Exploring the Formation of the Strategic Cooperation Among Japan, the United States, Australia and India and the Game of Check and Balance". *Journal of Liaoning University (Philosophy and Social Sciences Version)* 44 (1) (January): 168.

Rumley, Dennis (ed.). 2013. "The Indian Ocean Region: Security, Stability and Sustainability in the 21st Century", p. 33. http://www.aiidelhi.com/source/public/img/publication/IndianOceanSecurityTaskforceWeb.pdf. Access at 2 Apr 2018.

Swaine, Michael D. 2018. "Creating an Unstable Asia: The U.S. "Free and Open Indo-Pacific" Strategy". *Foreign Affairs*, March 2.

The White House. 2017. "President Trump's Trip to Asia", 3 November 2017. https://www.whitehouse.gov/blog/2017/11/03/president-trump-trip-to-asia. Access at 17 Nov 2017.

Tiezzi, Shannon. 2017. "In Japan, Trump and Abe Offer Alternative to China's 'Belt and Road'". *The Diplomat*, November 8. Access at 3 Apr 2018.

Tillerson, Rex. 2017. "Defining Our Relationship with India for the Next Century: An Address by U.S. Secretary of State Rex Tillerson", 18 October 2018. https://www.csis.org/analysis/defining-our-relationship-india-next-century-address-us-secretary-state-rex-tillerson. Access at 3 Apr 2018.

Tyler, Melissa Conley, and Samantha Shearman. 2013. "Australia's New Region: The Indo-Pacific", May 21. http://www.eastasiaforum.org/2013/05/21/australias-new-region-the-indo-pacific/. Access at 12 Apr 2018.

Wei, Zongyou. 2013. "The Strategic Adjustment of the United States in the Indo-Pacific Region and Its Geostrategic Impact". *World Economics and Politics* (10).

Yun, Joseph. 2013. "The Rebalance to Asia: Why South Asia Matters (Part 1)". In: *Testimony Before the House Committee on Foreign Affairs Subcommittee on Asia and the Pacific*, 26 February 2013.

Zhao, Qinghai. 2013. "The "Indo-Pacific" Concept and its Implications for China". *Contemporary International Relations* (7).

Locating China in the Indo-Pacific Debates: Perspectives from India

Swaran Singh

Abstract While the paradigm-shift from continental Asia-pacific to new maritime geopolitical framework of 'Indo-pacific' may be a dynamic discursive to ensure strategic equilibrium amongst multiple new and old stakeholders, continued exclusion of China remains its most formidable limitation. However, apart from this exclusion in Western discourse, there remain internal triggers to China's reluctance that reinforce such external responses treating China as trigger but not integral to their construction of the new Indo-Pacific paradigm. Also, driven by bean-counting of the realists, the contemporary discourses seem far too influenced by prophecies of inevitable Sino-US confrontation. These often miss nuanced responses in Chinese discourses that may not flow from its military might but imperceptible cultural and economic entwines. The central contention of this paper is that it remains a prerequisite for the peaceful development of both China and the Indo-Pacific framework that they mutually synergise their engagement towards maximising mutual benefits. Staying apart has only been counterproductive. This is where India—that has substantial security and economic engagements respectively with both US and China—can perhaps smoothen this interface in order to make Indo-Pacific an inclusive, effective as also a sustainable geopolitical proposition.

Keywords Indo-Pacific · India · China · Geopolitics

Rise of China has been the single most important new trigger for several recent geopolitical re-formulations. This includes the 'Indo-Pacific' paradigm which finds itself at the centre of recent regional security and development discourses amongst the United States friends and allies. Borrowed from geosciences, this term has come to be equally acceptable in geopolitics, representing largely a maritime view of the well-known continental Asia-Pacific region. The narrower definitions of Indo-Pacific restrict it to only the western Pacific Ocean while adding the Indian Ocean into it. (Chacko 2016: 1; Chen 2011: 3). There are, of course, expansive descriptions as well. These demarcate it from the eastern coast of Africa to western shores of the

S. Singh (✉)
Diplomacy & Disarmament, Center for International Politics, Organization and Disarmament (CIPOD), School of International Studies, Jawaharlal Nehru University, New Delhi, India

C. Zhu (ed.), *Annual Report on the Development of the Indian Ocean Region (2018)*, Research Series on the Chinese Dream and China's Development Path, https://doi.org/10.1007/978-981-13-7693-1_4

Americas. However, even when seriously contested and relatively nascent category in geopolitics, this new formulation shows great promise to unleash systemic changes in world politics and transform equations amongst the stakeholders in the Asia-Pacific region. Such potential of this debate is often measured from the speed with which it seems to develop a definitive character and connotations and the way growing consensus is being built amongst the littoral nations.

The most visible triggers for this rapid shaping-up of 'Indo-Pacific' paradigm are not far to seek. First of all, this has a direct co-relation with China's continued rise which stands re-enforced by Beijing's high-voltage economic growth that has continued even in the face of decade-long global economic slow-down since 2007. More recently, Brexit crisis in Europe and president Donald Trump's 'America First' policy on the one hand, and president Xi Jinping's ambitious Belt and Road Initiative on the other, have catapulted China to the eminence of a redeemer of the industrialised world. China's recent history supports its credentials: it played a critical role in East Asian financial crisis of 1997 which contributed to the revival of these tiger economies thereby accelerating the global power shift from the north-Atlantic to the trans-Pacific. This also marks the shift in international geopolitics from the old ways of military alliances to the newer themes of connectivity and co-prosperity. The fact that primary focus of China has not been on re-enacting the cold war military alliances makes hardcore realists miss China's real leverages in 'shaping' this emerging geopolitics of the Indo-Pacific region (Ali 2017: 37; Shambaugh 2013: 8; Dallmayr 2012: 3).

It is based on the premise that comprehensive power will determine their future equations in international politics, this paper contends that China's Belt and Road Initiative building partnerships from Africa to the Asia-Pacific has been the most potent new force in bridging cold war divides between the Indian and the Pacific Oceans. Moreover, the very sustenance of China's overarching economic partnerships has witnessed Beijing transforming 'Malacca dilemma' from being a barrier into a bridge between the Indian Ocean and the Pacific (Billington 2014: 67; Yuan 2013; Zhu 2010: 167–168). China's attempts to find alternatives to Malacca straits (e.g. bridges, pipelines or arctic sea routes) continues to be a work in progress even after launching of China's ambitious BRI. China's expanding economic footprint, however, promises to unfold a new arena of its shared objectives with the 'Indo-Pacific' geopolitics which also seeks to bridge old cold war divides. This provides avenues for both sides to explore how China's rise can synergise with emerging Indo-Pacific geopolitics. But for this to happen, Indo-Pacific debates must evolve an inclusive approach ensuring that China remains integral to their new geopolitical formulations.

1 Why Is China Seen as Outlier?

The reality of China emerging as the trigger as also integral part of the emerging geopolitics of the Indo-Pacific is perhaps not easy to internalise for the cold war realists who see China's 'hegemony' as the defining the future of the 'Indo-Pacific' paradigm. (Till 2016: 100; Prakash 2013: 279; Mohan 2012). They continue to overstate US 'offshore balancing' and completely miss China's subtle use of soft-power leverages especially Beijing's calibrating of its regional initiatives with the ASEAN that promise to "bring other and larger global benefits to China." (Mahbubani and Sng 2017: 102; Quayle 2013: 30). Nevertheless, China—the trigger—has remained an outsider to most of the Indo-Pacific discourses. At best, China is recognised as a stimulant to these new formulations but not integral to them; making Indo-Pacific debates as if prisoners of cold war mind sets; or worse, motivated monologues amongst friends and allies of the United States.

Major regional initiatives for the 'Indo-Pacific' paradigm are projected as triggered mainly by the United States attempts to 're-balance' Asia-Pacific, Australia's Look West, India's Look/Act East policies and sporadic reactions from Japan, South Korea and ASEAN members. Origins of this broader shift from Asia-Pacific to 'Indo-Pacific' again lies majorly in the rise of China and in search for alternative friends and frameworks to deal with rise of China. (Chacko 2016: 2; Panda 2012: 149–151; White 2010: 62–63). This has seen two parallel security and development architectures evolving led by the United States and China respectively. Their overlaps as also waxing and waning dynamics have kept regional situation in a constant flux for all stakeholders. Impulses of shrinking U.S. global leadership and BRI obtaining stronger endurance during the second term of president Xi Jinping starting 2018 is expected to make these dynamics all the more complicated.

While Australia has been on the lead in promoting 'Indo-Pacific' debates which make it the 'centre' of this geopolitical formulation, there has been a visible shift in Canberra's approach to China. Australia *Defence White Paper 2009* had once inspired a well-known Australian commentator to say: "Canberra has come to see China's rise as the central strategic challenge in the Indo-Pacific region, and it has thus become a major driver of Australia's maritime force modernization." He further alluded to how Prime Minister Julia Gillard's government agreeing during 2012 APEC Conference to allow 2500 US marines to be stationed in a new US naval base at Darwin in northern Australia (Medcalf 2011: 199; Fabey 2017: 28). Stories of Australia rebooting its security alliance had been galore for last few years. But while Australia may continue to play proxy for the Asia pivot and offshore balancing of the US, Australia has also reassessed its policy on China's rise. Its *Defence White Paper 2013* had marked the shift saying: "The Government does not approach China as an adversary. Rather, its policy is aimed at encouraging China's peaceful rise and ensuring that strategic competition in the region does no lead to conflict." (Department of Defence 2013: 11).

As regards, China's largest neighbour and also emerging peer power India, there has been a lukewarm shift in favour of inviting China into 'Indo-Pacific' discourse yet, New Delhi remains cautious of potentially having to choose between China and the US with both pulling in different directions. But unlike limiting policies to only lip service, India's track record since 1960s when it supported China's permanent seat on the United Nations Security Council has continued in spite of all hiccups in their bilateral ties. India (which has come closer to US) has had a record of having facilitated China's entry into the India Ocean Rim Association of Regional

Cooperation (IOR-ARC) in 2001, into the South Asian Association for Regional Cooperation (SAARC) in 2005 as also in India Ocean Naval Symposium. These are forums that have been integral to New Delhi's perceived core national interests.

Then there is Indonesia, that virtually stretches from Indian to Australian shores. Starting from May 2013 call by foreign minister R. M. Marty M. Natalegawa for an Indo-Pacific Treaty of Friendship and Cooperation, it sees Indo-Pacific as "the most relevant geo-strategic canvas for its emerging power status projection." (Shekhar 2018: 69). Jakarta also sees 'Indo-Pacific' having the potential to deliver a new 'dynamic equilibrium' and wishes to contribute to ensuring that it does not fall prey to either 'the unchecked preponderance of a single state" or "due to disorder or uncertainty" associated with multiple actors (Natalegawa 2013: 4). According to one columnist, simply for its location and archipelagic nature and long stretch, Indonesia may respond to US incentives and emerge as the hub to the Indo-Pacific geopolitics:

> This way, Indonesian entry in world arena as a promising economy and a vibrant democracy has stirred up the strategic environment of the whole region. The centrality of Indonesia has emerged in Indo-Pacific politico-security dynamics after American pivot to Asia and all the major powers whether it is US, China, India, Japan or Australia, are busy in developing a well-crafted strategic partnership with world's largest archipelago and redefining their policy engagements among themselves in the light of growing economic, political and military clout of Indonesia in Asia-Pacific. (Bhattarai 2012)

Other regional powers like Japan, South Korea, the Philippines, and Thailand that Hillary Clinton once described as "the fulcrum for its [US] turn to the Asia-Pacific" have remained generally tight-lipped about China being part of this process; let alone taking any leading role in facilitating China's entry into the Indo-Pacific discourses. Understandably these are not nations that are going to support China becoming integral to 'Indo-Pacific' paradigm.

As regards the United States, which has aptly blessed these new formulations of the 'Indo-Pacific' region, it has been supporting expansive definitions describing the 'Indo-Pacific' region "stretching from the Indian subcontinent to the western shores of Americas." (Clinton 2011: 57). By doing so the US hopes become integral to this geopolitical region and also to replicate here its leadership model of 20th century Europe. This would ensure that U.S. continues to be the leader as power shifts from trans-Atlantic to the Indo-Pacific region. Like Britain in 20th century Europe, it seeks to partner Australia or India as its leading mediators in 21st century Indo-Pacific discourse. This may seem music to Indian ears yet Indo-Pacific has never been India-centred. It is a combination of the Pacific Ocean and the Indian Ocean and later remains a shared asset for all the littoral nations together. Also, as US leaders seem choose India over China and shed their preference for divisive colonial expression 'South Asia' and return to a more traditional and inclusive term 'Indian subcontinent' is amply appreciated by Indian interlocutors. Yet, to the discomfort of the U.S., several Indian experts stress on the need to engage China and to ensure that China remains integral to the emerging geopolitics of the 'Indo-Pacific' region. Some of them believe that without engaging China, the Indo-Pacific would not even be sustainable. To quote an influential former diplomat, Shyam Saran, Indo-Pacific debates…

> "[must] not exclude China" [though it is for Beijing to] "decide whether it is ready to embrace an inclusive approach to dealing with the new challenges or insist on an exclusionary strategy, based on a narrow definition of its own security interests." (Saran 2011)

Given its shrinking global leadership and changing orientations of its friends and allies, coming years may see US policies going beyond simply endorsing or blessing the 'Indo-Pacific' paradigm. Recent years have seen the US not just hedging but edging towards offensive strategies. If prophecies made by Secretary of State Hillary Clinton about US being clear on expanding its military presence to ensure stability and security in the Indo-Pacific and, "China is depicted as not taking enough "responsibility" in its rise to the region" then US has to also heed to its globalists like George Soros who believe "there needs to be a shift in attitude among Western states that will encourage China to play its full, even dominant, part in a new international system." (Bolton 2013: 59; Clinton 2011). It is in this backdrop that Pentagon had announced its plans on how, by year 2020, roughly 60% of its naval fleet would be stationed in the Asia-Pacific and the first batches of US marines had already arrived in the region since September 2012 reaching 2500 by the time president Obama laid down office (Fels 2016: 379; Grevatt 2013; Welch 2012; White 2013). It seems that even such provocative deployments have not enticed China's into entering the Indo-pacific debates which makes this continued exclusion of China from the Indo-Pacific discourse perplexing.

2 Complications of the U.S. Outreach

Unlike the regular refrain of the relative decline of US in recent years, "China growing power" among other things had "driven the administration of President Barack Obama to "reengage"…in the Asia-Pacific region." (Kuik et al. 2012: 315; Green 2009: 27–28). Others described the US as the "resident power in the Indo-Pacific… committed to reinvigorating its capabilities …enhancing its maritime partnerships" (Lin 2016: 97; Bradford 2011: 203). This expansive outreach of US had ensured that China continued to be an outlier in US-blessed Indo-Pacific discourse. Indeed, for much of twentieth century, US had been the most influential underwriter of stability and security separately in the Indian Ocean and the Pacific Ocean. Its main engagement though remained trans-Atlantic. For maintaining such large footprint it followed a 'hub-and-spokes' strategy of bilateral and multilateral military alliances that were built in the name of containing spread of communism (Proctor 2016: 418; Mastanduno 2002: 194). With the collapse of former Soviet Union, rise of China, and particularly in face of unprecedented threat from the non-state actors since 9/11, this old US alliance-architecture of 'hub-and-spokes' no longer effectively addresses the US security concerns. Indeed, it appears increasingly becoming counterproductive and cumbersome. Excessive dose of military prowess seems to outstretch US commitments that no longer fit well with its relatively shrinking resources where bestsellers of Fareed Zakaria and Parag Khanna talk of the "post-American, multipolar world".

(Brooks and Wohlforth 2016: 3; Lundestad 2012: 5–7). The US accordingly has been exploring ways to downsize military expenditures and to evolve new methodologies of burden-sharing which has become the buzzword of the Donald Trump presidency (Deni 2017: 77). These are new concerns that are rapidly redefining US approach to offshore balancing and has already led to its abandonment of the trans-pacific partnership thereby introducing newer contours of the 'Indo-Pacific' geopolitics though even new strategies continue to be premised on its old anti-China theologies.

The US is increasingly seeking to maximise its regional outreach by realigning with new friends as also " urge them to make efforts to find a comprise with China on issues where China feels strongly that its interests are threatened." (Hu 2016: 81; Clinton 2011: 62). US recognises that shrinking of its footprint has accelerated in wake of advancing capabilities of several other regional stakeholders, especially the so-called emerging economies or Asia's rising powers like China, India, Indonesia, and so on. Besides, these recent decades have witnessed the rise of new asymmetric strategies where countries like North Korea or Iran are not necessarily seen as vulnerable to US diktat. Even before Donald Trump became president, the US had been reshaping its foreign policy and recalibrating its interests across the Asia-Pacific. At one level, it had even tried endorsing China as *primus inter pares* across the region but that experience did not go as per US wishes and the two continue to have serious differences. Since 2003, Beijing was asked to convene the non-proliferation Six Party Talks on North Korea. But US believes that China did not "bring to bear the full weight of its state to truly implement the existing UN imposed sanctions" and Pyongyang has continued with testing ballistic missiles and detonating nuclear devices (Christoffersen 2016: 177; Blank and Kim 2012: 272). Accordingly, US has been encouraging India to not just 'look' but also 'Act' East which has coincided with India's increasing participation in various ASEAN-centred forums. India's post-tsunami proactive regional diplomacy since 2005 witnessed India, for the first time, partnering in a coalition for relief and rehabilitation outside the United Nations, and it was led by the United States. This was new as India has never accepted such coalitions outside UN auspices.

Indeed, following long and tortuous diplomatic parlays since India's nuclear tests of May 1998, successive US administrations of both Republican and Democratic parties have come to promote closer relations with New Delhi. This has seen India gradually expanding its engagement with US allies; as also engage with these Indo-Pacific discourses. With the 2010 Indo-US nuclear deal taking the lead, India is now widely endorsed as a responsible power with advanced nuclear technologies though its procurement of nuclear reactors from US or France continues to be in jeopardy. Year 2011 witnessed Australia's ruling Labour Party's attitude towards India finally changing leading to lifting of the ban of sale of uranium to address India's power generation needs (Roy 2011: 125–127). Japan also signed a similar nuclear deal with Indian during July 2017 but, at least in short-term, no nuclear technologies are likely to be transferred to New Delhi. The fact that India's policies remain grounded in 'strategic autonomy', have not been to the full satisfaction of US and its Indo-Pacific discourse. For instance, even when India was in favour of East Asian summit allowing US membership yet it took US five years to be accepted as member of the East Asia summits in 2012. Similarly, US-Japan-India (and potentially US-Australia-India) triangles are projected to strengthen India's role in the Indo-Pacific yet caution continued to define India's policies (Singh 2013: 135–137). The fact that Beijing continues to stand disengaged has also triggered concerns in India which shares complex relations with Beijing. Australia's softening approach towards rising China can be instructive of future trajectories in engaging regional powers and for its possible realignments with China. The change of mood in the Philippines remains another case in point.

But this piecemeal softening of India and other powers does not show any response from the US administration. Obama administration's focus even on economic initiatives like the Trans-Pacific Partnership (TPP) was widely interpreted as another apt example of countering and excluding China from Indo-Pacific paradigm. But president Trump's desertion of the TPP has in no way made it pro-Beijing. Indeed, there is an increasing realisation amongst China's neighbours that it is difficult to imagine any economic partnership network in the region that does not include China which is the largest trading partner for most countries across the 'Indo-Pacific'. The region has witnessed two overlapping yet parallel networks emerging at the same time: China being the largest trading partner of every country that makes each of them see China's prosperity intertwined with their own prosperity, and US continuing to lead in most emerging and erstwhile security structures across the Indo-Pacific and source for military supplies. Meanwhile, most regional players, including China, prefer hedging strategies propagating being 'fine' in endorsing the US primacy. This can at best be a short-term arrangement and portends major recalibration in the Indo-Pacific paradigm if this has to become the guiding geo-political frame of reference for long-term regional peace and security.

3 China's Rise in US 'Pivot' to Asia Discourse

Rise of China since early 1990s witnessed US seeking to transform the pattern of political and security alignments across the Asia-Pacific by (a) introducing new trilateral dialogues, (b) exploring "new security partners", and (c) blessing "new alignments" in Asia (Wesley 2010: 229). This lay at the core of US 'pivot' to Asia from 2011 which further fuelled their popular scenario-building of Sino-US contestations that continue to be the staple-food for experts and media commentaries projecting their inevitable confrontation in the Indo-Pacific (Allison 2017: 309). This is what determines their mapping of China's military modernisation and its expanding strategic footprint across the Indo-Pacific. Michael Austin, for instance, popularised his reconstruction of the cold war divide by concluding that "How America and China react, along with the capabilities they employ, may determine which country emerges with the legitimacy and authority to set rule for the Indo-Pacific region in the coming decades." (Doyle 2011: 48). Similarly, columnist Peter Symonds believed that "Obama administration's "pivot" to Asia is nothing but a comprehensive military build-up throughout the Indo-Pacific region, greatly highlighting the danger of war with China."(Symonds 2012). But this was like comparing apples to oranges. No doubt China has expanded its presence across the Western Pacific and Indian Ocean but "China's strategy focuses on accumulating influence through efforts such as the Belt and Road Initiative, which seeks to build economic connections…while avoiding combat between uniformed militaries." (Cooper and Shearer 2017: 305).

There, no doubt, exist alternative voices, even within the US, yet these have not been most influential in their scheme of things. One such Asia expert Ashley Telis, for example, makes a relatively nuanced assessment of region's future. For him, the prospect of China successfully integrating the Indo-Pacific "through a network of trading relations that could become the foundations for an impermeable sphere of influence centred on Chinese economic, geopolitical, and cultural primacy in Asia is deeply threatening the US interests at a time when many regional states find themselves increasingly pulled by China's growing power-political mass." (Tellis 2011: 15). Then there are those who highlight what could be seen as possible Chinese perspectives of US assessments on China's rise. To quote another seasoned US diplomat, Chas and Freeman (2012):

> No one in Asia seeks to deny China an appropriate role in regional security architecture. But, in Chinese eyes, the aim of U.S. policy seems to be to perpetuate U.S. dominance, while confining China to the sidelines of a newly reinforced American sphere of influence. No one in the Indo-Pacific region wishes to see it divided between rival hegemonies, still less between foreign and Asian hegemonies. Yet that outcome is implicit in the current trajectory of U.S.-China relations.

In the US policy perspective, expanding footprint of China is seen to directly threaten core US interests and this makes confrontation between US and China a strong possibility. As early as in April 2003, speaking at the Shengri-La Dialogue at Singapore, US Secretary of Defence, Leon Panetta had reiterated that greater part of the US naval forces, including "six aircraft carriers…[and] a majority of our cruisers, destroyers, Littoral Combat ships and submarines" would be soon stations in this region. (Choong 2013). Others saw US 'pivot' to Asia as an attempt to focus on ever expanding economic opportunities which drives US initiatives away from continental military failures in Iraq and Afghanistan to the maritime visions of Indo-Pacific region that represents 40% of the total global trade and accounts for 60% of the US exports. So, any such confrontationist approach, military or economic, was seen as "likely to inflame Chinese nationalism" making it difficult for Beijing "to submit to US primacy indefinitely." (Santis 2012: 211–12; Yahuda 2013: 454). Such militaristic scenario-building has remained devoid of exploring any possibilities of complex interdependence involving multi-sectoral coordination between US and China though both sides sporadically do allude to these. This partially explains why China appears aloof and insulated from contemporary debates on the Indo-Pacific geopolitics. It is pertinent to ask here as to what could have facilitated Chinese engagement with the Indo-Pacific?

4 China's Engagement with Indo-Pacific Region

Other than these popular imaginations of the US-China military confrontation, the most convincing explanation for China's lack of engagement with Indo-Pacific 'discourses' lies in China's sensitivities towards the South China Sea especially in the wake of recent American campaign on freedom of navigation in this maritime territory. Right from very beginning, for instance, proponents of the Indo-Pacific have been projecting South China Sea as the "geopolitical hub and vital economic artery" as also the "critical part of the Indo-Pacific commons" (Medcalf 2012a, b: 8; Yahuda 2013: 458). Some Indian officials and analysts have also shown India's concerns for ensuring freedom of navigation in South China Sea being grounded in its economic interests which explain India's limited engagement with Indo-Pacific discourse (Puri and Sahgal 2011: 445). But India has never been at home with experts who describe South China Sea as the most possible 'tipping point' in the geopolitics of Indo-Pacific (Auslin 2010: 18). This is because China sees US naval presence as source of instability but not posing any existential threat nor they have any irreconcilable ideological differences.

There also remain other regional factors and forces that make it complicated for US and China to reconcile. From its very beginning, for instance, India has been reluctant to be seen integral part of US 'pivot' to Asia which explains its lukewarm approach to the 'Indo-Pacific' discourses. According to Indian security analyst C Raja Mohan, "the sustainability and credibility of US alliances in the Indo-Pacific region… is coming under stress amid the proliferation of advanced military capabilities by countries such as China and Iran, and their divergent strategies." (Mohan 2011: 2). Outcomes will depend also on how US and China respond to these challenges. As of now, in the emerging new areas like piracy and maritime terrorism affecting commerce and security, China is not expected to be anyone's partner, let alone China taking lead in any of these. Result is continued differences and divergences in their parallel and often unconnected responses. Unlike most countries in the Indo-Pacific that have always relied on the US for maintaining order in Asia's high seas, China, says Raja Mohan, is "building blue-water naval capabilities to secure its expanding interests." (Mohan 2011: 2). Other Indian commentator, Sanjaya Baru paints much more interesting scenario where, in the long run, the pull of China's geoeconomics is likely to outweigh against the geo-strategic push of the United States (Baru 2011). This is exactly the same sentiment that president Trumps 2017 *National Security Strategy* outlines as it alludes to how it sees, "China seeks to displace the United States in the Indo-Pacific region, expand the reaches of its state-driven economic model, and reorder the region in its favor." (National Security Strategy of the United States of America 2017: 25).

Its surprising that China's economic leverages have not incentivised its entry into the US-led 'Indo-Pacific' formulations. Even in trade driven formulations like the Trans-Pacific Partnership China's exclusion was seen as a glaring gap. But while China remains integral to Asia-Pacific Economic Cooperation India remains still outside it. New Delhi instead has preferred to promote China-led Regional Comprehensive Economic Cooperation. As regards TPP, India places "no great importance…though India's advantages in services trade can play better." (Dogra and Woo 2013). This, in spite of the fact that unlike China, India has no rivalry with the US and it is seen closer to the US which has since brought it the recognition from the 'other' emerging power in the Indo-Pacific region. This clearly further complicates Beijing's assessment of Indo-Pacific formulations. But this also enables India to facilitate China's engagement with the Indo-Pacific discourses which call for balancing its equations with both US and China. India being China's largest neighbour and being cautiously engaged with 'Indo-Pacific' discourse can engage Beijing to synergise its policies with India in order to energise its own engagement with the Indo-Pacific discourse. To quote Rory Medcalf, "China is arguably the quintessential Indo-Pacific power." (Medcalf 2012a, b). However he believes that,

> …the official Chinese position is to be circumspect if not suspicious about the Indo-Pacific, perhaps because it could be taken as legitimising India's role into China's Western Pacific neighbourhood, thus diluting a sense of the centrality of China in the Asian strategic order. (Medcalf 2012a, b)

5 India's Dilemma and Re-orientation

In spite of inheriting an imperial naval task force with two aircraft carriers and an imperial naval vision of British India which was the lynchpin of regional security across Indian Ocean, independent India largely remained an inward-looking only to gradually come up with rhetoric about need to remove great power naval presence from the Indian Ocean (Paleri 2013: 275; Ladwig III 2009: 90). It was form early 1990s that India's growing economic engagement with East Asia led to its growing recognition of its stakes in its extended neighbourhood including in the Indian Ocean rim. This was followed by India starting naval exercises with the US and other ASEAN navies that have since shaped India's geopolitical interests. In twenty-first century these are both necessitated and facilitated by the success of India's Look East policy since early 1990s which is now called the Act East policy with greater depth and expanse in building strategic partnerships with as many countries in as many sectors as possible. This also marks the shift in India's foreign policy from non-alignment to multi-alignment where India seeks to build stronger partnerships with as many countries in as many sectors as possible. As regards the expansive geo-strategic framework of the Indo-Pacific India's engagement with this nascent geopolitical paradigm remains largely viewed 'limited' maritime perspective of what has been the continental region of the Asia-Pacific. (Ibid.).

As regards India's strategic circle and policy makers it is only recently that the term 'Indo-Pacific' has gained some traction. It is generally seen as extension of India's geopolitical interests beyond Southeast Asia to reach out to the extended neighbourhood in the western Pacific. India's former foreign secretary, Shyam Saran, has called it a "logical corollary of India's Look East policy having graduated to an Engage East policy." (Saran 2011). However, today India's Act East policy's expanding footprint in Indo-Pacific is not only seen as "an attempt to balance and deter, but also, and perhaps more importantly, to engage China" (Grare 2017: 25). This represents fastest growing component of India's political and economic relations beyond ASEAN to include China, Japan, South Korea, Australia, New Zealand and so on and these have resulted in growing exchanges between Indian and the Pacific littorals. But, stretching of India's strategic space to include western Pacific has its consequences and such expansion needs caution. To the least this calls for ensuring that it is not viewed as bandwagoning US containment of China (Pant and Joshi 2016: 5).

A far more nuanced approach would call for India engaging China and facilitating its incorporation into Indo-Pacific discourses. This would at least mitigate some of their inevitable friction flowing from India's engagement with the Indo-Pacific region. India's economic engagement with East Asia followed by increasing interest in Indo-Pacific already underscores India's growing strategic interest in South China Sea which makes China sceptical of India's motives with China "urging India to stay out" of this disputed maritime theatre (Puri and Sahgal 2011: 445–446; Roy 2016: 63). But both sides have to appreciate that the clock of globalisation can not be turned back and in face of their deepening economic interdependence with regions and maritime spaces like Indo-Pacific "neither can afford to ignore the other's maritime policies." (Singh 2018). Also, "Delhi, for its part, needs to candidly reflect not the pre-modern geo-economic linkages in the Indian Ocean, which were inclusive and expansive, and China was often an integral part of those inter-regional exchanges. Put plainly, the notion of a closed or privileged Indian space between Aden and Malacca was an imperial aberration rather than the norm in the wider space of Asian history." (Singh 2018).

India's dilemma is to maintain fine balance amongst various stakeholders, especially China and the United States, who are often seen pulling in different directions. China's power projections as also its expanding operational capabilities in this islet-dotted maritime theatre of South China Sea get often exaggerated in view of its perceived concerns about US preponderance and proclivities threatening military confrontation (Hemmings 2011: 90–91; Dillon 2011: 66). This makes China not just assertive against US and its allies like Japan but increasingly weary of its new friends like India who displays increasing interest in the South China Sea and in the geopolitics of the Indo-Pacific region. And as US moves its focus from Iraq and Afghanistan to now 'Indo-Pacific' region, it has clearly communicated engaging India as a partner, if not as an ally and projecting China as its potential challenge or what Stephen Walt calls 'a peer competitor' (Ghimis et al. 2012: 103). However, in face of president Donald Trumps's 'America First', both China, and US remain sceptical of confrontation being their preferred course and both seem as yet amenable to alternative courses if possible. In this unrelated triggers like North Korea's missile and nuclear weapons program could also become their slippery space.

This is where India has an opportunity to work together with China. India should recognise China's entry into Indo-Pacific as a prerequisite for the success of this proposition. India can calibrate initiatives to facilitate China becoming integral to Indo-Pacific debates which is essential to make it an effective geopolitical frame of reference for 21st century security and development. Prima facie, both share several similarities at regional and global discourses and have gradually evolved stronger understanding on such issues. In view of their bourgeoning economic ties, both China and India have adopted strategies of hedging and accommodation. India represents a unique advantage that should encourage China into participating in debates on the geopolitics of the Indo-Pacific. Even in engaging China, India can further develop this niche of its deeply entrenched 'strategic autonomy' thesis of its foreign policy. Amongst the friends and allies of the United States, India may also stand a certain advantage in being the most acceptable to China as preferred interlocutor for facilitating China's participation in Indo-Pacific discourse. This holds promise for India-China bilateral ties as well.

6 Conclusion

Unlike many other stakeholders in the Indo-Pacific region, Indian experts see China's engagement into Indo-Pacific as an essential pre-requisite for ensuring long-term peace and stability of the region as also for the success of 'Indo-Pacific' paradigm as the new geopolitical frame of reference for future. India is sure not the first country to come up with such proposition but remains best suited to ensure China's participation. Given the nature of China's rising bilateral trade ($84.45 billion for 2–17) and burgeoning investments makes India a special partner of China in this entire Indo-Pacific region. China's inclusion into Indo-Pacific discourse also promises to facilitate China's peaceful rise. India believes that this new Indo-Pacific framework is more inclusive and represents twenty-first century equations much better; it is likely to be less contentious than the old Asia-Pacific frame which was restricted to only pacific-Asian nations. Besides, while it could be possible to achieve consensus on the conceptual level, these stakeholders will also need to build consensus at the operational level that will have its own challenges given that all issues of development and security are getting increasingly intertwined.

As regards, India, this seems unusual period in the history of independent India where New Delhi enjoys confidence of all major powers in the region. Robust and hyperactive foreign policy of prime minister Narendra Modi has also made India far more visible. But, while warming up of Indo-US ties have majorly redefined India's equations with most of US friends and allies in the region, the multi-alignment policy of India has insured that it is not done at the cost of India's relations with its other partnerships, even when some of these have been disconcerting to the successive leadership of the United States. More important, the gravitation point of India-China relations has since moved from bilateral to multilateral format, where their sense of camaraderie at addressing regional and global issues, has produced positive spina-offs for their bilateral ties. Increasingly, both sides are using this regional and global lens to assess and understand their bilateral equations. This marks the backdrop of State Counsellor Wang Yi's new formulation that China-plus-India do not make two but eleven. With this new warming up spirit between China and India, engaging in the

Indo-Pacific discourse could be one such inordinate goal for both China and India to begin working together and coordinate their strategies with direct positive spin-offs for their bilateral ties.

Finally, when it comes to discourses on the Indo-Pacific geopolitical framework, the US has, so far, failed to replicate its twentieth-century success of having led the Western bloc without contextualising it into the local nuances and equations. Those were different times that made Marshal Plan possible and North Atlantic Treaty Organisation became the main instrument of setting the post-World War II liberal order. In twenty-first century, these US initiatives in discoursing Indo-Pacific can not rely on old fashioned approach of looking for another Britain in Australia or seeing not-so-amiable France in India. US will need to use contemporary European model of Big-Three (Britain, France, Germany) and engage the core of major stakeholders in the Indo-Pacific region. This presumes China's inclusion as a must to ensure peace and stability in the Indo-Pacific. As the old wisdom tells us any new geopolitical framework to survive must assure that it does not hurt the core interest of any of its major stakeholders. Moreover, making China integral to Indo-Pacific discourses, may not necessarily mean end of primacy of the United States, at lest int the short term.

References

Ali, S. Mahmud. 2017. *US-Chinese Strategic Triangles: Examine Indo-Pacific Insecurity*. Cham, Switzerland: Springer International Publishing.

Allison, Graham. 2017. *Destined for War: Can America and China Escape Thucydides Trap?* New York: Houghton Mifflin Harcourt.

Auslin, Michael. 2010. Tipping Point in the Indo-Pacific. *The American Interest* 6 (4) (March/April): 17–24.

Baru, Sanjaya. 2011. "A Continent Adrift in the Western Pacific is Seeking a New Indo-Pacific Home". *Business Standard* (New Delhi), November 28.

Billington, Michael. 2014. "Connecting Indonesia to the Eurasian Mainland". In *The New Silk Road Becomes the World Land-Bridge*, edited by Nancy Spannaus. EIR Special Report, EIR News Service Inc.

Bhattarai, Keshav Prasad. 2012. "Indonesia and the Emergence of New Strategic Dynamics in Asia-Pacific—Analysis". *The Reporter* (Kathmandu), July 30–August 5.

Blank, Stephen, and Younkyoo Kim. 2012. "Restarting the Six-Party Talks: Russia's Dilemmas and Current Perspectives". *Korea Observer* 43 (2) (Summer): 253–277.

Bolton, Kerry. 2013. *Geopolitics of the Indo-Pacific: Emerging Conflicts, New Alliances*. London: Black House Publishing Ltd.

Bradford, John F. 2011. The Maritime Strategy of the United States: Implications for Indo-Pacific Sea Lanes. *Contemporary Southeast Asia* 33 (2) (August): 183–208.

Brooks, Stephen G., and William C. Wohlforth. 2016. *America Abroad: The United States' Global Role in the 21st Century*. Oxford: Oxford University Press.

Chacko, Priya. 2016. "Introduction: The Rise of the Indo-Pacific". In *New Regional Geopolitics in the Indo-Pacific: Drivers, Dynamics and Consequences*, edited by Priya Chacko. New York: Routledge.

Chen, Dake. 2011. "Indo-Pacific Tripole: An Intrinsic Mode of Tropical Climate Variability". In *Advances in Geosciences*, edited by Kenji Satake and Jianping Gan, 1–18. London: World Scientific Publishing.
Choong, William. 2013. "US Pivot to Asia Must Come with Reassurances". *The Straits Times* (Singapore), April 24.
Christoffersen, Gaye. 2016. "Pathways to a Northeast Asian Energy Regime". In *China's Rise and Changing Order in East Asia*, edited by David Arase, 173–196. New York: Palgrave Macmillan.
Clinton, Hillary. 2011. America's Pacific Century. *Foreign Policy* (Washington, DC), November, Issue 189, pp. 56–63.
Cooper, Zack, and Andrew Shearer. 2017. Thinking Clearly About China's Layered Indo-Pacific Strategy. *Bulletin of the Atomic Scientists* 73 (5): 305–311.
Dallmayr, Fred. 2012. "Introduction". In *Contemporary Chinese Political Thought: Debates and Perspectives*, edited by Fred Dallmayr and Zhao Thingyang. Lexington: The University Press of Kentucky.
Department of Defence, *Defence White Paper 2013*, Australian Government, Commonwealth of Australia, Canberra.
Deni, John R. 2017. *NATO and Article 5: The Trans-Atlantic Alliance and the Twenty-First-Century Challenges of Collective Defense*. Lanham, Maryland: Rowman & Littlefield.
Dillon, Dana R. 2011. Countering Beijing in the South China Sea. *Policy Review* (167) (June & July): 51–67.
Dogra, Suvi, and Jie Woo. 2013. "Where Does India Stand Amid Changing Asia-Pacific Trade Dynamics?" *Financial Express* (New Delhi), April 4.
Doyle, Randall. 2011. "The Asia-Pacific Region: "The Geographical Pivot of History" in the Twenty-First Century". In *Modern China and the New World: The Reemergence of the Middle Kingdom in the 21st Century*, edited by Randall Doyle and Zhang Boshu, 43–70. Lanham, Ml: Lexington Books.
Fabey, Michael. 2017. *Crashback: The Power Clash between the U.S. and China in the Pacific*. New York: Scriber.
Fels, Enrico. 2016. *Shifting Power in Asia-Pacific? The Rise of China, Sino-US Competition and Regional Middle Power Allegiance*. Cham, Switzerland: The Springer International Publishing.
Freeman Jr., Chas W. 2012. "Indo-Pacific Dynamics in Trans-Pacific Perspective". *Middle East Policy Council*, 16 April 2012, at http://www.mepc.org/articles-commentary/speeches/indo-pacific-dynamics-trans-pacific-perspective.
Grare, Frederic. 2017. *India Turns East: International Engagement and US-China Rivalry*. Oxford: Oxford University Press.
Grevatt, Jon. 2013. "Australia and US to Bring Defence Trade Treaty into Force". *Jane's Defence Industry* 30 (6), (June 1).
Ghimis, Ana-Maria., Monalisa Guiglea, Cristiana Maria and Alina Mogos. 2012. America's New Grand Strategy—An Inherited Step Back? *Strategic Impact* (3) (July/September): 98–110.
Green, Michael J. 2009. Asia in the Debate on American Grand Strategy. *Naval War College Review* 62 (1) (Winter): 14–29.
Hemmings, John. 2011. The Potential for Sino-US Discord in the South China Sea. *The RUSI Journal* 156 (2) (April/May): 90–95.
Hu, Richard Weixing. 2016. "The Chinese Response to the US Rebalancing Strategy: Sino-US Relations and Washington's Pivot to Asia". In *Asia Pacific Countries and the US Rebalancing Strategy*, edited by David W F Huang, 69–84. New York: Palgrave Macmillan.
Kuik, Cheng-Chwee, Nor Azizan Idris and Abd Rahim Md Nor. 2012. The China factor in the US "Reengagement" with Southeast Asia: Drivers and Limits of Converged Hedging. *Asian Politics & Policy* 4 (3): 315–344.
Ladwig, I.I.I., and C. Walter. 2009. Delhi's Pacific Ambition: Naval Power, "Look East", and India's Emerging Influence in the Asia-Pacific. *Asian Survey* 5 (2): 87–113.

Lin, Cheng-Yi. 2016. "Chinese Response to Obama's Rebalancing to Asia Strategy". In *Asia Pacific Countries and the US Rebalancing Strategy*, edited by David W F Huang, 85–102. New York: Palgrave Macmillan.

Lundestad, Geir. 2012. *The Rise & Decline of the American "Empire": Power and its Limits in Comparative Perspective*. New Delhi: Oxford University Press.

Mahbubani, Kishore, and Jeffery Sng. 2017. *The ASEAN Miracle: A Catalyst for Peace*. Singapore: NUS Press.

Mastanduno, Michael. 2002. "Incomplete Hegemony and Security Order in the Asia-Pacific". In *America Unrivaled: The Future of the Balance of Power*, edited by G. John Ikenberry, 181–210. New York: Cornell University Press.

Medcalf, Rory. 2011. "Grand Stakes: Australia's Future Between China and India". In *Asia Responds to its Rising Powers: China and India*, edited by Ashley J. Tellis, Travis Tanner and Jessica Keough, 195–226. Washington, DC: The National Bureau of Asian Research.

Medcalf, Rory. 2012a. "Chance to Calm South China Sea". *The Australian* (Sydney), July 12.

Medcalf, Rory. 2012b. "Indo-Pacific: What's in a Name?". *The Interpreter* (Sydney), August 16.

Mohan, C. Raja. 2011. India and Australia: Maritime Partners in the Indo-Pacific. *The Asialink Essays* 3 (7): 1–4. http://www.asialink.unimelb.edu.au/__data/assets/pdf_file/0008/505628/Maritime_Partners_in_the_Indo-Pacific.pdf.

Mohan, C. Raja. 2012. *Smudra Manthan: Sino-Indian Rivalry in the Indo-Pacific*. Washington, DC: The Brookings Institution.

Natalegawa, Marty M. 2013. "An Indonesian Perspective on the Indo-Pacific" [Keynote Address by Indonesia Foreign Minister at Conference on Indonesia, Center for Security and International Studies, Washington, DC], 16 May 2013, at http://csis.org/files/attachments/130516_MartyNatalegawa_Speech.pdf, 1–5.

National Security Strategy of the United States of America, President of the United States, December 2017.

Paleri, Prabhakaran. 2013. "Maritime Challenges and Priorities in Asia: An Indian Perspective". In *Maritime Challenges and Priorities in Asia: Implications for Regional Security*, edited by Joshua H. Ho and Sam Bateman, 272–283. New York: Routledge.

Panda, Rajaram. 2012. India and Australia: Security Dynamics in the Asia Pacific. *Asia Pacific Review* 19 (1) (May): 130–156.

Pant, Harsh V., and Yogesh Joshi. 2016. *The US Pivot and Indian Foreign Policy: Asia's Evolving Balance of Power*. New York: Palgrave Macmillan.

Prakash, Arun. 2013. On Indo-Pacific Maritime Security: 'We May Sink Together If We Do Not Swim Together. *Asian Politics & Policy* 5 (2): 275–283.

Proctor, Pat. 2016. *Containment and Credibility: The Ideology and Deception that Plunged America into the Vietnam War*. New York: Carrel Books.

Puri, Raman., and Arun Sahgal. 2011. The South China Sea Dispute: Implications for India. *Indian Foreign Affairs Journal* (New Delhi) 6 (4) (October–December): 437–448.

Quayle, Linda. 2013. *Southeast Asia and the English School of International Relations: A Region-Theory Dialogue*. New York: Palgrave Macmillan.

Roy, Edmond. 2011. Australian Uranium and India: Ideology Versus Pragmatism. *South Asia* 34 (1) (April): 113–140.

Roy, Nalanda. 2016. *The South China Sea Disputes: Past, Present and Future*. New York: Lexington Books.

Santis, Hugh. 2012. The China Threat and the "Pivot" to Asia. *Current History* 111 (746) (September): 209–215.

Saran, Shyam. 2011. "Mapping the Indo-Pacific". *The Indian Express* (New Delhi), October 29.

Shambaugh, David. 2013. *China Goes Global: The Partial Power*. Oxford: Oxford University Press.

Shekhar, Vibhanshu. 2018. *Indonesia's Foreign Policy and Grand Strategy in the 21st Century: Rise of an Indo-Pacific Power*. New York: Routledge.

Singh, Swaran. 2013. "US-Japan-India Trilogue: The China Factor". In *Strategic Convergence of Japan-India Relations and the Emergence of China*, edited by Takenori Horimoto and Lalima Varma, 133–152. New Delhi: Manohar.
Singh, Zorawar Daulet. 2018. India and China Can Coexist in the Indo-Pacific. *Economic & Political Weekly* (New Delhi) 53 (13) (March), http://www.epw.in/journal/2018/13/strategic-affairs/india-and-china-can-coexist-indo–pacific.html.
Symonds, Peter. 2012. "Military Build-Up in Indo-Pacific Region: US "Pivot" to Asia Threatens War with China". *Global Research*, 6 June 2012 at http://www.globalresearch.ca/military-build-up-in-indo-pacific-region-us-pivot-to-asia-threatens-war-with-china/.
Tellis, Ashley. 2011. "The United States and Asia's Rising Giants". In *Strategic Asia 2011–12: Asia Responds to its Rising Powers, China and India*, edited by Ashley J. Tellis, Travis Tanner, and Jessica Keough, 3–34. Washington, DC: The National Bureau of Asian Research.
Till, Geoff. 2016. "Reactions to the Re-balance: Asia in General and Southeast Asia in Particular". In *Assessing Maritime Power in the Asia-Pacific: The Impact of American Strategic Re-balance*, edited by Greg Kennedy and Harsh V. Pant. Surrey, UK: Ashgate Publishing Ltd.
Welch, Dylan. 2012, "Rules for US Troops in NT kept Secret". *The Age*, (Melbourne, November 11).
Wesley, Michael. 2010. "Australia Faces a Changing Asia". *Current History*, (September), 227–231.
White, Hugh. 2013. "Is Australia Ready for Asia's New Strategic Realities? Australia's Defence Policy Ignores the Strategic Implications of China's Rise". *The Straits Times*, (May 22).
White, Hugh. 2010. Power Shift: Australia's Future Between Washington and Beijing. *Quarterly Essays, Issue* 39: 1–74.
Yahuda, Michael. 2013. China's New Assertiveness in the South China Sea. *Journal of Contemporary China* 22 (81): 446–459.
Yuan, Jingdong. 2013. China and the Indian Ocean: New Departures in Regional Balancing. In *Deep Currents and Rising Tides: The Indian Ocean and International Security*, edited by John Garofano and Andrea J. Dew, (see Chap. 7). Washington, DC: University of Washington Press.
Zhu, Zhiqun. 2010. *China's New Diplomacy: Rationale, Strategies and Significance*. Surry, UK: Ashgate.

Australia's Cognition of the "India-Pacific Strategy", Reasons and Countermeasures

Zhang Jiegen and Li Hongmei

Abstract Australia is a traditional ally of the US, and a key participator of the "Indo-Pacific Strategy", so, it is of practical significance to study Australia's cognition of the "Indo-Pacific Strategy", and the reasons behind such cognition. This paper first reviews the process of emerging of the "Indo-Pacific" concept, and the putting forward and evolution of the "Indo-Pacific Strategy". On this basis, this paper conducts a systematic analysis about Australia's cognition of the "Indo-Pacific Strategy", and mainly analyzes Australia's official attitude and its academic community's attitude toward this strategy. The analysis finds that Australian authority held a positive attitude toward the US-dominated "Indo-Pacific Strategy"; while, there are mainly three types of attitudes toward the strategy, namely, approval, middle and opposition, in the academic community; and in the academic community, to some extent, those who hold an approving attitude toward the strategy are the most influential. Then, this paper analyzes the factors that influence Australia's cognition of the "Indo-Pacific Strategy". The factors can be classified into domestic factors and international factors. Domestic factors include Australia's special geographic location of bordering two oceans, and the fact that Australia's internal politics is getting increasingly conservative and populist; and external factors mainly include: regarding China, Australia follows the principle of "high level politics" overweighing "low level politics"; Australia relies on the US in security, and follows the US in strategy; and Australia gives high attention to India's rising. Lastly, regarding China's counter-measures, this paper attempts to put forward 3 suggestions: first, economy still can be considered an effective tool in China's foreign policy regarding Australia; second, a tacit acceptance of the "Indo-Pacific" concept promotes the normalization of China's presence in the Indian Ocean Region; third, China should maintain strategic composure and strategic flexibility.

Z. Jiegen (✉)
Center for South Asia Studies and the Center for Pakistan Studies, The Institute of International Studies, Fudan University, Shanghai, China

L. Hongmei
Department of International Relations and Public Affairs, Fudan University, Shanghai, China

C. Zhu (ed.), *Annual Report on the Development of the Indian Ocean Region (2018)*, Research Series on the Chinese Dream and China's Development Path, https://doi.org/10.1007/978-981-13-7693-1_5

Keywords Australia · Indo-Pacific strategy · Quadrilateral security dialogue · Follower policy

1 Emerging of the "Indo-Pacific" Concept, and Putting Forward of the "Indo-Pacific Strategy"

As early as in August 2006, right before his first term as Japanese prime minister, Shinzo Abe conceived of the Indo-Pacific region as one separate strategic entity, which jointly led by countries "in the same camp", namely, the US, Japan, India and Australia. This proposal actually aims to establish a "democracy club" to counter-balance the rising China, but it was later rejected by the Bush Administration and the Obama Administration.[1] However, since the "Indo-Pacific" concept has gradually accepted by relevant countries, and the China-US relations, China-Japan relations, China-Australia relations and China-India relations have suffered setbacks from time to time over the recent years, the "Indo-Pacific Strategy" is eventually proposed by the US. Before analyzing Australia's cognition of the "Indo-Pacific Strategy", it is necessary to conduct a review about the process of how "Indo-Pacific" concept and "Indo-Pacific Strategy" has been put forward. The "Indo-Pacific" concept had been gradually accepted, and ultimately replaced the "Asia Pacific" concept in Australia, which provides some basis for Australia's subsequent active participation in the "Indo-Pacific Strategy".

(1) **Emerging of the "Indo-Pacific" concept**

In October 2006, think tanks from India and Japan held a seminar on strengthening strategy and security cooperation between India and Japan to address the rising of China at the Institute for Defense Studies and Analyses of India (IDSA). At the seminar, the "Indo-Pacific" concept was firstly put forward and discussed. In January 2007, Scholar Gurpreet S. Khurana from India National Maritime Foundation (NMF) wrote an article entitled "Maritime Route Security: The Prospects of India-Japan Cooperation", in which, the "Indo-Pacific" concept was formally used.[2] Since then, "Indo-Pacific" began to be publicly used as a brand new academic term. This concept has a clear geopolitical color since its appearance. Just as it is pointed out by some scholars, the birth of the "Indo-Pacific" concept is triggered by China's increasing political and economic influence.[3] Besides, to some degree, it is also connected to India's desire to change its disadvantaged position of being marginalized in the "Asia Pacific" concept. The strong politically realistic color doesn't reduce this concept's potential influence; on the contrary, it has gradually gained recognition of relevant countries.

[1] Swaine (2018).

[2] Khurana (2017).

[3] Guo (2018).

On August 22, 2007, in a speech at the Indian Parliament, then Japanese Prime Minister Shinzo Abe called on building a "Broader Asia" that included the Indian Ocean and the Pacific Ocean, and advocated building a huge network that not only included India and Japan, but also included the US and Australia.[4] In November 2012, Professor Rory Medcalf, who served as the director of the International Security Program of the Lowy Institute at the time, a well-known think tank in Australia, and currently serves as Director of the School of National Security, Australian National University, published an article entitled "Pivoting the Map: Australia's Indo-Pacific System", in which, he states an opinion that, Australia finds itself in an objective and active Indo-Pacific regional system.[5] In 2013, in a Defense White Paper, Australian government officially accepted the Indo-Pacific concept for the first time, which made Australia the first country to add the term of "Indo-Pacific" in an official document, or the first country to acknowledge that the Indian Ocean and the Pacific Ocean belong to the same regional system. According to the data from the Department of Defense of Australia, so far, Australian government has issued a total of 7 defense white papers (issued respectively in 1976, 1987, 1994, 2000, 2009, 2013 and 2016), and the interval between different white papers shows a trend of being shortened. This explains that in Australia's perception, the current international strategic environment is changing at an increasingly faster rate, so, strategic adjustment must be made timely. In its *Defense White Paper 2013*, Australian government mentioned the "Indo-Pacific" concept for the first time (the concept was never mentioned in previous defense white papers), and the term appears as many as 58 times in the whole document. In this white paper, Australia believes that a new "Indo-Pacific Strategic Arc" is emerging, and that this is mainly a result of India's rising and the deepening of interdependence between relevant countries in economy and security due to increase of exchange of trade, investment and energy resources between them. Moreover, Australia believes that its security environment will be deeply influenced by the evolution of the strategy structure in the Indo-Pacific area. This report stresses that, the "Indo-Pacific" concept is only a logical extension of the "Asia Pacific" concept used in the *Defense White Paper 2009*.[6] This sufficiently shows that, Australia has expanded the scope of its strategic interest to the Indo-Pacific area, and formally included the Indian Ocean into its scope of interest. The *Defense White Paper 2016* goes even further. In the white paper, the term of "Indo-Pacific" appears as many as 70 times, gradually becoming a common term. What on earth "Indo-Pacific" is? How should the concept be defined? Rory Medcalf is of an opinion that, "use of the term of 'Indo-Pacific' means acknowledgement of the rapidly developing economic and security connection between the West Pacific Ocean region and the

---

[4]"Confluence of the Two Seas", Speech by H.E. Mr. Shinzo Abe, Prime Minister of Japan at the Parliament of the Republic of India, *Ministry of Foreign Affairs of Japan*, August 22, 2007. http://www.mofa.go.jp/region/asia-paci/pmv0708/speech-2.html.

[5]Medcalf (2012, p. 471).

[6]Defense White Paper 2013, *Australia Government, Department of Defense*, May, 2013. p. 7. http://www.defence.gov.au/whitepaper/2013/docs/WP_2013_web.pdf.

Indian Ocean region".[7] We can see that, the definition of "Indo-Pacific" is mainly made geographically, and it mainly covers Indian Ocean and Pacific Ocean regions.

Actually, before Australia officially included the "Indo-Pacific" region into its scope of strategic interest, discussion about the "Indo-Pacific" concept had become very common, and it was generally realized that, the transition from the "Asia Pacific" concept to the "Indo-Pacific" concept is a general trend, and use of the "Indo-Pacific" concept is becoming very common. This is a main result of the judgment that Australia made about India's rising and increase of the Indian Ocean's strategic value. The Defense White Paper that the Department of Defense of Australia issued in 2009 pointed out that the Indian Ocean's strategic value will increase, and the white paper made a forecast that by 2030, just like the Pacific Ocean, the Indian Ocean will occupy a core position in Australia's maritime strategy, and defense deployment.[8] The *Australia Defense Force Posture Review* that Australian government published in 2012 stresses that Australia should lay more emphasis on the Indian Ocean in defense deployment.[9] On January 23, 2013, Australia issued its first national security strategy Document—*Strong and Secure: A Strategy for Australia's National Security*. In the document, the term "Indo-Pacific" appears frequently, which proves that Australia is gradually including the Indian Ocean into its scope of interest.[10] Generally speaking, a wide consensus has been basically established regarding acceptance of the "Indo-Pacific" concept and recognition of the Indo-Pacific region's importance; while, regarding the specific "Indo-Pacific Strategy" and resumption of Quad, there are still some different opinions in Australia, and the differences mainly exist in the academic circle and the strategic study circle; to a certain extent, the support school wins by being politically right, which will be specifically analyzed in later parts of this paper.

(2) **Putting forward of the "Indo-Pacific Strategy"**

Trump almost opposes "any policies that Obama put forward". In order to put forward an Asia strategy that is different from the "returning to the Asia Pacific" strategy put forward by the Obama administration, Trump adopted the "Free and Open Indo-Pacific" strategy that was firstly proposed by Japan, which will become the US's new Asia strategy. The Indo-Pacific Strategy, the whole name of which is "a free and open Indo-Pacific" strategy, mainly stresses the freedom and openness principle. Just as one senior official from the White House said, "the strategy's basic principles are: respecting the freedom of voyage and flight; respecting international laws and national sovereignty; exempted from coercion; and promoting private enterprises and

---

[7]Medcalf (2014, p. 472).

[8]Defending Australia-In the Asia Pacific Century: Force 2030 (Defense White Paper 2009). *Department of Defense, Australia Government.* 2009, p. 37. http://www.defence.gov.au/whitepaper/2009/docs/defence_white_paper_2009.pdf.

[9]Hawke and Smith (2013).

[10]Strong and Secure: A Strategy for Australia's National Security, *Department of the Prime Minister and Cabinet, Australia Government,* January 23, 2013. p. 30. https://www.files.ethz.ch/isn/167267/Australia%20A%20Strategy%20for%20National%20Securit.pdf.

freedom and opening of market",[11] while, a complete strategy should at least include definition of specific strategic interests, setting of strategic objectives and the means and methods to achieve the objectives. Viewed from these several aspects, the current "Indo-Pacific Strategy" is still quite vague, which is also one of the reasons why there are some debating about the strategy in Australia, which will be discussed later. And the academic community also conducted wide discussion about the "Indo-Pacific Strategy", especially the analysis about its objectives. Just as Felix K. Chang, a senior researcher at the Foreign Policy Research Institute of the US, believes, the "Indo-Pacific Strategy" is a strategy to balance against China's influence in the region.[12] Zack Cooper, a senior researcher at the Center for Strategic and International Studies of the US (CSIS), also believes that, viewed from the geopolitical perspective, the core of the "Indo-Pacific Strategy" is to expand the US's participation in the region by strengthening strategic containing of China.[13] When this paper's authors conducted exchange about relevant aspects with scholars from the US and India, these scholars plainly said that, the strategy is a policy response to China's gradually increasing influence.

Viewed from the perspective of the US's intention, the "Indo-Pacific Strategy" may consist of two parts: Firstly, regarding the security aspect, the strategy mainly aims to establish a security dialogue and negotiation mechanism through resumption of the Quadrilateral Security Dialogue (Quad), which includes the 4 countries of the US, Japan, India and Australia, and to build a so-called "freedom and democracy" club that is based on common values and ideas (although so far, no routine mechanism has been established), and to ultimately build the mechanism into a 4-country security cooperation alliance, although the possibility is uncertain. Regarding specific military cooperation, it may take such forms as Malabar joint military exercise. Currently, the trilateral and bilateral security dialogue between the 4 countries provides some cooperation basis for resumption of the Quad. Secondly, in economic aspect, in order to counter against China's "One Belt and One Road" plan, the US may, jointly with the other 3 countries, establish an alternative infrastructure investment plan in the Indo-Pacific area, especially Southeast Asia,[14] so as to reduce the influence of China's "One Belt and One Road" plan from economic perspective. While, the economic content part currently is still in the conception stage, and whether it can be put into practice is still to be seen. It can be readily seen that, the "Indo-Pacific Strategy" actually was put forward in a context that the "Indo-Pacific" concept has gotten wide recognition. This paper is of a view that, to some extent, there is no substantial difference between this strategy and the "returning to the Asia Pacific" strategy put forward during the Obama administration. Both of the two strategies' cores are to contain China's increasing military and economic influence, and their difference lies in that, geographically, the strategic scope of the Indo-Pacific strategy is extended

[11]Cooper (2018, p. 7).

[12]Chang (2017).

[13]Cooper (2018, p. 7).

[14]Australia, U.S., India and Japan in talks to establish Belt and Road alternative: report, *Reuters*, February 18, 2018.

to cover the Indian Ocean region. Just as Ph.D. Andrew Phillips from Queensland University of Australia pointed out in a research report submitted to the Australian senate in 2012, that to ensure maritime business security in the Indian Ocean region is of vital importance for Australia's national security interest.[15] Moreover, regarding the participating countries, India is included into the scope of dialogue. Besides, the US's Asia strategy adopts a China Containing Strategy that equally stresses military aspect and economic aspect. Militarily, the strategy stresses rebalancing, while, economically, the strategy supports TPP that has the characteristic of multilateralism. From the above analysis, we can see that, Trump administration's "Indo-Pacific Strategy" is not quite different from the previous Asia Pacific Strategy, and its ideal strategy design is still equally stressing military and economic aspects.

Currently, the strategy mainly involves military security cooperation level, especially, the resumption of Quad provides an chance to incubate the "Indo-Pacific Strategy". During the ASEAN Meeting held in Manila of Philippine in November 2017, the US, Japan, India and Australia separately held a security dialogue during the interval of the sessions. As the Quadrilateral Security Dialogue (Quad 1.0) was forced to suspend due to the withdrawal of Australia 10 years ago, this dialogue was called Quad 2.0, and it is a key part of President Trump's "Indo-Pacific Strategy". Similar to the Quad 1.0 of 10 years ago, Quad 2.0 was also produced targeting at a third country, which, however, to some extent, has intensified uncertainty and competition in the "Indo-Pacific" area. Geng Shuang, spokesperson of the Ministry of Foreign Affairs of China, said, "China expects to see that relevant countries develop friendly relations and cooperation, which, nevertheless, will not target at any third party".[16] Historically speaking, Japan is the originator of this dialogue: in 2007, Shinzo Abe put forward the proposal during his "one-year term" as prime minister, and the proposal got strong support of then US's Vice President Dick Cheney, Australian Prime Minister John Howard and Indian Prime Minister Manmohan Singh. The four parties held a security dialogue for the first time in the year; besides conducting dialogue at diplomatic level, the four parties also conducted joint military exercises, such as the "Malabar" military exercise, as the main content of cooperation at military level. Thus, the "Asia Pacific version of NATO", which mainly consists of democratic countries, began to take shape. However, due to its clear intention of attempting to contain China's quickly growing military and economic influence in the area, the strategy encounters diplomatic protest from China. On November 11, 2007, after Australia's new prime minister Kevin Rudd came to power, Australia voluntarily exited from the dialogue out of consideration of the overall situation of the China-Australia relations. At the time, Kevin Rudd mainly worried about that the close economic cooperation relations between China and Australia may become a victim of the informal dialogue, so, Australia exited from this initiative during the

[15] Andrew Phillips, Australia and the Challenges of Regional Order-Building in the Indio-Pacific Age, A submission prepared to contribute to the Senate Inquiry into the Indian Ocean region and. Australia's foreign, trade and defense policy, 2012. p. 3.

[16] Routine press meeting given by the spokesperson of the Ministry of Foreign Affairs of China Geng Shuang on November 13, 2017, the Ministry of Foreign Affairs of the P.R.C, November 13, 2017. http://www.fmprc.gov.cn/web/fyrbt_673021/jzhsl_673025/t1510045.shtml.

formal discussion in 2008, and refused to take part in the joint military exercise. Then, the quadrilateral security dialogue was declared "coming to an untimely end" before even forming a mechanism. From this, we can see that, in the early stage, Australia became a key variable in determining whether the multilateral security dialogue will work. Australia returns to the Quadrilateral Security Dialogue, which proves that Australian government's stance regarding the Quad has shifted from hesitation to determination.[17]

The Quad 2.0 dialogue is themed on "a free and open Indo-Pacific", and it mainly discusses subjects in the following 7 aspects: a rules-based order; voyage and flight freedom; international law; interconnectivity; ocean security; North Korea nuclear issue and terrorism.[18] From the official statements that the four countries' governments issued, it can be seen that Australia maintains active strategic accordance with the US. The two countries' statements both cover subjects in 7 aspects, and their expressions are almost the same; while, Japan and India have some reservations and different emphases in these 7 aspects. Actually, the US is in a primary position in Australia's strategic consideration, which determines that the US's foreign strategy is, to a far extent, of important reference for Australia. However, Joshua Kurlantzick, a senior researcher at the US Foreign Relations Commission, is of an opinion that, regarding the main carrier of the Indo-Pacific Strategy—the Quadrilateral Security Dialogue, Trump administration has not provided a clear development path yet. The relevant parties are still not sure whether Quad can develop into a substantial security cooperation mechanism. Besides, probably due to Australia's past "record" of withdrawing from the previous Quad cooperation in the middle, Joshua Kurlantzick considers Australia "a weak link" in the Quad cooperation, since China is the largest trading partner of Australia, and there is no fundamental conflict of interest between Australia and China, and there is no maritime and ashore conflict between the two countries.[19]

2 Australia's Cognition of the "Indo-Pacific Strategy"

As a "new born", the "Indo-Pacific Strategy" is currently still in an early stage of development, and precisely speaking, it has not taken a primary form yet. In order to understand Australia's cognition of the "Indo-Pacific Strategy", we need to conduct a study about the attitude of the Australian government and the Australian academic community toward the strategy. This paper attempts to get a glimpse into Australian government's cognition of the "Indo-Pacific Strategy" by analyzing Australia's official attitude and stance toward Quad, and Australia's change and adjustment of its strategic interest. Meanwhile, like the US's political and academic community, Australia's political and academic community also has the "revolving door" feature;

[17]Wyeth (2017).

[18]Panda (2017).

[19]Kurlantzick (2018).

specifically, there are frequent interactions between think tanks, research institutions and government decision-making entities. This determines that to conduct a study about the Australian academic community's cognition of the "Indo-Pacific Strategy" is of practical significance.

2.1 Australian government's cognition of the "Indo-Pacific Strategy"

Since Quad is an important constituent of the Indo-Pacific Strategy security framework, this paper will firstly conduct a brief combing through and review of Australia's official attitude toward Quad.1, so as to get a better understanding about the process of change of Australian government's stance. In May 2007, with driving by then Japanese Prime Minister Shinzo Abe, the 4 participating parties, namely, the US, Japan, India and Australia, held a quadrilateral security dialogue for the first time. This dialogue attempts to build a so-called "freedom and democracy" alliance in Asia, so as to jointly address the security challenge; while, since the strategy has a clear feature of targeting at a third party, China responded to it strongly. In order not to provoke China, in July 2007, Australia's then Secretary of Defense Brendan Nelson assured China that the so-called Quad.1 is not what Australia pursues during his visit to China. Then, Brendan Nelson clarified during his visit to India that Australia's interest in Quad.1 is only limited to issues like peace maintaining and economy.[20] In September 2007, the US and India invited Australia, Japan and Singapore to participate in the "Malabar" joint naval exercise in the Bengal bay, the largest naval exercise so far in the history. In November of the same year, Kevin Rudd became the prime minister of Australia. In order to continue to develop friendly relations with China, Australia unilaterally withdrew out of Quad.1, intending to isolate and counterbalance China. In February 2008, Australia's then foreign minister Stephen Smith publicly said that there will not be another Quad meeting, and promised that Australia will not advocate similar dialogues in the future.[21] Although it is still a close ally of the US, Australia's attitude toward Quad in this stage appeared to be rather cautious and careful. However, analyzing the subsequent a series of official documents of Australia, we can find that, Australia experienced a process of gradual acceptance of the "Indo-Pacific" concept, which results in that Australia's scope of strategic interest extends from the Asia Pacific region to the whole Indo-Pacific region. This provides some basic conditions for Australia's subsequent return to Quad.2. A systematic study of this change process will be conducted in following parts.

In *Australia Defense Force Posture Review* issued by the Australian government in March 2012, the Asia Pacific concept is mentioned for as many as 32 times, and although the "Indo-Pacific" concept doesn't appear in the document, the document's

---

[20]Madan (2017).

[21]See Footnote 20.

emphasis on the Indian Ocean has become very obvious, since the concept is mentioned for 16 times, and the report clearly stated that the Indian Ocean region is becoming more and more important to Australia.[22] In the *Australia in the Century of Asia* white paper issued by the Australian government on October 28, 2012, the "Indo-Pacific" concept is mentioned for 4 times. This document is of an opinion that, emerging of the "Indo-Pacific" concept was driven by the increasing economic interaction between South Asia, Southeast Asia and Northeast Asia regions, and the rising importance of the Middle East-Asia maritime passageway for energy transportation. And it is of an opinion that the "Indo-Pacific" concept considers the West Pacific Ocean and the Indian Ocean as an integrated strategic arc, which can effectively shape Australia's economic, political, security and environmental interest.[23]

While, in the *Defense White Paper 2013*, when the concept of "Indo-Pacific" is mentioned, apparent differences can be found between the *Defense White Paper 2013* and the *Defense White Paper 2009*, among which, two places should be especially noted: Firstly, in the *Defense White Paper 2013*, the "Indo-Pacific" concept officially replaces the "Asia-Pacific" concept, and the "Indo-Pacific" concept is mentioned for 58 times, while, the "Asia Pacific" concept is only mentioned in 3 places. The Indo-Pacific region was firstly separately stressed as one part of Australia's strategic outlook, and was placed in a primary position in the content of the outlook. This is the first time that Australian government defines Australia's interest considering Indo-Pacific as an integrated strategic system. On the basis of the *Defense White Paper 2009*, the *Defense White Paper 2013* points out three fundamental characteristics of the development of order in the Indo-Pacific region: firstly, over the next dozens of years, development of the China-US relations is of vital importance for shaping Australia's strategic environment, and evolution of the China-US relations is under dual influence of the US's regional commitment and China's rising. Secondly, a new Indo-Pacific Strategic Arc that connects the Indian Ocean and the Pacific Ocean, and runs across Southeast Asia is forming. The document points out that, "Indo-Pacific" is a logical extension of the Asia Pacific concept, and Australia's strategic priority areas after adjustment will include a wide arc-shaped belt, including areas from India to Southeast Asia, to Northeast Asia, and include relevant maritime transportation routes. "Indo-Pacific is rising as a system. Considering its diversity and universality, undoubtedly, its security structure is composed of a series of sub-regions and relevant arrangements, rather than being a monolithic whole".[24] At the same time, the white paper also points out that, the security in the Indo-Pacific region is faced with a dual development trend of cooperation and competition going in parallel. Thirdly, besides the influence from the China-US relations and India's rising, the influence of other regions and countries on the strategic environment, like Japan, South Korea and Indonesia, is also becoming more and more important. "For Australia, the environment's getting increasingly more complicated will result in that it will become more challenging to achieve the objective and to influence the outcome. Asian countries

---

[22]Hawke and Smith (2012).

[23]Australia in the Asian Century White Paper, *Australia Government*, October, 2012. p. 74.

[24]Defense White Paper 2013, *Department of Defense, Australia Government*, 2013. p. 7.

will balance wider interest and partnership, and Australia's voice needs to be louder and clearer". Meanwhile, it stresses that Australia will be committed to promoting regional multilateralism and developing bilateral relations.[25]

Secondly, what's more important is that Australia included the Indo-Pacific region into its scope of strategic interest for the first time, namely, Australia extended its scope of strategic interest from the previous Asia Pacific region to the Indian Ocean Region, and stressed that to seek a stable Indo-Pacific is in line with Australia's strategic interest. This is fundamentally different from Australia's definition of its strategic interests in the Asia Pacific region in the *Defense White Paper 2009*. In its *Defense White Paper 2013*, Australia states that its development of defense policies is mainly based on its 4 strategic interests: a secure Australia; a secure South Pacific and East Timor; a stable Indo-Pacific region; and a rules-based and stable global order. Regarding the Indo-Pacific region, the white paper writes: "Australia has a lasting strategic interest with stability in the Indo-Pacific region, especially Southeast Asia, and with a good maritime environment in the region". And it clearly points out that Australia has interests with peacefully solving territorial and maritime disputes according to international laws, including in the South China sea region, and Australia strongly supports the US to continue to intervene in and strengthen strategic presence in the Indo-Pacific region, and the white paper reiterates that security in the Indian Ocean Region is of vital importance for Australia's strategic interest.[26]

Australia's emphasis on the Indo-Pacific region is not only manifested in its series of official documents, but is also displayed in its officials' public statements about Australia's stance. In 2015, Australia's then Secretary of Defense Kevin Andrews declared in a speech, "In the current world, one major development trend is the continued shift of strategic and economic forces to the Indo-Pacific region; in such a context, the security and prosperity in the region is closely related to Australia".[27] Regarding the Indo-Pacific region, Australia's *Defense White Paper 2016* basically continues the principles that were adopted in the *Defense White Paper 2013*, but lays a higher stress on the region's freedom, openness, order and security, and attaches a higher importance on the maritime order in the Indo-Pacific region.[28] Compared with the fact that the Indo-Pacific concept is mentioned for 70 times in the *Defense White Paper 2013*, the *Defense White Paper 2016* completely abandoned the Asia Pacific concept, which is not mentioned at all in the document. To some degree, these subtle changes and adjustments of Australia's foreign policy provide a policy basis for subsequent security dialogue. After the Quadrilateral Security Dialogue meeting that the US, Japan, India and Australia held on November 12, 2017, viewed from the contents of the statements that the Australian Department of Foreign Affairs and Trade issued, the formulation of these statements is almost exactly the same with that of relevant statements that the US issued; the authors believe this is because that the US's regional policies serve as a reference for Australia, and Australia even

[25]Defense White Paper 2013, *Department of Defense, Australia Government*, 2013. p. 8.

[26]Defense White Paper 2013, *Department of Defense, Australia Government*, 2013. pp. 25–26.

[27]Dobell (2015).

[28]Defense White Paper 2016, *Department of Defense, Australia Government*, 2016, p. 70.

completely follows the US in development relevant policies, the discussion about which shall be conducted in following parts, rather than because that Australia and the US have same interests, which results in that their stances happen to be the same. Viewed from the contents, this statement mainly consists of 3 parts: (1) Vision: promote prosperity and security in the Indo-Pacific region, and be committed to ensuring freedom and openness in the region; (2) Common goal: maintain a rules-based order in the Indo-Pacific region; respect international law, and freedom of voyage and flight; promote inter-connectivity; coordinate counter-terrorist activities and maintain maritime security in the region; work together to address the threat that are posed to the world's peace and security by North Korea's nuclear arms and such weapons of mass destruction as missiles; (3) Means: All participating parties shall be committed to conducting persistent Quadrilateral Security Dialogue and deepening the cooperation relations based on shared values and rules.[29]

One week after the holding of the Quadrilateral Security Dialogue, Australia soon issued a foreign policy report, namely, the *2017 Foreign Policy White Paper*. This is the first comprehensive policy report about Australia's participation in global affairs that Australia issued since the *2003 Foreign Policy White Paper*.[30] In the *2003 white paper*, the Indo-Pacific concept was not mentioned at all, but in the *2017 white paper*, the "Indo-Pacific" word appears for as many as 74 times, far more than its times of appearing in the *Defense White Paper 2016*. In the *2017 Foreign Policy White Paper*, Australia states that China's economic growth is changing the power balance in the Indo-Pacific region, which results in the situation that the US's dominant position in the region is facing a challenge. This white paper lists 5 major objectives that are of vital importance to Australia's security and prosperity, among which, the objective in the primary position is to "promote an open, inclusive and prosperous Indo-Pacific region, and to ensure the rights of all countries are respected."[31] For this purpose, the white paper continues to list strengthening the US-Australia alliance as the core of Australia's regional policy, and it considers Australia's alliance relations with the US as the core guarantee for Australia's national security, and an important basis for developing Australia's strategy and defense plan; the white paper writes, Australia should encourage and support the US's maximum participation in the Indo-Pacific region in economy and security aspect, and stresses that Australia shall benefit from the primarily rules-based international order that is dominated by the US after World War II. Regarding the roles of the US, India and Japan, this white paper is of an opinion that the US plays a stabilizer role in the Indo-Pacific region, and Japan and India play an active role in ensuring regional stability, and the white paper believes that Australia's security and prosperity depends on a regional environment with the features of respecting international law and relevant rules and an open market.[32] To

[29] Australia-India-Japan-United States consultations on the Indo-Pacific, *Department of Foreign Affairs and Trade, Australia Government,* November 12, 2017. http://dfat.gov.au/news/media/Pages/aus-india-japan-us-consultations-on-the-indo-pacific.aspx.

[30] See Footnote 12.

[31] 2017 Foreign Policy White Paper, *Australia Government*, 2017. p. 3.

[32] 2017 Foreign Policy White Paper, *Australia Government*, 2017. p. 37.

some extent, this white paper states Australia's advocacy and support for the US's dominance in the regional order; in other words, it expresses Australia's desire to maintain the "status quo". Compared with previous series of documents, in this white paper, when talking about China, Australia's attitude is almost straightforward, and the white paper states that, "we encourage China to exercise its rights on the following conditions: promote regional stability; strengthen international law; and respect small countries' interests and their rights to peacefully pursue their interests".[33] From this, we can observe the trend that Australia is gradually getting tougher with China. A logical outcome of this development trend is that Australia is changing from its previous practice of pursuing of a subtle balance between its relations with the US and its relations with China to almost completely following the US with its tough policies regarding China. A clear manifestation is that, since 2017, Australia is active in promoting resumption of Quad, calling for reestablishment of an "alliance of freedom and democracy". The US gave a positive response to this calling. On October 18 of the year, the US's then Secretary of State Rex Tillerson responded that, there is enough space for inviting other countries, including Australia, to join in the US, India and Japan bloc. Then, Japan, India and Australian Foreign Minister Julie Bishop all said that they would like to cooperate with countries from the same camp, which finally made the holding of Quad.2 a thing that will realize naturally when the conditions permit.

2.2 *Australian Academic Community's Cognition of the "Indo-Pacific Strategy"*

The time when Australian academic community began to discuss about the "Indo-Pacific" concept is generally earlier than the time when the Australian authority began to discuss about the concept. Among the academic institutions, the Lowy Institute, a well-known Australian think tank, is an institute that discussed about and paid attention to the "Indo-Pacific" concept relatively early. As early as in 2011, Professor Micheal Wesley, then executive director of the Lowy Institute, said, Australia should realize that it is in a new Indo-Pacific era. In the Indo-Pacific region, more and more countries are facing a common dilemma: on one side, they are getting increasingly more dependent on China economically; on the other side, they made a series of diplomatic and security commitments that deviate from China.[34] Some other scholars even doubt the Indo-Pacific Strategy's practicability for Australia, and they are of the opinion that Australia is not capable of shouldering this important task due to Australia's small scale and political culture, and the only way for Australia is to link its strategy with the US's global strategy.[35] Then, the discussion and use of the Indo-Pacific concept began to gain momentum in Australia, and a general

[33] 2017 Foreign Policy White Paper, *Australia Government*, 2017. p. 39.

[34] Wesley (2011).

[35] Scott (2013).

consensus has been established. Like in the US, in Australia, the think tanks are active, and the political community and the academic community frequently interact, and mutually influence each other. Australia's academic community plays a certain role in promoting Australia's transition to adopting the Indo-Pacific Strategy, and Australia's participation in the US-dominated Indo-Pacific Strategy.

In 2013, 4 think tanks, namely, Heritage Foundation of the US, Vivekananda International Foundation of India, Tokyo Foundation of Japan, and Australian Strategic Policy Institute (ASPI), jointly held the "Quad+" dialogue, which aims to expand consensus and promote restart of Quad by inviting experts in relevant fields from the 4 countries to discuss about common strategic concern. Since 2013, this dialogue began to be held in one of the 4 countries in rotation, which serves as a "dual track" level extension mechanism of the Quad official dialogue.[36] To some extent, this "dual track" mechanism serves the role of promoting, supplementing and coordinating with "one track" mechanism. Besides, Australian Defense Force Academy is also one of the institutions that pay attention to the "Indo-Pacific Strategy" in an early period. Since 2015, this institution publishes 1–2 issues of Indo-Pacific Strategy Compilations every year, which cover very wide issues, mainly focusing on discussion and study about countries in the Indo-Pacific region and relevant issues.[37] Australian academic community began to widely pay attention to the Quadrilateral Security Dialogue (Quad), which is a main content of the strategy, since November 2017, when Trump put forward the "Indo-Pacific Strategy". The "Indo-Pacific Strategy" stirred wide discussion in the academic community, but there is a wide divergence between the views of relevant parties. This paper classifies the views into 3 schools based on the degree of their support for reviving Quad:

1. Approval school: This school is of an opinion that Australia should strengthen cooperation with the US, Japan and India in the region, because: firstly, it can give much play to Australia's unique geographic advantage of "bordering two Oceans", and increase Australia's regional influence; secondly, to strengthen cooperation with these countries is in line with Australia's national interest, and can help address their common threats by cooperation. The worry about China's "expanding" strategic presence in the Indo-Pacific region is a main driving factor for proposing of the Indo-Pacific strategy, which, conversely, constitutes a proof of Quad's geopolitical nature and its aim of guarding against a third party. Australia considers Quad a political opportunity. For example, Euan Graham, director of the international security program of Lowy Institute, holds a very positive attitude toward the strategy. He is of an opinion that Australia should not miss this hard-to-get geopolitical opportunity once again, and that Australian government should coordinate the stances of the two political parties in Australia, so as to achieve cooperation between the two parties regarding the subjects of the Quadrilateral Security Dialogue. Regarding to what degree the Quadrilateral Security Dialogue should develop, he is of the opinion that this depends on

[36]The Quad-Plus, *Heritage Organization*, https://www.heritage.org/the-quad-plus.

[37]Indo-Pacific Strategic Digest, *Australia Defence College*. http://www.defence.gov.au/adc/publications/Indo-Pacific_Strategic_Digest.asp.

whether China shall strengthen its strategic presence in the East Indian Ocean region, and implement maritime coerce.[38] Professor Ian Hall from Griffith University agrees that Australia should strengthen its participation in Quad, but he doesn't think that Quad is of a military alliance nature for containing China, rather, he thinks the strategy is more like a relatively loose inter-country coordination mechanism designed to address a common challenge.[39] Associate Professor Sarah Percy from Queensland University is of the opinion that Australia should be committed to building Quad into a cooperation platform that focuses on fighting against crimes on the sea, and she believes that this is a main way to increase cooperation between the 4 countries and to achieve substantial progress with the cooperation.[40]

2. The middle school: This school's stance in the discussion about Quad is relatively moderate. They do not clearly approve or oppose Australia's joining in Quad, but they are concerned about whether Australia can have a place in future development of rules in the Indo-Pacific region; moreover, they believe that the Australia-India relations that were not adequately stressed should be deepened. One main characteristic of this school's view is that it stresses Australia's developing its independent foreign policy and strategy based on its own interest. For example, Researcher Graeme Dobell from Australian Strategic Policy Institute (ASPI) said, he doesn't oppose Australia's participating in any regional bloc or group, but the key issue is what role Australia shall play in Asia's future process. He believes that Australia should pursue independent foreign policy based on its own national interests, rather than determine its strategy from the perspective of another country, and he thinks that Australia should actively participate in development of rules in the Asia region.[41] Senior researcher Anthony Bergin from Australian Strategic Policy Institute (ASPI) is of an opinion that the US's replacing the "Asia-Pacific" concept with the "Indo-Pacific" concept amounts to an explicit acknowledgement of India's importance. He is of an opinion that India is a key force in the Indo-Pacific region, and the bilateral cooperation between Australia and India in the Indo-Pacific region should be strengthened.[42] Regarding the prospect of Quad, Australia's former diplomat Geoffrey Miller AO FAIIA is of an opinion that only time can prove whether Quad is beneficial for Australia or not, but the prospect is not so promising.[43] James Curran from the Lowy Institute is of a relatively cautious opinion, and he thinks that to expect Quad to

---

[38]Debating the Quad, the Center of Gravity Series, *Strategic and Defense Studies Center, Australia National University,* March 2018. pp. 2–7.

[39]Debating the Quad, the Center of Gravity Series, *Strategic and Defense Studies Center, Australia National University*, March 2018. pp. 12–14.

[40]Debating the Quad, the Center of Gravity Series, *Strategic and Defense Studies Center, Australia National University,* March 2018. p. 25.

[41]Dobell (2018).

[42]Bergin (2018).

[43]Geoffrey Miller AO FAIIA, Singapore, Australia, "the Quad" and ASEAN: Same Same But Different, *Australia institute of International Affairs*, January 16, 2018. http://www.internationalaffairs.org.au/australianoutlook/singapore-australia-quad-asean-different/.

develop into an Asia version of NATO is likely to be just an illusion. Regarding the US, the Trump Administration's governing principle of "the US's interests come first" makes it possible that the US may ignore Australia's interests in critical periods of time, and such precedents do occur between the US and Australia in history.[44]

3. Opposition school: This school's attitude basically is explicitly opposing Australia's joining in Quad, and they make their analyses mainly from the perspective of benefit and cost, and they calculate the possible negative impact of Quad mainly from the economic perspective, worrying about that Australia's closely following the US in adopting China containing policies in security may result in Australia's economic interests being ultimately harmed, and that for Australia, the potential loss may exceed the gains. For example, Professor Huge White from Australia National University holds a critical view regarding Quad. He is of an opinion that the continued growth of China's GDP will increase Australia's cost of countering against China. According to the forecast of Australian Department of Treasury, China's GDP may reach about 42.2 trillion dollars by 2030, far more than that of the US, India, Japan and Australia. In addition, as one key party of Quad, whether India will be willing to support the US's countering against China in the future is uncertain,[45] In other words, there is a worry about whether Quad can maintain its internal unity and consistency of stance. In addition, regarding the US's willingness to participate in affairs in the Indo-Pacific region, Huge White holds a view that is completely opposite to that of the Australian government. He judges that it is an inevitable trend for the US to withdraw from Asia; while on the contrary, Australian government strongly believes that the US will continue to maintain its participation and its strategic presence in Asia, and will successfully dominate and maintain the world order. Associate Professor Chengxin Pan from Deakin University of Australia refuted the two fundamental premises for establishment of the Quad dialogue. Undoubtedly, this dialogue is a strategic response to the so-called "China challenge", and the judgment about "China challenge" is based on two presupposed premises, which respectively are: (1) The challenge that China may bring essentially is in the military aspect; (2) China's rising brings a threat to the survival of the rules-based world order. He is of an opinion that there are two fundamental faults with these two hypotheses, which may bring a security predicament for relevant parties, and get the Quad dialogue to achieve what is right opposite to the objective it is intended to achieve. Therefore, he suggests that Australia should not invest too much in the Quadrilateral Security Dialogue; on the contrary, regarding the China issue, Australia should implement a pragmatic, multi-faceted, and cautious policy.[46]

---

[44]Curran (2017).

[45]Huge White, The White Paper's grand strategic fix: Can Australia achieve an Indo-Pacific pivot? Nov. 28, 2017. https://johnmenadue.com/hugh-white-the-white-papers-grand-strategic-fix-can-australia-achieve-an-indo-pacific-pivot/.

[46]Debating the Quad, the Center of Gravity Series, *Strategic and Defense Studies Center, Australia National University,* March 2018. p. 8–11.

Researcher Benjamin Zala from Australian National University is of an opinion that Quad doesn't have a clear objective, and the potential risk of its participation overweighs the potential benefit, therefore, he suggests that Australia should not invest time, resources or even its reputation for this initiative.[47]

From the views of these three schools, it can be clearly noted that: The approving school mainly considers issues from the security perspective, and their attitude toward China is relatively tough; the middle school more stresses independence of Australia's foreign policy, and they oppose that Australia's foreign strategy is too much influenced by the China-US relations; the opposing school mainly considers the issues from an economic perspective, featuring pragmatism. Viewed from the perspective of their actual influence on the Australian government, it seems that the approving school is more popular with the Australian government, and better suits the actual needs of the Australian government. This, to some degree, explains that, high level politics (security) seems to be more likely to be stressed than low level politics (economy), and sometimes, the latter may become a victim of the former. The fact that Australia participated in the Quad.2 dialogue last year, and that the statement the Australian government gave during the dialogue is highly in line with that of the US, proves the Australian government's acceptance and approval of the "Indo-Pacific Strategy". This is clearly different from Australia's attitude toward Quad 10 years ago, and explains that the Australian government's cognition of the Indo-Pacific strategy has changed.

3 Main Factors Influencing Australia's Cognition of the "Indo-Pacific Strategy"

It should be noted that, this part mainly analyzes the factors that influence Australia's cognition of the "Indo-Pacific Strategy"; actually, this part mainly analyzes those factors that influence Australia's official cognition of the strategy, since the official perception directly determines Australia's direction of strategy, and development of strategy. From the above discussion, we can see that Australia's acceptance of the "Indo-Pacific Strategy" actually is a logical outcome of the transition of its cognition of the strategy. Presently, the "Indo-Pacific Strategy" is still in an early stage, namely, the popularization and publicity stage, which is one of the causes that result in the current situation that although the Australian authority is active about the "Indo-Pacific Strategy", it has not conducted much discussion about it yet. Meanwhile, think tanks and research institutions are still debating fiercely about the strategy. In such a context, this paper mainly focuses on analysis of the factors that cause the change of Australia's stance regarding Quad. Specifically, this paper will mainly analyze the domestic and foreign factors that influence the transition of Australia's cognition of the Indo-Pacific strategy; and domestic factors include geographic factors and

[47] Debating the Quad, the Center of Gravity Series, *Strategic and Defense Studies Center, Australia National University*, March 2018. p. 22.

internal political factors, while, foreign factors include the US factor, China factor and India factor.

3.1 Domestic Level

1. **Geographic advantage of "bordering two oceans"**

That Australia is expanding its strategic scope from Asia Pacific to Indo-Pacific, expressing its concern over the order in the Indo-Pacific region, and giving active response to the "Indo-Pacific Strategy" proposed by the US, is a result of geographic factors. Geographically speaking, among the 4 countries of the US, Japan, India and Australia, Australia is the only country that "crosses over the two oceans", enjoying an exceptional geographic advantage. Being located in a junction area between the Indian Ocean and the Pacific Ocean, Australia is the country most qualified to develop an "Indo-Pacific Strategy", since such a geographic advantage results in a necessity for Australia to be concerned about maritime security on the two oceans. In an article that was published in 2014, Rory Medcalf wrote, "Indo-Pacific is an objective description of Australia's geographic location of crossing over the two oceans, and of an area that includes a rising China". "The Indo-Pacific concept recognizes that Australia is an integral part of this region, rather than being in a marginal location".[48] Viewed from Australia's developing and discarding of the Indo-Pacific concept and the Asia-Pacific concept, Australia's definition of "Indo-Pacific" is in a process of continuously self-reinforcing. Both of the political community and academic community are working hard to stress the legitimacy and inevitability of Australia's "Indo-Pacific status", for which, Australia's geographic advantage is cited as the best proof. Besides, this also can be well explained by the geographic deployment of the royal Australian navy. Australia's naval bases are generally deployed on the east side and west side of Australia, and they can be mainly grouped into east navy fleet and west navy fleet. The east fleet base (HMAS *Kuttabul*) is located in Sydney in the Pacific Ocean region, and it began to be built in 1913. The west fleet base (HMAS Stirling), which is located in the nearby of Perth at the coast of the Indian Ocean, officially went into service in July 1978, and over half of Australia's ground and submarine forces are deployed at this base. In 1987, Australian government officially announced the "Two-Ocean Basing Plan", which aims to build the royal Australian navy into a major fleet that is capable of continued operation along its east coast and west coast.[49]

2. **Australia's internal politics is getting more conservative**

For a long time, Australia's political field has been dominated by two political parties, namely, the Liberal Party and the Labor Party. The Liberal Party is usually considered a center-right conservative party, and the Labor Party is considered a center-left

---

[48]Medcalf (2014).

[49]Fleet Base West, *Australia Navy*, http://www.navy.gov.au/establishments/fleet-base-west.

party. During their respective ruling periods, the two parties adopted different policies regarding China. Generally speaking, the Liberal Party is relatively tough, while, the Labor Party is relatively moderate. Starting from September 2013, the Liberal Party has ruled Australia continuously for years, while, the spreading of populism across the world over the recent years has had some impact on Australia. For example, the Brexit and Trump's coming to power in the US have to some extent had some motivating effect on development of populism in Australia, which results in the populist development of Australia's domestic political circle. The most prominent feature is that over the recent years, some right wing small parties are continuously rising in Australia, and their main characteristics are "plebification" and conservatization, which to some degree, shows a discontent with the ruling by the Liberal Party. For example, in February 2017, Cory Bernardi, an outspoken right wing politician, publicly criticized the Liberal Party for its abandoning traditional values, and announced his breaking away from the Liberal Party-National Party alliance led by Malcolm Turnbull, and he planned to independently build a party of a pure ideology. Bill Shorten, a leader of the opposition party—Labor Party of Australia, also advocates building Australia and developing Australia's manufacturing industry, etc.[50] Besides, Australia experienced much political instability over the recent years, which mainly stems from fierce internal political fight, for example, Australia's Prime Minister Turnbull once had a fight with Australia's vice prime minister due to the latter's scandals. Moreover, like Trump, as a politician with business background, the Australian Prime Minister and the US's president have a common feature of being good at assessing specific policies in an economic way, and they especially stress cost and gains, and pursue maximization of the gains. All these factors can influence Australia's foreign policy. And increase of Australia's internal political instability and uncertainty also had some impact on Australia's external relations. In order to divert internal contradictions, countries often try to divert attention of its citizens by relatively tough foreign policies, or use it as a tool to unite different parties.

3.2 External level

In analyzing external influencing factors, this paper will mainly focus on analyzing change of the relations between Australia and China, the US and India. The three countries shall be considered key variables that influence Australia's cognition of the "Indo-Pacific Strategy". While, in spite of Japan's close cooperation relations with Australia, this paper shall not consider Japan a key variable regarding its influence on Australia's cognition of the "Indo-Pacific Strategy", therefore, this paper shall not conduct much discussion about Japan. In the National Security Strategy that Australia issued in 2013, the number of times that China is mentioned is only less than that of the US: the document mentions China in 28 places, and it is of an opinion that the China-US relations will become the most important influencing factor for shaping the

[50]Marks (2017).

environment for the "Indo-Pacific Strategy".[51] To some extent, deterioration of the China-US relations is one of the factors that cause deterioration of the China-Australia relations; and to some extent, the development of Australia's foreign strategy is profoundly influenced by the US' regional strategy, and strategically follows the U.S. policy. In this context, China's rights asserting behavior in the South China Sea, and China's "Belt and Road" related projects in Southeast Asia are all given a negative label by Australia, and China is accused of interfering in Australia's internal politics. These factors jointly result in deterioration of the China-Australia relations, and that to support the "Indo-Pacific Strategy" advocated by the US is considered "politically correct".

1. **Regarding China, "high level" politics overweighs "low level" politics**

Over the recent years, the China-Australia relations experienced subtle change, which is mainly represented in the description of the China issue in Australia's relevant official documents. In the *Defense White Paper 2013*, Australia clearly acknowledges that China's economic transformation is a key factor that causes the shift of global strategic center towards the Indo-Pacific area, and believes that the growth of China's defense capacity and development of military modernization is a natural and reasonable outcome of the continued growth of China's economy.[52] To some extent, development of the China-US relations will have some influence on Australia's foreign strategy. The *Defense White Paper 2016* writes, by 2035, the US, China and China-US relations will continue to be one of the most important factors that influence the security and economic development in the Indo-Pacific region. Regarding Australia's addressing of its relations with the US and China, it is apparent that, Australia's development of its relations with the US stresses the security and military aspect, "The US-Australia alliance is based on their common values, and that to establish an alliance with the US is the core of Australia's defense policy, and Australia will continue to consolidate its alliance with the US by supporting the US to better play its role in solidifying stability in the region".[53] Australia lays a higher stress on the economic aspect in developing China-Australia relations, and it hopes that the continued growth of China's economy will bring more opportunity for Australia. At the same time, Australia believes that, by 2035, the stability in the Indo-Pacific region will be mainly influenced by China's policies and behavior.[54]

Over the recent years, Australia's attitude toward China is getting increasingly tougher, of which, a basic characteristic is that in Australia, "high level politics" (security) is overweighing "low level politics" (economy), and becomes a main consideration in Australia's policy regarding China. Australian officials once publicly criticized and accused China in various occasions, which resulted in that the China-Australia relations has almost fallen to a historic low in the recent decade. On March

[51] Strong and Secure: A Strategy for Australia's National Security, *Australia Government, Department of the Prime Minister and Cabinet*. p. iii.

[52] Defence White Paper 2013, *Department of Defence, Australia Government*, 2013. p. 11.

[53] Defence White Paper 2016, *Department of Defence, Australia Government*, 2016. p. 44.

[54] Defence White Paper 2016, *Department of Defence, Australia Government*, 2016. p. 42.

13, 2017, Australian Foreign Minister Julie Bishop made outspoken criticism of China's institution in a speech he gave during attending the Fullerton Lecture in Singapore, which was organized by the International Institute for Strategic Studies (IISS), "However, when an undemocratic country like China joins in the current system, it may benefit a lot,", and he believes that the rules-based international order established after the World War II is full of uncertainty.[55] In its *Foreign Policy White Paper* issued in November 2017, Australian government made acute criticism of China's behavior regarding the South China sea issue, and it "......calls on relevant parties to stop sea reclamation and building activities, and Australia is especially concerned over that China is conducting such activities at an unprecedented speed and scale".[56] And "Australia is concerned over the potential possibility of use of force in the East China Sea and Taiwan Strait".[57] These comments that are unfriendly to China result in deterioration of the China-Australia relations, and what's worse is that in Australia, the voice that accuses China of its influence on Australia's domestic political process is very loud. In this context, on December 5, 2017, Australian Prime Minister Malcolm Turnbull held a press conference, at which he announced that Australia will reform its Foreign Interference Act, which resulted in worsening of the China-Australia relations.[58] A few days later, Australia Prime Minister Malcolm Turnbull said when making an introduction about the Foreign Interference Act, "Australian people are standing up".[59] In such an atmosphere, Australian media even poured oil on the flames by publishing all kinds of negative reports about China, which accelerated deterioration of the China-Australia relations.

Generally speaking, deterioration of the China-Australia relations is mainly due to the following several reasons: firstly, with China being strengthening protection of its interests in the South China Sea, Australia's attitude toward China experiences a process of gradual change. Regarding the South China Sea dispute, Australia chose to stand in the same line with the US and its allies, publicly stating that China should observe the ruling that was made by the arbitration tribunal in July 2016; secondly, over the recent years, Australia often accused China of attempting to directly or indirectly influence its internal politics; thirdly, Australia holds a contradictory attitude toward the Belt and Road initiative: on one hand, Australia wants to increase China-Australia economic cooperation and promote domestic investment and economic development by participating in the Belt and Road initiative; on the other hand, it refuses to sign relevant memoranda with China due to security concern.[60] Besides, Australia is to some extent disappointed at the US's reduction of its regional com-

---

[55]Bishop (2017).

[56]2017 Foreign Policy White Paper, *Australia Government*, 2017. p. 46.

[57]2017 Foreign Policy White Paper, *Australia Government*, 2017. p. 47.

[58]Press Conference With Senator The Hon. George Brandis QC, Attorney-General and senator The Hon. Mathias Cormann, Minister For Finance, *Prime Minister of Australia*, December 5, 2017. https://www.pm.gov.au/media/press-conference-senator-hon-george-brandis-qc-attorney-general-and-senator-hon-mathias.

[59]Tom Phillips (2017).

[60]Bisley (2018).

mitments after the Trump administration came to power; specifically, it worries that the US may reduce its strategic participation in the Indo-Pacific region, especially security commitments, since after all, Australia considers its relations with the US and the US's regional participation one of the important guarantees for its national security, which is very apparent in Australia's defense white paper.

However, in Australia, the attitude towards China is not a monolithic whole, and Australian people seem to be more pragmatic. According to the opinion poll conducted by the Lowy Institute in 2017, Australian people's cognition of China displays a trend of becoming increasingly more contradictory, and this situation is becoming increasingly more apparent with continuously strengthening of China's military power. For example, in an opinion poll of Australian people's cognition of China, the percentage of people who believe that "China constitutes a military threat" is rising; 46% of Australian people believe that China may constitute a military threat to Australia in 20 years, increasing by 7 percentage points than that in 2015. While, 79% of Australian people believe that to Australia, China is more like an economic cooperation partner, rather than a military threat.[61] China is Australia's largest trade partner and largest export market, and Australia is China's second largest destination of investment. Australia's former Prime Minister Tony Abbott once said the two things that influence Australia's policy regarding China are "fear" and "greed", which result in that Australia's policy regarding China is full of indecisiveness and contradictions. Wesley also holds a similar view. He is of an opinion that Australia is facing a contradictory reality: Australia's main source of economic prosperity is potentially challenging their most sacred values.[62]

2. **Rely on the US in security, and follow the US in strategy**

Undoubtedly, as one "close ally" of the US in the Asia Pacific region, the development of Australia's external strategy is influenced by the US's foreign strategy to a high extent. Since Australia adopts a policy of following the US in strategy, Australia's foreign strategy actually lacks independence and autonomy. In Australia's view, over the past more than 60 years, the US plays a key role in maintaining stability in the Asia region.[63] The US's importance and role are placed at a core position in Australia's development of its foreign strategy. From a series of official documents that Australia issued over the recent years, it can be seen that, the number of times the US is mentioned is continuously rising, and that Australia's attitude of following the US in policy is becoming more apparent. According to primary statistics, in the recent 3 defense white papers that Australia issued over the recent years, the number of times the US was mentioned respectively are: in the white paper 2009, the US is mentioned for 80 times; in the white paper 2013, 85 times; and in the white paper 2016, 129 times. In its national security strategy document—*Power and Security: Australia's National Security Strategy* that Australia issued in 2013,

[61] 2017 Lowy Institute Poll, *Lowy Institute*, June 21, 2017. https://www.lowyinstitute.org/publications/2017-lowy-institute-poll.

[62] Valencia (2017).

[63] Defence White Paper 2013, *Department of Defence, Australia Government*, 2013. p. 10.

the US-Australia alliance was listed as one of the 8 backbones that ensure Australia's national security.[64] The document points out that, "the alliance with the US is the core of our efforts to ensure national security, and it contributes a lot to ensuring regional security and stability; therefore, we need to continue to consolidate this relations."[65] In Australia's view, the US-Australia alliance is the main cornerstone of Australia's defense and security cooperation since World War II. The two countries deepen their alliance cooperation mainly through regular dialogues, joint military exercises, information sharing, defense technology sharing, complementary diplomacy, and research and development cooperation.[66] On May 16, 2013, the U.S.-Australia Defense Trade Cooperation Treaty officially came into effect, which gives Australia a special right to get the US's advanced defense technology.[67] http://www.defence.gov.au/ustradetreaty/aboutthetreaty.asp. During this period, due to that the Obama administration announced the "returning to the Asia-Pacific" strategy, Australia's assessment about the US's policy is that the US will increase its attention and investment in Asia, which is in line with Australia's national interests.

The *Defense White Paper 2016* clearly states that Australia seeks to expand and deepen its alliance relations with the US, and that Australia supports the US to play a key role in maintaining security order in the Indo-Pacific region by means of military rebalancing.[68] The US is considered a "stabilizer" by Australia in the Indo-Pacific region, and "Australia welcomes and supports the US to play a key role in ensuring lasting peace in the Indo-Pacific region".[69] In Australia's view, to unswervingly support the US is in line with Australia's interest in the Indo-Pacific region, and the US is considered an important guarantee for Australia's security interest. The enthusiasm that Australia shows toward Quad.2 and the active response Australia made regarding the "Indo-Pacific Strategy" proposed by the US reflect Australia's implementing a policy of "following the US". But, Trump's coming to power brings much worry for Australia. It worries that the Trump Administration's "US first" policy will reduce the US's strategic presence in the Indo-Pacific region, and reduce its security commitments to its allies, which may result in that Australia faces uncertainty in security. Previously, Australia was deeply disappointed by the US's withdrawing from the TPP, and it hopes that the US can return to the TPP. In its *2017 Foreign Policy White Paper*, Australia expressly states that, "Our alliance with the US is the core of our participation in the Indo-Pacific region, without the US's wide participation in the region in politics, economy and security, the transfer of power in the Indo-Pacific region will accelerate, which will result in that the objective

[64] Strong and Secure: A Strategy for Australia's National Security, *Australia Government, Department of the Prime Minister and Cabinet*. January 23, 2013. p. vii.

[65] Strong and Secure: A Strategy for Australia's National Security, *Australia Government, Department of the Prime Minister and Cabinet*. January 23, 2013. p. 38.

[66] Strong and Secure: A Strategy for Australia's National Security, *Australia Government, Department of the Prime Minister and Cabinet*. January 23, 2013. p. 22.

[67] Australia-US Defence Trade Cooperation Treaty, *Department of Defence, Australia Government*.

[68] Defence White Paper 2016, *Department of Defence, Australia Government*, 2016. p. 15.

[69] Defence White Paper 2016, *Department of Defence, Australia Government*, 2016. p. 123.

of security and stability in the region that Australia pursues will be very difficult to achieve".[70]

It is not difficult to find that, in many cases, especially regarding the subject of regional security, Australia basically adheres to a policy of "speaking in a same voice" with the US, which is especially obvious regarding the South China Sea issue; moreover, as it is mentioned in previous parts, Australia maintains a stance that is highly in line with that of the US in its official statement about the Quadrilateral Security Dialogue in 2017. Needlessly to say, security and defense cooperation is a major part of the two country's cooperation, and among Australia's allies, the Australia-US relations is only next to the US-Britain relations in terms of their importance to the US. Just as the US State Department said, the US and Australia have established extremely close defense relations and cooperation, and Australia has been fighting shoulder to shoulder with the US in every major conflict since World War I. In 2014, the two countries signed the U.S.-Australia Force Posture Agreement, so as to strengthen their military cooperation.[71] At the 30th U.S.-Australia Minister-level Dialogue that was held on October 2015, the two countries signed a joint statement about strengthening defense cooperation, which reiterates that the US will comprehensively implement the military power deployment action in Australia.[72] In July 2017, the two countries held the 7th "Talisman Sabre"-code named large scale joint military exercise.[73] In addition to the continuously deepening US-Australia military cooperation relations, Australia's leaders have called on the US to strengthen its participation in the Indo-Pacific region on different occasions. For example, when Australian Prime Minister Malcolm Turnbull was attending the US Governors Association Meeting in Washington in February 2018, he urged the US not to reduce its presence in the Indo-Pacific region, believing that the US is a guarantee for regional peace and prosperity, and he stressed the active role that the US-dominated principles and rules-based international system have played, and expected companies from the US and Australia to conduct more infrastructure building in the Pacific and Southeast Asia.[74]

Moreover, that to continue to consolidate the US-Australia alliance enjoys wide public support in Australia. According to the public opinion poll that was conducted by the Lowy Institute of Australia, the support ratio of the US-Australia alliance among Australian people has maintained at a high level for a long time. During the 10 years period from 2008 to 2017, the support ratio of the US-Australia Alliance among Australian people always maintained at above 70%, and even maintained at over 80% in most years (for details, please refer to Fig. 1). These jointly provide a

[70]2017 Foreign Policy White Paper, *Australia Government*, 2017. p. 4.

[71]U.S. Relations With Australia, *U.S Department of State*, February 24, 2017. https://www.state.gov/r/pa/ei/bgn/2698.htm.

[72]Fact Sheet: United States–Australia Cooperation: Deepening Our Strategic Partnership, *the White House*, January 19, 2016. https://obamawhitehouse.archives.gov/the-press-office/2016/01/19/fact-sheet-united-states-%E2%80%93-australia-cooperation-deepening-our-strategic.

[73]Exercise Talisman Sabre 2017, *Department of Defence, Australia Government,* http://www.defence.gov.au/Exercises/TS17/.

[74]Probyn (2018).

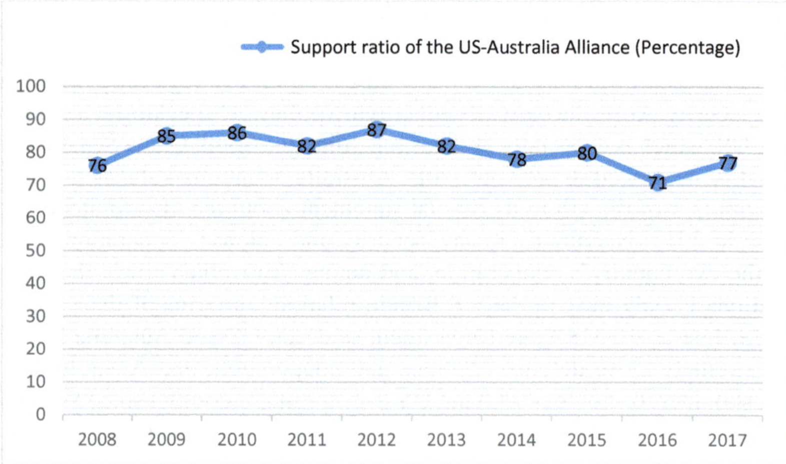

Source of data: 2017 Lowy Institute Poll. *Lowy Institute*,
https://www.lowyinstitute.org/publications/2017-lowy-institute-poll

Fig. 1 The Public Opinion Support Ratio of the US-Australia Alliance in Australia Support ratio of the US-Australia Alliance (Percentage)

solid political base and public base for Australia's adopting a policy of "following the US" in strategy, and it can be said that the close security relations between Australia and the US is almost unbreakable. Trump's "Indo-Pacific Strategy" precisely meets Australia's strategic needs for the US to continue to dominate the order in the Indo-Pacific region.

3. **Regarding India, from strategic separation to strategic cooperation**

India's rising is one of the key factors that lead Australia to attach high importance to the Indian Ocean region, and it is also a main influencing factor that leads Australia to expand its scope of strategic interest to the whole Indo-Pacific region. In relevant documents that are mentioned above, you can find that Australia is attaching increasingly higher importance to India and the Indian Ocean. Although India and Australia are the two countries with the strongest naval power in the Indian Ocean Region, substantial security cooperation between the two countries started relatively late. The two countries have held dialogues at different levels and in different fields, for example, in November 2009, when then Australian Prime Minister Kevin Rudd visited India, the two countries issued the joint statement of "India-Australia Security Cooperation", and established several cooperation mechanisms, including regular mutual visit and dialogue between the two countries' ministers, defense policy exchange between the two countries' high level officials, consultation between the two countries' national security advisors, and joint counterterrorism workgroup dialogue,[75] but these cooperation activities are all in a dialogue or negotiation stage, and they are seldom implemented into specific actions. The two countries conducted their first bilateral naval exercise in history in the Bengal bay in September 2015,[76] which is really late in coming. The main reason for the two countries' slow progress in conducting substantial cooperation lies in that there are fundamental differences between the two countries in their strategy tradition, decision-making process, and their stances regarding China and Pakistan, and in most time in the past, there is basically no crossing between their scopes of strategic interest. In the past, Australia's scope of strategic interest mainly focuses on the Pacific Ocean region, and the Indian Ocean region was not sufficiently stressed; while, India's scope of strategic interest has been limited to the South Asia region for a long time, then, it was slowly expanded to the Indian Ocean region, but it seldom mentioned the Pacific Ocean region.[77] This results in that the two countries' foreign strategy is basically in a separated state of mutual independence, namely, being in different geographic systems, and that the necessity for the two countries to develop a close strategic cooperation relations is not high.

With India's rising, and popularization and wide use of the "Indo-Pacific" concept, the scopes of strategic interests of Australia and India are continuously converging, which drives the two countries to gradually come to a stage of practical strategic cooperation. And the Indian Ocean's importance to Australia is continuously rising, which is not difficult to be noted from Australia's frequent mentioning of the Indian Ocean in its various documents. In 2016, senior researcher David Brewster from the School of National Security of Australia National University advocated building a bottom-to-top security and defense cooperation mechanism in the Indian Ocean Region between the US, Japan and Australia.[78] Moreover, the two countries' common concern about China's rising is also one of the key factors that promote them to go to strategic cooperation. For Australia, India is an ideal cooperation partner in the Indian Ocean Region. With continued growth of India's economic strength, Australia is seeking to expand economic cooperation and business and trade exchange with India. In addition, Australia believes that, Australia and India have common interests in security in the Indian Ocean Region, and they both stress an international law-based regional order, and seek to strengthen the security structure in the region; meanwhile, Australia strongly encourages India to participate in the East Asia, and supports the US-India cooperation.[79] Although Australia and India have not conducted much substantial cooperation in the field of defense yet, they have established security dialogue by different channels. The two countries even agree to establish a 2 + 2 model of dialogue, including secretaries of defense and foreign affairs; currently,

[75]India-Australia Joint Declaration on Security Cooperation During Visit of Prime Minister Kevin Rudd, *Institute for Defense Studies and Analysis.* November 12, 2009. https://idsa.in/resources/documents/India-AustraliaJointDeclaration.12.11.09.

[76]Khurana (2015).

[77]Brewster (2014).

[78]Brewster (2016).

[79]2017 Foreign Policy White Paper, *Australia Government*, 2017. p. 42.

India has established dialogues of a similar model only with Japan and the US, which shows that the two countries all recognize the importance of each other. The "Indo-Pacific Strategy", especially, restart of the Quadrilateral Security Dialogue, provides to some extent a platform for the cooperation between Australia and India. This is also one of the reasons for the change of Australia's attitude toward Quad, and Australia's enthusiasm for the "Indo-Pacific Strategy".

4 Several Suggestions

Before proposing China's possible policy options, it is necessary to firstly make a primary judgment about the possible development trend of the "Indo-Pacific Strategy". As is well-known, the "Indo-Pacific Strategy" is dominated by the US, and Australia adopts a policy of "following the US in strategy"; therefore, the US's any measure regarding the "Indo-Pacific Strategy" shall influence Australia's relevant policies. On April 2, 2018, at the US State Department's media briefing on the "Indo-Pacific Strategy", the US's Deputy Assistant Secretary of State Alex N. Wong said, looking back on the past year, we really think that the first year of the Trump administration is a year for introducing the strategic concept, and during the second, third and fourth year of the Trump administration's first term, our work will focus on building and implementing this strategy.[80] This strongly proves the US's determination to implement the "Indo-Pacific Strategy". As is mentioned in previous parts, no specific strategic plans have been developed for the "Indo-Pacific Strategy" yet, which caused Australia's deep worry about the strategy's future. Alex N. Wong explained that the core of the "Indo-Pacific Strategy" lies in its freedom and openness, which involves the opening up of infrastructure projects and investment in the region. Regarding the reasons why the US accepts the "Indo-Pacific" concept, he said: firstly, this concept acknowledges the key role that South Asia, especially India, plays in East Asia, Southeast Asia and the Pacific region; secondly, it is in line with the interests of the US and countries in this region that India plays an increasingly important role in this region.[81] To some extent, Australia also acknowledges the importance of India. As is analyzed in previous parts of this paper, this is also one of the reasons why Australia favors the "Indo-Pacific Strategy". For China, regarding how to address Australia's participation in the "Indo-Pacific Strategy", or how to address the "Indo-Pacific Strategy" itself, this paper attempts to give the following suggestions:

(1) **Economy still can be considered as an effective tool in China's policy regarding Australia**

Objectively speaking, although Australia comprehensively follows the US in security and strategy, it is impossible for Australia not to consider its economic interest at

[80] Wong (2018).

[81] See Footnote 80.

all; besides, the China-Australia economic cooperation is real, and constitutes an important interest of Australia. In such a context, only economic factor can become a key element to influence Australia's policy regarding China. According to the statistical data issued by the Australian government, viewed from the China-Australia bilateral trading value of goods, in 2016–2017 fiscal year, Chinese mainland is the largest trading partner of Australia, accounting for 27.6% of Australia's total bilateral trading value. When counting Hong Kong of China (2.4%) and Chinese Taiwan (2.3%), the total percentage shall be 32.3%, next come Japan with 11%, and the US with 7.5%.[82] Moreover, according to the data of the 2016–2017 fiscal year, Chinese Mainland is the largest single market of Australia's export of services, accounting for 18% of Australia's total export value of services; when counting Hong Kong of China (3.5%) and Chinese Taiwan (1.6%), the total percentage shall be 23.1%. The US comes next with 10.4%. In terms of total bilateral trade value of services, Chinese Mainland is Australia's second largest trading partner, accounting for a percentage of 10.5%; when counting Hong Kong of China (3.5%), the total percentage shall be 14%, second only to the US (14.3%).[83] The services that Australia exports to China are mainly education related foreign study tour services: in this year, this type of services account for about 53.8% of all exported services, and personal tour services come next, accounting for a percentage of 30.2%.[84] These numbers show that, China and Australia have a close economic relations, and depend on each other economically, while, this is an asymmetrical type of interdependence, namely, Australia depends on China more. This asymmetrical interdependence gives China a big power over Australia, since, comparatively, China enjoys more initiative in this interdependence relations, and Australia shall pay a high price for deterioration of the China-Australia relations. China only needs to maintain the steady growth of its domestic economy, and make Australia really understand that Australia will suffer a loss bigger than potential gains in its confronting against China, just as some people in Australia worry about. Just as it is forecasted by the Department of Treasury of Australia, China will become the biggest economy in the world by 2030.

Moreover, Australia doesn't conduct as much economic cooperation with the US, Japan and India as with China, and these countries are not expected to develop as well as China in the future, so, in the long term, it will harm Australia's national interest to expand its hostility towards China from the security field to the economic field. China only needs to continue to maintain the growth of its domestic economy, and with strengthening its economic power, China may use economy an effective tool in its foreign policy regarding Australia; after all, for Australia, none of the US, Japan and India can replace China in terms of the importance, volume, or potential of their bilateral trades with it.

---

[82]Composition of Trade-Australia 2017, *Australia Government, Department of Foreign Affairs and Trade,* p. 74. http://dfat.gov.au/about-us/publications/Documents/cot-2016-17.pdf.

[83]Composition of Trade-Australia 2017, *Australia Government, Department of Foreign Affairs and Trade,* p. 47. http://dfat.gov.au/about-us/publications/Documents/cot-2016-17.pdf.

[84]Composition of Trade-Australia 2017, *Australia Government, Department of Foreign Affairs and Trade,* p. 9. http://dfat.gov.au/about-us/publications/Documents/cot-2016-17.pdf.

(2) **It will promote normalization of China's presence in the Indian Ocean to tacitly accept the "Indo-Pacific" concept**

Since the "Indo-Pacific" concept has a gene of "countering against China" since it was firstly proposed, Chinese authority has always held a reserve attitude toward the concept. However, that India is rising and the importance of the Indian Ocean Region is rising is an undisputed fact, especially in the context that the "Maritime Silk Road" plan proposed by China seems to cover the whole "Indo-Pacific" region geographically. The importance of the Indian Ocean for China is apparent, and the Indian Ocean and the Pacific Ocean have gradually become an integrated system. In addition, driven by the US, this concept has gradually been accepted by other countries in the region, and it is getting wide use. China cannot change this fact. Moreover, to consider the "Indo-Pacific" region an integrated whole can help clear the Indian Ocean of its "India status", namely, weaken India's perception that "the Indian Ocean is an Ocean of India". This perception resulted in that China's any action in the region shall be considered by India as a challenge to its sphere of influence. In this context that the popularization of the "Indo-Pacific" concept cannot be stopped, China may as well accept its use, and further promote legalization and normalization of China's presence in the Indian Ocean Region. It needs to be noted that the acceptance of the "Indo-Pacific" concept doesn't equal to acknowledgement of the legitimacy and justifiability of the "Indo-Pacific Strategy", which has an objective of containing China. China's tacit acceptance of the "Indo-Pacific" concept only means China acknowledges that the "Indo-Pacific" region belongs to a same geographic system; therefore, to use the "Indo-Pacific Strategy" concept and to oppose the strategy at the same time don't contradict with each other, and it is only a tactics of China for taking advantage of a momentum that is favorable for China.

(3) **Maintain strategic composure and strategic flexibility**

Actually, although the voices advocating the "Indo-Pacific Strategy" are loud, there is still some uncertainty about it. Whether it can produce substantial containing effect upon China still needs to be seen. This uncertainty is mainly shown in the following several aspects: firstly, will the "Indo-Pacific Strategy" become an empty framework? Currently, the US is very active and determined to increase its strategic presence in the region, since in the US's view, this concerns with its national security interest, and Australia spares no efforts to support the US. But, just like past security cooperation between India and Australia, which often stops at desktop or on paper, often with much talk but very little virtual action, whether the US-dominated "Indo-Pacific Strategy" will repeat this model still needs to be seen. Secondly, it contradicts the "Indo-Pacific Strategy" that the US follows a reverse globalization policy regarding economy inherently. The former is domestically oriented, and turns from advocating multilateral trade to supporting bilateral trade; while, the economic contents that the latter contains advocate collectively building an alternative multilateral and regionalist cooperation mechanism that can balance against the "One Belt and One Road" initiative, which results in a situation that there are logic contradictions in the US's policy. In a word, the "Indo-Pacific Strategy" that the US advocates is totally incompatible with the trade protectionist policy it follows; the former stresses freedom and opening up, while the latter stresses weakening the competitiveness of foreign products by tariff and other means. For example, recently, the US initiated a Section 301 investigation on some products that are imported from China, and tried to protect domestic enterprises by high duty. Thirdly, despite that the US still has very strong hard power and soft power, it is an undisputed fact that the US is continuously declining. Therefore, a problem that may arise is that: The US's ambition to implement the "Indo-Pacific Strategy" doesn't match its available resources, and according to the forecast made by the Department of Treasury of Australia, by 2030, the US's gross economic output will be equivalent to only about one half of China's economic output.[85] In addition, compared with the "returning to the Asia Pacific Strategy" put forward during the Obama administration, the "Indo-Pacific Strategy" requires more resources to implement. Even if the US may ask Australia, Japan and India to share the burden as much as possible, whether these countries have the capability and willingness to share the burden is a question, which may further influence the strategy's validity.[86] Moreover, assuming the "Indo-Pacific Strategy" develops just as the US hopes, China may dilute the strategy's effects by strengthening its bilateral security cooperation with India, Japan and Australia respectively, and China even may try to crumble the strategy's intention of "allying to contain China" from the inside by voluntarily joining in the strategy. Therefore, what China needs to do is to maintain its strategic composure and strategic flexibility.

References

Bergin, A. 2018. *Towards an Indo-Pacific Strategic Partnership*. Australia Strategic Policy Institute (ASIP), 2 Feb 2018. https://www.aspi.org.au/opinion/towards-indo-pacific-strategic-partnership.

Bishop, J. 2017. *Change and Uncertainty in the Indo-Pacific: Strategic Challenges and Opportunities*. Minister for Foreign Affairs, 13 Mar 2017. https://foreignminister.gov.au/speeches/Pages/2017/jb_sp_170313a.aspx.

Bisley, N. 2018. *"Australia Faces Contested Asia". Regional Security Outlook 2018*, pp. 30–31. Council for Security Cooperation in the Asia Pacific (CSCAP). http://www.cscap.org/uploads/docs/CRSO/CSCAP2018WEB.pdf.

Brewster, D. 2014. The India-Australia Security and Defence Relationship: Developments, Constraints and Prospects. *Security Challenges* 10 (1), 65–71.

Brewster, D. 2016. *Australia and India: Forging a Stronger Relationship*. Australia Institute of International Affairs, 1 Sept 2016. http://www.internationalaffairs.org.au/australianoutlook/australia-and-india-forging-a-stronger-relationship/.

Chang, F.K. 2017. *What's in a Name? Strategy Behind the "Indo-Pacific"*. Foreign Policy Research Institute (FPRI). 11 December 2017. https://www.fpri.org/2017/12/whats-name-strategy-behind-indo-pacific/.

[85] 2017 Foreign Policy White Paper, *Australia Government*, 2017. p. 26.

[86] See Footnote 1.

Cooper, Z. 2018. "U.S. Strategy in Asia: Mixing Economic Nationalism with Security Internationalism". *Regional Security Outlook 2018*. Council for Security Cooperation in the Asia Pacific (CSCAP). http://www.cscap.org/uploads/docs/CRSO/CSCAP2018WEB.pdf.

Curran, J. 2017. *Trump Exhumes the Quad*. Lowy Institute, 17 Nov 2017. https://www.lowyinstitute.org/publications/trump-exhumes-quad.

Dobell, G. 2015. *Australia's Indo-Pacific Understanding*. *Australia Strategic Policy Institute (ASPI)*, August 17, 2015. https://www.aspistrategist.org.au/australias-indo-pacific-understanding/.

Dobell, G. 2018. *Asia's Rise: The Rules and The Rulers*. Australia Strategic Policy Institute(ASIP), February 15, 2018. https://www.aspi.org.au/opinion/asias-rise-rules-and-rulers.

Guo, M.A. 2018. The Origin of 'Indo-Pacific' as Geopolitical Construct. *The Diplomat*, January 25. https://thediplomat.com/2018/01/the-origin-of-indo-pacific-as-geopolitical-construct/.

Hawke, A., Smith, R. 2012. *Australia Defense Force Posture Review*. Australia Government, March, 2012. http://www.defence.gov.au/Publications/Reviews/ADFPosture/Docs/Report.pdf.

Hawke, A., Smith, R. 2013. *Australia Defense Force Posture Review*, 7. Australia Government, March 30, 2013. http://www.defence.gov.au/Publications/Reviews/ADFPosture/Docs/Report.pdf.

Khurana, G.S. 2015. *Ausindex-2015: Australia Pivots to the Indian Ocean*. Australia Naval Institute, 1 Nov 2015. http://navalinstitute.com.au/ausindex-2015-australia-pivots-to-the-indian-ocean/.

Khurana, G.S. 2017. *The 'Indo-Pacific' Concept: Retrospect and Prospect*, 1. National Maritime Foundation. February 2, 2017.

Kurlantzick, J. 2018. Trump's Indo-Pacific Vision: A Solid Idea, Hard to Pull Off. *Aspenia Online*, February 19. http://www.aspeninstitute.it/aspenia-online/article/trumps-indo-pacific-vision-solid-idea-hard-pull.

Madan, T. 2017. The Rise, Fall, and Rebirth of the 'Quad'. *War on the Rocks*, November 16. https://warontherocks.com/2017/11/rise-fall-rebirth-quad/.

Marks, K. 2017. The Rise of Populist Politics in Australia. *BBC News*, March 1. http://www.bbc.com/news/world-australia-39111317.

Medcalf, R. 2012. Pivoting the Map: Australia's Indo-Pacific System. *The Center of Gravity Series*, p. 3. November 2012. https://www.files.ethz.ch/isn/175987/COG1_Medcalf_Indo-Pacific.pdf.

Medcalf, R. 2014. In Defense of Indo-Pacific: Australia's New Strategic Map. *Australia Journal of International Affairs* 68 (4).

Panda, A. 2017. U.S, Japan, India and Australia Hold Working-Level Quadrilateral Meeting on Regional Cooperation. *The Diplomat,* November 13. https://thediplomat.com/2017/11/us-japan-india-and-australia-hold-working-level-quadrilateral-meeting-on-regional-cooperation/.

Probyn, A. 2018. Malcolm Turnbull urges US not to diminish presence in Indo-Pacific. *ABC News (Australia Broadcasting Corporation)*, February 24. http://www.abc.net.au/news/2018-02-25/malcolm-turnbull-urges-us-not-to-diminish-presence-indo-pacific/9482428.

Scott, D. 2013. Australia's Embrace of the 'Indo-Pacific': New Term, New Region, New Strategy? *International Relations of the Asia-Pacific* 17. June 26, 2013.

Swaine, M.D. 2018. *Creating an Unstable Asia: The U.S. "Free and Open Indo-Pacific" Strategy*. Carnegie Endowment for International Peace, 2 Mar 2018. http://carnegieendowment.org/2018/03/02/creating-unstable-asia-u.s.-free-and-open-indo-pacific-strategy-pub-75720.

Tom Phillips, C.K. 2017. Turnbull Says Australia will 'Stand Up' to China as Foreign Influence Row Heats Up. *The Guardian*, February 8. https://www.theguardian.com/australia-news/2017/dec/09/china-says-turnbulls-remarks-have-poisoned-the-atmosphere-of-relations.

Valencia, M.J. 2017. Joining the Quad: Fear Versus Greed. *The Diplomat*, December 15. https://thediplomat.com/2017/12/joining-the-quad-fear-versus-greed/.

Wesley, A. 2011. Irresistible Rise of the Indo-Pacific. *Australian Literary Review*, 5. May 4, 2011. https://www.lowyinstitute.org/sites/default/files/pubfiles/Wesley%2C_Irresistible_rise_of_the_Indo_Pacific_1.pdf.

Wong, A.N. 2018, April 2. *Briefing on The Indo-Pacific Strategy*. U.S Department of State. https://www.state.gov/r/pa/prs/ps/2018/04/280134.htm.

Wyeth, G. 2017. Why Has Australia Shifted Back to the Quad. *The Diplomat*. November 16. https://thediplomat.com/2017/11/why-has-australia-shifted-back-to-the-quad/.

Connotation and Dilemma of the US Indo-Pacific Strategy and China's Responses

Peng Liu

Abstract The collective rise of the eastern countries represented by China and India has caused the shift of world's center of gravity. In response to this situation, the Indo-Pacific region with the ocean as the main boundary has become the central stage for the game of all countries. Indo-Pacific has also quickly transformed from a geographic concept into geographic reality and entered into national strategies of various countries. The name of the US's Indo-Pacific strategy may change with the change of the Trump administration, but the core content of the Indo-Pacific strategy will remain unchanged. In other words, the US strengthens the existing alliances and establishes new alliances to contain China's rapid rise, thus preventing any force in the Indo-Pacific region from threatening the US hegemony. The US' current Indo-Pacific strategy is the concentric circles of the US-Indo-Pacific, the US-South Asia, and the US-India established according to the realism and the Cold War mentality based on the Obama administration's "pivot to Asia-Pacific". The Australia-India-Japan-US alliance or Quad, which has been greatly discussed in China, may not be established realistically. However, the United States is increasing its military presence in Indo-Pacific region and establishing the bilateral or multilateral networks through alliances in the Indo-Pacific region. The Indo-Pacific order, aimed to establish a "free and open Indo-Pacific", is actually an exclusive system design against China, which will have a direct impact on China's "Belt and Road" and Indo-Pacific maritime cooperation. To this end, while prudently and resolutely promoting the implementation of the "Belt and Road", China should encourage the institutional design of ASEAN-dominated Indo-Pacific structure and support the establishment of an open Indo-Pacific system arrangement based on the existing East Asia Summit. This should become the main content of China's Indo-Pacific strategy.

Keywords Indo-Pacific strategy · Concentric circle · Transactional diplomacy · The quad · Indo-Pacific system design

---

P. Liu (✉)
Research Institute for Indian Ocean Economies, Yunnan University of Finance and Economics, Kunming, China

C. Zhu (ed.), *Annual Report on the Development of the Indian Ocean Region (2018)*, Research Series on the Chinese Dream and China's Development Path, https://doi.org/10.1007/978-981-13-7693-1_6

Since the concept of "Indo-Pacific" was proposed, the academic community in China has conducted continuous follow-up research on it, and generated a lot of relevant research results.[1] However, the peak of the "Indo-Pacific" study is the resumption of "Indo-Pacific" by the US Trump administration in 2017. The key words of Indo-Pacific research have changed from "Indo-Pacific concept" to "Indo-Pacific strategy". Various papers published on Indo-Pacific since 2017 have been entitled with the "Indo-Pacific Strategy", where the tentative "Indo-Pacific concept" has been no longer used. This reflects the gradual deepening of the Indo-Pacific study in the academic circles in China, and also indicates the consensus on the transformation of "Indo-Pacific" from concept to practice.

The United States has always been the "top priority" of the studies on international studies in China, and the US "Indo-Pacific strategy" is certainly the focus of the research on "Indo-Pacific" in China. The United States' Indo-Pacific, South Asia and India strategies are the three concentric circles which are interrelated and mutually supported. In addition, the interaction between the US and India plays a core role in the mutual constructions among the three. The interpretation and analysis of United States' "Indo-Pacific strategy" from the perspective of mutual connections can present a more complete picture.

1 Emergence of Indo-Pacific 2.0

1.1 Atypical Region: Indo-Pacific

According to the theory of international relations, Indo-Pacific is not a typical region, and is still being shaped. In the field of international studies, regional research has mainly sprung up after World War II. With the re-building and integration of Europe after World War II and the emergence of a lot of independent nation-states in Asia, Africa and Latin America, regional consciousness has been increasingly recognized in many regions. The region has gradually become an independent object between the global order and nation-states. Correspondingly, the concept of the international system/global system has also been applied into the region, thereby resulting in a "regional system".[2]

From the definition of regional system in international relations, it can be found that it is not entirely applicable to Indo-Pacific. In 1973, William R. Thompson analyzed 32 papers on regional issues in international relations in his article, where he summarized the four necessary and sufficient conditions for becoming a regional system: (1) There are certain rules for the interactions or the relationships among the actors in a region, and the change of one actor in the region can lead to the corresponding change of another actor; (2) there is the similarity among actors; (3) actors

[1]Relevant research results and translations include: Zhao (2013), Taylor et al. (2014), Wu (2014), Liu (2014), Xia (2015).

[2]Liu (2015).

inside and outside the region have recognized the region as a unique region; (4) there are at least two actors in a regional system.[3] Barry Buzan and Ole Waever argued that the core structure of the regional security complex contains the four variables: the boundary (which separates a regional security complex from its immediate neighbors), and the anarchy structure (which means that a regional security complex must include more than two autonomous units), polarity (which involves the distribution of power among units), and social construction (which involves friendly and hostile patterns among units).[4]

From these concepts, "Indo-Pacific" has not become a typical regional system, but the denial of the formation of Indo-Pacific according to the theory is obviously inappropriate like "cutting one's feet to suit the shoes". The important contribution of the constructivist school to the theory of international relations is that the international relations theory is an interpretation rather than an interpretative theory, and is a summary of experience rather than a science in the material sense.[5] In general, the Indo-Pacific region still basically conforms to the regional security complex defined by Barry Buzan and Ole Waever, but the new characteristics of Indo-Pacific as a "regional system" are as follows: First, the border of Indo-Pacific is not determined by land, but by the ocean. The boundaries of traditional regional divisions (such as South Asia, Northeast Asia and West Asia) are mainly determined by land while the boundaries of Indo-Pacific are mainly defined by ocean. Secondly, the openness of Indo-Pacific; In the Indo-Pacific region, because its main boundary is determined by ocean, there is some uncertainty that the countries and scopes are included in the Indo-Pacific region. Coastal countries, neighboring countries, and landlocked countries that rely mainly on ocean can be classified as Indo-Pacific countries in different definitions. These two characteristics make the Indo-Pacific region an "atypical" international region, which is the fundamental attribute that affects the Indo-Pacific interactions and studies.

1.2 Evolution from Indo-Pacific 1.0 to Indo-Pacific 2.0

Since the Indo-Pacific was proposed, it has experienced the two stages. At the first stage, the "Indo-Pacific" was mainly promoted by Japan and Australia, which continued from 2007 to around 2010. The second stage of "Indo-Pacific" mainly presented after Trump was elected. "Indo-Pacific" has evolved from concept to strategy.

---

[3]Thompson (1973).

[4]Barry and Weaver (2010).

[5]Jackson and Sorenson (2010).

1.2.1 Indo-Pacific 1.0

The core concept of "Indo-Pacific" is the Quad cooperation, which began in the Indian Ocean tsunami in 2004.[6] In the process of the post-tsunami disaster relief, the United States, Japan, Australia and India provided equipment and personnel such as navies, warships and aircrafts, and they were the four biggest contributors. So, the "Tsunami Core Group" was established by the four countries, and more than 40,000 soldiers and other personnel participated in the disaster relief. This may be the initial impetus for the cooperation of the four countries in the ocean.[7]

Japan is the main advocate of the Indo-Pacific concept during this period, and Prime Minister Shinzo Abe plays a particularly prominent role in this regard.[8] 2006 is the beginning of Abe's first term. During his visit to India, Abe said in his speech delivered at the Indian Parliament that "the Indian Ocean and the Pacific Ocean have converged as a sea of freedom and prosperity. Japan and India have the capability and responsibility to ensure that the Indian Ocean and the Pacific Ocean can become the most transparent ocean."[9] To this end, Japan has developed the "Japan's Free and Open Indo-Pacific Strategy".

Shinzo Abe has been the longest-serving prime minister in Japan since 1960. One of the main manifestations of Abe's values diplomacy during its first term of office is to introduce the Indo-Pacific with the so-called "Arc of Freedom and Democracy", of which the main concept is a "Democratic Diamond". In other words, the four democracies of the United States, Japan, Australia and India work together to maintain the Indo-Pacific order. In September 2007, the four countries and Singapore jointly held a naval exercise in the Bay of Bengal. After the concept of the Indo-Pacific with an Arctic of Freedom and Democracy was proposed, it's strongly protested by China because of its distinctive attribute that contains China. Subsequently, the standard-bearers of the cooperation of the four countries resigned or left office: In 2007, Abe resigned, Australian Prime Minister Howard failed to be elected again, and George W. Bush's term was coming to an end. The Obama administration did not fully support the alliance of the four countries, but proposed and implemented a "rebalancing strategy." Australia's new Prime Minister Kevin Rudd announced his withdrawal from the cooperation of the four countries. The cooperation of the four countries has been tentatively suspended.[10]

Since then, the "Indo-Pacific region" has not attracted the attention of many countries. Australia is the only country in this period that has discussed Indo-Pacific as a

---

[6]The Indian Ocean tsunami occurred on December 26, 2004. It's the second largest earthquake since 1900. The earthquake triggered a tsunami as high as 30 m, which spread into Oman in the Persian Gulf, Somalia and Mauritius on the east coast of Africa, Reunion and others. The earthquake and the post-earthquake tsunami caused huge casualties in Southeast Asia and South Asia, with at least 290,000 people dead and missing.

[7]Emma Chanlett-Avery, "Japan, the Indo-Pacific, and the Quad," The Chicago Council on Global Affairs, Feb. 2018.

[8]See Footnote 7.

[9]Li (2014).

[10]See Footnote 7.

serious concept in official documents. The Indo-Pacific concept is mentioned repeatedly and specifically addressed in such documents as *White Paper on Australia in the Asian Century* released in October 2012 and the *National Security Strategy* published by the Australian Government in January 2013.[11]

During this period, the Indo-Pacific concept was mainly proposed and promoted by Japan and Australia. It was mainly at the conceptual stage, and did not cause any active response from the "superpower" of the United States. The strategy of the US Obama administration during this period was "Asia-Pacific rebalancing." Although this strategy has certain overlaps with Indo-Pacific, it is not the same as Indo-Pacific. At the time, India was uncertain about "Indo-Pacific", worrying that the great powers may further enter the Indian Ocean and squeeze India's strategic space.

1.2.2 Indo-Pacific 2.0

Indo-Pacific have once again emerged and become a "hot topic" due to the joining of the United States and India. From 2015, a new round of the "Indo-Pacific" concept has emerged again and gradually shifted from concept to strategy. This is mainly manifested in the four aspects.

First, the release of "Indo-Pacific" strategy by the US. During the Obama administration, "Indo-Pacific" was also mentioned in the speeches by the Secretary of State Hillary Clinton, President Obama and other political figures, but it's not addressed too much in the official documents. In this period, the key of the US foreign strategy was "Rebalancing to Asia-Pacific". After the Trump administration took office, the goal of the US in the Indo-Pacific region was clearly stated in the *US National Security Strategy* released in November 2017 and the *US National Defense Strategy* released in early 2018, where the Indo-Pacific region is expounded in the first place as a separate region. This marks the shift of the United States from the indifference to the dominance and shaping of Indo-Pacific.

Secondly, India's change from cautious observation to limited participation. India initially held a cautious observation attitude toward the Indo-Pacific concept because it mainly worried that the United States would expand its presence in the Indian Ocean region, thus threatening Indian advantage in the Indian Ocean region. However, with Japan's persuasion and the clear attitude of the US, India came to realize that Indo-Pacific is mainly targeted at China and poses little treat to India. Furthermore, the structural contradictions between China and India have also offered India a strong interest in participating in the strategy of containing China. In November 2017, India participated in the "US-India-Japan-Australia Indo-Pacific Consultation Dialogue", and the Indian Navy Think Tank National Maritime Foundation held the "Indo-Pacific Regional Forum" for the two consecutive years in 2017 and 2018, which indicates the change of attitude in India.

Thirdly, the Indo-Pacific coordination between the US and India, and between India and Japan. In 2015, the United States and India jointly published the *U.S.-*

---

[11] See Footnote 1.

India Joint Strategic Vision for the Asia-Pacific and Indian Ocean Region, stating that "both countries believe that it's of great importance in guaranteeing the freedom of navigation and overflight, especially in the South China Sea; they call for the avoidance of the use of force to resolve territorial disputes and compliance with the United Nations Convention on the Law of the Sea.[12] In 2017, the Indian Prime Minister Modi paid a visit to the United States. During the visit, the two countries released the joint statement, of which the first part is entitled *Democratic Stalwarts in the Indo-Pacific Region*, stating the four principles that the two countries believed should be followed in the Indo-Pacific region.[13] It can be treated that the positions of the two countries in the Indo-Pacific region have been coordinated and a lot in common has been found. The deepened India-Japan relations, especially the rapid development of foreign ties between the two countries under the efforts of Abe and Modi, have currently become the most frequent and effective bilateral relationship in the Indian-Pacific region. India believed that the two countries have never been hostile in history and that there is no ideological, cultural and territorial dispute between the two countries. Abe's grandfather, Nobusuke Kish, had close ties with India. As Prime Minister of Japan, he paid a visit to India in 1957. He was very grateful to India for its policy toward Japan after World War II, and India has become the first country for which Japan provided official development assistance.[14] Abe often said that his grandfather Nobusuke Kish is his idol. In addition, Abe was also grateful to the Indian judge Pal in the Far East International Military Court for the trial of Japanese war criminals after World War II. In 2007, Abe specifically mentioned Judge Pal in his speech at the Indian Parliament and also visited Pal's son. In 2015, Japan became a permanent member of the India-US Malabar exercise. In the exercise of 2017, Japan sent the "Izumo" helicopter carrier to participate.[15] In 2015 and 2016, Japan's Official Development Assistance to India reached its historical maximum for two consecutive years. Furthermore, the two countries also signed an agreement on the peaceful use of nuclear energy, which is a major compromise for Japan, because Japan has been staunchly opposed to the nuclear proliferation.

Fourthly, the launch of the four-nation alliance (the Quad)/consultation; Previously, Shinzo Abe proposed the "democratic diamond", but it's too high-minded to be popular, and finally ended up with no results. In the Indo-Pacific 2.0, the cooperation among the four countries was launched again. In November 2017, during the East Asia Summit, the four countries held the "US-India-Japan-Australia Indo-Pacific Consultation Dialogue". In addition, several trilateral dialogue mechanisms

---

[12]"U.S.-India Joint Strategic Vision for the Asia-Pacific and Indian Ocean Region," Jan., 2015. https://obamawhitehouse.archives.gov/the-press-office/2015/01/25/us-india-joint-strategic-vision-asia-pacific-and-indian-ocean-region. (Date of Visit: January 10, 2018).

[13]A detailed analysis is made in the next section of this paper; for the joint statements by the two countries, please refer to: United States and India: Prosperity Through Partnership, June 2017 https://www.whitehouse.gov/briefings-statements/united-states-india-prosperity-partnership/. (Visit Date: January 10, 2018).

[14]Krishnan (2016).

[15]Rong (2017).

have been established among the four countries, including the Japan-India-Australia Trilateral Dialogue, the US-Japan-Australia, and the US-India-Australia.

The first round of Indo-Pacific and the second round of Indo-Pacific have generated different responses for which the reasons are as follows: First, the perception for China has changed. In 2007, the four countries' views on China were relatively positive. The United States hoped that China would become a "responsible great power", and India and Australia also desired to benefit from China's development. In 2017, China's strength was further enhanced. The "Belt and Road" has led China's proactive diplomacy to be further clarified. In such a case, the four countries' perception for China tends to be negative. Despite the cooperation with China, there are increasing factors that contain China. Secondly, other countries are not very sure whether the United States will provide the main force and resources for maintaining the existing order. Obama's Asia-Pacific rebalancing attempts to alleviate the anxiety of regional countries, but Trump's moves such as the US First and the withdrawal from the TPP have exacerbated such anxiety. In the Indo-Pacific region, the use of institutional arrangements to hold the United States and to prevent the regional dominance of China has become the consensus of Japan, Australia and India.

2 Manifestation of the US Indo-Pacific Strategy: Three Concentric Circles

For the first time in its first Trump's *National Security Strategy Report*, the Trump administration alone used Indo-Pacific as a separate region and defined Indo-Pacific as a region ranging from the west coast of India to the west coast of the United States.[16] From the existing US statements on the Indo-Pacific strategy, it can be found that its stated goal is to maintain or establish "a rules-based order that promotes transparency, respect for sovereignty and international law, stability, and free and fair trade" in the Indo-Pacific region.[17] These concepts are not new concepts in themselves, but the United States' interpretation of these concepts varies from time to time. The core of these concepts is to maintain the regional order which is under the leadership of the United States and gives priority to the interests of the United States, and to prevent the emergence of any challenger to the US hegemony in the Indo-Pacific region. The path to achieve this goal is the "transactional diplomacy/defense policy" under the guidance of "principled realism". The Indo-Pacific strategy, the South Asia strategy, and the Indian strategy of the United States are the three concentric circles around this core.

[16]"National Security Strategy of United States," Dec. 2017. http://nssarchive.us/wp-content/uploads/2017/12/2017.pdf. (Date of Visit: January 10, 2018).

[17]Singh et al. (2018).

2.1 *The US Indo-Pacific Strategy*

In the *National Security Strategy Report*, which was released at the end of 2017, the US goal for the Indo-Pacific strategy is stated as follows: "The free and open Indo-Pacific region provides prosperity and security for all. The United States will strengthen the ties with the allies and other partners in the Indo-Pacific region, and build a complete network and structure to curb any aggression, to maintain stability, and to guarantee the free use of open space."[18] The inherent logical contradiction of this goal lies in that the United States is the only nation which has the strength to threaten the freedom and openness of the Indo-Pacific region, but the US has first excluded itself, believing that it does not have such intention. Therefore, any country which poses a threat to the United States or has the national strength equivalent to the United States is regarded as a threat to the "free and open Indo-Pacific" and should be contained through the network of allies. However, the so-called allied network and the exception of the United States have made the Indo-Pacific region neither free nor open, but have caused hostility and exclusion in the originally free and open Indo-Pacific region. Under the guidance of this contradictory goal, the United States has carried out a series of deployments in the Indo-Pacific region, and the starting point of such deployments is always the increased armament, alliance and containment in a realism sense.

2.1.1 Distinguish Friendly Nations from Hostile Ones

The guiding principle of the US' Indo-Pacific strategy is the so-called "principled realism", so the first move of its policy is to distinguish friendly nations from hostile ones.

In the Indo-Pacific region, the United States hopes to maintain a "free and open Indo-Pacific", and regards China and North Korea as the two major threats.[19] The most fundamental reversal in this regard is the change in the policy of the United States toward China. Earlier, the United States positioned the Sino-US relations as a coexistence of competition and cooperation. In some areas, there might be a non-zero-sum game while in other areas there might be a zero-sum game. Currently, the United States has positioned China as a major competitor/threat. The rise of China is the biggest adjustment in the global power structure since the US became a world power in the late 19th and early 20th centuries.[20] If we compare the definition of China set out in the *US National Security Strategy* in 2015 and 2017, it can be seen

---

[18]See Footnote 16.

[19]See Footnote 16.

[20]Michael Green, Kathleen Hicks, Mark Cancian, "Asia-Pacific Rebalance 2025 Capabilities, Presence, and Partnerships: An Independent Review of U.S. Defense Strategy in the Asia-Pacific," Center for Strategic and International Studies, pp. 1–25. 2018.01.05. https://csis-prod.s3.amazonaws.com/s3fs-public/legacy_files/files/publication/160119_Green_AsiaPacificRebalance2025_Web_0.pdf. (Date of Visit: January 15, 2018).

that the policy of the United States for China has changed significantly. It's stated in the *US National Security Strategy* released in 2015 that "the United States is glad to see the rise of a stable, peaceful and prosperous China. The United States seeks to build a constructive partnership with China, which is beneficial to the two peoples and is also conducive to promoting the security and prosperity of Asia and the world—Despite the competitions between China and the United States, the United States does not believe that the conflicts between the two countries are inevitable. Meanwhile, the United States will manage competition and require China to abide by international rules".[21] In the *2017 US National Security Strategy* and *2018 US National Defense Strategy*, China is clearly identified as a competitor and rival, and the original cooperation has been replaced by complete containment and hostility. Especially, it's clearly stated in the *US National Defense Strategy* released in 2018 that: "it is increasingly obvious that China and Russia hope to transform the world into a dictatorial model like them, and gain the veto power over other countries in terms of economic, diplomatic and security affairs. China is using military modernization, infiltration influence, and predatory economy to force its neighbors to reshape the Indo-Pacific region for their own interests. As China's economic and military strength increases, China will continue to promote military modernization; its near-term goal is to establish hegemony in the Indo-Pacific region, and its long-term goal is to replace the United States as a global hegemony".[22]

The major US allies in the Indo-Pacific region include: South Korea, Japan, Australia, New Zealand, the Philippines, and Thailand. In addition, Vietnam, Indonesia, Malaysia and Singapore are the security and economic partners of the United States. India is a global strategic partner of the United States. "The United States welcomes India to rise as a global leader. The United States hopes India to become its closer strategic and defense partner. The United States will strengthen the cooperation among the United States, Japan, Australia and India".[23]

2.1.2 Increase the Military Deployments in Indo-Pacific

The US military investment in the Indo-Pacific region serves as a sign directly reflecting its strategic direction. The US military and defense arrangements in the Indo-Pacific region include: the evaluation of the existing military deployments, an increase in military spending for the Indo-Pacific region, and an increase in the military deployment in the Indo-Pacific region.

First, evaluate the existing military deployments of the United States in Indo-Pacific region. The US Congress passed a special bill in 2012 and 2016, requiring

[21] See Footnote 16.

[22] US Department of Defense, "Summary of the 2018 National Defense Strategy of the United States of America: Sharpening the American Military's Competitive Edge" https://www.defense.gov/Portals/1/Documents/pubs/2018-National-Defense-Strategy-Summary.pdf. (Date of Visit: February 10, 2018).

[23] See Footnote 16.

the Department of Defense to hire independent third parties to evaluate the US military deployments in the Asia-Pacific region. Although the evaluation report is aimed at the Asia-Pacific region, in the "Special Report on Indo-Pacific" on the official website of the US Department of Defense, the Asia-Pacific defense strategy assessment is directly replaced by the assessment of "the US Defense Strategy in Indo-Pacific",[24] indicating the US Department of Defense has automatically identified that the assessment report is also applicable to the Indo-Pacific region.

In 2012, the Center for Strategic and International Studies (CSIS) was commissioned by the US Congress to evaluate the strategic and military presence of the United States in the Asia-Pacific region. In 2015, the US Congress once again required the US Department of Defense to entrust an independent third party to evaluate the Asia-Pacific security environment, and the evaluation is expected to cover 2025. According to the report, on the whole, both parties in the Congress support the increased attention to the region, but both parties are worried whether the US administration has developed a strategy to increase the US presence in the region. The US interests in the Asia-Pacific region include: protecting Americans and US allies, promoting trade and economic development, and supporting the universal democratic values. Frontier military deployment is indispensable for the realization of the above three goals. However, the current rebalancing policy of the US administration is not sufficient to safeguard the above interests. China and North Korea often challenge the US's local security commitments, and the development of military strength in the region is going against the United States. The US Congress should go beyond the administration and one presidential term, form a long-term support, and improve the bipartisan consensus on military presence in the region.[25]

Secondly, increase special military spending for the Indo-Pacific region. In January 2017, US Senate Armed Services Committee Chairman McKinn proposed $7.5 billion military budget to support the US military spending for the Asia-Pacific region and its Asia-Pacific allies.[26] The funds are expected to increase by $1.5 billion each year for five consecutive years, which will continue until 2022. The funds will be used to increase the US military's arms reserves in the Asia-Pacific region, to build new military infrastructure, and to enhance the capabilities of the Asia-Pacific allies.[27] Trump's inauguration as the US president in January 2017 did not change the implementation of the plan. For Trump, who is always "anti-Barack Obama", this is quite unusual. In March 2017, the US Department of Defense officially adopted the plan. Senator McCain pointed out that the main reason for the Trump administration to adopt and support the plan is "China's challenge and the feasibility of maintaining

[24]US Department of Defense, "Special Report on Indo-Pacific" https://www.defense.gov/News/Special-Reports/0118_the-indo-pacific/. (Date of Visit: February 10, 2018).

[25]See Footnote 20.

[26]See Footnote 17.

[27]David Brunnstrom, "McCain proposes $7.5 billion of new U.S. military funding for Asia-Pacific," *Reuters* https://www.reuters.com/article/us-usa-asia-mccain/mccain-proposes-7-5-billion-of-new-u-s-military-funding-for-asia-pacific-idUSKBN15802T. (Date of Visit: February 18, 2018).

US security commitments in the Asia-Pacific region." The main purpose of the plan is to respond to the rise of China and North Korea.[28]

Thirdly, increase the military deployments in the Indo-Pacific region. The Indo-Pacific region is within the jurisdiction of the US Pacific Command. The US Pacific Command covers 52% of the world and needs to respond to threats from China and North Korea.[29] In the early 2014, the US Department of Defense included Pakistan and Afghanistan which were formerly under the jurisdiction of the US Central Command into the jurisdiction of the US Pacific Command.[30] At present, the US Air Force, Navy, Army, Marine Corps, Special Forces, Missile Force, Satellite, Intelligence, Surveillance, and Nuclear Proliferation forces have all increased their deployments in the Indo-Pacific region.[31] There are 11 aircraft carrier battle groups in the United States, and the home ports of five battle groups are located in the Indo-Pacific region.[32] The US Air Force increased the number of Air Force in the Pacific Command and promised to first apply the latest Air Force armament to the Pacific Command.[33] In 2012, the First Division of the US Army was transferred from the Central Command to the Pacific Command,[34] to increase the strength of the Army in the Pacific Command. In addition, the United States has also upgraded the hierarchy of the Pacific Command. In 2013, Vincent Brooks was appointed the Commander of the Pacific Command, who has been the first four-star general to hold this position since the end of the Vietnam War. In 2016, his successor, Robert Brown, was also a four-star general.

2.1.3 Bilateral and Multilateral Alliance/Partnership Programs

In order to maintain the absolute dominance in the Indo-Pacific region, especially its military dominance, the United States has established several bilateral and multilateral alliance network relations with its allies, with increasing its military investment in the Indo-Pacific region.

At the bilateral level, the military alliances between the US and Japan, and between the US and Australia are particularly important for the US Indo-Pacific strategy. The

---

[28] Yun Sun, "China and the Asa Pacific Stability Initiative," *China US Focus*, https://www.chinausfocus.com/finance-economy/2017/0523/15028.html. (Date of Visit: February 18, 2018).

[29] See Footnote 20.

[30] See Footnote 1.

[31] See Footnote 20.

[32] The home port of Reagan Aircraft Carrier is located at Yokosuka, Japan; the home ports of Theodore Roosevelt and Carl Vinson Aircraft Carriers are both located at Santiago; the home port of John Stennis Aircraft Carrier is located at the Bremerton Naval Base and the home port of Nimitz Aircraft Carrier. The home port is at the Everett Naval Base.

[33] Chuck Hagel, "The U.S. Approach to Regional Security," https://www.iiss.org/en/Topics/shangri-la-dialogue/chuck-hagel-862d. (Date of Visit: March 10, 2018).

[34] Jacqueline Fennell, "I Corps to Re-focus on Asia-Pacific," *Northwest Guardian*, http://www.nw-guardian.com/2012/11/15/14337/i-corps-to-re-focus-on-asia-pacific.html. (Date of Visit: March 10, 2018).

total number of the US soldiers stationed in Japan is about 100,000, and Japan is the country with the largest number of the US soldiers stationed abroad. In April 2015, the US-Japan Security Consultative Committee revised and released a new version of the *US-Japan Defense Cooperation Guidelines*, which further expands the scope of joint defense between the two countries. Australian decision-makers generally support the expansion of security cooperation with the United States. Australia encourages and supports the US Indo-Pacific strategy, believing that it's important for Australia's security to make the United States remain in Indo-Pacific. The deployment of the US Marine Corps in Darwin is only the first move in strengthening US-Australian military cooperation. Polls showed that 80% of Australians believe that their alliance with the US is of great significance for Australia's security.[35] In 2013, an Australia general was appointed as the deputy commander of the US Pacific Command, highlighting the close military relations between the United States and Australia.

At the trilateral level, the established dialogue mechanisms include the Trilateral Dialogue among the US, India and Japan, the Trilateral Dialogue among Japan, the US and Australia, the Trilateral Dialogue among Japan, India and Australia, and the Trilateral Dialogue among the US, Japan and South Korea. The US-Japan-India Trilateral Dialogue was launched in Washington in December 2011 and the second, third and fourth dialogues were held in Tokyo, New Delhi and Washington in April 2012, October 2012 and May 2013 respectively. The trilateral cooperation is moving towards institutionalization. The Japan-US-Australia trilateral dialogue has also been conducted for many times since its launch in 2012. The trilateral dialogue among Japan, India and Australia was also established in 2015. The maritime security of the Indo-Pacific is the top priority of those dialogues.[36]

In addition, the United States has launched a series of other multilateral maritime initiatives and cooperation. The Global Maritime Partnership (GMP) is flexible and is also a complement to the existing alliances and partnerships of the United States. The United States hopes to foster and strengthen the Maritime Partnership in the "Indo-Pacific" region by jointing hands with its allies, partners and non-governmental international organizations, so as to cope with common security threats and to respond quickly to possible crises. Regional Aligned Forces was launched in 2012, with the aim of deepening US military's contacts with other countries in the region and conducting relevant language and cultural training.[37] In 2015, the United States announced the establishment of the Maritime Security Initiative to enhance maritime cooperation between the United States and its regional allies and partners, and to promote its allies and partners to improve their capacity and bear more responsibility in terms of maritime security.

[35]Peter Jennings et al., Guarding against Uncertainty: Australian Attitudes towards Defence (Canberra: External Panel of Experts on the 2015 Defence White Paper, 2015). 117.

[36]Xu (2017).

[37]Field et al. (2013).

2.1.4 The Quad

In the US Indo-Pacific strategy, the Quad (US-Japan-India-Australian alliance) has received more attention. From the perspective of the United States, the Quad cooperation is only a part of the network of the Indo-Pacific bilateral and multilateral allies. In view of India's "ambiguous" attitude, it is unlikely that the four-party cooperation will turn into a four-nation alliance. In November 2017, after a lapse of 10 years, the dialogue between the four countries was restarted and the dialogue was hosted by Japan, which is themed with the "Free and Open Indo-Pacific". Judging from the press releases issued by the four countries after the conference, the four countries have reached consensus on the Indo-Pacific issues such as freedom, openness, freedom of navigation, and maritime security, but their cooperation still focuses only on broader issues.

2.1.5 The US Version of the Connectivity

The US Indo-Pacific strategy also includes the economic dimension. It's an important part of the US India-Pacific strategy to integrating the power of allies and propose an alternative plan for the "Belt and Road Initiative" (BRI). However, it has not yet been established, its main feature is to demonize and generalize some of the weaknesses in China's current construction of "Belt and Road Initiative". In January 2018, Daniel Rosenblum, Assistant Secretary of State for the South Asian and Central Asian affairs in the US State Department, gave a special explanation in his speech in Bangladesh. Economic connectivity is one of the main goals of the US Indo-Pacific strategy, and the key is infrastructure. "Infrastructural construction must comply with international standards and norms, must be financially sustainable, and must ensure the sovereign integrity of any host country, and prevent predatory economics."[38] The United States relies heavily on a number of projects funded by it to evaluate the "sustainability" of infrastructure, including the Commercial Law Development Program supported by the US Department of Commerce, the Trade Facilitate project and the Trade Promotion Authorization Act supported by the USAID, and the project supported by the US Department of State which evaluates the price/performance ratio of infrastructure.[39] The main function of such projects is to criticize China's overseas infrastructure construction model, and to ultimately get these projects to be suspended or cancelled.

[38] Daniel Rosenblum, "The United States and the Indo-Pacific Region," Jan 30, 2018. https://www.state.gov/p/sca/rls/rmks/2018/277742.htm. (Date of Visit: March 1, 2018).

[39] See Footnote 38.

2.2 *The United States' South Asia Strategy*

Maintaining the absolute dominance of the United States in the Indo-Pacific region is the overall goal of the United States in the Indo-Pacific region. The inclusion of South Asia is one of the most important differences between the Indo-Pacific strategy and the Asia-Pacific rebalancing strategy. According to the policy logic of the US "principled realism", the United States' South Asia strategy is to achieve the goal of getting the US away from Afghanistan as soon as possible. Meanwhile, Afghanistan will no longer become a terrorist base threatening the security of the United States. The path to achieve this strategy is through the "transactional diplomatic security policy." Specifically, the US hopes to abandon the democratic transformation for Afghanistan in exchange for the negotiations of the various factions in Afghanistan, to recognize and support India's leadership in South Asia and the Indian Ocean in exchange for India's greater investment in Afghanistan affairs, and to blame Pakistan for the poor performance of anti-terrorism.

On August 21, 2017, the Trump administration announced its South Asia strategy. Trump said that after his inauguration in January, he began to study and develop the South Asian strategy, which was finally determined at the Camp David meeting on August 18. According to Trump's speech, the core of its South Asia strategy is the Afghan issue. Its core goal is to decently get the US out of Afghanistan as soon as possible. This is the short-term goal of the US strategy for South Asia. The medium-term goal is to prevent the emergence of another terrorist nation threatening the United States in South Asia, and to put nuclear proliferation under control.

2.2.1 Decent Troop Withdrawal from Afghanistan

Trump said that "the three core interests of the United States in Afghanistan are as follows: first, The glorious and lasting end that matches the United States' sacrifice in Afghanistan; secondly, The rapid withdrawal may lead to the re-control by terrorists of Afghanistan; thirdly, it should prevent reappearance of terrorist shelters threatening the United States; and prevent nuclear weapons and materials from falling into the hands of terrorists".[40] In order to achieve the above goals, Trump listed the four pillars of the US South Asian policy: "The time limitation on troops withdrawal is no longer imposed; the United States does not care about national construction (democratic promotion), but is concerned about killing terrorists; it no longer uses US military power to build democracy in a foreign land far away from the United States, or to rebuild any other country based on our imagination; it has changed the policy toward Pakistan and requested NATO allies to support its new strategy".[41] In order to achieve the above policy objectives, the United States no longer opposes the

---

[40]Donald Trump, "No place is beyond the reach of American might and American arms," https://www.theatlantic.com/politics/archive/2017/08/full-transcript-donald-trump-announces-his-afghanistan-policy/537552/. (Date of Visit: March 1, 2018).

[41]See Footnote 40.

Afghan government's negotiations with the Afghan Taliban. The key is not whether there is democracy or not. The key is to establish a government that can control the situation and stop its land from becoming a breeding ground for terrorism. At the same time, the United States also requires India and NATO allies to invest more resources in Afghanistan so that the US pressure can be eased.

2.2.2 Comprehensively "Suppressing the Pakistan but Supporting India"

The war in Afghanistan has lasted for 17 years and has become the longest overseas war in the US history. The war in Afghanistan in the name of counter-terrorism has not achieved fundamental victory in terms of counter-terrorism. This is the true meaning of what Trump called it "the glorious and lasting end that matches the American sacrifice in Afghanistan".[42] In order to achieve counter-terrorism and prevent nuclear proliferation, the Trump administration is not interested in the construction of long-term and slow-moving mechanism and the promotion of India-Pakistan reconciliation. Instead, it attempts to solve issues by supporting India and suppressing Pakistan according to the logic of realism. The suppression of Pakistan can give the United States an excuse to attribute its poor long-term anti-terrorism "results" to Pakistan as a way of coping with the domestic pressure; suppressing Pakistan is also one of the costs paid by the US so that the United States can require India to increase its investment in Afghanistan and join the US for containing China. "India is the world's largest democracy and is a key security and economic partner of the United States. The United States is grateful to India for its important contribution to the stability of Afghanistan, but India has also earned billions of dollars from trade with the United States. The hope is that India can provide more help for the US in Afghanistan, especially in economic aid and economic development".[43] In terms of the Trump administration's South Asia strategy, India has become a strategic asset while Pakistan has become a strategic burden. At present, the United States has stopped all kinds of assistance to Pakistan, which is about 2.2 billion US dollars. India has also carried out a comprehensive blocking strategy for Pakistan in South Asia and the Indian Ocean region.

3 The India Policy in the US Indo-Pacific Strategy

The biggest difference between the Trump administration's India-Pacific strategy and the Obama administration's "Asia-Pacific rebalancing" strategy lies in that India's role became more significant. Since 2017, there have been growing interactions between the United States under the rule of Trump and India under the rule of Modi.

[42] See Footnote 40.

[43] See Footnote 40.

There are some intersections between Trump administration's transactional foreign policy and the Modi government's pragmatic diplomacy. The strongman politics of the US and India and their overlap in the Indo-Pacific strategy can give rise to a new trend in US-Indian relations. After the Trump took office, Prime Minister Modi paid a visit to the United States in June 2017, which is the first direct interaction between the two sides. On August 21 of the same year, the Trump administration officially released its South Asia strategy, which is the first regional strategy issued by the present US government. In September 2017, US Defense Secretary Matisse paid a visit to India. On October 18, the US Secretary of State Tillerson delivered a speech entitled *Determining the US-India relations in the Next Century.*, Tillerson paid a visit to India in October 24 2017. On November 23, Kenneth Juster became the new US ambassador to India. On November 28, Trump's daughter Ivanka paid a visit to India. On December 19th, the Trump administration released the first *US National Security Strategy*, which contains a lot of information about India.

3.1 India's Position in the US Indo-Pacific Strategy

The overall background of the warming US-Indian relations is the rapid rise of China. This is the biggest pressure on the US global strategy since the end of the Cold War. Under the circumstances where it fails to individually cope with the rise of China, the US hopes to share the pressure with others as much as possible by winning over other countries to cope with the rise of China. In this way, the US can continue to maintain its dominance. India has the willingness to contain China and has considerable strength, which is one of the few policy options for the United States. India has long pursued "strategic autonomy" as the core of its diplomacy. Therefore, in the face of the United States' years of enthusiasm and temptation, India only talks about projects/interests with the US but does not involve any strategy. Faced with a rising China, the US can only continue to increase its offer to India, hoping to further integrate India into its global strategy. This is why the Trump administration has increased its investment in India.

The main content of the Trump administration's Indian strategy is: to take the Indo-Pacific strategy as a starting point, to further bribe India to contain China from the strategic perspective, to work with India to contain Russia from the military and defense perspectives, to support India and suppress Pakistan from counter-terrorism perspective, and to encourage India to share its burden from the maritime perspective. The general idea of the United States is to transfer part of the power in the Indo-Pacific region to India, to recognize and support India to become the "lieutenant" of the Indo-Pacific region, to encourage India to play a greater role in balancing China, to reduce Russia's share and increase US's share in the Indian military and defense market, to attribute the unsuccessful counter-terrorism results to Pakistan, and trap India to contribute more for the counter-terrorism in Pakistan and Afghanistan, and to get India to actively share the burden of the US and to contain the expansion of China in the maritime field.

The Trump administration's strategy of supporting India to act as the lieutenant of the Indo-Pacific region is largely in line with India's interests and needs. Therefore, it is expected that the two countries will interact with each other more frequently in many fields.

3.2 *Adjustment of the US and India Strategic Goals in Context of India-Pacific Strategy*

3.2.1 Adjustment of Cooperation Goals

There are obvious differences in the strategic positioning and diplomatic goals between the United States and India in today's world. The United States hopes to maintain a unipolar world while India desires to be a pole in a multipolar world.[44] India's strategic goal toward the United States is to achieve a strategic rise with the help of the United States and to become a great power that is friendly to but independent of the United States. The US's strategic goal for India is to use the strength of India to hedge the pressure of China's rise on the US and to encourage India to share US burden in South Asia and the Oceans, thereby ultimately maintaining its global dominance in the case of relative decline in the US strength. However, under the guidance of pragmatic foreign policy, the differences in their goals do not hinder the cooperation between the two countries. What's more, the two countries are still adjusting their respective strategic cooperation goals.

In the early days of US-India strategic cooperation, the US hoped to get India on the track of US, but the US gradually realized that the strategic goals of the two countries are incompatible: the US hopes to form a strategic alliance while India hopes to remain strategically independent. Therefore, the United States adjusts its strategic goal for India as the friendliness to the United States and the in-depth cooperation in some areas. To this end, the US has offered the term for India "to become a non-NATO ally of the US"; it has greatly increased the standards and scale of arms sales and technology transfer to India. Accordingly, India no longer insists on a rigid non-alignment policy. In 2016, India signed a Logistics Support Agreement with the US, allowing the US to make a limited use of India's bases; and conducting soft military cooperation such as joint military exercises.

Modi's coming to power has further created conditions for India's diplomatic adjustment to the US. The Bharatiya Janata Party (BJP) itself has no historical burden. The Bharatiya Janata Party has never taken the traditional Indian non-aligned foreign policy as its diplomatic principle.[45] From 1998 to 2004, during the ruling of the Indian Bharatiya Janata Party (BJP), its foreign policy was bold and aggressive. In 1998, it conducted nuclear tests and became a country with nuclear weapons. Subsequently, India and the US government signed *The Next Steps in Strategic Partnership* in 2004,

[44] Liu (2016).

[45] See Footnote 20.

which has opened up a new pattern of strategic cooperation between India and the US.[46]

The expansion of Indian interests and the changes in the Sino-Indian relations also constitute the internal and external drivers of the Modi government to adjust its policy goal toward the United States. In the Indo-Pacific region, India is constantly expanding its security interests. Previously, India regarded South Asia as its security sphere. Apart from participating in UN peacekeeping operations, India rarely participated directly in security affairs outside South Asia. But this phenomenon is changing. India's interactives with the rest of the world are increasing. Foreign residents of India spread across the world and India's trade and investment are also increasing. India is one of the world's largest energy importers. Therefore, it can be seen that India's military operations outside South Asia are emerging and increasing: in April 2015, India successfully carried out evacuation of its own citizens and other foreign citizens in Yemen. Since 2008, the Indian Navy has begun to fight piracy in the Gulf of Aden.[47] In addition, the structural contradictions between China and India and the occasional outbreak of border disputes have caused many Indians to realize that India's largest and long-term security competitor is China. Previously, the tension between China and India mainly consisted in the land border areas. In recent years, India has also felt the maritime threat from China. The emergence of Chinese submarines in the Indian Ocean, China's links with Indian neighbors and especially the growing relations between China and Pakistan have always made India nervous.

3.2.2 Adjustment of Cooperation Pace

After more than 10 years of experiences with India, the United States has not only adjusted its strategic goals for India, but has also adjusted the pace of cooperation. The US military cooperation with India has been at a slower pace and has gradually adapted to India's national conditions. The US has not urged India to participate in activities outside the direct sphere of Indian influence. India has been worried that its military cooperation with the US may force India to be involved in some areas beyond its strategic interests. Therefore, the US cooperation with India is mainly concentrated in South Asia and the Indian Ocean. In the US defense cooperation with India, the "Slow and Steady" cooperation has become a new policy, which has left the two defense relations not to be affected by the change of Indian government.[48]

---

[46] See Footnote 44.

[47] Indian Ministry of External Affairs, "External Affairs Minister and Overseas Indian Affairs Minister Smt. Sushma Swaraj's Suo-Motu Statement in Lok Sabha on Recent Development in the Republic of Yemen and Efforts Made for Safe Evacuation of Indian Nationals from There," http://pib.nic.in/newsite/PrintRelease.aspx-?relid=118364. (Date of Visit: December 10, 2017).

[48] See Footnote 20.

3.3 New Contents of US-India Cooperation in the Context of the Indo-Pacific Strategy

3.3.1 Increased Strategic Coordination Marked with 2 + 2 Model

In June 2017, during the visit of Indian Prime Minister Modi to the United States, the two countries announced that they would establish a 2 + 2 defense and foreign ministerial-level strategic dialogue mechanism. The first 2 + 2 dialogue was originally planned to be held in Washington, DC, in April this 2018. However, the dialogue had to be delayed due to the sudden resignation of Secretary of State Tillerson. The 2 + 2 dialogue mechanism is a new "top-level design" for India and the United States to strengthen the Indo-Pacific strategic coordination.

In 2009, the US and India launched the Strategic and Economic Dialogue (2 + 2). In June 2017, the two countries agreed to launch a new 2 + 2 dialogue. The participants were the foreign ministers and the defense ministers. The new dialogue mechanism focuses on defense and strategic areas, and the economic dialogue will be conducted separately. The original strategy and economic dialogue is updated into a strategic dialogue attended by the foreign ministers and defense ministers of the two countries, which is an important signal for the two countries to strengthen the strategic coordination.

The establishment of the 2 + 2 mechanism mainly results from the efforts of India, which is conducive to further establishing the status of India as a world power. In the eyes of India, the establishment of 2 + 2 dialogue mechanism with the US is a "standard" practice of becoming a world power. At the same time, through the 2 + 2 mechanism, India also hopes to confirm that it has the same status as China in the US foreign policy.[49] Through the 2 + 2 mechanism, the US hopes to expand the cooperation with India beyond specific issues such as technology transfer, and encourages India to assume greater responsibility and to reduce the US burden. It also hopes that India will assume greater responsibility in South Asian and counter-terrorism, that India will play a bigger role in containing China, increasing the US' arms exports, reducing Russia's market share, and helping US domestic military development.

3.3.2 Bilateral Defense Cooperation

The Trump administration has inherited the US bilateral defense cooperation with India and has deepened it in some areas.

[49] India's diplomacy toward the US is closely related to China's diplomacy toward the US. As long as China and the US have established relevant mechanisms, India will request to establish the same mechanisms with the US. The establishment of the India-US 2 + 2 Dialogue was proposed after the China-US leaders met and confirmed the establishment of diplomatic security dialogue at Mar-a-Lago in April 2017. India's logic is that since the US considers itself a world power, then India's status should equal to that of another world power—China.

Military Sales and Technology Transfer

In 2018–2019, India's military spending was as high as 62.8 billion U.S. dollars, and its military spending ranked fifth in the world.[50] India has been the world's largest importer of arms for many years. In 2016, the United States and India issued a joint statement, clearly stating that India is the "major defense partner of the United States" and that the United States will "continue to transfer technology to India. A large number of military-civilian dual-use technologies can be transferred without permission. The bilateral weapon technology cooperation and transfer covers the naval system, the air force system, and the weapon system".[51] India is the main defense partner of the United States. This status has been authorized by the US Congress. To this end, the Trump administration has offered a list of defenses for India to consider purchasing.[52] In September 2017, during the visit of US Defense Secretary Matisse to India, one of the two major topics discussed was to further strengthen the US-India cooperation in defense equipment and technology so as to enhance India's military capabilities. In the next step, the focus of technology transfer between the two countries is on fighter aircraft, submarine and aircraft carrier technology. Moreover, the two countries have established a working group for aircraft carrier technology cooperation and a working group for jet engine technology cooperation.[53]

Signature and Implementation of Relevant Defense Cooperation Agreements

Since the end of the Cold War, the US and India have signed seven types of medium- and long-term military defense cooperation agreements,[54] including the Logistics Exchange Memorandum of Agreement (LEMOA) signed in 2016. However, the defense cooperation between India and the United States from the beginning of 2005 shows that it's always very difficult to carry out such agreements. India's complex bureaucracy and inefficiency are the main reasons for the difficult implementation. Although the US has been forced to accept the India's slower pace of cooperation, it still need to continuously promote the implementation of the agreements.

In addition, the signature of a new defense cooperation agreement is also a significant part of the bilateral defense cooperation. The United States and India have

---

[50] Laxman K Behera, "Defence Budget 2018–19: The Imperative of Controlling Manpower Cost," Institute for Defence Studies and Analyses, https://idsa.in/issuebrief/defence-budget-2018-19-controlling-manpower-cost-lkbehera-020218. (Date of Visit: February 10, 2018).

[51] "Joint Statement—The United States and India Enduring Global Partners in the 21st Century," June 7, 2016. https://obamawhitehouse.archives.gov/the-press-office/2016/06/07/joint-statement-united-states-and-india-enduring-global-partners-21st. (Date of Visit: February 10, 2018).

[52] Rex Tillerson, "Defining Our Relationship with India for the Next Century: An Address by U.S. Secretary of State Rex Tillerson," Center for Strategic and International Studies, October 18, 2017. https://www.csis.org/analysis/defining-our-relationship-india-next-century-address-us-secretary-state-rex-tillerson (Date of Visit: February 10, 2018).

[53] See Footnote 44.

[54] See Footnote 44.

negotiated the *Communication and Information Security Memorandum of Agreement* (CISMOA) and the *Basic Exchanges and Cooperation Agreement for Geospatial Information* (BECA) for many years. The United States has repeatedly urged that "India as a main defense partner of the United States" needs to sign the above two agreements as soon as possible. The above two agreements will involve the bilateral defense affairs and intelligence sharing, which is an important step in the strategic cooperation between the two countries. In the future, India and the United States may embrace these two agreements.[55]

Anti-terrorism Cooperation

At present, the US Federal Bureau of Investigation, the Department of Homeland Security, and the military are all engaged in the anti-terrorism cooperation with relevant departments of India. Former US Secretary of State Tillerson revealed that "currently, the anti-terrorism cooperation between the two countries has increased dramatically. Thousands of Indian security personnel have received training in the United States. They have also made joint monitoring of terrorists. In 2017, the two countries will also launch a new counter-terrorism identification dialogue. The US and India will play a leading role in anti-terrorism cooperation in their own regions".[56]

Joint Exercises

There are 11 routine military exercises between the US and India, including the bilateral navies, coastal guard, and air force.[57] The Malabar military exercise in 2017 is the most complicated one between the US and India, and Japan has become a permanent member of the exercise, which will take in other countries in the future.

3.3.3 Cooperation in Regional and Global Affairs

The important feature of US-India cooperation under the India-Pacific strategy is that the cooperation in regional and global affairs has become a new highlight of the US-India cooperation. In order to encourage India to assume greater responsibility in regional and global affairs, the US has spoke highly of the role of India. Former Secretary of State Tillerson said to create the US-Indian relations for the next 100 years. The US and India are increasing their cooperation on a global scale, and the consistency of the bilateral strategic interests is increasing, which will affect the situation in the next 100 years. The US and India not only share democracy, but also have the same vision for the future. The US-India strategic partnership is based on common

---

[55]Zhang (2018).

[56]See Footnote 52.

[57]See Footnote 44.

principles: the rule of law, free navigation, universal values, and free trade. The US and India are the protectors for the stability for the eastern and western hemispheres, and the US-India cooperation will bring security and prosperity to their people and the people in the remaining world.[58]

The topics of the bilateral cooperation in regional and global affairs include Afghanistan and Pakistan issues, and the Indian Ocean order. The pillar of the Trump administration's South Asia policy is to decently withdraw troops from there and to incidentally deal with the cause of terrorism on the premise of increasing no resources. Therefore, the cooperation between India and the United States on the Afghan issue, India's increased development and security aids to Afghanistan, have exerted pressure on Pakistan to crack down on terrorism, and the cooperation with India on Iran and Afghanistan issue will also become the content of the cooperation between the two countries. During the visit to India by US Secretary of Defense Matisse in September 2017, one of the two issues discussed by the two sides is that US hopes that India will provide more assistance for the peace and stability in Afghanistan and implement the new Afghan and South Asian policies proposed by Trump.

The most critical strategic issue between India and the US in Indo-Pacific region is the maritime and regional order. The two countries have repeatedly emphasized the freedom, the rule-based international law, and the opposition to any unilateral change of current situation in Indo-Pacific. In the joint statement released by Modi during his visit to the US in 2017, the four principles were clearly set for the Indo-Pacific region: "Reaffirming the importance of free navigation, free overflight, and free trade in the Indo-Pacific region; requiring all countries to peacefully resolve territorial and sea disputes according to international law; developing economic connectivity through transparent infrastructure, responsible financial and debt measures, the respect for the sovereignty and territorial integrity of other countries, the respect for the rule of law, and environmental protection; calling on all the countries in the Indo-Pacific region to follow the above principles".[59] These so-called principles are highly targeted, and the two countries attempt to jointly design the order of the Indo-Pacific region.

3.3.4 Alternative Program of "Belt and Road Initiative"

It's well known that India resists the "Belt and Road Initiative". The Trump administration has also sharply criticized the "Belt and Road Initiative". India and the US have a lot in common in boycotting China's "Belt and Road Initiative". In October 2017, when Tillerson gave a speech at the Center for Strategic and International Studies, he made a lot of criticisms on China's Belt and Road Initiative. "We have been observing the behaviors and activities of other countries, especially China. China's financing mechanism has led many countries to bear huge debts. These projects create no new jobs. However, infrastructure projects have created a lot of jobs for

---

[58] See Footnote 52.

[59] "United States and India: Prosperity Through Partnership," https://www.whitehouse.gov/briefings-statements/united-states-india-prosperity-partnership/. (Date of Visit: March 10, 2018).

laborers, including Chinese laborers. China-dominated financing structure makes it difficult for host countries to obtain financing support in the future, and it is easy to fall into debt trap. Therefore, such structure does not support the future growth of those countries. We believe that some counter-financing methods and structures should be established. At the East Asia Summit in August this year, we have started some quiet conversations about how to create new mechanisms. We may not be able to compete against the conditions set by China, but the countries where such projects are located must consider the price they are willing to pay to guarantee their sovereignty and control over the future economy."[60] The US accusation of China's "predatory economy", India's "Monsoon Plan", "SAGAR", "the Growth Corridor in Asia and Africa" and so on has shown that the two countries have begun to take the countermeasures against the "Belt and Road Initiative". The United States and India should cooperate to provide various kinds of help for other countries, so that such countries can protect their sovereignty, enjoy better connectivity, and have greater voice in the regional structure to protect their own interests and promote economic development. This is also the natural composition of India's Act East policy.[61]

4 Dilemma of the US Indo-Pacific Strategy

4.1 The Purpose and Means of the United States' Indo-Pacific Strategy Do not Match Each Other

One of the main reasons why the Trump administration's so-called "Free and open Indo-Pacific" strategy has replaced the "Pivot to Asia" strategy is that China's rise has exerted a huge pressure on the United States, the US's policy toward China has changed from engagement plus containment to containment as a main part. At the same time, it hopes that other non-alliance powers such as India can be introduced to maintain the existing hegemony. Its fundamental purpose is to continue to maintain the original global power structure and dominated by the US absolutely in the context of a relative decline of the US strength. Its main means are traditional unilateralism, military means and alliances. However, there is a natural mismatch between the purpose and means of the US Indo-Pacific strategy:

First, the existing global power that US enjoyed is to great extent the institutional power and soft power. It relies on the power generated by various global institutions, organizations, and mechanisms established after World War II. The international system and soft power have largely ensured that the United States can still enjoy the "dominant power" inconsistent with its strength in the context of relative decline in its strength. The guiding ideology of the Trump administration's Indo-Pacific strategy is the pragmatic "principled realism", and its unilateralism, military means, and

[60] See Footnote 52.

[61] See Footnote 52.

alliances are also accelerating the decline of its institutional power and soft power. The Trump administration's withdrawal from the TPP and from the Paris Climate Agreement, trade war against China in violation of WTO rules, response to hot issues in the Indo-Pacific region by military means (Iranian nuclear issue, and the military patrol in the South China Sea), willful blindness to India's hegemony in South Asia, and so on, are weakening the foundation of its "power structure".

4.2 The Tension Between the Eastward Movement of the Economic Center and the Western-Dominated International Order

The world's economic center moves eastward because of the collective rise of the eastern countries represented by China and India. Meanwhile, the development of globalization has made the connections between the East and the West much closer. There is a tension between the eastward movement of the world economic center and the existing US-led international order. The US Indo-Pacific strategy should have focused on resolving this imbalance and realizing the redistribution of rights and obligations. However, the current US Indo-Pacific strategy is committed to stagnating the collective rise of the Eastern countries by military alliances, economic sanctions, strategic containment and other Cold War mentality instead of solving the problem of imbalance of the order, while the US divides Asia-Pacific region by the old and new alliance system, and adopts political and military means to break through the established production networks in Asia and Indo-Pacific. For the United States, "Indo-Pacific" is far from a geo-economic reality, but is a strategic plan to contain the realization of the "Indo-Pacific Era".[62]

4.3 The US Transactional Policy Cannot Cope with the Anxiety of the Indo-Pacific Allies

The Indo-Pacific allies of the US have realized that although the United States is still the biggest power in the world, its strength is declining, and the Trump administration's "US First" strategy also makes the allies further question whether the US will continue to provide security protection for them. The main focus of the US Indo-Pacific strategy is to maintain or create a new alliance system, which will address the concerns of the allies. The main way for the United States to create and maintain the alliance system is "transactional diplomacy and principled realism." This means that the US's commitment to the security of the allies is price tagged and has negotiation space, and the allies must pay the corresponding price according to the

[62]Liu (2014).

needs of the United States. The US requires the NATO allies and the Indo-Pacific allies to increase military spending and purchase more US arms. This is a realistic portrayal of this situation. These strategic issues such as the reliability of the US commitment to the allies, the US strategy toward China, the US support for the free trade system, and the determination of the US to maintain its leadership, cannot be solved through transactional policies. What is needed is the US's firm support of the principles.[63] The Indo-Pacific allies still meet the requirements of the US due to their security reliance on the United States, but the security guarantees based on inequality and transaction are ultimately unreliable. There is still no institutional arrangement beyond the alliance system. Therefore, the "security anxiety" of the allies cannot be alleviated.

4.4 The Concentric Circles of the Indo-Pacific Strategy Cannot Be Formed

The Trump administration has always advocated the "free and open Indo-Pacific region" strategy, which aims to maintain a rule-based international order, liberal values and free navigation. The United States believes that the rising China threatens the realization of these goals. It is very clear that the Chinese Navy is currently not capable of projecting strength and achieving maritime control in the Indian Ocean, and is not eager to grasp the above capabilities.[64] The US Indo-Pacific strategy is likely to be counterproductive because it may also irritate China and cause other Asian countries to worry, which will then intensify conflicts in the region and even lead to zero-sum competition. The Trump administration has adopted an ideological and conflicting stance toward China, and is adventuring to wage a round of meaningless cold wars. But what Asia needs is a more constructive regional policy based on the balance of power and mutual benefits. The US Indo-Pacific strategy has actually undermined the "free, open and rule-based Indo-Pacific order" always advocated by the US, thus splitting Asia-Pacific and Asia.[65]For the United States, confrontational China will eventually become a self-fulfilling promise because of the hostile policy adopted by the United States. Under such circumstance, Indo-Pacific will be neither free nor open, but will become a closed and divided Indo-Pacific region.

---

[63]See Footnote 28.

[64]Gupta (2017).

[65]Michael D. Swaine, "A Counterproductive Cold War With China Washington's "Free and Open Indo-Pacific" Strategy Will Make Asia Less Open and Less Free," *Foreign Affairs*, https://www.foreignaffairs.com/articles/china/2018-03-02/counterproductive-cold-war-china?amp. (Date of Visit: March 18, 2018).

4.5 *Incompatibility Between India's Indo-Pacific and the US' Indo-Pacific Strategy*

In terms of the US Indo-Pacific strategy, the US is trying to build India into the "lieutenant" in the Indo-Pacific region, but the Indo-Pacific strategies between the two countries are incompatible.

First of all, there are no foundations for the formation of the India-US alliance or the US-India-Japan-Australian alliance (the Quad). There are two key factors in forming an alliance: common interests or threats; shared views of order/goals. In the case of the Indo-Pacific strategies of the US and India, the two countries may have common interests or threats, but they have different views of order. In addition, India is still wary of the cooperation with the US. Many Indians are still worried that the defense cooperation with the US will make India a "loyal follower" of the United States. On the other hand, the United States is a potential rival to India's security policy. India's security policy is unusual, not only because it's not always in hesitation about defining different countries as a primary threat, but also because these countries are divided into the three different levels: Pakistan at the regional level, China at the super-regional level, and the US at the global level.[66] Its ultimate national security goal is to "eliminate Pakistan, defeat China, and challenge the US".[67]

Secondly, India's Indo-Pacific strategy is a combination of the "Security and Growth for All in the Region" (SAGAR) and the Act East strategy. The Modi-led government's Indian Ocean strategy is the "Security and Growth for All in the Region" (SAGAR), which aims to create a connectivity plan for the Indian Ocean region, highlighting India's dominant position in the region. After reviewing the press release issued in November 2017 after the "US-India-Japan-Australia Indo-Pacific Consultation Conference", the press releases issued by the United States, Japan and Australia were roughly the same, while it's mentioned in the press release issued by India: "The Indian side emphasizes India's Act East Policy is the cornerstone of its involvement in the Indo-Pacific region."[68] It can be seen that on the one hand, India's Indo-Pacific strategy is to maintain its dominant position in the Indian Ocean; on the other hand, it's to pragmatically absorb the high-quality resources of other parties and realize its own development as soon as possible. In order to achieve the above objectives, India adopted the "Parallel Track Strategy", also known as Multi-

---

[66] See Footnote 4.

[67] See Footnote 4.

[68] Press release issued by the Indian Ministry of Foreign Affairs, QUESTION NO.653 MEETING WITH OFFICIALS ON THE SIDELINES OF ASEAN, http://www.mea.gov.in/rajya-sabha.htm?dtl/29212/question+no653+meeting+with+officials+on+the+sidelines+of+asean; Press release issued by the US Department of State, Australia-India-Japan-U.S. Consultations on the Indo-Pacific, https://www.state.gov/r/pa/prs/ps/2017/11/275464.htm; Press release issued by the Australian Ministry of Foreign Affairs and Trade, Australia-India-Japan-United States consultations on the Indo-Pacific, http://dfat.gov.au/news/media/Pages/aus-india-japan-us-consultations-on-the-indo-pacific.aspx; Press release issued by the Japanese Ministry of Foreign Affairs, Australia-India-Japan-U.S. Consultations on the Indo-Pacific, http://www.mofa.go.jp/press/release/press4e_001789.html.

Pivot Strategy or Multi-aligned Diplomacy.[69] At the second "Indo-Pacific Regional Dialogue" hosted by India, India clearly stated its understanding of Indo-Pacific: "In the Indo-Pacific region, there are the three rising powers (China, India and Iran), the two countries with unchanged strength (Japan and Russia), the four key neutral countries (Indonesia, Singapore, South Korea and Vietnam), a revisionist country (North Korea), and a superpower (The United States)".[70] In the case of India's Indo-Pacific strategy, its foreign policy is to establish cooperative relations with all key countries in the Indo-Pacific region; its economic policy is to lay equal emphasis on security and economy, and economic and trade development is one of India's main demands in the region. From the Indo-Pacific strategies of India and the United States, there are at least the three differences: First, the US focuses on security while India attaches equal importance to economy and security. Secondly, the US excludes Russia and Iran while India hopes to maintain contacts with Russia and Iran. Thirdly, the United States advocates containing China while India upholds to continue economic contacts with China.

5 Impact of the US Indo-Pacific Strategy on China and Its Countermeasures

The main starting point of the US Indo-Pacific strategy is to contain China and to maintain its "hegemonic bonus" in the context of a relative decline of the US strength. It should be recognized that despite the factors such as the change of the US government, from the "Asia-Pacific rebalancing" of the Obama administration to the "Indo-Pacific strategy" of the Trump administration, the containment against China has not changed, with only the difference in their degree. Therefore, the US Indo-Pacific strategy and the corresponding policy adjustments by other countries in the region will have a long-term impact on China.

[69] Zhang Jiadong: "New Expansion Tendency of India: Status, Characteristics and Limitations", *People's Tribune · Frontiers*, Issue 01, 2018, pp. 6-18.

[70] The 2nd Indo-Pacific Forum was jointly organized by the Indian Maritime Foundation and the Indian Navy, which was attended by the Indian Minister of Defense, Chief of Staff, Minister of Water Resources, and the former Foreign Secretary Dr.S. Jaishankar. The author was invited to be present at the Forum. The above content is from the concept text of this conference released by the conference organizer, which can basically represent the current Indian officials' opinions and views on the Indo-Pacific region.

5.1 Impact of the US Indo-Pacific Strategy on China

5.1.1 Propose an Alternative Plan for the "Belt and Road Initiative"

Under the guidance of the "Belt and Road Initiative", the geopolitical consequences brought about by the improved international economic influence of China are the primary threats that the US Indo-Pacific strategy needs to address. Although the United States uses military and security methods such as alliance strategy to curb the expansion of China's influence, the use of military means to deal with economic cooperation is contrary to the tide of international economic cooperation supported by most countries in the world, of which the result is also very limited. Therefore, in the US Indo-Pacific strategy, the US may integrate the power of allies and propose an alternative plan for the "Belt and Road Initiative". In fact, the former US Secretary of State Tillerson once clearly proposed to introduce an alternative plan for the "Belt and Road Initiative". His criticism of China's "predatory economy" in developing countries in Africa is merely to create a paradox for the introduction of an alternative plan. To this end, the United States, Japan and India individually or jointly put forward the "high-quality infrastructure", or the "Asia-Africa Growth Corridor", "Open and Free Indo-Pacific", "effective aid", and so on, which are all the slogans and plans against the "Belt and Road Initiative". Furthermore, they will also continuously bring forth new ones to interfere with the countries along the "Belt and Road", and to disrupt the construction of projects relating to "Belt and Road initiative". The United States will also use its advantage of controlling the power of international discourse to continuously promote the concepts of transparency, democracy, popular participation, and civil society, and to look for and enlarge the weaknesses of the "Belt and Road Initiative".

For an alternative plan for "the Belt and Road Initiative" proposed by the US, it may not necessarily make substantial inputs, but it can still increase the hesitation of countries along the Belt and Road. Countries along the "Belt and Road", especially small and medium-sized countries, mostly pursue a balanced strategy of great powers and adopt a pragmatic attitude toward the "Belt and Road Initiative". As the United States, India and Japan work together to promote the alternative plans for "the Belt and Road Initiative" in the Indo-Pacific region, projects proposed under the "Belt and Road Initiative" will face greater uncertainty in the above-mentioned countries, and those projects already in place will be faced with greater risks.

The US and India cooperate to proceed with the alternative plans for "the Belt and Road Initiative" may be only an empty promise, it can still add new chips to the negotiations with the countries along "the Belt and Road". As a result, the political risks and operating costs of "the Belt and Road" projects will increase. The suspension and then restart of the Colombo Port City project in Sri Lanka has proved that under the intervention of external forces, the project is restarted but its cost has been increased further.

5.1.2 The "Quad" May Further Limit China's Maritime Cooperation in the Indo-Pacific Region

Under the great support of the United States and Japan, the cooperation between the United States, Japan, India and Australia will be further strengthened and will develop in the direction of the loose "Group Four." The "Quad" is mainly aimed at the growing expansion of the Chinese navy and Chinese interests in the Indo-Pacific region. At the Raisina Dialogue held in India from January 17–18, 2018, the US Pacific Commander and the Indian Navy Commander both claimed that "China is a destructive force in the Indo-Pacific region". The Australian Navy Commander and the Japanese Chief Staff also participated in the conference. This is just the latest case of the "Quad" to jointly squeeze China's maritime forces. Similar forums, exercises, initiatives, and interactions on multilateral occasions will continue. It's clear that the four countries will have a common voice over the top two priorities of the South China Sea and China's presence in the Indian Ocean, and will also try to establish some preliminary cooperation mechanisms of the "Quad". In terms of future port construction, and the expansion and existence of naval power in the Indo-Pacific region, China will confront the common pressure and opposition of the four countries.

5.1.3 More Pressure Will Be Exerted on China in Terms of Pakistan and Afghanistan Issues

In the Indo-Pacific strategy, Pakistan has become a scapegoat for the United States' poor performance of counter-terrorism activates, and is suppressed and abandoned by the US. The first step for the US-India cooperation in Indo-Pacific region is to further increase the pressure on Pakistan. At present, the United States has stopped all kinds of assistance to Pakistan for a total of about 2.2 billion U.S. dollars. India is also implementing a comprehensive blockade strategy for Pakistan in South Asia and the Indian Ocean region. As an all-weather strategic partner of China, Pakistan faces an unprecedented strategic environment. China's various projects, investments and military cooperation projects with Pakistan are criticized by the United States and India, especially on various international occasions. The topic of requiring China to exert pressure on Pakistan and reduce the cooperation will be continuously put forward. The US and India cooperate with each other to jointly suppress Pakistan. This has added external pressure to the construction and operation of the China-Pakistan Economic Corridor.

In terms of the Afghanistan issue, the United States and India will jointly request China to provide more aid for Afghanistan, but they will also limit the scope and fields of China's investment in Afghanistan. The US will make greater efforts to win over India under the India-Pacific strategy. The US arms sales and strategic support for India have greatly enhanced India's capability and willingness to confront China. Consequently, India may continuously adventure to cause similar "Doklam confrontation" on the border issue and Tibet issue. Therefore, China may face greater long-term pressure in its southwest territory.

5.1.4 China's Action of Safeguarding Its Rights in the South China Sea and Its Normal Activities in the Indian Ocean Are Under Greater Pressure

The main excuse for the US strategy to strengthen and establish a military alliance is China's action of safeguarding rights in the South China Sea. China's rightful demands in the Indian Ocean are thought to have taken up India's "cheese". In the Indo-Pacific consultation conference of the four countries held in 2017, the four countries jointly referred to the "rules-based Indo-Pacific order and the Indo-Pacific ocean security". In the US-India joint statement released in 2017, it's also officially noted that the United States and India believed that the four principles should be abided by in the Indo-Pacific region. These four principles include the freedom of navigation, peaceful settlement of territorial and sea disputes, and respect for the sovereignty and territorial integrity of other countries. Even if there is no substantive action in the short-term under the Indo-Pacific Ocean cooperation established under the leadership of the United States for the sake of excluding China, it will still exert greater pressure on China's South China Sea policy and activities in the Indian Ocean region.

5.2 Response to the US Indo-Pacific Strategy

5.2.1 Advocate the Establishment of an Open Indo-Pacific Order Based on the "East Asian Summit"

The core demands of China's Indo-Pacific strategy are the openness of the Indo-Pacific order and no institutional arrangement which excludes China from the Indo-Pacific region. If China sets up a new set of Indo-Pacific system, it's both difficult and unnecessary to do so. The existing East Asia Summit takes the form of "10 + 8" (the ten countries of ASEAN plus China, Japan, South Korea, Australia, New Zealand, India, the United States, and Russia), covering all core countries of the Indo-Pacific region. The East Asia Summit is hosted by ASEAN and is not dominated by any major power. This can guarantee the openness of the Indo-Pacific system and China will have full opportunities for participation in the mechanism. Moreover, this proposal is easily to have support from the 10 ASEAN countries. Such institutional design is also supported by Australia. The Secretary of the Australian Department of Foreign Affairs and Trade Varghese and other scholars believed that the Indo-Pacific system has a ready-made institutional foundation - that is, the East Asia Summit (EAS). Therefore, promoting the further institutionalization and improvement of the East

Asia Summit will become the key way for Australia to construct the Indo-Pacific system.[71]

In view of the small groups established by bilateral and multilateral means in the US Indo-Pacific strategy, China should make full use of existing multilateral mechanisms such as Shanghai Cooperation Organization (SCO) and BRICS. At present, the multilateral mechanisms jointly attended by China, Russia and India include the China-Russia-India Trilateral Dialogue Mechanism, the Shanghai Cooperation Organization, the BRICS, and the United Nations. The main containment targets of "Indo-Pacific" and "the Quad" are China and Russia. India is still "vague" about the "Quad" at present. Therefore, the existing multilateral mechanisms of China, Russia and India should be fully utilized to enhance the functional cooperation among the three countries, to mitigate the Sino-Indian relations and to increase the difficulty and divergence of the cooperation between India, and the rest three nations of the US, Japan and Australia.

5.2.2 Prudently and Resolutely Promote the Integration of the "Belt and Road Initiative" with Existing International Mechanisms

The construction of the "Belt and Road Initiative" is a century-long plan and is also a long-term strategy for the rise of China. Therefore, there may be long-term encroachment and dissatisfaction of other great powers about it. China must adhere to the principle of "gradual advancement" in prudently and resolutely carrying out various projects of the "Belt and Road Initiative". China shall also avoid the eagerness for quick results.

China shall take the success of the Asian Infrastructure Investment Bank as an example, and avoid the self-centered view in the process of constructing the "Belt and Road Initiative". China must integrate the construction of the "Belt and Road" into the development of various types of international organizations and international mechanisms, or realize the co-construction of the "Belt and Road Initiative" through the creation of a new international mechanism, thereby changing the China-centered nature.

5.2.3 Prevent the Materialization of the "Quad"

Under the Indo-Pacific framework, there is an increase in the possibility of "the United States, India, Japan and Australia" forming a group of four nations (the "Quad"). In the case of the US and Japan tying to win over India and the widening gap between China and India, it's inevitable for India to join the Quad. At present, China should prevent the materialization of the "Quad" and stop it from becoming an alliance mechanism against China. To this end, we must further make high-profile opposition to the Cold War mentality and ideology on various international occasions

[71] Song (2016).

by equating the behavior of the "Quad" to the Cold War mentality, thereby winning a certain moral force. Meanwhile, it is necessary to continue to carry out functional cooperation with India and Australia, and strive to play a certain balancing role in the "Quad", thus mitigating the intensity of containing China.

5.2.4 Intensify the Diplomatic Relations Between China and Russia and Between China and Pakistan

The US-Indian relations and the Indo-Pacific strategy not only directly targeted China, but also aimed at Russia. The US taking over the Indian arms market directly engagers the interests of Russia. The investigation of Trump's Russia Scandal further deepened the hostility against Russia in all walks of life in the United States. Therefore, the originally-expected improvement of US-Russia ties after Trump's successful election is impossible. To this end, China and Russia should warm up their ties and further enhance the bilateral relations. In particular, they must complement the shortcomings of bilateral relations and create better conditions for the strategic cooperation between the two countries.

The US-India cooperation has exerted the greatest direct pressure on Pakistan. China should continue to implement the existing China-Pakistan cooperation projects, especially the China-Pakistan Economic Corridor. On multilateral occasions, China should endeavor to ease the pressure of Pakistan. In addition to providing assistance for Pakistan, China shall also encourage Pakistan to improve its self-development capability, increase secularization level, and gradually remove the conditions for extremist forces, thus contributing to the long-term stability of Pakistan.

5.2.5 Maintain a Self-restriction Strategy Toward India

It is necessary to recognize that there is the long-term and widespread hostility and hatred of Indian elites toward China. It is impossible to achieve a major change in India's attitude toward China. Meanwhile, there is also the long-term and widespread distrust of the Indian elites toward the United States. Furthermore, there is still a huge difference in the cooperation between India and the United States. The US-Indian relationship is far from reaching the level of allies. And it's also very unlikely that they will become an alliance in the future without the breakout of major wars. Therefore, to some extent, there is still some space for China to win over India and prevent the US-Indian relations from developing too fast and too deep. Specifically, while making contacts with India, China should fully respect India's state of mind and dignity of being a great power, and give more respect for India on some occasions. In addition, at this stage, China should temporarily restrain itself to maintain the status quo and avoid "being caught in double fronts" in terms of sensitive issues such as border issues.

6 Conclusion

The name of the US Indo-Pacific strategy may change with the replacement of the Trump administration, but the core content of the US Indo-Pacific strategy will remain unchanged. In other words, it's still to prevent any country that threatens US hegemony in the Indo-Pacific region and to contain the rapid rise of China by strengthening the existing alliances and establishing new alliances. The current US Indo-Pacific strategy is the three concentric circles of the US-Indo-Pacific, the US-South Asia, and the US -India established based on the Obama administration's original "Pivot to Asia-Pacific" strategy and according to the realism and the Cold War mentality. The Quad or four-nation alliance of Australia, India, the US and Japan, which has been discussed a lot in China, may not be established in reality. However, it's true that the United States has increased its military presence and established the bilateral and multilateral networks through alliance in the Indo-Pacific region. The Indo-Pacific order, aimed to establish a "free and open Indo-Pacific", is actually an exclusive institution design against China, which will have a direct impact on China's "Belt and Road Initiative" and Indo-Pacific maritime cooperation. To this end, while prudently and resolutely the implementing the "Belt and Road Initiative", China should support the institutional design of ASEAN-dominated Indo-Pacific architecture and encourage the institutional arrangement to establish an open Indo-Pacific based on the existing East Asia Summit. This should become the main content of China's Indo-Pacific strategy.

Acknowledgements Supported by: Study on the Impact of Southeast Asian Security Pattern on China's Implementation of the 21st Century Maritime Silk Road (16ZDA091), a major project of the National Social Science Fund of China (NSSFC) in 2016; Study on the Impact of International Mechanisms of the Indian Ocean Region on Maritime Silk Road Construction (15CGJ030), a youth project of the National Social Science Fund of China (NSSFC) in 2015.

References

Barry, Buzan, and Ollie, Weaver. 2010. "*Regions and Powers: The Structure of International Security*", trans. Pan Zhongyu, et al., 118–120. Shanghai: Shanghai Century Publishing Group.

Field, Kimberly, James Learmont, and Jason Charland. 2013. "Regionally Aligned Forces: Business not as Usual", *Parameters*, (3).

Gupta, Sourabh. 2017. "US-India Defense Ties: Setting the Table for Secretary Mattis' Visit to New Delhi", *Pacific Forum CSIS*, Honolulu, Hawaii, September 25, 2017.

Jackson, Robert, and Georg, Sorenson. 2010. *Introduction to International Relations: Theories and Approaches,* 4th ed. trans. Song Dexing, et al., 150–175. Beijing: China Renmin University Press, 2010.

Krishnan, Ananth. 2013. "Coming Full Circle: Shinzo Abe in India", *The Hindu*, May 13, 2016.

Li, Xiushi. 2014. "Preliminary Analysis of Japan's Strategic Expansion in the Pacific Ocean and the Indian Ocean—from "Anti-piracy" to "Defending the Sea Routes in the Two Oceans", *International Review* (02):121–134.

Liu, Peng. 2015. "Assessment of the International System in the Indian Ocean Region," Doctoral Dissertation of Jinan University, pp. 28–29.

Liu, Peng. 2016. "Evaluation on Military Security Cooperation in the Global Strategic Partnership between India and the United States", *South Asian Studies* (04):29–50.

Liu, Zongyi. 2014. "Conflict or Cooperation?—Geopolitical and Geoeconomic Choices in the "Indo-Pacific" Region", *Indian Ocean Economic and Political Review* (4):4–20.

Rong, Ying. 2017. "New Situation of Indo-Pacific Strategic Interactions From the "Malabar" Military Exercise", *Peace and Development* (05):48–61.

Singh, Abhijit, Aparna Pande, Jeff M. Smith, Samir Saran, Sunjoy Joshi, and Walter Lohman. 2018. *The New India-US Partnership in the Indo-Pacific: Peace, Prosperity and Security*, 1–59. Observer Research Foundation, Observer Research Foundation, Hudson Institute.

Song, Wei. 2016. "On the Australian Indo-Pacific System Concept and Strategic Path Selection", *Journal of Shanghai Jiaotong University (Philosophy and Social Sciences Version)* (02):13–22.

Taylor, Melissa Conley, et al. 2014. "Divergences on Indo-pacific between Australia and India", *Indian Ocean Economic and Politic Review* (01):138–143.

Thompson, William R. 1973. "The Regional Subsystem—A Conceptual Explication and a Propositional Inventory", *International Studies Quarterly* 17(1):89–117.

Wu, Zhaoli. 2014. "The Origin of "Indo-Pacific" and Multi-Country Strategic Game", *Pacific Journal* (1):29–40.

Xia, Liping. 2015. "The US "Indo-Pacific Strategy" from the Dual Perspective of Geopolitics and Geo-Economics", *American Studies Quarterly* (02):32–51.

Xu, Juan. 2017. "The US-India-Japan Maritime Security Cooperation in the Context of "Indo-Pacific", *South Asian Studies* (02):95–112.

Zhang, Jiadong. 2018. "New Expansion Tendency of India: Status, Characteristics and Limitations", *People's Tribune Frontiers* (01):6–18.

Zhao, Qinghai. 2013. "The "Indo-Pacific" Concept and Its Implications for China", *Contemporary International Relations* (7):14–22.

Historical Changes of "Indo-Pacific" Geo-economics and Development Demands of India

Yang Yishuang

Abstract India is anxious to strengthen the relations with the Asian-Pacific region, yet the "Act East Policy" doesn't perform as well as it expected. Moreover, because it is difficult to gain an edge on the competition with China on regional economic presence, India prefers to see a new cooperation framework, which could let India play a more important role in it, and meanwhile provide India with the alternative proposals in various aspects to make up for India's inadequacies. The introduction of "Indo-Pacific" concept is just in line with such demands of India. But the "Indo-Pacific" concept is vague at the economic level and has no practical effect on improving India's economic presence in this region. For the existing Asia-Pacific cooperation mechanism, "Indo-Pacific" is purely a destructive factor and lacks the ability to build a new mechanism. At time of pursuing the profits brought by "Indo-Pacific", India could hardly leave such factors out of account. Due to the independence of its development goals, India's participation in "Indo-Pacific" must be limited.

Keywords Indo-Pacific · Geo-economics · India · The Indian Ocean

1 Geo-economic Background of "Indo-Pacific": Historical Changes of Economic Center Shift

Though "Indo-Pacific" is a strategic concept, the geo-economic factor played a vital role in shaping the concept, because the introduction of a strategic concept itself reflects the changes of world political and economic landscape. The rise of "Indo-Pacific" is based on the historical shift of economic center, but the shift is not a process of moving from "Asia-Pacific" to "Indo-Pacific" but a process of moving towards Asia.

Y. Yishuang (✉)
Research Institute for Indian Ocean, Yunnan University of Finance and Economics, Kunming, China

C. Zhu (ed.), *Annual Report on the Development of the Indian Ocean Region (2018)*, Research Series on the Chinese Dream and China's Development Path, https://doi.org/10.1007/978-981-13-7693-1_7

(I) Increasing importance of the Indian Ocean depends on the development of the "Asia-Pacific" region

"Indo-Pacific" region includes the most important maritime trade routes across the world. However, before China, India and other developing countries experience the rapid economic growth and swift strength increase, no one would regard the Indian Ocean and the Pacific Ocean as a whole. The Indian Ocean and the Pacific Ocean were always regarded as two independent strategic and economic regions.

The introduction of "Indo-Pacific" is said to be due to the increasing importance of the Indian Ocean. Yet as a matter of fact, after a careful investigation at the economic level, the increasing importance of the Indian Ocean isn't mainly due to the rapid economic growth of economies around the Indian Ocean, but substantially depends on the development of Asia-Pacific. There are two major reasons: first, the economic rise of China and East Asia manufacturing hubs; second, the uneven distribution of production factors (including energy and minerals) and markets on a global scale.

Nowadays, two-thirds of the world's oil shipments and one-third of world's bulk cargo traffic pass through the Indian Ocean. Protecting their own economic and route security becomes an important reason for major countries who want to project power on the Indian Ocean. This also changes the geopolitical landscape of the Indian Ocean. However, Asia serves as the place of departure or destination of most of energy and cargoes which pass through the Indian Ocean.[1] Take the data of February 2017 as an example, 48% of oil shipment of OPEC members was exported to China, India, Japan and South Korea, and most of the oil shipment need pass through the Indian Ocean.[2] China has seven of the world's top ten busiest container terminals, while India's Jawaharlal Nehru Port near Bombay ranks the 30th in the world and is also the only Indian port among the world's top 50 ports. Just the rapid rise of Asia results in the rapid expansion of energy and market demands in the Asia-Pacific region, while the uneven distribution of production factors makes the Asia-pacific countries have to go across the Indian Ocean and the Pacific Ocean to realize their energy allocation and to seek market in the world. That makes the Indian Ocean "overtaking the Atlantic Ocean and the Pacific Ocean and becoming the world's busiest trade corridor of great strategic significance",[3] and also makes the maritime corridor and navigation safety of the Indian Ocean become an important global issue.

In other words, as a trade and energy corridor, the increasing importance of the Indian Ocean is tightly connected with the economic prosperity and rapid rise of Asia-Pacific. Compared with the Atlantic Ocean and the Pacific Ocean in the past, the particularity of the Indian Ocean lies in that the increasing importance of the Indian Ocean doesn't depend solely upon the economic growth and regional integration of the economies around the Indian Ocean. The economic growth of East Asia and Southeastern Asia play the main driving role.

---

[1]"Plenty of Fish in the Sea Food Security in The Indian Ocean", *Diplomat*, https://thediplomat.com/2012/08/plenty-of-fish-in-the-sea-food-security-in-the-indian-ocean/.

[2]"Fossil Fuel Global Flow Oil Data Used Track," Thomsonreuters, https://blogs.thomsonreuters.com/answerson/fossil-fuel-global-flow-oil-data-used-track/.

[3]Zhao (2013).

(II) "Indo-Pacific" concept has nothing to do with economic Integration of Indian Ocean region and Pacific region

The introduction and promotion of the "Indo-Pacific" concept make the scholars of India, Australia and the US to discuss the economic relations of "Indo-Pacific" and how to promote the economic integration of the region. However, there are no signs of deep integration between Indian Ocean region and Pacific region at all.

First, the intraregional trade in both the "Indo-Pacific" region and the Indian Ocean seems sluggish compared with that in the Asia-Pacific region. In recent decade, 65–70% of the total trade volume of APEC members is the internal trade among the APEC members (see Table 1), and the intraregional trade comprises 27% of total GDP; by contrast, if we define "Indo-Pacific" region as the ASEAN + 3 and the Indian Ocean Rim Association (IORA), the total intraregional trade volume respectively comprised 23.46 and 22.75% of total trade volume in 2016, hovering at around 25% throughout the year (see Table 2). The economy is less integrated in this region.

Second, the Indian Ocean Rim economies are not the major trade partners of Asia-Pacific counties. In fact, most of Indian Ocean Rim economies, including South Asia and Gulf countries, are even less related with their neighboring countries in comparison with Asia-Pacific countries, especially the APEC members (Table 3).

There are many factors that lead to the phenomenon. Between the Indian Ocean region and the Asia-Pacific region, there are gaps in economic development and differences in factor endowment. According to the traditional international economic theory, there should be greater complementarity between the two regions. In fact, it is reflected in the trade characteristics between the Indian Ocean Rim economies and the Asia-Pacific economies. However, the basis of all economic activities is the expansion of labor division and market scale. As the vertical separation degree and modular technology continue upgrading during the production process, the vital role of competitive interindustry trade is gradually overtaken by that of intra-industry trade and even inter-product trade. The development of value chain and the global distribution of production network make the complementarity less important and the relations between investment and trade increasingly close. By contrast, the "institutional distance", the requirements on infrastructure, and the similarity in economic development exert growing influences on trade. But, lots of the Indian Ocean Rim economies are underdeveloped in those fields and suffer from universally inadequate infrastructure and relatively backward economic development. Even if parts of economies adopt a political system similar to that of the West, there is still "institutional distance" between the Indian Ocean region and the economically developed Asia-Pacific region in market openness and business environment.

Such gap is also shown by the lack of mutual investment in the "Indo-Pacific" region. Currently, there are three major countries engaged in foreign direct investment (FDI), namely the US, Japan and China, which all belong to Asia-Pacific countries. In terms of their main FDI destinations, most top-ranking destinations are Asia-Pacific and European countries (see Table 4), while the low-ranking partners are the Indian Ocean countries. By contrast, the Indian Ocean Rim economies attract relatively a small amount of investment, most of which concentrates on the energy sector in India

Table 1 Intraregional trade of APEC members

Year	2006	2007	2008	2009	2010	2011	2012	2013	2014	2015	2016
APEC's total trade value (hundred million dollars)	112,663	126,678	144,365	113,598	146,034	173,133	178,887	182,228	184,303	165,511	159,438
APEC's intraregional trade value (hundred million dollars)	77,954	86,268	94,777	76,525	99,451	115,496	120,415	123,077	125,454	116,096	111,266
Proportion of Intraregional trade (%)	69.19	68.10	65.65	67.37	68.10	66.71	67.31	67.54	68.07	70.14	69.79

Source United Nations Comtrade Database

Table 2 Intraregional trade of ASEAN and IORA

Year	2006	2007	2008	2009	2010	2011	2012	2013	2014	2015	2016
Proportion of ASEAN's intraregional trade (%)	25.41	25.46	25.21	24.76	24.90	24.34	24.63	24.55	24.30	23.75	23.46
Proportion of IORA's intraregional trade (%)	25.71	25.36	25.82	27.53	26.97	27.08	25.32	25.03	24.46	24.05	22.75

Source United Nations Comtrade Database

Table 3 Trade relations between APEC members and IORA members

Year	2013	2014	2015	2016	2017
APEC members' gross export value to the world (US dollars)	8932470783.00	9108093171.00	8313051759.00	8021007162.00	6096597329.00
APEC members' gross export value to IORA members (US dollars)	1277726211.00	1310296780.00	1186272962.00	1115829659.00	791474718.00
Proportion (%)	14.30	14.39	14.27	13.91	12.98
APEC members' gross import value from the world (US dollars)	9293309159.00	9322946371.00	8239469250.00	7997099699.00	6655686286.00
APEC members' gross import value from IORA members (US dollars)	1453147005.00	1453147005.00	1453147005.00	1453147005.00	1453147005.00
Proportion (%)	15.64	15.59	17.64	18.17	21.83

Source United Nations Comtrade Database

Table 4 Top 8 countries in FDI Stock of Japan, China and the US

Japan		China		The US	
Ranking	Stock (hundred million dollars)	Ranking	Stock (hundred million dollars)	Ranking	Stock (hundred million dollars)
The US	4541.39	Hong Kong, China	7807.45	The Netherlands	847,391
The UK	1207.47	Cayman Islands	1042.09	The UK	682,361
China	1087.63	British Virgin Islands	887.66	Luxembourg	607,849
The Netherlands	1056.67	The US	605.80	Ireland	387,092
Australia	663.25	Singapore	334.46	Bermuda	288,822
Thailand	552.28	Australia	333.51	British Caribbean Islands	265,548
Singapore	417.86	The Netherlands	205.88	Singapore	258,864
South Korea	319.73	The UK	176.12	Switzerland	172,608

Source www.mofcom.gov.cn, www.bea.gov

and gulf countries. Furthermore, the Indian Ocean region rarely invests in the Asia-Pacific countries. As mentioned, such investment could hardly bring about trade, especially intermediate products trade or inter-industry trade, and also hardly realize the market scale expansion in the real sense so as to weaken the boundary effect. The Asia-Pacific region and the Indian Ocean region, which are included in the so-called "Indo-Pacific" region, are two relatively independent regions in economy. Just as the Australian scholar said, the shaping of "Indo-Pacific" has a strong maritime safety foundation, but its economic logic is indeed under-developed.[4]

(III) **The "Indo-Pacific" concept reflects the control and intervention attempts of the concept promoter on the shift process of economic center**

As mentioned above, it is not wrong to regard the "Indo-Pacific" as the expansion of Asia-Pacific at the economic level, or, the core of "Indo-Pacific" is Asia-Pacific. The "Indo" part of "Indo-Pacific" refers to still a relatively independent geo-economic region, while the Indian Ocean is only the derivation or rim of Asia-Pacific economic center. We could even say that the so-called "Indo-Pacific" only connects the manufacturing hubs of East Asia with the key energy of Western Indian Ocean via the transportation routes of "Maritime Asia". Besides that, Asia-Pacific economies

[4]Wilson (2017).

have relatively weak economic radiation power on the economies around the East Indian Ocean, while the economies around the Indian Ocean have extremely remote economic radiation power on the Asia-Pacific economies. The fundamental goals and reasons for the "Indo-Pacific" concept promoters to include the Indian Ocean and India in the concept have nothing to do with the economic integration process of the Indian Ocean and India. When Hillary Clinton used the term "Indo-Pacific" in formal presentations in 2010 and said that the Pacific Ocean and the Indian Ocean have associated by shipping and strategy and advocated that India and the US should build the "Indo-Pacific Economic Corridor", she didn't focus on the economic relations between the Indian Ocean and the Pacific Ocean, because compared with the regionalism and integration in other regions of the world, such economic relations are not enough to be considered strategically in both density and breadth. Actually, the main reason for the those promoters to launch and lay stress on the regional concept of "Indo-Pacific" is China's rise and the increase of East Asia's economic and strategic weight in the world, which would not only change the geo-economic landscape but also affect the maritime interests of many countries.

Thus, "Indo-Pacific" concept is created, adopted and promoted for the security and strategic reasons and lacks the substantial economic foundation when compared with other important geopolitical concepts. In other worlds, in the "Indo-Pacific" concept, the truly and only important economic factor in fact is the promoter's intervention and control attempts on the historical shift process of economic centers, because the shift process of economic centers is often the shift process of economic hegemony and the process of the major changes to strategic value of some region. First, the emerging of new economic hegemony means the adjustment of "International property structure" and the reallocation of the world's resources.[5] However, what the western scholars are more concerned about is that after the new hegemony gains dominance, it would plunder the resources of other countries by means of seigniorage, or in other words, economic hegemony is linked with predatory behaviors.[6] Second, the rise of new regions and new economic centers in the world means not only changes to the landscapes of both economic hegemony and maritime hegemony in regional market, the changes to original balance of the region, but also a sharp increase in the cost for maintaining the original world system. During this process, relevant countries also have to take countermeasures to prevent hegemony from falling into the hands of others, or prevent others from plundering the resources, or maximize the benefits as much as possible during the process.

Therefore, the economic aspect of "Indo-Pacific" focuses not on the development of economic integration or cooperation prospect of the regions but on the attitudes of main participants towards the shift process of economic hegemony.

(1) **For the US**, though "only a few American scholars look at the concept Indo-Pacific from the perspective of geo-economics", it is because the final goal of American "Indo-Pacific" strategy in economy is how to strengthen the economic combination between India and ASEAN members, so as to counterbal-

[5]Cai (2009).

[6]Cai (2011).

ance China's presence on Southeast Asia, South Asia and the Indian Ocean region.[7] No matter whether the US government adjusts its domestic or foreign policies, or whether American foreign policy shows relatively large uncertainty in a period of time, in the medium and long term, the US government could not sit idly by to watch the shift of economic centers and economic hegemony. According to Satter, an American scholar, currently the US believes that the goal of China is to "enhance its strength in Asia-Pacific region" and "try to push the US to withdraw from Asia"; and the China Case introduced by China in international economy also poses a challenge to the US.[8] Thus, under the circumstance of dual separation that Asia "depends on China in economy and the US in security", it is imperative to intervene in the process of economic growth in Asia-Pacific region. That is fully embodied in the policy mix launched by the US: first, it is to give a heavy blow to the external economy of China and Asian economies through the trade protectionism and a trade war, so as to refuse to advance the bilateral market access negotiations and other behaviors under the US-China Comprehensive Economic Dialogue (CED) and take the opportunity to practice blackmail and extortion, or it is to put pressure through direct negotiations or oral instructions to ask Asian economies to change their economic and trade modes; second, it is to stop China to popularize the "China Case" via the "Belt and Road", and Trump said in his report to the Congress that the US would use all "available tools" to pressure China on its global popularization of Chines economic mode[9]; third, it is that the US has gradually given up its old stand that asks China to take on more responsibilities in the US-led world order and launched a new concept to try to build new international economic order to replace and resist China; forth, considering the importance of Asia-Pacific region towards the rise of China's economy, it is to marginalize Asia in the new international economic order to resist or cover the existing integration system of Asia and interfere with the construction of regionalism in this region, so as to "stop Asia from shaping the regional trade groups excluding the US".[10] Though the US gives up TPP temporarily, it only shows that **the means by which the US seeks to maintain its dominance in the global economy has transformed from "reshaping and leading the process of economic integration in the Asia-Pacific region through economic instruments" to "interfering with and intervene in the process of regional integration mechanism in Asia-Pacific region through non-economic instruments"**. By doing so, the US once again grasps the initiative in the mechanism and order construction in Asia-Pacific region and the Indian Ocean region in future.

---

[7]Liu (2014).

[8]"*US Policy towards China Enters a Major Transition Period*", Reference News, March 23, 2018, original from a report of Japanese Sankei, March 22, 2018.

[9]"Trump Says U.S. to Use All Tools to Pressure China on Trade", *Bloomberg*, https://www.bloomberg.com/news/articles/2018-02-28/trump-says-u-s-will-use-all-tools-to-pressure-china-on-trade.

[10]Xia (2015).

(2) **For Australia, Australia itself is the beneficiary of the economic center shift process, so it pays more attention to the economic implication of "Indo-Pacific"**. Lying between the Pacific Ocean and the Indian Ocean, Australia has channel advantages in maritime trade, and its export is especially driven by East Asian. For instance, in 2016, China, Japan and South Korea of East Asia made up over half the merchandise export of Australia (52.2%); China-Australia trade volume totaled US$107.8 billion; Australia's trade surplus exceeded US$33.5 billion; the Chinese tourists spent as much as RMB46 billion in Australia. Despite the increasingly close economic ties between Australia and Asia, as a country in Oceania, Australia has always faced the difficulties in integrating into the existing economic cooperation mechanism in Asia. Besides the definition of "Middle Power", Australia needs a new framework to highlight its geo-economic advantages and particularity and to lead or at least participate in the formulation of rules in this new framework. "Indo-Pacific" satisfies such demands of Australia.

(3) **For Japan, first, Japan is unwilling to sit idle to see it being marginalized in the process of the rise of new economic center; second, after launching the Fukuda Doctrine, Japan has grown its economic presence on Southeast Asia for a long time and now needs a bigger framework to support its Asia-Africa Growth Corridor**. As early as Shinzo Abe's first term, in a speech entitled as "Confluence of the Two Seas" at the Parliament of India in August 2007, Abe emphasized the constantly-strengthened importance of the Indian Ocean and the Pacific Ocean and the increasingly-underpinned relationship between the two oceans, and then launched the "Free and Open Indo-Pacific" Strategy. From the economic perspective, Abe stressed that the US, Australia, Japan and India should join hands to usher in the "freedom and prosperity" of "Broader Asia" and hoped to build the broader network covering Indo-Pacific region to realize the mobility of personnel, capital and goods. Japan also expected to further expand the economic mechanism of Asia to Africa. At time of elaborating Japan's "Indo-Pacific" Strategy at the 6th Tokyo International Conference African Development in 2016, Abe said that let us made this stretch that was from Asia to Africa a main artery for growth and prosperity. As a matter of fact, Japan is expecting to be the leader of this process.

Overall, at time of shaping and launching the "Indo-Pacific" concept, from the economic perspective, the US considers how to counterbalance China's economic presence and marginalize the regional mechanism of "Asia-Pacific" to intervene in the shift process of economic centers; Australia seeks to enjoy greater say and decision-making power in this process; Japan seeks to consolidate its position in the region where China's influence is relatively weak to prevent its position in world economic system from falling into the hands of others; **and India takes into consideration more complicated factors in terms of the connotation of "Indo-Pacific"**.

2 The Development Needs and Eastward Expansion of India

From "Asia-Pacific" to "Indo-Pacific", one of the most important changes is to include India (and surrounding areas) into the concept. This is not only because and promoters of "Indo-Pacific" deliberately want to win over India, but also because India aggressively seeks to validate its presence eastward. India has witness the historical shift in fields of geopolitics and geo-economics during the shift process of economic centers. In terms of its lofty ambition, India prefers itself would be the next economic center in the shift process. The high economic growth rate, young population structure, huge domestic market and linguistic and institutional advantages give India the confidence. India's goal of becoming a global power with a great say and characteristics is in line with India's long-term economic development goal. Seeing that Modi won the election by banking on Vikas (development) and nationalism, this goal can still be widely recognized.

To achieve this goal, India must expand its strategic space and regional presence to extend its interests "from the Indian Ocean to southern region of South China Sea and West Pacific Ocean".[11] Economically speaking, India has also to develop its own economic strength to guarantee the rapid and stable economic growth at home and improve its position in international economic system, so as to counterbalance the regional economic presence of its opponents (no matter imaginary or real).

Therefore, all the foreign policies of India are to serve this goal and require India to face the relationships between India and Asia-Pacific region squarely, because "a country with great power ambitions can grow its presence in not only faraway lands but also surrounding areas—particularly when it has two-thirds of the world's population, a rising military power, and a considerable part of the world's wealth across its vast land".[12] This makes "Act East" become one of India's key foreign policies.

(I) **In term of economic space expansion, India must expand eastward**. In the late 20th century, Asian production network were gradually formed. This vast production network has three functions: first, it realizes the rapid industrialization of developing countries in Asia; second, it helps Asia resume its position of world economic center; third, it accelerates the construction process of Asian regional integration and regionalism. For all these reason, the concept "Asia-Pacific" is shaped quickly, and the Asia-Pacific region also becomes an engine of world economic growth. However, India and other south Asian countries are always on the margins of this economic circle and production network and lag behind this heartland in both industrialization and regional integration.

Though the Indian scholars often complain about the concept "Asia-Pacific" and claim that this concept ignores India's rapid growth and economic importance and excludes India, such result was caused by India itself. Throughout India's economic

[11]Zhao (2009).

[12]"India Acts East", Foreign Policy, http://foreignpolicy.com/2016/05/17/india-acts-east/.

development history, the long-term closed-door economic policy after its independence cuts off the traditional business contact and traffic links with Asia-Pacific region. Moreover, the big differences in growth mode further cut India off from other Asian regions during the rapid growth of the emerging economies in East Asia and Southeast Asia. Furthermore, due to its years of intentional and unintentional acts of omission and numerous barriers generated by complicated political structures of South Asia, regional integration in South Asia has remained weak on all fronts, and the institutional construction of regionalism even becomes a stage for competitions between India and Pakistan. Substantively, due to the special framework of economic geography, there is no real trade and investment integration in South Asia, and all important economic relations lie in the bilateral economic and trade relations between India and other South Asian countries. The separation between production and market makes it difficult for South Asian region to integrate into the Asia production network, while India even feels proud of not being an "export-driven economy". Therefore, for quite a long time, South Asia is not only a geopolitical plate separated from other part of Asia but also a relatively independent economic plate.

Even though India has a vast domestic market and the middle class which India is proud of, its underdeveloped industrial sector and single domestic market still fail to satisfy the development demands of India, a populous country with 1.3 billion people. Just as former RBI Governor Raghuram Rajan said, even if India achieves an economic growth rate of 7.5%, it is still not enough to create jobs for the Indian workforce.[13] According a McKinsey Repor in 2014, in order to improve the industrial structure and meet the population growth demands, India need to add 111 million non-agricultural jobs before 2022.[14] In the context of globalization, it will also be difficult for India to realize its development goal of becoming a center of world economic development, if India neither opens to the outside world nor actively seeks new markets. This requires India to overtake South Asian region and integrate itself into a vaster market. The policies adopted by the Modi Government show that Modi has also realized that.

As mentioned above, among the regions surrounding India, South Asian is featured by small economic weight, backward economic development and lack of integration mechanism (see Table 5) and fails to meet the demands of India on market expansion. Though India maintains close economic relations with the gulf countries, such economic tiles are mostly built on basis of labor export and energy import. In the northwest, though in recent years India has greatly enhanced the economic and trade exchanges with Afghanistan on the occasion of the deterioration of Afghanistan-Pakistan relations, considering the political unrest in West Asia, security will still be the primary consideration of India in this region. By contrast, the resistance from "eastward" market and economic space expansion is much smaller. Asia-Pacific

[13]"Growth rate of 7.5% not enough to create jobs for the Indian workforce, Raghuram Rajan tells CNBC", *Scroll*, March 20, 2018, https://scroll.in/latest/872743/growth-rate-of-7-5-not-enough-to-create-jobs-for-the-indian-workforce-raghuram-rajan-tells-cnbc.

[14]"Indias Path from Poverty to Empowerment", McKinsey Report, February 2014, https://www.mckinsey.com/global-themes/asia-pacific/indias-path-from-poverty-to-empowerment.

Table 5 Proportion of intraregional trade volume to total trade volume of south Asian countries (unit: %)

Year	2010	2011	2012	2013	2014	2015
South Asian countries	8.81	7.58	9.07	8.80	9.88	9.53
South Asia countries excluding India	4.14	4.53	3.95	3.85	3.62	4.48

Source Prepared by author on basis of UNCTAD data

region has a large population and vast territory and enjoys prosperous economy and relatively stable political and social order. Southeast Asia serves a bridge connecting India with the heartland of Asia-Pacific region. The ASEAN member countries have up to 6 million overseas Indians. India has also maintained friendly relations with Australia and Japan.

Furthermore, if India wants to maintain a high-speed growth in future, its energy demand will be tripled or quadrupled over today's demand. However, Australia and Indonesia can strengthen the energy security of India. India lacks direct traffic links with the countries in Central Asia and Central Europe, while Australia is largest LNG supplier in the world. Meanwhile, though India is making great efforts to develop its clean and green energy, coal will still be one of its most important resources within a long time, and 60% of coal imported by India is from Indonesia. Just like China's demand for resources, India's economic growth demand for resources facilitates the maritime transportation, but geographical proximity provides India with more advantages and motivations to establish its economic presence on Straits of Malacca and other strategic passages.

(II) **From the historical and psychological perspectives**, it's an inevitable choice for India to rebuilt economic relations with Asia-Pacific region. Indian scholars believe that before the 19th century, there was geo-economic network covering West Asia, South Asia, Southeast Asia and East Asia, among which Indian folk merchants-led marine trade played a vital role, but that network was dissembled later.[15] In history, India did build the multiple trade-based relations with most of Asian countries, especially Southeast Asian countries in fields of politics, society and culture. Such relations were not broken even after the Islamzation of Indonesia and Malaysia. However, after the decline of Indian southern dynasties and the invasion of western colonial forces, South Asia and east Asia were separated by the Bay of Bengal and the Himalayas and South Asia became an independent geo-plate; the northwest of India was isolated from the inner Asia by the strategic buffer zone that was intentionally made by the US in the Great Game; the southeast of India was cut off by the colonial forces that controlled the sea routes. Deeply impressed by the invaders from the sea in the post-colonial era, India attached more weight to the preparedness for ocean affairs and less weight on the importance of marine economy in a long period of time. India would prefer to expel all foreign forces from the

[15]Singh (2018).

> Indian Ocean to realize its so-called "Closed Sea" but forgot that the historical geo-economic network built in this region was depending on the openness of the Indian Ocean. After India's independence, the India-Pakistan confrontation and the Southeast Asia Treaty Organization built by the US in Southeast Asian region didn't give Nehru a chance to realize the strategic conception of "Pan-Asianism", while succeeding Prime Minister Indira Gandhi mainly focused on building the regional power in South Asia. Those actually made India miss the opportunity to forge closer relations with Southeast Asian countries that rose economically in that period. Meanwhile, India always has a good opinion of its role in international community and invests heavily in major-country diplomacy, but pay less attention to its neighbors. The immediate consequence is that India misses the early stage of a shift of the world economic center to Asia-Pacific region.

The lack of such relations is even more significant in South East Asia, which has long been under the interaction between two cultural circles of India and East Asia in history. However, India has been so busy stabilizing its supremacy in Indian subcontinent and seeking an important role in international system that East Asian region has wield greater economic clout in Southeast Asia during the shaping of the concept "Asia-Pacific". Nowadays, India eagerly expects to play an influential role in Asia-Pacific region. Psychologically speaking, to integrate into the economic circle of "Asia-Pacific" is just like to integrate into the cultural circle of East Asia. It is unacceptable for India. **For India, to restore its charisma and core role in such regions where India has ever established important presence in history, India must realize that "geo-economic dimension" and "geo-cultural dimension" are interdependent and mutually supported. Therefore, if India wants to restore its geo-status, it should also rebuild the India-centered economic network**.

For the above two reasons, since the 1990s, India has gradually cemented its economic and trade relations with the ASEAN, Japan and South Korea. In 1992, India become a sectoral dialogue partner of the ASEAN; in 1994, Rao's government put forward the "Look East Policy" in its foreign policy decision-making and launch the high tide of moving eastward towards Southeast Asia; in 1996, India joined the Asean Regional Forum and became a full dialogue partner of the ASEAN; in June 1997, India together with Bangladesh and Sri Lanka joined the "BIMSTEC" with an aim to strengthen the economic relations between South Asia and Southeast Asia; since 2003, India has started to strengthen its diplomatic and military cooperation with those regions to focus on strategic security, energy acquisition and economic interaction, and expanded its target regions to the entire Western Pacific Region including Australia in a bid to include this stretch that was from Australia to China and East Asia into its cooperation scope; in August 2009, India signed the India—ASEAN Free Trade Area Agreement with the ASEAN; moreover, India had also successively launched the "Project Mausam" and the "Spice Route" to seek to rebuild the geo-economic and geo-cultural links.

3 Limited "Act East" and India's Acceptance and Interpretation of "Indo-Pacific"

Prime Minister Modi had spent a lot of time to visit the ASEAN, Japan and South Korea when he was the chief minister of Gujarat, so he was well aware of the importance of "Eastward" policy for India. Among his first 40 visits after Modi assumed office, nearly half of destinations were in South Asia, Southeast Asia and South Asia. However, Modi has also thought that the "Look East" is limited and India must make the "Look East Policy" go up to a new level. In November 2014, Modi brought forward the "Act East Policy" to replace the "Look East Policy" at the ASEAN Blockchain Summit, with an aim to bridge the gaps between India and East Asian and Indo-Pacific countries.

The upgraded "Act East Policy" scales up India's eastward expansion in following aspects. First, its geographical scope is expanded from the Southeast Asia to the stretch including Australia, Japan, South Korea and China later; second, its cooperation area is also expanded from single economic dimension in the beginning to a multi-dimension including strategy, security, mechanism and others. Modi has repeated to make commitments to inject new energy into the cooperation between India and Asia in fields of economy, politics and security on various occasions. When he assumed office, Modi actively invited the business leaders and delegations from East Asia and Southeast Asia to India to make investment; at time of meeting the leaders from Myanmar and the ASEAN, he made a commitment to geographically deepen the interconnectivity with those regions; he also extended the scope and scale of development assistance provided by India to the less-developed ASEAN member countries and Pacific Islands; during Obama's visit to India in 2015, he on behalf of India expressed the willingness to join the APEC; on January 26, 2018, he also invited the governmental leaders from the ASEAN member countries to New Delhi to attend the Republic Day Parade ceremony. All of those moves manifest India's determination to continue strengthening the relations with the East.

Though India has the determination and provide the commitment, a report released by Lowy Institute in 2014 points out that India "must demonstrate that Act East is more than just a rebranding of an existing policy."[16] Just as Indian scholar Raja Mohan said, in India's "Act East Policy", the gap between the potential and reality hasn't been narrowed,[17] while there are always gaps between India's willingness and ability to play a vital role in Asia. Take the ASEAN as an example, India only accounted for 2.6% of the ASEAN's foreign trade volume in 2016. Among the dialogue partners of the ASEAN, India is the latest to sign the free trade agreement with the ASEAN. India gives the priority to protecting its domestic market and industries in almost all important economic and trade negotiations because of the existing large trade deficit and pressures from domestic interest groups. Such attitude by no means can convince everybody that India has revolutionized its economic idea. Though India has

[16] "India Acts East", Foreign Policy, http://foreignpolicy.com/2016/05/17/india-acts-east/.

[17] Raja Mohan (2016).

made great efforts in providing the interconnectivity and the international assistance, including India-Myanmar-Thailand highway and KMMTTP, India's construction progress and commitment fulfillment have been always one step behind China. In the opinion of some scholars, the fact that India becomes a formal member of the East Asia Summit and the ASEAN Defense Ministers Meeting Plus marks that "India has been gradually accepted as a member of "Asia-Pacific", but, as mentioned above, **it is presently difficult for India to become a member of the Asia-Pacific region both economically and psychologically**. India is absent from the key economic and security arrangements of "Asia-Pacific", and the "Act East Policy" cannot change the situation quickly. To some Indian scholars, the term "Asia-Pacific" is an "East Asian or Western Pacific formulation" and forces India to seek for a broader concept framework.[18] However, the fact that India is located on the edge of Asia-Pacific economic circle is still unchanged. It is a reflection and reason of the limited "Act East Policy".

Thus, we have to consider the limitation and real purpose of India's "Act East Policy". India has long been realized that in comparison with existing geo-strategic differences, there has been huge gap between China and India in the economic presence on Asia including Southeast Asia. Such gap lies not only in trade and investment in this region but also in the system presence including international assistance, education and vocational training, even in the motivation and ability of both China and India in organizing the Track 1.5/II dialogue.

In fact, it has long been said in India that China extends its presence in Asia at the expense of India. So we can see that to counterbalance China's presence is still one major objective of India and countries in Southeast Asia and Asia-Pacific region. Such intention has also resulted in the ambiguous attitude of India in the multilateral cooperation in this region. Besides domestic policy disputes or security considerations, the cloud on the horizon is that China will benefit more from it depending on its solid economic base, though those regional integration arrangements work as a huge boost for India's market scale expansion, multilateral trade growth and external economic sector development. Once India participates in such regional economic arrangements, the gap between India and China in economic presence would be widened. It is why India on the one hand always expresses its desire to deepen its economic relations with its eastern neighbors and surrounding countries in a high profile, and on the other hand impedes the construction of lots of regional cooperation institutions in which China play a vital role.

So it is no surprise that India connects its "Act East Policy" with "Indo-Pacific". Gurpreet Khurana, the earliest interpreter and promoter of "Indo-Pacific" concept, believes "Indo-Pacific" concept can showcase the importance of the Indian Ocean and ultimately help India play a more important role in Asia-Pacific affairs, especially a role in protecting the maritime security in field of regional economic growth and

---

[18]Aaron Jed Rabena, "Is the 'Indo-Pacific' Construct Trump's Pivot to Asia Policy?", CSIS NEWSLETTER https://www.csis.org/analysis/pacnet-13-indo-pacific-construct-trumps-pivot-asia-policy.

development.[19] India is anxious to strengthen the relations with Asia-Pacific region due to its own development needs; however, the "Act East Policy" doesn't perform as well as it expected, and it becomes difficult to win the regional economic presence competition between India and China, so India is unwilling to join existing Asia-Pacific cooperation mechanism but prefers a new framework that can not only avoid or counterbalance China's presence but also help India play a more important role in it, meanwhile can offer the alternative plans in various aspects to make up for India's own inadequacies. The introduction of "Indo-Pacific" concept falls in with the demand of India.

Thus during Obama's visit to India in 2015, the US and India signed the *US-India Joint Strategic Vision for the Asia-Pacific and Indian Ocean Region*; during Modi's visit to Japan in December 2015, Japan and India issued a joint statement on *Japan and India Vision 2025 Special Strategic and Global Partnership Working Together for Peace and Prosperity of the Indo-Pacific Region and the World* (hereinafter referred to as the "Vision 2025") and reiterated their unwavering commitment to build "a peaceful, open, equitable, stable and rule-based order in the Indo-Pacific region" and realize "the peace, security and development in the Indo-Pacific region"; during Modi's visit to the US in June 2017, Modi and Trump made a joint statement to "work together for the peace and stability in Indo-Pacific region"; during the visit of US Secretary of State Rex Tillerson to India on October 25, 2017, Tillerson and Indian Foreign Minister Sushma Swaraj made a joint statement to work together for "a free, open and prosperous Indo-Pacific region".

For India, the "Indo-Pacific" concept supported by quadrilateral cooperation can do a job that none of the four countries can do alone, that is to prevent China becoming the sole provider of infrastructure products and the leading power in the regions; the commitments the US provides to promote the interconnectivity and economic growth and build the energy network in South Asia, Southeast Asia and Central Asia through "Indo-Pacific Strategic Conception" and the cooperation between Japan and India on infrastructure construction projects in South Asian region can provide these regions with the "alternative" plans that India cannot offer due to lack of funds or ability; to play such a vital role in geo-strategic framework and become a rule maker and system builder can also meet India's self-esteem needs for its goal of becoming a "global power".

4 India's Efforts in Bilateral and Multilateral Regional Economic Cooperation in the Context of "Indo-Pacific"

Presently, "Indo-Pacific" is mainly a strategic and security cooperation framework. As mentioned above, due to India's objectives and development needs in term of "Indo-Pacific", "India's "Indo-Pacific" includes not only geo-political factors but

---

[19] "The Origin of 'Indo-Pacific' as Geopolitical Construct: Insights from Gurpreet Khurana", Diplomat, https://thediplomat.com/2018/01/the-origin-of-indo-pacific-as-geopolitical-construct/.

also quite important geo-economic contents",[20] while India also pays equal attention to the "Indo-Pacific" concept in geo-economic field. India currently has also manages to promote multiple bilateral and regional cooperation on infrastructure construction and interconnectivity in "Indo-Pacific" region. But for now, except the appreciable progress in economic cooperation between India and Japan, the economic and trade cooperation between India and Australia face not only a relatively narrow foundation but also huge pressure from the US. In term of regional cooperation, India has participated in the ambitious "Asia-Africa Growth Corridor" and "Indo-Pacific Economic Corridor", but the two projects are limited to visions and initiatives and have no practical implementation plans and policies temporarily.

(I) **In term of bilateral economic cooperation, besides defense and strategic cooperation India has also cemented the economic and trade relations with "Indo-Pacific" partners, but except a great stride in the cooperation between India and Japan, there are twists and turns in the economic and trade relations between India and both Australia and the US.**

1. **Japan. Japan and India are working on strengthening a series of cooperation in term of economy, trade, investment and infrastructure construction**. During Modi's visit to Japan in 2014, Modi and Abe reached an agreement to double Japan's investment in India before 2019; and Abe made a commitment to provide India with the private investment and assistance worth 3.5 trillion yen, including official development assistance, in the next five years. In response, India set up the Japan Plus Office in October 2014 to provide Japanese enterprises with the one-stop investment services. In 2015 and 2016, the two countries held a series of discussions and cooperation on the establishment of industrial towns. The Mumbai–Ahmedabad high-speed rail corridor which adopts Japanese high-speed rail system is about to be built in India formally. Only in 2017, Japan provided India with the loan amounting to 384.1 billion yen, the largest loan Japan provided to one country in one year, of which a loan totaling 149.2 billion yen (equivalent to US$1.4 billion) was used for Mumbai subway construction. According to the official data from India, Japan invested US$4.7 billion in India, up 80% year on year, in 2016–2017 fiscal year. Moreover, during the same period, the bilateral trade volume between Japan and India hit US$13.6 billion. Overall, in recent years, Japan's investment in India has increased rapidly, while the trade between Japan and India has grown relatively stable (Table 6).
   Actually, the cooperation between Japan and India develops rapidly in term of overseas infrastructure construction. The Vision 2025 issued by Japan and India in 2015 said that the two countries would work together for the construction of industrial network and regional value chain and an open, equitable, transparent business environment in Indo-Pacific region. Currently, their main cooperation projects includes Colombo LNG Power Generation Project in Sri Lanka, a core

[20]Liu (2014).

Table 6 Goods trade between Japan and India in recent years (unit: Thousand Dollars)

Year	2010	2011	2012	2013	2014	2015	2016
Indian exports from Japan	8,265,086	11,218,263	12,362,967	10,489,824	9,963,998	9,635,158	9,808,531
Indian exports to Japan	4,805,077	5,592,608	6,415,550	7,325,476	5,756,879	4,529,718	3,827,283

Source UN CAMTRADE

country of the "Free and Open Indo-Pacific Strategy"[21]; Trincomalee Port Development Project; New Container Terminal Project in Colombo Port; Chabahar Port Expansion Plan and Neighboring Special Economic Zone Construction Project in Iran; and Dawei Port Development Plan on the Thai-Myanmar border in future. Japan has often expressed in its official documents that Japan would strive to connect India's "Act East Policy" with Japan's "Partnership for Quality Infrastructure" worth US$200 billion to realize the strategic interconnectivity in South Asia and Southeast Asia by means of cooperation. Japan hopes to continue to consolidate and expand its economic bases in South Asia, while India hopes to further strengthen its presence on neighbors by providing investment and infrastructure. India shares common cooperation goals with Japan in providing these regions with "an alternate source of infrastructure construction partnerships" other than China.

2. **Australia**. Australia is one major energy sources of India. Due to its rapid development in recent years, India's domestic iron and steel production grows at an annual rate of 6.8%; the gap between coal production and consumption has been widened (23% in 2016), particularly lack of industrial coal, so India imports large quantities of coals from Australia.[22] In 2016, India served as the fifth largest export market of Australia, and Australian exports to India hit US$12.9 billion. The major export commodities of Australia to India include coals, vegetables, gold and copper ores, of which coals comprised 56% in 2016. The educational sector led the service trade. Thus, the foundation for bilateral trade is relatively narrow. Furthermore, due to the problems on trade structure, there are also high trade deficits between India and Australia. Currently, India and Australia is negotiating to sign the Comprehensive Economic Cooperation Agree-

[21]On March 8, 2018, India, Japan and Sri Lanka signed the tripartite MoU and agreed to set up a JV near Colombo with an aim to build the facilities integrating LNG import, storage and power generation. India-based Petronet LNG, Japan-based Mitsubishi Corporation and Sojitz Corporation, and the Government of Sri Lanka respectively hold a stake of 47.5, 37.5 and 15% in the JV. This project is the first LNG power generation project in Sri Lanka and is expected to be completed in 2021.

[22]The coal India imports from Australia is mostly metallurgical coal (90%), while the coal for heating and power generation only accounts for 10% of total imports.

Table 7 Stock of US' investment in India from 2010 to 2016 (unit: Million Dollars)

Year	2010	2011	2012	2013	2014	2015	2016
Total investment in Asia-Pacific region	570,111	591,657	672,777	709,623	764,077	803,269	846,680
India	24,666	19,000	25,413	24,850	27,812	29,939	32,939
Percentage (%)	4.33	3.21	3.78	3.50	3.64	3.73	3.89

Source Website of U.S. Bureau of Economic Analysis (BEA) (www.bea.gov)

ment (CECA), which includes the substantive contents of India-Australia FTA. However, because there are substantial divergences between the two countries in protecting India's agriculture and granting visas (concerning the protection of Australian labor market), no further progress has been made in the negotiation. In April 2017, Australian Prime Minister Malcolm Turnbull visited India and sought to deepen the economic cooperation between India and Australia. Meanwhile, Australia also tailored the Australia-Indian economic strategy, but in comparison with the defense cooperation, the economic and trade cooperation between the two countries hasn't developed so rapidly. Such situation hasn't changed much under the framework of "Indo-Pacific".

3. **The US**. In the wake of India's rapid economy growth and the improvement of India-US relation, the economic and trade relations between India and the US has developed quickly in recent years, and the US has become the largest export market of India at present. The bilateral trade volume between India and the US was only US$4.8 billion in 1980 and hit US$114 billion in 2016. Moreover, the bilateral goods trade volume between China and the US was down by 6.7% year on year and still hit US$519.61 billion in 2016. Thus we can see that US is the most important overseas market of India, but India is not the most importance trade partner of the US. In addition, the US's direct investment in India grows relatively slow. In recent years, India has only accounted for around 4% of US's total investment in Asia-Pacific region (Table 7).

India and the US share common outlooks and viewpoints in strategy and security, but they don't have much in common in economy and trade. First, India is also under the pressure of US trade protectionism. As the bilateral trade volume rises, India's trade surplus with the US also floats high. When Modi was elected as prime minister in 2014, he made a commitment to strengthen the trade relations with the US, and Modi's tax reform and National Intellectual Property Rights policy also created favorable conditions for US goods to enter Indian market. However, before Trump announced tariffs on US$50 billion worth of Chinese goods in early March 2018, Trump also put India on a par with China and said that if the two countries didn't lower tariffs on imports from the US, the US would impose retaliatory tariffs on them. The US also required India to reduce its average tariff rate from 13.4%

to "match the global standard".[23] In order to pacify the US, India has repeatedly clarified and pledges to reduce the trade deficit by increasing natural gas imports and civilian airliner orders from the US. Nevertheless, India still worries that the trade war between the US and China would indirectly harm the interests of India.[24] Second, there are also differences between the Us and India in trade policy. The business groups in the US prefer putting pressure on India via platforms such as US-India Trade Policy Forum (TPF) to make India better implement the intellectual property protection policy and then reduce the protection of its domestic industries, thereby entering India's retail, pharmaceutical and entertainment industries. Due to such differences, two countries are often involved in public disputes over WTO. Meanwhile, India also expects the US to relax visa policy. There are big differences between the two countries in these two aspects. When the US makes plans for the TPP, India, just like China, is also excluded.

(II) **In term of multilateral and regional cooperation**, under the framework of "Indo-Pacific", India participates in two major projects: the Asia-Africa Growth Corridor and Indo-Pacific Economic Corridor. The two projects are essentially to promote and implement the "non-China-led infrastructure development Initiative". Though both purport to build an India-centered interconnectivity network from South Asia to Southeast Asia, India tries to exclude China from such regions to prevent China becoming a single dominant force in term of infrastructure construction among the developing countries in Indo-Pacific region.

1. **Asia-Africa Growth Corridor (AAGC) Initiative**. AAGC is a collaborative effort by India and Japan to promote multilateral cooperation. During Modi's visit to Japan in November 2016, the two countries reach a consensus to work together for the construction of infrastructures and industrial corridors in Asia and Africa. Modi pitched the AAGC at the 52th Annual General Meeting of the African Development Bank Group held more than ten days after China's Belt and Road Forum for International Cooperation in May 2017 to call for cooperation to promote the "quality" infrastructure and industrial network construction in vast Asian-African region from Southeast Asia to Western Indian Ocean, so as to realize the goal of the so-called "Free and Open Indo-Pacific Region". Because the AAGC greatly overlaps with the "Belt and Road" in term of the geographical coverage and construction-oriented areas (interconnectivity), adding the subtle launch time, the AAGC is regarded as an alternative to China's "Belt and Road". However, up to this date, this ambitious initiative has only the Vision 2025 document jointed issued by Japan and India and has no specific implementation plans and policy documents.[25]

---

[23] "Don't Equate Us with China, India Tell Us", *Economic Times*, https://economictimes.indiatimes.com/news/economy/foreign-trade/dont-equate-us-with-china-india-tells-us/articleshow/63423141.cms.

[24] "Why New Delhi welcomes a cando Canberra", *Live Mint*, https://www.livemint.com/Opinion/EDBEEYwr3AOUjbH4jV06rJ/Why-New-Delhi-welcomes-a-cando-Canberra.html.

[25] Lou (2018).

2. **Indo-Pacific Economic Corridor (IPEC) Conception**. In the US-India Strategic Dialogue in 2013, US Secretary of State John Kerry pointed out that the US would cooperate with India to "realize the potential of IPEC, which would not only promote the trade and interconnectivity among the dynamic economies in South Asia and Southeast Asia but also stimulate development and investment". Around 2015, a large number of Australian and Indian scholars made the feasibility studies on this conception. After Trump administration came into power, its first annual budget also included the construction funds for the "New Silk Road" and "IPEC". During Trump's visit to China in 2017, he was also popularizing the concept "IPEC". But so far, IPEC is still at the "conceptual" level and seemed not to find the framework and link of implementation. Indian academic circle and media take a welcoming and optimistic attitude to the concept, but India hasn't expressed the willingness to connect the conception with the "Act East Policy" in any official speech so far.

Besides, India also imitates China to frequently hold various regional and international summits (e.g. India-Africa Summit, International Energy Summit and etc.) and expresses its positive willingness different from the past to participate in the international cooperation by means of Track 1.5 dialogue.

5 Participation with a Grain of Salt

As mentioned above, "Indo-Pacific" satisfies the strategic demands of India, so India welcomes the "Indo-Pacific" concept and responded enthusiastically to "Indo-Pacific". It is a natural choice. However, currently India still takes "Indo-Pacific" with a grain of salt. From the perspective of Indian official documents, at time of welcoming "Indo-Pacific", India always lays stress on the importance of the "Act East Policy" for it. So, "Indo-Pacific" is very important for India, but India is still evaluating what the conceptual framework can offer and how much India can participate in it.

(I) **India also needs stable peripheral environment to achieve its economic development goal**.

For India, one of its major goals of participation in "Indo-Pacific" is to prevent China becoming an order leader in Asia-Pacific region and curb the economic presence expansion of China in Asia-Pacific in South Asia and Southeast Asia and the military presence of China in the Indian Ocean under the Indo-Pacific framework. However, India don't want a war in this region, **because the Indian Ocean is of unparalleled economic and security importance for India**. India has the double-edged goals of curbing the expansion of China and guaranteeing the maritime safety in the Indian Ocean, but there are differences in priority between the two goals. India never wants the massive conflicts in the Indian Ocean region, firstly because of the limited military might of China, it is difficult for India to form the limited control over the conflicts;

and secondly because India needs to transport around 75% of its oil import via the Indian Ocean, the affected energy and trade routes will give a great bow to India’s development needs. That is why India puts forward the “Think West” at time of proposing the “Act East”. India still gives the top priority to the Northwestern Indian Ocean region (including the Persian Gulf, Gulf of Oman, Gulf of Aden and the Red Sea) which is closely related to energy security. Anyhow, India needs a peaceful and stable peripheral environment to realize its development goals. Moreover, India also knows that India’s overmuch involvement in “Indo-Pacific” strategy will make China feel a serious threat to its interests in this region and thus give China not only the reasons to grow its presence in the Indian Ocean but also the motivation to “boldly reconstruct the security framework in this region. That will make the Indo-Pacific region take a longer road to peace, prosperity and stability”.[26]

(II) **Currently, the “Indo-Pacific” concept is still vague and lacks of practical effect to improve India’s economic presence in this region**.

As mentioned in the first part of this article, at the economic level, there is no highly integrated and real regionalism in the “Indo-Pacific” region, so the truly and only important economic factor in fact is **the promoter’s intervention, involvement and control attempts on the shift process of world economic centers to Asia**. So, the concept itself means not only that the Indian Ocean countries has already missed the opportunities to develop the reciprocal bilateral trade and investment relations with the economies in Asian manufacturing centers, but also that due to the innate weakness in the construction of regional economic mechanism, the “Indo-Pacific” concept is less possible to surpass the concept “Asia-Pacific” that it attempts to replace. If the “Indo-Pacific” concept becomes a two-wheel engine, one wheel of the engine is naturally disabled. Thus, “Indo-Pacific” is essentially a kind of military cooperation on the basis of the Quadrilateral Security Dialogue (Quad). In both US and India, some people think that the “Indo-Pacific” concept has no serious economic component but only conceptually depends on a complex India.[27] If “Indo-Pacific” has no good economic agenda but only focuses on military, the Quad can’t achieve its goal.[28]

The US, Australia, Japan and India attempt to put forward a plan under the framework of “Indo-Pacific” to counterbalance and replace China’s “Belt and Road” Initiative, but it has made little headway. In fact, “Indo-Pacific” is a mechanism that attempts to encircle China and marginalize China in maritime security and regional affairs, but it is impossible to completely put China’s presence aside from the Asia-Pacific region. China’s role as an economic growth engine in Asia-Pacific region

[26]“Indias Role and Chinas Roads in the Indo Pacific”, Diplomat, https://thediplomat.com/2018/02/indias-role-and-chinas-roads-in-the-indo-pacific/.

[27]“No One Commenting Big Idea Trump Put Forward Apec”, South China Morning Post, http://www.scmp.com/business/companies/article/2119540/no-one-commenting-big-idea-trump-put-forward-apec.

[28]“Quad Needs Both Economic Military Plan for Indo Pacific”, *Economic Times*, https://economictimes.indiatimes.com/news/defence/quad-needs-both-economic-military-plan-for-indo-pacific/articleshow/63049831.cms.

can't be replaced in the short run. Neither the international economic cooperation initiative launched by Japan nor the economic weight of India can replace China's leading role in this region.

Moreover, as mentioned above, at present, India makes great efforts to promote the bilateral and multilateral cooperation mechanisms in "Indo-Pacific" region, but none of such efforts and cooperation must be built under the framework of "Indo-Pacific". For the eastward development needs of India, whether or not there is the "Indo-Pacific" concept, India has to strengthen the bilateral relations with the Pacific Ocean countries such as Japan and Australia, and needs to settle the trade disputes with the US. In term of multilateral economic cooperation, India is now keen to imitate China to show its initiative in participating in multilateral cooperation by means of Track 1.5 Dialogue, but India has no clearer plans and policies in practical mechanism construction currently. No doubt India claims to offer "an alternative source" and calls its investment a "less aggressive political system and overseas ambition[29]", but so far its economic efficiency is unconvincing. Therefore, India currently enjoys the strategic and security benefits from the "Indo-Pacific" concept, but it also knows the "one-wheel" characteristics of the concept. India's "Indo-Pacific" ambition needs the support of geo-economics, while one major goal of its "Act East" is still to deepen the economic relations with the Asia-Pacific region. So, India won't and can't completely depend on the economically vague "Indo-Pacific" concept to achieve its goal.

(III) Inconsistent goals of quadrilateral cooperation under the framework of "Indo-Pacific"

There are still differences among the four countries in application of the "Indo-Pacific" concept. As mentioned above, at the economic level, the US only considers counterbalancing China's presence and marginalizing "Asia-Pacific" with the "Indo-Pacific" concept, so as to intervene in the shift process of economic centers. So, the US pays less attention to geo-economics and regional cooperation mechanism construction. Australia seeks to enjoy greater say and decision-making power during the process of Asia-Pacific economic integration and hopes to play a greater role in economic affairs in Indo-Pacific region. Japan hopes to advance its economic cooperation mechanism in Indo-Pacific region and gives full play to its advantages in such region where China's influence is relatively weak, so as to cement its position in world economic system. India seeks, by means of the "Indo-Pacific" concept, to strengthen its ability building and become the next economic center to realize its dream of being a great power. In other words, Australia and Japan still hope to make a difference in term of geo-economics, while India hopes to pursue more economic interests.

However, if the US, regardless of objective conditions, presses ahead with its "America First" policy, it must have a negative impact on the prospect of economic development and regional cooperation in this region. **As mentioned above, the only economic reason for the US to pursue the "Indo-Pacific" concept is to copy with**

[29]"Indias Role And Chinas Roads in the Indo Pacific", Diplomat, https://thediplomat.com/2018/02/indias-role-and-chinas-roads-in-the-indo-pacific/.

the shift of both economic centers and power gravity, which are brought by the rise of Asia. For the "Indo-Pacific" concept builds a new framework on basis of the existing regional cooperation and integration system in Asia, it must play a counterbalancing and disruptive role in existing regional cooperation.[30] For the US, the "Indo-Pacific" concept is a geopolitical concept that is tailored for the US and parts of its allies to better reshape the leadership of the US in regional order[31] and centers on American interests. So, that brings nothing but harm to the process of economic integration in Asia. In fact, when the US put forward the "IPEC" and the "New Silk Road" Initiative, due to the "America First" policy pursued by the Trump Government, Japan and India of the quadrilateral cooperation are still under constant pressure from the US. In November 2017, at time of announcing his "Indo-Pacific Dream" and "Indo-Pacific Economic Partnership" at APEC CEO Summit, Trump emphasized that "fairness and reciprocal opening" should be the core of "Indo-Pacific Economic Partnership". He believes that it is not fair and reciprocal for the US to unilaterally open the market and lower the trade barriers in the past and requires the Indo-Pacific countries to "follow the rules". This is in fact to bring pressure on Indo-Pacific countries to force them to change their trade and economic mode. Some scholars think that the contradiction between India and the US in the field of economy and trade will not be alleviated due to the "Indo-Pacific Strategy Conception" but be strengthened probably due to the "Indo-Pacific Economic Partnership in America's favor" pursued by Trump.[32]

In short, for the existing regional mechanisms in this region, the "Indo-Pacific" concept is a destructive factor while lacks of the ability to build a new mechanism. Therefore, the US expresses a very strong attitude towards China at time of announcing the concept, but Australia, India and Japan still hope to improve the relationship with China under the framework of "Indo-Pacific".[33] Though the three countries worry about China's ever-increasing presence, and there are more or less deterioration or twists and turns in the relations with China, they still hope to benefit from the China-led economic growth in Asia-Pacific region. In other words, they only hope, through a proactive strategy, to change or upgrade their role in the shift process of economic centers, but would not like to see the process is sabotaged by others. This determines that India is bound to choose its own path and will not cater to the US-led "Indo-Pacific" Strategy.

[30]Zhao (2013).

[31]Zhou and Wang (2018).

[32]Yang and Wang (2018).

[33]"Can Indo Pacific Compete China", *Japan Times*, https://www.japantimes.co.jp/opinion/2018/01/10/commentary/japan-commentary/can-indo-pacific-compete-china.

6 Conclusion

India faces contradictions in geo-economic change in Indo-Pacific region. All parties of the quadrilateral cooperation hope to benefit from the historical shift of economic centers, but their economic agendas differ from one another. The US hopes to use this strategic conception and other policy mixes to sabotage and thwart the process; Japan and Australia hope to change their role in this process; and India has also its own plans and ideas. In the past, India, for a variety of reasons, became a marginalized country during the historical shift process of economic centers to the Asia-Pacific region, but now India not only wants to participate in the process to share the benefits from it but also hopes and dreams to become the next center. For this purpose, on the one hand, India is anxious to expand and guarantee its strategic and economic space in the Indo-Pacific region under the framework of "Indo-Pacific", which also serves the needs of its "Act East" goal; on the other hand, India increasingly expects and even asks for a share from the rapid growth in the Asia-Pacific region. So, if "Indo-Pacific" Strategy fails to provide India with its desired economic guarantee and support or help strengthen its construction ability, India's participation will also be limited. In order to counterbalance China's presence, it is a natural choice for India to join the "Indo-Pacific Strategy". However, India has a clear understanding of its pursuit under the framework of "Indo-Pacific". Since the pursuit is limited, India's participation will also be limited.

Furthermore, for India, the Modi Government has greatly strengthened the diplomatic relations with the US, Australia and Japan in recent years, but India still strategically maintains its Independence and autonomy. That is a basic principle in Indian diplomacy and totally in line with its development goal of being a great power. At time of participating in the negotiations concerning international cooperation mechanism, India always shows a high degree of protective attitude towards its policy independence and domestic affairs. This is why India always has an ambiguous attitude, takes a negatively aggressive stand and is even called "Naysayer" at time of participating in various regional mechanisms including RCEP negotiations. If the Trump Government brings growing economic and trade pressure to India, there is no telling whether India changes its attitude from a flatterer now to a defender later. In fact, in the face of the trade disputes between China and the US, India doesn't crow it. When the Indian Government makes concessions to the US and repeatedly expresses the willingness to solve the trade deficit, the press and academic circles of India become wary and uneasy about the trade protectionism of the US.

So, it is unnecessary for China to fear India's participation in "Indo-Pacific", or try to win over India or even come between India and the other three parties of QUAD by means of benefit shift. Whether to shift benefits or not, India is bound to join "Indo-Pacific" but certainly not totally involved in it. Overmuch concession will give India the reason and motivation for interest blackmail. That's what China need to keep an eye on.

References

Cai, Yiming. 2009. A Study on the Alternation of Economic Hegemonic Powers in the World. *Economic Review 5*: 93–102.

Cai, Yiming. 2011. Hegemony Cycle in World Economy: One Model for Single Country. *Journal of International Trade* 9: 169–176.

Liu, Zongyi. 2014. Conflict or Cooperation?—Geopolitical and Geo-economic Choices in ‘Indo-Pacific Region. *Indian Ocean Economic and Political Review* 4: 4–20.

Lou, Chunhao. 2018. Asia-Pacific Growth Corridor” Initiative: Connotation, Motivation and Prospect”. *International Studies* 1.

Raja Mohan. 2016. *Modi’s World*. Translated by C. Zhu and Y. Yang. Social Sciences Academic Press, p. 118 (India).

Singh, Z.D. 2018. India and China Can Coexist in the Indo–Pacific. *Economic and Political Weekly* 53 (13).

Wilson, Jeffrey D. 2017. Investing in the economic architecture of the Indo-Pacific. *Indo-Pacific Insight Series* 8: 4. http://perthusasia.edu.au/ipis-8.

Xia, Liping. 2015. U.S. Indo-Pacific Strategy from Geopolitical and Geo-economics Perspectives. *The Chinese Journal of American Studies* 2: 32–51.

Yang, Rui, & Wang, Shida. 2018. India and ‘Indo-Pacific Strategic Conception’—Positioning, Intervention and Limitation. *Contemporary International Relations* 1: 46–53.

Zhao, Gancheng. 2009. India: Major Country Prestige and Major Country Diplomacy. *Shanghai People’s Publishing House* 1: 3.

Zhao, Qinghai. 2013. Concept ‘Indo-Pacific’ and Implications for China. *Contemporary International Relations* 7: 14–22.

Zhou, Fangyin, & Wang, Wan. 2018. Indo-Pacific Strategy and China’s Response from the Perspective of Australia. *Contemporary International Relations* 1: 29–36.

Economic Development and Evolution of Geo-economic Pattern of the "Indo-Pacific" Region

Yanfang Li

Abstract This paper mainly discusses three issues from the perspective of geo-economics: First, discuss the two arguments of "the transfer of world economic centers" and the "counterbalancing China's increasing geo-presence" through comparing the economic development dynamics of "Indo-Pacific" and "Asia-Pacific" and analyzing the economic interaction between the two regions; second, provide evidences that containing China with "Indo-Pacific" strategy may impede regional economic development by analyzing the periodic changes of the "Indo-Pacific" geo-economic pattern and comparing the influence and contribution of "Indo-Pacific" strategic partners (the U.S., Japan, Australia and India) and their balancing object (China); third, put forward some thoughts on strengthening the geo-economic cooperation in the "Indo-Pacific" region by comparing the economic inputs of China, the U.S., Japan, Australia and India in the "Indo-Pacific" region and analyzing their different attitudes towards the "Indo-Pacific" strategy. The main conclusions are that: first, despite no obvious transfer trend of the world economic center, the increased dependence of the "Asia-Pacific" region on the "Indo-Pacific" region enhances the geo-economic importance of the latter; second, the origin of the "Indo-Pacific" concept is resulted from not only the geo-economics itself but also the realistic or perceived threat on the U.S., Japan, Australia and India caused by China's development model successfully driven by the geo-economics; third, as China has surpassed and become the leading force and defender in the regional economic cooperation years ago, the U.S., Japan, Australia and India are the challengers to the current order of the geo-economic pattern; fourth, the "Indo-Pacific" region is more important to the geo-economics of China, Japan, Australia and India than that to the U.S.; fifth, if the "Indo-Pacific" strategy attempts to contain China, it will inevitably lead to the tearing of geopolitics

---

Yanfang Li, Ph.D., associate professor, Research Institute for Indian Ocean Economies, Yunnan University of Finance and Economics. Her main research field is south Asia Economy.

Note: To avoid confusion, we regard "Asia-Pacific" and "India-Pacific" as region and regard ASEAN, South Asian Association for Regional Cooperation, Gulf Cooperation Council and Common Market for Eastern and Southern Africa as area.

Y. Li (✉)
Research Institute for Indian Ocean Economies, Yunnan University of Finance and Economics, Kunming, China

C. Zhu (ed.), *Annual Report on the Development of the Indian Ocean Region (2018)*, Research Series on the Chinese Dream and China's Development Path, https://doi.org/10.1007/978-981-13-7693-1_8

and geo-economics, and then damage the economic growth and integration of the region; sixth, China shall pay attention to the strategic direction of the "Indo-Pacific" strategy, seek the converging points of common interests with other countries, and dissolve the adverse factors. Meanwhile, efforts shall also be made to continuously drive a more open and inclusive geo-economic cooperation model.

Keywords "Indo-Pacific" · "Asia-Pacific" · Geo-economic pattern · Geo-economic influence · One belt one road

In the late 20th century, active globalization promoted the rapid development of international trade and international investment, which therefore led to the prosperity of the world economy. In recent years, as globalization has become increasingly difficult, all countries have paid more attention to bilateral and regional multilateral economic and trade cooperation, and accelerated the economic cooperation process at sub-regional, regional and trans-regional levels. In particular, in the vast area from African continent to the east coast of Asia and Oceania, the pace of trans-regional economic cooperation between countries and regional economies has been constantly accelerated; the joint participation of international economies within and outside a region has profoundly affected the overall economic pattern of the region, while reshaping the current economic and geopolitical situations of various countries and regions. Since 2013, the U.S., Japan, Australia and India have officially adopted the concept of the "Indo-Pacific" to the region, and successively put forward the idea of targeted geo-strategic cooperation. This has not only raised the global attention to the region, but also triggered heated discussions on the "Indo-Pacific" from all communities. At present, the "Indo-Pacific" cooperation between the U.S., Japan, Australia and India has still mostly focused in the field of geo-security. However, any substantial and broader strategic cooperation is bound to have a profound impact on the geopolitical, geo-security and geo-economic patterns of the "Indo-Pacific" region as well as China's cooperation in the region. From the perspective of geo-economics, this paper tentatively adopts the analysis indicators of international economics and the analysis logics of geo-economics to discuss three issues on the basis of clarifying the "geo-politics application" process of the "Indo-Pacific" concept: first, analyze the economic interactive relationship between the two regions by comparing the dynamic changes of regional economy between "Indo-Pacific" and "Asia-Pacific" to discuss the two theories of "the transfer of world economic centers" and the "counterbalancing China's increasing geo-presence"; Second, analyze the periodic changes of the "Indo-Pacific" geo-economic pattern and compare the influence and contribution of "Indo-Pacific" strategic partners (the U.S., Japan, Australia and India) and their balancing object (China) to provide evidences that containing China with "Indo-Pacific" strategy may impede regional economic development; third, compare the economic inputs of China, the U.S., Japan, Australia and India in the "Indo-Pacific" region and analyze their different attitudes towards the "Indo-Pacific" strategy thus to put forward some thoughts on strengthening the geopolitical and geo-economic cooperation in the "Indo-Pacific" region.

1 Changing "Indo-Pacific" Concept from Geography to Geo-politics

In the application of the "Indo-Pacific" concept, the subjects are policy makers, scholars or strategic analysts. The former focuses on the geostrategic development of the "Indo-Pacific" concept, while the latter interprets the "Indo-Pacific" strategy and its development process from the perspectives of geopolitics, geo-security and geo-economics.

At the decision-making level, although the U.S., Japan, Australia and India are the main drivers of the "Indo-Pacific" geo-strategy, they have different "Indo-Pacific" geo-strategic progress. Since 2009, although the governments of the four countries have released policy signals about the importance of the "Indo-Pacific" region, they have only expounded the Indian Ocean region as a new key area of the "Asia-Pacific" region, without explicitly using the concept. For example, in 2007, Shinzo Abe, Japan's Prime Minister, proposed linking the Pacific Ocean and the Indian Ocean into a sea of freedom and prosperity using the concept of the "Arc of Freedom and Prosperity"[1]; in 2012, Shinzo Abe continued to stress the importance of the Indian Ocean to Japan's diplomatic strategy using the concept of "Asia's Democratic Security Diamond"[2]; in 2009, Australia's Defense White Paper began mentioning the region, but still referred to it as the "Wider Asia-Pacific Region"[3]; over the same period, the "Indo-Pacific" that the Obama administration considered was merely a dependent of the U.S. "Asia-Pacific" "rebalancing strategy"; in 2011, then-Secretary of State Hillary Clinton still called the area stretching from the Indian subcontinent to the west coast of the America as the "Asia-Pacific" when writing an article for a foreign affairs magazine[4]; in 2012, Indian Prime Minister Manmohan Singh mentioned that the stability, security and prosperity of the "Indo-Pacific" region are crucial to the development and prosperity of countries in the region at ASEAN-India Commemorative Summit, but his focus is only the "Look East Policy".[5]

Since 2013, the "Indo-Pacific" region has gradually risen to the level of geo-strategy. Although the U.S., Japan, Australia and India have been the main drivers of this strategy, they have still been out of step in strategic cognition and implementation enthusiasm. Among them, Japan and Australia are the most active promoters of

---

[1] Abe (2007).

[2] Shinzo A. Asia's Democratic Security Diamond [EB/OL]. Project-Syndicate, 2018-03-15, https://www.project-syndicate.org/commentary/a-strategic-alliance-for-japan-and-india-by-shinzo-abe.

[3] Department of Defence of Australia Government, Defence White Paper 2009, http://www.defence.gov.au/whitepaper/2009/docs/defence_white_paper_2009.pdf.

[4] Hillary Clinton, "America's Pacific Century", Foreign Policy, November 2011, http://www.foreignpolicy.com/articles/2011/10/11/americas_pacific_century?page=full.

[5] Opening Statement by Prime Minister at Plenary Session of India-ASEAN Commemorative Summit, [EB/OL] 2012-12-20, http://www.mea.gov.in/Speeches-Statements.htm?dtl/20981/opening+statement+by+prime+minister+at+plenary+session+of+indiaasean+commemorative+summit.

the "Indo-Pacific" strategy. In 2013, Australia published the Defense White Paper,[6] became the first country to endow the "Indo-Pacific" region with the geostrategic significance at the level of policy, and included it into the "one-track" operation. Till 2017, the country's Foreign Policy White Paper[7] mentioned the "Indo-Pacific" region for more than 120 times. In Japan, during visit to the U.S. in 2013, Shinzo Abe regarded "Indo-Pacific" and "Asia-Pacific" as a whole, and mentioned that Japan must play a dominant role in the region.[8] In 2016, Shinzo Abe officially proposed the "Free and Open India-Pacific" Strategy at the 6th Tokyo International Conference on African Development.[9] In 2018, in his speech for policy proposal for the parliament, Shinzo Abe mentioned in the section of overlook of global diplomacy to "work with countries with such basic values as freedom, democracy, human rights and rule of law, like the U.S., Europe, ASEAN, Australia and India, so as to ensure peace and prosperity from the Asia-Pacific region to the Indian Ocean region", and frankly said that "Japan will push a 'free and open India-Pacific strategy'".[10]

Compared with Japan and Australia, India is not very positive about the "Indo-Pacific" concept, but pays more attention to the Act East Policy.[11] In 2015, the country issued the maritime security strategy to expand its maritime interests to the entire Western Pacific,[12] but still did not independently propose the "Indo-Pacific" strategy. In fact, India only mentions "Indo-Pacific" in bilateral and multilateral cooperation. For instance, in 2015, India and Japan jointly announced the establishment of a special strategic and global partnership to maintain the peace and prosperity in the "Indo-Pacific" region and the world[13]; in 2017, during his visit to the U.S., Narendra Modi proposed that the U.S. and India promote the stability of the "Indo-Pacific"

[6]Australian Government Department of Defence, Defence White Paper 2013, http://www.defence.gov.au/whitepaper/2013/docs/WP_2013_web.pdf.

[7]2017 Foreign Policy White Paper, https://www.fpwhitepaper.gov.au/foreign-policy-white-paper.

[8]Shinzo Abe, Japan Is Back (policy speech at Center for Strategic and International Studies) [EB/OL]. 2013-02-23, https://www.kantei.go.jp/cn/96_abe/statement/201302/23speech.html.

[9]Shinzo Abe, speech at the opening ceremony of the 6th Tokyo International Conference on African Development (ITCAD VI), [EB/OL]. 2016-08-27, https://www.kantei.go.jp/cn/97_abe/statement/201608/1218963_11159.html.

[10]Shinzo Abe, Policy Speech by Prime Minister Shinzo Abe to the 196th Session of the Diet [EB/OL]. 2018-01-22, https://www.kantei.go.jp/cn/98_abe/statement/201801/20180122siseihousin.html.

[11]Manish Chand, Act East: India's ASEAN Journey, [EB/OL]. 2014-12-10, http://www.mea.gov.in/in-focus-article.htm?24216/act+east+indias+asean+journey.

[12]Ensuring Secure Seas: Indian Maritime Security Strategy, https://www.indiannavy.nic.in/sites/default/files/Indian_Maritime_Security_Strategy_Document_25Jan16.pdf.

[13]Joint Statement on India and Japan Vision 2025: Special Strategic and Global Partnership Working Together for Peace and Prosperity of the Indo-Pacific Region and the World, [EB/OL]. 2015-12-12, http://www.mea.gov.in/bilateral-documents.htm?dtl/26176/joint+statement+on+india+and+japan+vision+2025+special+strategic+and+global+partnership+working+together+for+peace+and+prosperity+of+the+indopacific+region+and+the+worlddecember+12+2015.

region[14]; in 2017, while the U.S., Japan, Australia and India focused on common interests of the "Indo-Pacific" region in negotiations, India adhered to the "Act East Policy" as the cornerstone of its participation in the "Indo-Pacific" region.[15]

Regardless of the attitudes of Japan, Australia and India, it is the U.S. that is the decisive force in advancing the "Indo-Pacific" strategy. After holding the office, Donald Trump had not explicitly mentioned the "Indo-Pacific"; until Narendra Modi visited the U.S. in 2017, Donald Trump used the concept for the first time on diplomatic occasions. In the same year, then-Secretary of State Rex Tillerson made several references to "Indo-Pacific" in his speeches on the U.S.-India relations and subsequent visits to India. In November 2017, Donald Trumpbegan promoting the U.S.-led "Indo-Pacific" strategy in Asia, and specifically elaborated the "Indo-Pacific" concept in the National Security Strategy Report,[16] and officially substituted Obama administration's "Asia-Pacific" strategy with the "Indo-Pacific" strategy. The shift in the U.S. attitudes may be conducive to achieving the strategy with the help of the "four-country cooperation". In fact, the "four-country cooperation" launched by Japan in 2007 was a tentative security cooperation across the "Indo-Pacific", which however was not achieved due to different strategic goals among the countries. Along with the constant frustration in the globalization over the subsequent decade, the "four-country cooperation" only makes a comeback this time. On November 12, 2017, the U.S., Japan, India and Australia discussed the "common interests of the Indo-Pacific region" during the APEC Economic Leaders' Meeting.[17] A decade later, the four-country security cooperation dialogue restarted, marking that the "Indo-Pacific" concept was officially accepted by the four countries.[18]

Compared with policy makers, strategic analysts and scholars conducted more advanced researches on the geopolitical significance of the "Indo-Pacific". In early 1900s and around 2007, they made discussions, but failed to further continue the discussions. After 2010, the governments of the four countries successively introduced the "Indo-Pacific" into the regional strategic framework, which unleashed the third upsurge of exploring the geopolitics of the "Indo-Pacific" in the academic circles. On the basis of literatures, these academic researches focused on the "Indo-Pacific" concept, the origin of the "Indo-Pacific" and the forming process of the "Indo-Pacific" strategy mainly in dimensions of time and space from perspectives of geopolitics, security and economics.

[14] Joint Statement-United States and India: Prosperity through Partnership, [EB/OL]. 2017-06-27, http://www.mea.gov.in/bilateral-documents.htm?dtl/28560/joint+statement++united+states+and+india+prosperity+through+partnership.

[15] India-Australia-Japan-U.S. Consultations on Indo-Pacific, [EB/OL]. 2017-12-12, http://www.mea.gov.in/press-releases.htm?dtl/29110/indiaaustraliajapanus+consultations+on+indopacific+november+12+2017.

[16] National Security Strategy of the United States of America. https://www.whitehouse.gov/wp-content/uploads/2017/12/NSS-Final-12-18-2017-0905.pdf.

[17] Australia-India-Japan-United States Consultations on the Indo-Pacific, http://dfat.gov.au/news/media/Pages/aus-india-japan-us-consultations-on-the-indo-pacific.aspx.

[18] Lin (2018).

There are controversies in the origin of the "Indo-Pacific" concept in the academic circles. Some scholars (Chacko 2016)[19] tended to believe that Indian scholar Khurana (2007) first proposed the "Indo-Pacific" concept, while the first state head who used the concept is Shinzo Abe, Japan's Prime Minister.[20] However, as Australian scholar Scott (2012) said, the "Indo-Pacific" concept is not a new creation,[21] because the bio-geographical concept of "Indian Ocean-Pacific Ocean" emerged long time ago, the region refers to the lands and oceans connecting the Indian Ocean to the Western Pacific.[22] Therefore, the "Indo-Pacific" concept involved in this paper only applies the original geographical concept in exploration of geopolitics or policy practice. From the perspective of the origin of use the conceptual geo-development, more researches (Scott 2012; Medcalf 2012, 2015) discovered that the first person who used the "Indo-Pacific" concept in the field of geopolitics is German geopolitician Karl Haushofer. Since 1924, he mentioned the concept of Indopazifischen Raum (the "Indo-Pacific" region/space)[23] in more than 30 geopolitics papers; relevant researches were scattered in a few academic discussions in early and mid-20th century, but later suspended. In 2017, Indian scholar Khurana acknowledged that Australians used the geopolitical concept of "Indo-Pacific" first, but pointed out that he was the first scholar to introduce and interpret the concept in recent years (Khurana 2017).

Scholars generally believe there are two reasons for the originality of the "Indo-Pacific".[24] First, scholars believe that the implementation of the "Indo-Pacific" concept and strategy is an objective result of the global development, because the shift of global geostrategic emphasis and geo-economic center towards "Indo-Pacific" leads to common strategic concerns of all countries. Second, the rapid rise of China and its rising influence in the "Indo-Pacific" region become common concerns of the U.S., Japan, Australia and India. In this case, balancing China's influence in the region becomes the main reason for promoting the "Indo-Pacific" strategy. Therefore, China is selectively excluded from most of relevant security cooperation and economic cooperation discussions. In addition, although the "Indo-Pacific" strategy has common target objects, the four countries have different strategic objectives. For example, the U.S. focuses on geopolitics and military security, but not economic

[19]Mercy A. Kuo, The Origin of 'Indo- Pacific' as Geopolitical Construct, THE DIPLOMAT, 2018-1-25, https://thediplomat.com/2018/01/the-origin-of-indo-pacific-as-geopolitical-construct/.

[20]Abe (2007).

[21]Scott (2012).

[22]Wikipedia, Indo-Pacific, https://en.wikipedia.org/wiki/Indo-Pacific.

[23]Weigert (1942).

[24]Note: As for the origin of "Indo-Pacific", scholars of various countries have some similar conclusions, reference: C Raja Mohan, Samudera Manthan: Sino-Indian Rivalry in the Indo-Pacific, http://carnegieendowment.org/files/Samudra_Manthan_Brief1.pdf; Scott (2013); Wu (2014); Saroj Bishoyi, Geosrategic Imperative of the Indo-Pacific Region: Emerging Trends and Regional Responses, https://idsa.in/system/files/jds/jds_10_1_2015_geostrategic-imperative-of-the-indo-pacific-region.pdf; Yellow River, Containment Thinking in Evolution of U.S. Geopolitical Strategy: from "Selective Containment" to "Indo-Pacific Strategy" [J]. Journal of Shenzhen University (Humanities & Social Sciences), January 2018, pp. 72–78; Xia (2015).

integration and prosperity in the region[25]; Japan expects to restore its geo-economic influence, in addition to imposing the strategic containment on China on a larger scale[26]; India is unsatisfied with China's expansion in the Indian Ocean and wants to extend its influence eastward into the western Pacific, but doesn't unreservedly promote the "Indo-Pacific" strategy because it is unwilling to become a chess piece against China under the U.S.-led strategic framework[27]; Australia's strategic objectives are to balance China's influence, maximize its geographical advantages in the two oceans, and become a moderator among big countries in the "Indo-Pacific" region, while make profits in security and economy.[28,29]

So far, during the research and practice of the "geo-politics application" for the "Indo-Pacific" concept, both decision makers and scholars have endowed significance the "Indo-Pacific" geopolitics, geo-security and geo-economics with significance. Therefore, the "Indo-Pacific" is both a geopolitical concept and a geo-economic concept.[30] Nevertheless, existing researches only adopt the perspectives of geopolitics and geo-security rather than the geo-economic perspective. The main reasons may be as follows. First, the concept of geo-economics was proposed in 1990s, and there has still not been a complete analytical framework and theory up to now; second, scholars mostly believe that geo-economics is at the service of geopolitics and geo-security and there's no need to discuss as a special topic; third, the function of economics is mainly post-event explanation, and "Indo Pacific" is only a concept with a vague regional scope and there's no substantive cooperation even in the seemingly solid "quadrilateral cooperation". At present, in researches for the "Indo-Pacific", the content involving geo-economics mainly analyzes the origin of the strategy. In 2013, only American and Indian scholars proposed the concept of Indo-Pacific Economic Corridor (IPEC) from the perspective of cross-regional economic cooperation,[31,32] but with no subsequent practice or further discussion. In fact, the two explanations for the origin of the "Indo-Pacific", namely the "shift of the world's economic center" and the "counterbalancing China's increasing geo-presence", still remain in qualitative researches or common sense recognition of scholars. This paper chooses to verify the two theories of origin with the international economic indica-

[25]Liu (2014).

[26]Zhu (2016).

[27]C. Raja Mohan, Donald Trump's 'Indo-Pacific' and America's India Conundrum, https://www.isas.nus.edu.sg/wp-content/uploads/media/isas_papers/ISAS%20Insights%20No.%20476-%20Donald%20Trump's%20'Indo-Pacific'%20and%20America's%20India%20Conundrum.pdf.

[28]Hu Xin, "Australian Dream": Being A Middle Power in the "Indo-Pacific" Region [J] Around China, pp. 32–34.

[29]IPCS Book Discussion, The Indo-Pacific: Political and Strategic Perspective, http://www.ipcs.org/pdf_file/issue/SR162-BookReview-IndoPacific.pdf.

[30]Scott (2013).

[31]USAID, Indo-Pacific Economic Corridor: Coordinated Regional Trade Analysis. https://banyanglobal.com/wp-content/uploads/2017/06/Indo-Pacific-Economic-Economic-Corridor.pdf.

[32]Shankari Sundararaman, Indo-Pacific Economic Corridor: A Vision in Progress. http://www.orfonline.org/research/indo-pacific-economic-corridor-a-vision-in-progress/.

tor analysis method; based on that, it tries to explain the cognitive bias of the four countries in the "Indo-Pacific" strategy with the geo-economic logic.

2 "Indo-Pacific" Regional Economic Development Analysis: "Asia-Pacific" as Reference

2.1 "Indo-Pacific" Geo-economic Scope Definition

Up to now, although the U.S., Japan, Australia and India have different definitions of the "Indo-Pacific" region, they have made changes along with the adjustment in their foreign strategic emphasis, but shown a general trend of increasingly broadening of the scope. For example, in 2007 and 2012, Japan proposed "the convergence of the two oceans" and the "Asia's Democratic Security Diamond" respectively, and proposed scope generally included the western Pacific and the eastern Indian Ocean; when Japan advocated the free navigation in Africa in 2016, it obviously extended the scope of "Indo-Pacific" to the east coast of Africa. Indian has always emphasized "Look East" and "Act East", and actually focused on the eastern Indian Ocean and the Southeast Asia. The Australian government explicitly proposed that the "Indo-Pacific" refers to the western Pacific and the entire Indian Ocean region in 2012; but now it prefers the broad scope of "Indo-Pacific" proposed by the U.S., namely from the eastern Pacific coast to the western Indian Ocean coast.

Because the ambiguous regional scope is not conducive to the research of geo-economics, this paper selected representative regional organizations or regional organizational groups for an alternative research. First, "Indo-Pacific" and "Asia-Pacific" regional scopes shall be defined according to the research content. Specifically, the 21 official members of APEC will represent the "Asia-Pacific" region,[33] ASEAN, South Asian Association For Regional Cooperation (SAARC), Gulf Cooperation Council (GCC), Common Market for Eastern and Southern Africa (COMESA) and some regional important countries, such as China, Japan, Korea, Australia, New Zealand, Iran and Iraq will represent the "Indo-Pacific" region,[34] and the area, population, GDP, per capita GDP, trade import and export quotas, and FDI inflow and outflow were taken as comparative indicators. Among them, the representativeness of APEC

[33]Note: 21 official APEC members are Australia, Brunei, Canada, Chile, China, Hong Kong, China, Indonesia, Japan, South Korea, Malaysia, Mexico, New Zealand, Papua New Guinea, Peru, the Philippines, Russia, Singapore, Chinese Taipei, Thailand, the U.S., Vietnam.

[34]Note: A total of 50 countries, including ASEAN 10 + 3 countries: Brunei, Cambodia, Indonesia, Laos, Malaysia, Burma, the Philippines, Singapore, Thailand, Vietnam and China (excluding Hong Kong, Macao and Taiwan), Japan, South Korea; 2 Australian countries: Australia, New Zealand; 8 SAARC countries: India, Nepal, Bhutan, Bangladesh, Pakistan, Afghanistan, Sri Lanka and Maldives; GCC 6 + 2 countries: Iran, Iraq, Bahrain, Kuwait, Oman, Qatar, Saudi Arabia, UAE; 19 COMESA countries: Burundi, Comoros, Democratic Republic of Congo, Djibouti, Egypt, Eritrea, Ethiopia, Kenya, Libya, Madagascar, Malawi, Mauritius, Rwanda, Seychelles, Sudan, Swaziland, Uganda, Zambia and Zimbabwe.

for "Asia-Pacific" is high recognized; ASEAN and China, Japan and Korea are the most representative regional cooperation organizations in the western Pacific region; Australia and New Zealand are in the junction of the eastern Indian Ocean and the western Pacific; SAARC contains all of countries in the eastern Indian Ocean region; GCC, Iran and Iraq are the most important economic combinations in the northern Indian Ocean and the Gulf regions; and COMESA represents the cluster of important countries on the west bank of the Indian Ocean.

2.2 *"Asia-Pacific" and "Indo-Pacific": Comparison of Economic and Trade Development, and Intra-regional Economic Integration*

2.2.1 From "Asia-Pacific" to "Indo-Pacific": Comparison of Economic and Trade Development

"Asia-Pacific" covers a total area of about 60.136 million km^2, taking up 46.35% of the global total. Its total population is about 2.898 billion, taking up 40.68% of the global total. Its GDP is about US$45.41 trillion, occupying 60.02% of the global total; the per capita GDP is about US$15,767, which is 1.54 times of the global level; its FDI inflow and outflow were US$926.273 billion and US$875.528 billion respectively, accounting for 53.04 and 60.28% of the global totals; the trade import and export quotas were US$801.905 billion and US$7992.271 billion respectively, taking up 49.65 and 49.99% of the global totals. "Indo-Pacific" covers a total area of about 40.692 million km^2, taking up 31.37% of the global total. Its total population is about 4.706 billion, taking up 66.05% of the global total. Its GDP is about US$27.13 trillion, occupying 35.86% of the global total; the per capita GDP is about US$19,109, which is 1.87 times of the global level; its FDI inflow and outflow were US$391.003 billion and US$430.560 billion, accounting for 22.39 and 29.64% of the global totals; the trade import and export quotas were US$508.513 billion and US$571.554 billion respectively, taking up 31.49 and 35.75% of the global totals. "Indo-Pacific" and "Asia-Pacific" have regional overlapping in East Asia, ASEAN and Australia.[35] The region's global GDP share is 28.57%, import and export respectively account for 24.10 and 24.84% of the world's totals, and FDI inflow and outflow take up respectively 17.61 and 27.33% of the world's totals.

The analysis shows that based on such indicators as land area, total GDP, trade value and FDI, "Asia-Pacific" still boasts the largest economic magnitude, trade vol-

[35]Note: In this research, the cross countries in both the "Asia-Pacific" and the "Indo-Pacific" are China, Japan, Korea, Brunei, Indonesia, Malaysia, Singapore, the Philippines, Thailand, Vietnam, Australia and New Zealand. The influence of the two regions on the global economy cannot be simply added up, and the impacting factors of overlapping regions are not necessarily excluded from the comparison. In subsequent researches, data of overlapping regions will be processed when necessary.

ume and investment volume. "Indo-Pacific" features a large population, but with an unbalanced interregional development. Among them, ASEAN 10 + 3 countries show high economic indicators, with a good comprehensive development; SAARC witnesses a fast-growing GDP, with a low trade level; GCC records a high per capita GDP, but with a low economic growth rate and a narrow market; and COMESA registers backward development in general (see Table 1). In terms of trade structure, "Asia-Pacific" occupies a larger export share of manufactured goods, while "Indo-Pacific" accounts for higher export proportions of primary products and labor-intensive products (see Table 2). In terms of Ease of Doing Business Index, "Asia-Pacific" boasts a generally better business environment, and the remaining countries, except for Papua New Guinea, have a higher rank; on the contrary, "Indo-Pacific" countries have a lower business environment score in general; particularly, SAARC and COMESA countries have a very lower Ease of Doing Business Index, which pulls down the regional average level (see Table 3). With respect to the development trend, in recent years, the "Indo-Pacific" region' has higher comprehensive GDP growth rate and average trade growth rate than "Asia-Pacific", but with a lower average growth rate of FDI than "Asia-Pacific" (see Fig. 1).

2.2.2 From "Asia-Pacific" to "Indo-Pacific": Comparison of Economic and Trade Influence Development

Through the comparison between "Asia-Pacific" and "Indo-Pacific" in the 10-year economic development, it can be seen that the influence of both regions on global import and export declined in 2016, whereas the influence on GDP, and FDI inflow and outflow slightly increased. Specifically, the weight of APEC in global total GDP accounted for 60.02%, that of import and export trade still took up half of the total (49.65 and 49.99%), that of FDI inflow and outflow occupied 53.04 and 60.28%, and that of FDI stock inflow and outflow also accounted for 53.87 and 55.32%, respectively. In addition, the development trend of recent years suggested increasing proportions of investment invitation and investment in the region.

In comparison, the contribution of "Indo-Pacific" to global economy and trade is much lower than that of "Asia-Pacific". In 2016, its proportion in global GDP was 35.86%, that in global import and export were 31.49 and 35.75%, those in FDI inflow and outflow were 22.39 and 29.64%, and those in FDI stock inflow and outflow were only 11.02 and 5.70% respectively. In fact, the region only have stronger investment invitation and investment strengths in ASEAN, but with lower FDI flow and stock levels in the other three areas and limited increases in the past decade (see Table 4). In terms of the growth rate, the momentum of "Indo-Pacific" exceeds that of "Asia-Pacific". For example, during 2006 and 2016, the global proportions of GDP, import, export, FDI inflow and FDI outflow of "Asia-Pacific" increased by 4.87 percentage points, 2.51 percentage points, 5.06 percentage points, 11.70 percentage points and 24.21 percentage points, whereas those "Indo-Pacific" increased by 10.58 percentage points, 6.10 percentage points, 5.36 percentage points, 4.40 percentage points and 18.47 percentage points, respectively (see Fig. 2).

Table 1 General table of economic and trade situations of "Indo-Pacific" and "Asia-Pacific" (2016)

Country	Total GDP (US$1 million)	GDP growth rate (%)	Per capital GDP (US$)	Land area (1000 km^2)	Total population (1 million people)	FDI inflow (US$1 million)	FDI outflow (US$1 million)	Trade import (US$1 million)	Trade export (US$1 million)
ASEAN	2,555,865	4.73	3990	4325	640	101,093	35,405	1,085,700	1,151,831
SAARC	2,891,893	6.85	1637	4771	1766	50,363	5448	489,471	332,191
GCC	1,346,509	2.13	24,927	2572	54	17,910	26,745	455,733	588,255
COMESA	693,664	4.07	1333	9168	520	17,777	968	141,591	67,521
Iran	42,5402	13.40	5299	1628	80	3372	104	40,000	69,000
Iraq	160,021	10.99	4301	434	37	−5911	304	38,713	43,890
Australia	1,304,463	1.98	54,069	7682	24	48,190	6011	196,137	191,152
New Zealand	187,517	3.04	40,232	263	5	2291	−43	36,062	33,740
China	11,218,281	7.25	7993	9388	1403	133,700	183,100	1,587,925	2,097,632
Japan	4,936,212	1.02	38640	364	127	11,388	145,242	607,602	644,899
Korea	1,411,246	2.83	27,784	97	50	10,826	27,274	406,192	495,426
"Indo-Pacific" region's total	**27,131,073**	**4.75**	**19,109**	**40,692**	**4706**	**39,1003**	**430,560**	**5,085,128**	**5,715,539**
APEC	**45,403,700**	**2.84**	**15,666**	**60,136**	**2898**	**926,273**	**875,528**	**8,019,053**	**7,992,271**
Global total	**75,648,868**	**2.45**	**10,189**	**129,733.92**	**7124.54**	**1,746,423**	**1,452,463**	**16,150,393**	**15,986,094**

Source Population, trade and investment data is sourced from UNTCAD STAT, and other data is sourced from World Bank Database

Table 2 Comparison of regional foreign trade structure between "Indo-Pacific" and "Asia-Pacific" (2016)

Product category	SITC0	SITC1	SITC2	SITC3	SITC4	SITC5	SITC6	SITC7	SITC8	SITC9
APEC	5.20	0.79	4.59	9.81	0.34	10.01	10.55	42.89	12.18	3.64
Import and export structure	4.99	0.48	3.69	6.86	0.58	8.30	11.94	43.77	13.87	5.53
ASEAN	6.50	0.69	2.90	11.77	0.55	10.47	14.19	43.41	7.38	2.14
Import and export structure	7.38	0.79	3.43	9.93	3.08	8.56	8.84	41.07	14.44	2.48
SAARC	4.77	0.18	5.59	21.25	3.09	12.14	17.87	23.91	5.13	6.07
Import and export structure	10.15	0.45	3.24	8.60	0.34	11.59	24.74	13.61	25.64	1.63
GCC	9.35	1.02	2.07	3.26	0.45	7.71	15.60	38.25	13.68	8.61
Import and export structure	2.67	0.47	1.57	54.33	0.25	10.94	9.97	7.25	4.60	7.96
COMESA	12.98	0.92	3.63	11.91	1.98	13.06	17.11	29.10	7.40	1.92
Import and export structure	18.66	3.40	7.87	16.72	0.65	7.72	22.70	4.93	7.34	9.68

Source Calculation and tabulation are based on UNCTAD Stat

Notes

SITC is an international trade standard classification

SITC0–4 refers to primary products, and SITC5–9 refers to manufactured products (SITC5 and SITC7 refer to capital-intensive products, SITC6 and SITC8 refers to labor-intensive products, and SITC9 refers to other unclassified products).Specifically, SITC-0 is food and live animals; SITC-1 is beverages and tobaccos; SITC-2 is non-edible raw materials (excluding fuel); SITC-3 is fossil fuels, lubricants and related fuels; SITC-4 is animal and vegetable oil, grease and wax; SITC-5 is chemicals and relevant products; SITC-6 is manufactured products classified by raw materials; SITC-7 is machinery and transport equipment; SITC-8 is miscellaneous products; SITC-9 is other commodities not otherwise classified by Standard International Trade Classification

Table 3 Ranking of "Indo-Pacific" and "Asia-Pacific" countries in Ease of Doing Business Index in 2017

Region	APEC		ASEAN countries		GCC, Iran, Iraq and SAARC		COMESA	
No.	Country	Ranking	Country	Ranking	Country	Ranking	Country	Ranking
1	New Zealand	1	Singapore	2	UAE	26	Mauritius	49
2	Hong Kong, China	4	Malaysia	23	Bahrain	63	Rwanda	56
3	Korea	5	Thailand	46	Oman	66	Kenya	92
4	The U.S.	8	Brunei	72	Qatar	83	Seychelles	93
5	Taiwan, China	11	Vietnam	82	Saudi Arabia	94	Zambia	98
6	Australia	15	Indonesia	91	Kuwait	102	Uganda	115
7	Canada	22	The Philippines	99	Iran	120	Egypt	122
8	Japan	34	Cambodia	131	Iraq	165	Malawi	133
9	Russia	40	Laos	139	Bhutan	73	Comorin	153
10	Mexico	47	Myanmar	170	Nepal	107	Burundi	157
11	Peru	54			Sri Lanka	110	Ethiopia	159
12	China	78			India	130	Zimbabwe	161
13	Chile	57			Maldives	135	Madagascar	167
14	Papua New Guinea	119			Pakistan	144	Djibouti	171
15					Bangladesh	176	Libya	174
16					Afghanistan	183	Congo Democratic	177
17							Sudan	168
18							Libya	188
19							Eritrea	189

Source Tabulation is derived from World Bank Database
Note APEC has a total of 21 members, and 7 of them belong to ASEAN

According to the main index data, economic aggregate and global weight of "Asia-Pacific" were much higher than those of "Indo-Pacific", indicating that the global economic center is obviously still in "Asia-Pacific". In terms of growth momentum, GDP and trade influence of "Indo-Pacific" increased faster, while the contribution of "Asia-Pacific" to FDI still increased much faster than that of "Indo-Pacific".

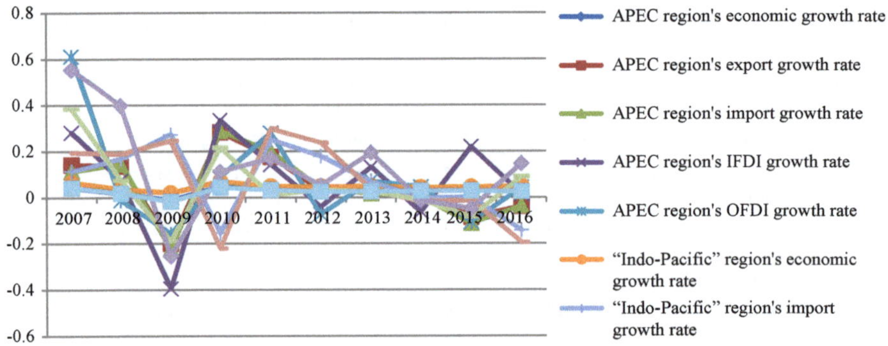

Fig. 1 Economic and trade growth trend of "Indo-Pacific" and "Asia-Pacific". *Source* Calculation and charting are based on UNCTAD Stat

2.2.3 From "Asia-Pacific" to "Indo-Pacific": Comparison of Economic and Trade Openness Development

Regional economic and trade openness can be analyzed based on the foreign trade dependence index and the foreign capital dependence index of regional organizations. (FDI stock index is adopted in this paper).

In terms of foreign trade, APEC's foreign trade dependence in 2016 was 34.39%. The trade dependences of ASEAN, SAARC, GCC and COMESA were 82.87, 28.80, 79.20 and 30.40% respectively. The figures of all regions except for ASEAN and GCC were below the global average of 41.06%. In recent years, the foreign trade dependences of these regional organizations have shown a trend of sharp decline, indicating that all regions haven been trying to reduce their dependence on foreign trade. To some extent, it can also be seen as the result of the slowdown of the globalization process.

In terms of foreign capital, APEC's FDI stock inflow and outflow dependences in 2016 were respectively 31.71 and 31.87%. ASEAN's dependences were 73.25 and 40.72%, SAARC's dependences were 13.31 and 5.12%, GCC's dependences were 30.24 and 20.36%, and COMESA's dependences were 34.96 and 6.38%, respectively. Among them, the dependences of ASEAN and GCC were higher than the global average of 35.07 and 34.56% (see Fig. 3). According to the trend analysis, the foreign capital contribution to the regional economic growth has increased rapidly. As the GDP level has been rising, the increased foreign capital dependence indicates that all parties have increased their efforts in investment attraction.

Table 4 Comparison of investment strength development between "Indo-Pacific" and "Asia-Pacific"

Year	2006	2007	2008	2009	2010	2011	2012	2013	2014	2015	2016
Global proportions of APEC's FDI inflow and outflow											
Inflow	41.34	39.13	53.46	40.68	46.66	46.36	44.37	55.37	56.62	51.49	53.04
Outflow	36.07	36.31	45.43	59.48	51.47	57.82	60.80	64.56	75.31	52.75	60.28
Inflow stock	48.39	47.23	41.31	42.98	45.64	45.05	46.75	49.23	51.11	51.69	53.87
Outflow stock	50.42	50.47	41.27	45.04	46.90	45.87	49.06	51.85	53.97	53.79	55.32
Global proportions of ASEAN's FDI inflow and outflow											
Inflow	4.48	4.39	3.33	3.92	7.99	5.96	6.78	8.74	9.85	7.14	5.79
Outflow	2.15	2.88	1.82	4.37	4.48	3.93	4.07	5.85	7.08	3.49	2.44
Inflow stock	3.94	4.11	5.06	4.87	5.65	6.01	6.50	6.54	7.00	7.20	7.00
Outflow stock	2.12	2.27	2.53	2.55	2.88	3.11	3.36	3.46	3.74	3.78	3.87
Global proportions of SAARC's FDI inflow and outflow											
Inflow	1.86	1.71	3.64	3.32	2.26	2.52	1.74	2.26	2.97	2.75	2.88
Outflow	–	–	1.24	1.47	1.16	0.80	0.62	0.14	0.96	0.48	0.38
Inflow stock	0.67	0.79	1.00	1.10	1.19	1.16	1.17	1.11	1.24	1.36	1.45
Outflow stock	–	–	–	0.43	0.47	0.52	0.53	0.49	0.54	0.57	0.56
Global proportions of GCC's FDI inflow and outflow											
Inflow	2.78	2.49	3.59	4.08	3.28	1.85	1.71	1.68	1.80	0.83	1.03
Outflow	1.50	1.42	2.00	1.36	1.12	1.70	1.22	2.85	1.15	2.03	1.84
Inflow stock	0.85	0.89	1.43	1.47	1.55	1.64	1.63	1.59	1.65	1.70	1.66
Outflow stock	0.37	0.44	0.70	0.62	0.64	0.75	0.74	0.80	0.89	1.03	1.14
Global proportions of COMESA's FDI inflow and outflow											
Inflow	1.20	1.26	1.39	1.48	1.39	0.59	1.28	1.17	1.20	1.02	1.02
Outflow	0.05	0.22	0.47	0.19	0.38	0.07	0.21	0.15	0.08	0.08	0.07
Inflow stock	0.52	0.54	0.76	0.74	0.76	0.77	0.79	0.80	0.84	0.90	0.91
Outflow stock	0.03	0.05	0.12	0.11	0.13	0.13	0.13	0.13	0.13	0.13	0.13

Source Calculation and tabulation are based on UNCTAD Stat

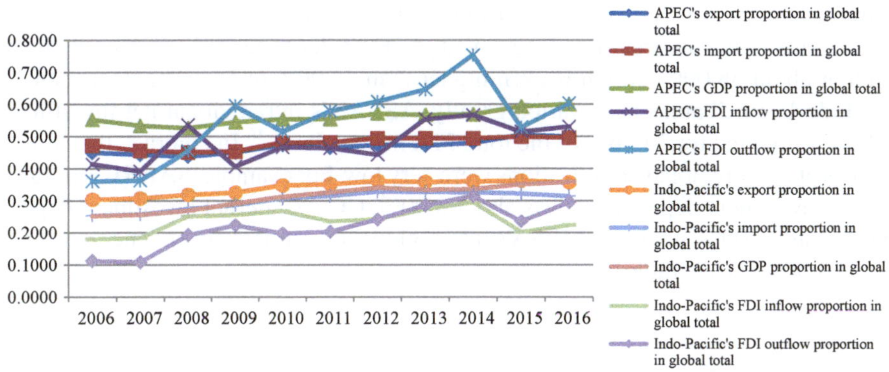

Fig. 2 Comparison between "Asia-Pacific" and "Indo-Pacific" in economic importance. *Source* Calculation and charting are based on UNCTAD Stat

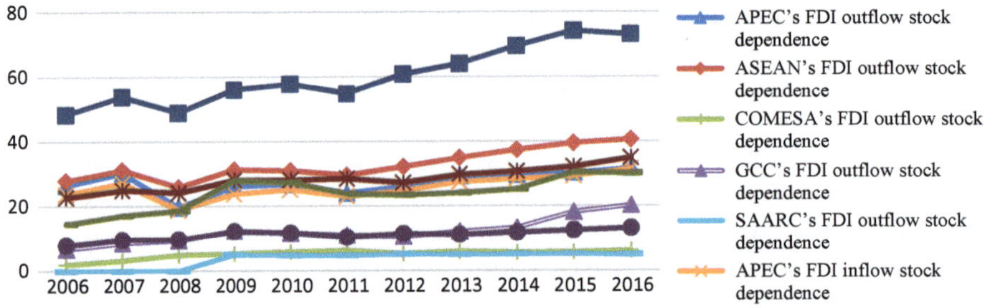

Fig. 3 Comparison of foreign capital dependence between the "Asia-Pacific" and the "Indo-Pacific". *Source* Calculation and charting are based on UNCTAD Stat

2.2.4 From the "Asia-Pacific" to the "Indo-Pacific": Comparison of Intra-regional Economic Integration Development

The indicators measuring regional economic integration are complicated. Due to the space limitation, two general indicators—regional trade dependence and regional investment dependence are selected in this paper.

According to the data of UNCTAD, the intraregional trade level of APEC has been very stable. Since 1990s, UNCTAD's intraregional import and export ratios in the total regional import and export have remained above 70%. Despite of slight declines in recent years, the figure has still maintained at around 69%. The intraregional trade ratio in the "Indo-Pacific" has been basically on the rise. From 2006 to 2016, ASEAN's intraregional import share increased from 18.68 to 22.71%, and its intraregional export share decreased from 24.76 to 24.17%; SAARC's intraregional import share increased from 4.40 to 5.18%, and its intraregional export share increased from 6.32 to 6.96%; GCC's intraregional import share decreased from 11.15 to 10.92%, and its intraregional export share increased from 5.68 to 10.44%; and COMESA's intraregional import share decreased from 6.23 to 5.27%, and its intraregional export share increased from 5.30 to 10.24%.

In terms of the intraregional investment, APEC's dependence has been relatively high or about 58.00%, which is even higher than 42.00% of EU. The dependences of "Indo-Pacific" areas have varied greatly. ASEAN's intraregional net investment inflow accounted for 24.76% of the total FDI in actual use.[36] In contrast, the dependences of other regional organizations were very low. For example, SAARC's intraregional investment dependence was about 3.00%, GCC's internal investment dependence was 23.00%, while COMESA's intraregional investment dependence was only about 8.00%[37] (see Table 5).

[36]UNCTD, ASEAN investment report 2017, http://unctad.org/en/PublicationsLibrary/unctad_asean_air2017d1.pdf.

[37]UNCTAD's bilateral investment data are only updated to 2011. http://unctad.org/meetings/en/SessionalDocuments/ciimem4d2_en.pdf.

Table 5 Intraregional investments of the "Indo-Pacific" areas and the "Asia-Pacific" areas

Area	Period	Intraregional investment proportion (%)
APEC	2003–2005	61.00
	2009–2011	58.00
ASEAN	2003–2005	11.00
	2009–2011	12.00
	2016	24.76
SAARC	2003–2005	2.00
	2009–2011	3.00
GCC	2003–2005	16.00
	2009–2011	23.00
COMESA	2003–2005	1.00
	2009–2011	8.00

Source Calculation and tabulation are based on UNCTAD Stat

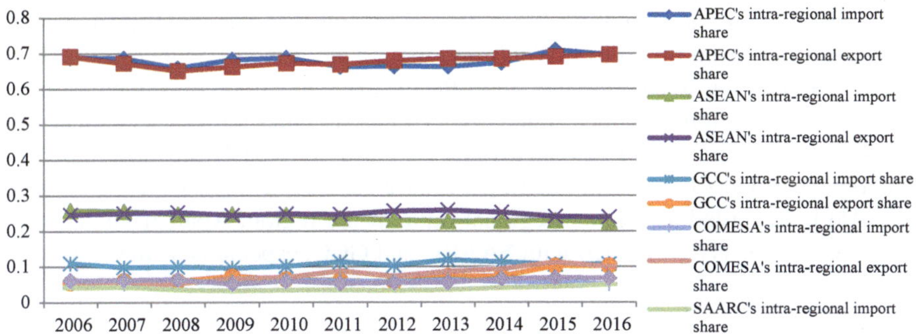

Fig. 4 Comparison of intraregional trade share between the "Asia-Pacific" and the "Indo-Pacific". *Source* Calculation and charting are based on UNCTAD Stat

On the whole, APEC's intraregional trade dependence and intraregional investment dependence have been on the decrease. However, over the years, they have maintained a high ratio, and the intraregional import and export ratios have been relatively symmetrical, indicating that the regional production structure and trade structure have become mature and stable to some extent. Besides, the intraregional trade share was also much higher than that of other regions (including EU), and the intraregional investment capacity and momentum have remained robust. In addition, by 2016, there have been 62 intraregional free trade agreements signed and implemented within APEC, with a more obvious intraregional growth trend. Meanwhile, although the two indicators of the "Indo-Pacific" areas are still improving, the development level in the region is obviously low (see Fig. 4).

2.3 *Development Analysis of Interregional Economic Relations Between the "Indo-Pacific" and the "Asia-Pacific"*

2.3.1 Interregional Trade Level Calculation of the "Indo-Pacific" and the "Asia-Pacific"

According to UNCTAD's data, in 2016, APEC imported a total of US$1.31 trillion of commodities from four areas of the "Indo-Pacific". Specifically, imports from ASEAN, SAARC, GCC and COMESA accounted for respectively 68.02, 11.26, 19.40 and 1.32%. It exported a total of US$1.39 trillion of commodities, with an interregional surplus of more than US$80 billion. Specifically, the proportions of exports to ASEAN, SAARC, GCC and COMESA took up respectively 64.44, 17.86, 13.76 and 3.94%. During 2006 and 2016, the proportion of APEC's export to ASEAN, SAARC, GCC and COMESA in its total export increased from 13.1 to 17.47%, and the proportion of its import from these areas decreased from 17.31 to 16.48%. Meanwhile, the proportion of the "Indo-Pacific" region's export to APEC in its total export reduced from 66.16 to 60.04%, and that of the import declined from 60.48 to 64.86%. It is fair to say that the "Indo-Pacific" region's trade dependence on the "Asia-Pacific" region remained much higher than the latter's trade dependence on the former. In addition, ASEAN or ASEAN 10 + 3 are obviously the most important economic partners of the "Asia-Pacific". Because the area belongs to APEC, its trade can also be regarded as the intraregional trade of the region. Apart from ASEAN, APEC is not closely correlated with SAARC and GCC, especially with COMESA.

2.3.2 Analysis of Inter-regional Trade Structure of the "Indo-Pacific" and the "Asia-Pacific"

According to the calculation based on the Standard International Trade Classification (SITC), from 2010 to 2016, the proportion of primary products in the two-way trade between APEC and the "Indo-Pacific" region was decreasing, while the proportion of manufactured goods was increasing. Specifically, the proportion of primary products imported from ASEAN decreased from 31.51 to 23.09%, whereas the proportion of primary products exported to ASEAN decreased from 21.26 to 18.65%; the proportion of primary products imported from SAARC fell from 36.34 to 19.24%, while the proportion of primary products exported to SAARC reduced from 23.59 to 19.59%; the proportion of primary products imported from GCC decreased from 91.41 to 84.30%, and the proportion of primary products exported to GCC decreased from 8.40 to 7.93%; the proportion of primary products imported from COMESA decreased from 72.52 to 44.81%, and the proportion of primary products exported to the market decreased from 23.72 to 15.30%.

As a whole, APEC mainly exports manufactured products to the "Indo-Pacific" region, especially six categories of labor-intensive products (manufactured prod-

Table 6 Import and export structures between APEC and ASEAN (*Unit %*)

	Imported commodity structure			Exported commodity structure		
Year	2010	2013	2016	2010	2013	2016
SITC0	5.27	5.35	6.16	4.67	4.91	5.77
SITC1	0.25	0.32	0.37	0.63	0.74	0.89
SITC2	5.41	5.31	3.98	2.43	2.22	2.32
SITC3	18.85	21.43	11.03	12.83	14.72	9.06
SITC4	1.73	1.53	1.55	0.70	0.51	0.61
SITC5	6.96	7.55	7.08	8.84	8.79	9.11
SITC6	7.18	7.35	7.51	14.87	15.69	16.63
SITC7	42.35	38.77	45.30	42.69	39.33	42.23
SITC8	9.22	10.66	13.74	7.68	9.50	9.42
SITC9	2.78	1.73	3.29	4.66	3.59	3.96

Source Calculation and tabulation are based on UNCTAD Stat

ucts classified by raw material) and seven categories of capital-intensive products (machinery and transportation equipment categories). Meanwhile, APEC mainly imports industrial manufactured products from ASEAN, SAARC and COMESA and primary manufactured products from GCC. For example, APEC mainly imports categories 3 (fossil fuel), 7 and 8 (miscellaneous) products from ASEAN, and exports categories 6 and 7 products to ASEAN; mainly imports categories 5 (chemical), 6, 7 and 8 products from SAARC, and exports categories 5, 6, 7 and 8 products to SAARC; intensively imports category 3 products from GCC (accounting for 83.33% of the total import from GCC), and mainly exports categories 6, 7 and 8 products to GCC; mainly imports categories 3, 6 and 8 products from COMESA, and mainly exports categories 6, 7 and 8 products to this market (see Tables 6, 7, 8 and 9).

2.3.3 Interregional Trade Complementarity Calculation Between the "Indo-Pacific" and the "Asia-Pacific"

To measure the trade complementarities between the "Asia-Pacific" and the "Indo-Pacific", the trade complementarity index (TCI) of APEC and the four areas of the "Indo-Pacific" can be calculated respectively. The results are shown in Tables 10, 11, 12 and 13.

In terms of primary products, the complementarities between APEC and the "Indo-Pacific" areas are quite different, but strong at both the export level and the import level. Besides, the overall complementarities are still rising.

With respect to export, APEC and ASEAN have strong complementarities in categories 0, 2 and 3 of primary products, and their complementarities are gradually increasing; and they weak complementarities in category 1 of products, and almost no complementarity in category 4 of products; APEC and SAARC have strong com-

Table 7 Import and export structures between APEC and SAARC (*Unit %*)

	Imported commodity structure			Exported commodity structure		
Year	2010	2013	2016	2010	2013	2016
SITC0	5.91	7.66	6.69	2.85	2.64	3.45
SITC1	0.28	0.27	0.27	0.14	0.09	0.11
SITC2	14.75	7.67	4.22	5.70	5.52	5.09
SITC3	14.95	13.43	7.58	10.52	10.88	7.44
SITC4	0.45	0.45	0.48	4.38	4.32	3.50
SITC5	10.17	12.61	14.03	13.49	13.45	12.64
SITC6	28.01	31.42	33.18	19.43	21.03	22.54
SITC7	8.68	8.59	10.50	32.15	29.46	33.87
SITC8	16.20	17.25	22.36	5.91	7.92	8.22
SITC9	0.59	0.65	0.69	5.43	4.70	3.13

Source Calculation and tabulation are based on UNCTAD Stat

Table 8 Import and export structures between APEC and GCC (*Unit %*)

	Imported commodity structure			Exported commodity structure		
Year	2010	2013	2016	2010	2013	2016
SITC0	0.09	0.07	0.16	4.99	4.51	4.64
SITC1	0.01	0.01	0.03	0.32	0.26	0.41
SITC2	0.56	0.44	0.78	1.17	1.08	1.19
SITC3	90.73	90.84	83.33	1.27	1.61	1.20
SITC4	0.02	0.05	0.02	0.65	0.47	0.49
SITC5	5.73	5.58	9.88	4.82	4.28	4.27
SITC6	1.35	1.36	3.23	17.34	16.48	15.74
SITC7	0.51	0.64	0.56	50.32	47.55	46.81
SITC8	0.20	0.29	0.52	13.64	15.99	15.84
SITC9	0.79	0.72	1.49	5.48	7.79	9.41

Source Calculation and tabulation are based on UNCTAD Stat

plementarities in categories 2 and 3, particularly category 4, weak complementarities in category 0, and almost no complementarity in category 1; APEC and GCC have strong complementarities in category 0, weak complementarities in category 1 and 2, almost no complementarity in category 3, and declining complementarities in category 4; APEC and COMESA have very strong complementarities in categories 0 and 2, especially category 4, but weak complementarities in categories 1 and 3.

In the aspect of import, APEC and ASEAN have very strong complementarities in categories 2, 3 and 4 of products, and relatively strong complementarities in categories 0 and 1 of products; APEC and SAARC have very strong complementarities in categories 0, 2 and 4 of products, relatively strong complementarities in category

Table 9 Import and export structures between APEC and COMESA (*Unit %*)

	Imported commodity structure			Exported commodity structure		
Year	2010	2013	2016	2010	2013	2016
SITC0	3.76	5.32	11.68	11.67	10.61	8.25
SITC1	1.30	3.35	5.43	0.19	0.28	0.18
SITC2	7.13	8.82	12.87	4.14	3.73	2.00
SITC3	60.32	48.09	14.76	3.54	3.79	1.47
SITC4	0.01	0.04	0.14	4.18	3.89	3.41
SITC5	2.44	2.07	1.96	6.73	7.75	7.27
SITC6	18.46	22.16	36.00	17.79	20.73	21.74
SITC7	0.47	0.95	1.39	36.63	32.42	35.39
SITC8	4.99	6.11	10.71	10.26	13.41	15.99
SITC9	1.11	3.08	5.05	4.87	3.38	4.31

Source Calculation and tabulation are based on UNCTAD Stat

3, and no complementarity in category 1; APEC and GCC have very strong complementarities in categories 3 and 4, and relatively weak complementarities in other categories; APEC and COMESA have very strong complementarities in categories 0–4 of products, especially increasing complementarities in categories 0, 1, 2 and 4.

With regard to manufactured products, APEC and the "Indo-Pacific" areas have relatively high overall complementarities, but with no big change in the complementarity degree in recent years.

In terms of export, APEC and ASEAN have very strong complementarities in categories 7, 8 and 9 of products, but mediocre complementarities in categories; APEC and SAARC have very strong complementarities in categories 6 and 9, certain complementarities in categories 5 and 7, and relatively weak complementarities in category 8; APEC and GCC have very strong complementarities in categories 6, 7, 8 and 9, but relatively weak complementarities in category 5; APEC and COMESA have very strong complementarities in category 6, certain complementarities in categories 5, 7 and 8, and relatively weak complementarities in category 9.

With respect to import, APEC and ASEAN have very strong complementarities in categories 7 and 8; APEC and SAARC have very strong complementarities in categories 6 and 8; APEC and GCC's complementarities are mainly reflected in category 9; APEC and COMESA have very strong complementarities in categories 6 and 9, and mediocre complementarities in other categories.

2.3.4 Energy and Transport Contributions of the "Indo-Pacific" to Economic Development of the "Asia-Pacific"

The importance of the "Indo-Pacific" to the "Asia-Pacific" and even the whole world comes more from its energy output, commodity transportation and relevant added

Table 10 Trade Complementarity Index between APEC and ASEAN in 2006–2016

Product category	2006	2007	2008	2009	2010	2011	2012	2013	2014	2015	2016
SITC0	0.51	0.55	0.56	0.54	0.56	0.59	0.58	0.58	0.61	0.63	0.67
	0.71	0.71	0.77	0.75	0.72	0.77	0.79	0.74	0.78	0.80	0.83
SITC1	0.29	0.28	0.28	0.28	0.28	0.29	0.32	0.33	0.33	0.36	0.37
	0.42	0.45	0.48	0.48	0.52	0.56	0.63	0.66	0.70	0.78	0.79
SITC2	0.71	0.72	0.75	0.82	0.68	0.69	0.71	0.70	0.70	0.71	0.80
	1.36	1.37	1.33	1.36	1.38	1.50	1.29	1.35	1.12	1.19	1.23
SITC3	0.43	0.46	0.50	0.52	0.58	0.70	0.58	0.44	0.55	0.62	0.65
	5.64	6.97	7.41	6.75	6.85	6.79	6.28	5.93	6.36	5.50	5.48
SITC4	0.20	0.20	0.23	0.24	0.26	0.31	0.29	0.20	0.23	0.25	0.27
	3.11	4.40	4.50	4.17	4.05	3.83	3.75	3.46	3.45	3.18	2.98
SITC5	0.62	0.62	0.65	0.60	0.64	0.67	0.66	0.65	0.65	0.64	0.64
	0.60	0.60	0.55	0.55	0.59	0.67	0.68	0.65	0.65	0.62	0.63
SITC6	1.07	1.00	0.99	0.95	0.96	0.97	0.96	0.93	0.94	0.88	0.86
	0.53	0.53	0.54	0.59	0.56	0.55	0.57	0.59	0.59	0.59	0.58
SITC7	0.98	0.99	1.07	0.99	1.05	1.13	1.08	1.10	1.11	1.07	1.06
	1.31	1.29	1.18	1.31	1.24	1.17	1.26	1.29	1.26	1.28	1.25
SITC8	2.23	2.30	2.31	2.29	2.16	2.14	2.09	2.10	2.06	1.92	1.78
	1.08	1.10	1.08	1.07	1.07	1.08	1.10	1.11	1.11	1.15	1.21
SITC9	1.11	1.19	0.74	1.55	1.19	1.06	1.77	1.72	2.07	1.95	2.31
	0.50	0.51	0.76	0.42	0.71	0.80	0.58	0.59	0.67	0.50	0.40

Source Calculation and tabulation are based on UNCTAD Stat
Notes
ASEAN's data is excluded from APEC's data in the calculation of the table
In the complementarity calculation of each category in the table below, the upper line represents the trade complementarity index of APEC's export and import, while the lower line represents the trade complementarity index of APEC's import and export

value. The Indian Ocean is considered to be the world's most strategic seaway, and half of global containers, 1/3 of bulk cargo and above 80% of oil products are shipped through sea areas of the "Indo-Pacific". According to data of BP, in 2016, about 34.20% of global oil production came from the Middle East, about 8.60% came from Africa, and 8.70% from came Australia and Southeast Asia; while about 38.50% of global oil exports came from the Middle East and North Africa in the Indian Ocean region. UNCTAD data also shows that in 2016, APEC imported about US$411.2 billion of oil from ASEAN, SAARC, GCC, Iran, Iraq, Australia, New Zealand and other main areas or countries of the Indian Ocean, accounting for 52.60% of the organization's total oil imports of the year. Among main East Asian countries, China imported about 65.38% of oil from countries in the Indian Ocean region, including 35.95% from GCC, Iran and Iraq, about 6.03% from Australia, about

Table 11 Trade Complementarity Index between APEC and SAARC in 2006–2016

Product category	2006	2007	2008	2009	2010	2011	2012	2013	2014	2015	2016
SITC0	0.50	0.45	0.41	0.42	0.41	0.35	0.33	0.35	0.42	0.48	0.53
	1.32	1.31	1.39	0.96	1.07	1.15	1.29	1.32	1.30	1.27	1.19
SITC1	0.09	0.08	0.06	0.05	0.07	0.07	0.08	0.07	0.08	0.09	0.11
	0.35	0.35	0.42	0.46	0.45	0.35	0.40	0.40	0.39	0.43	0.45
SITC2	1.88	1.70	1.39	1.46	1.27	1.18	1.29	1.29	1.38	1.45	1.52
	1.85	2.02	1.96	1.87	1.87	1.45	1.83	1.40	1.23	1.10	1.10
SITC3	1.20	1.36	1.31	1.35	1.23	1.22	1.23	1.33	1.45	1.49	1.62
	0.91	1.06	0.99	0.89	1.03	0.97	0.90	1.03	1.06	0.85	0.94
SITC4	4.98	5.49	4.66	5.53	5.70	5.15	5.32	5.24	5.84	5.52	5.56
	45.09	37.94	27.78	18.31	19.35	19.29	20.16	20.53	19.43	15.17	10.52
SITC5	0.73	0.71	0.83	0.72	0.75	0.75	0.71	0.71	0.77	0.76	0.75
	0.76	0.73	0.76	0.66	0.70	0.71	0.81	0.79	0.76	0.84	0.86
SITC6	1.09	1.04	1.04	1.18	1.30	1.25	1.09	1.24	1.24	1.33	1.41
	1.90	1.74	1.69	1.72	1.85	1.63	1.66	1.73	1.69	1.72	1.72
SITC7	0.85	0.83	0.81	0.82	0.74	0.72	0.66	0.66	0.64	0.70	0.75
	0.26	0.29	0.36	0.42	0.40	0.41	0.41	0.41	0.44	0.42	0.42
SITC8	0.42	0.40	0.38	0.39	0.38	0.39	0.49	0.45	0.42	0.45	0.46
	2.29	2.14	1.98	2.20	1.84	1.90	2.03	1.72	1.77	1.92	2.03
SITC9	1.98	1.66	1.58	1.93	2.48	2.79	2.53	1.93	1.80	2.07	1.41
	0.19	0.19	0.21	0.42	0.25	0.73	0.14	0.32	0.19	0.44	0.25

Source Calculation and tabulation are based on UNCTAD Stat

10.83% from ASEAN and 12.57% from the African continent; top 10 oil exporters to Japan included 8 countries in the Indian Ocean region, taking up 75.65% of Japan's total oil import; top 10 oil exporters to South Korea included 9 countries in the Indian Ocean region, occupying 67.70% of the country's oil import. In terms of energy and commodity transportation channel, the "Asia-Pacific" region, especially countries in the Western Pacific region, has been increasingly dependent on the Indian Ocean.

3 Geo-economic Pattern Development and Subject Analysis of the "Indo-Pacific"

Since 1990s, economic globalization and regional integration have deeply influenced the global geo-economic pattern. Under the competitive and cooperative geo-economics logics, major countries within and outside the region with an international economic capacity and geo-economic strategic adjustment are the main forces to change the geo-economic pattern, while trade and investment are the most direct and primary means. In this chapter, the development of the geo-economic pattern of the

Table 12 Trade Complementarity Index between APEC and GCC in 2006–2016

Product category	2006	2007	2008	2009	2010	2011	2012	2013	2014	2015	2016
SITC0	1.21	1.13	1.14	1.03	1.18	1.17	1.10	1.09	1.10	1.06	1.05
	0.20	0.20	0.19	0.24	0.26	0.19	0.17	0.17	0.18	0.29	0.31
SITC1	0.48	0.41	0.35	0.36	0.44	0.44	0.49	0.52	0.56	0.58	0.61
	0.19	0.20	0.17	0.29	0.21	0.18	0.37	0.41	0.48	0.42	0.47
SITC2	0.55	0.52	0.49	0.53	0.58	0.60	0.61	0.61	0.61	0.60	0.56
	0.26	0.32	0.38	0.33	0.34	0.36	0.33	0.32	0.38	0.53	0.53
SITC3	0.13	0.13	0.14	0.14	0.17	0.19	0.15	0.22	0.21	0.21	0.25
	5.87	6.03	5.11	5.39	5.00	4.49	4.11	4.20	4.52	5.33	5.91
SITC4	1.14	1.16	1.05	0.97	1.21	1.22	0.96	0.83	0.91	0.73	0.81
	14.86	12.30	11.99	11.12	12.07	11.72	8.58	9.19	10.21	8.31	7.64
SITC5	0.53	0.51	0.50	0.46	0.53	0.55	0.54	0.53	0.54	0.49	0.47
	0.46	0.49	0.46	0.51	0.62	0.61	0.62	0.56	0.60	0.75	0.81
SITC6	1.41	1.38	1.56	1.44	1.41	1.48	1.44	1.35	1.29	1.22	1.23
	0.34	0.36	0.35	0.52	0.53	0.44	0.39	0.42	0.44	0.65	0.69
SITC7	1.42	1.50	1.53	1.45	1.37	1.36	1.43	1.41	1.40	1.30	1.20
	0.14	0.15	0.14	0.22	0.15	0.13	0.19	0.23	0.24	0.22	0.22
SITC8	1.06	1.10	1.13	1.30	1.26	1.39	1.48	1.36	1.37	1.24	1.23
	0.15	0.16	0.15	0.19	0.16	0.14	0.21	0.18	0.20	0.31	0.36
SITC9	1.30	0.86	1.11	1.32	1.66	1.90	1.82	1.72	1.73	1.72	2.00
	0.43	0.33	0.34	0.46	0.49	0.63	0.66	0.72	0.62	0.88	1.22

Source Calculation and tabulation are based on UNCTAD Stat

"Indo-Pacific" will be analyzed by area and country. Due to the difficulty in obtaining bilateral data for FDI inflow, outflow and stock of each area, the changes in the geo-economic pattern of "Indo-Pacific" areas will be analyzed with trade indicators; and then the influence of major countries on the changes in the geo-economic pattern of this region will be analyzed with both trade and investment indicators.

3.1 Geo-economic Pattern Development of the "Indo-Pacific": Analysis at Regional Level

In this chapter, the average level of 1990s is represented by the level of 1995, the regional geo-economic pattern changes are compared with the 10-year development level, and the time points of 2000, 2010 and 2016 that is the latest year of data available are selected for analysis. Moreover, due to the big number of trading partners in each area, it is difficult to analyze them one by one and unnecessary to make a comprehensive analysis. This has no impact on the analysis results because the international trade concentration of these regions has always been high; no matter

Table 13 Trade Complementarity Index between APEC and COMESA in 2006–2016

Product category	2006	2007	2008	2009	2010	2011	2012	2013	2014	2015	2016
SITC0	1.57	1.64	1.61	1.38	1.58	1.89	1.79	1.55	1.64	1.51	1.46
	1.14	1.06	0.95	1.21	1.20	1.62	1.21	1.34	1.66	2.14	2.18
SITC1	0.59	0.54	0.51	0.48	0.59	0.60	0.60	0.61	0.59	0.60	0.55
	1.40	1.30	1.21	1.66	1.63	2.23	1.75	2.33	2.63	3.18	3.37
SITC2	1.18	1.14	1.41	1.24	1.13	1.19	1.15	1.26	1.26	0.98	0.99
	1.80	1.57	1.88	2.28	1.74	2.21	1.70	1.98	2.49	2.76	2.66
SITC3	0.61	0.54	0.49	0.50	0.56	0.57	0.59	0.51	0.58	0.74	0.91
	4.63	4.99	4.29	4.29	3.96	2.41	3.10	2.83	2.23	2.08	1.82
SITC4	4.05	4.15	4.77	3.95	4.78	5.98	4.39	4.09	3.78	3.31	3.55
	14.19	15.12	16.79	17.96	14.83	28.12	22.38	24.32	30.46	20.11	19.88
SITC5	0.73	0.75	0.80	0.73	0.75	0.85	0.82	0.89	0.83	0.81	0.80
	0.27	0.29	0.34	0.38	0.37	0.50	0.39	0.46	0.51	0.54	0.57
SITC6	1.03	1.04	1.28	1.50	1.29	1.26	1.41	1.44	1.38	1.38	1.35
	0.66	0.61	0.60	0.75	0.86	1.20	0.98	1.10	1.42	1.52	1.58
SITC7	1.03	1.04	1.12	1.12	1.05	0.95	0.98	1.01	0.98	0.94	0.91
	0.06	0.05	0.07	0.08	0.07	0.10	0.07	0.09	0.14	0.15	0.15
SITC8	0.67	0.69	0.65	0.67	0.71	0.67	0.75	0.79	0.76	0.77	0.67
	0.40	0.39	0.37	0.44	0.35	0.48	0.33	0.37	0.45	0.54	0.58
SITC9	1.97	1.78	0.62	0.46	0.68	0.53	0.35	0.53	0.41	0.31	0.45
	0.77	0.64	0.21	0.32	0.53	0.87	0.67	0.68	0.96	1.10	1.48

Source Calculation and tabulation are based on UNCTAD Stat

for import or export, the total ratio of top 10 trading partners exceed at least half of the region's total. Therefore, top 10 import and export trading partners of each area are only selected in this paper, so as to analyze the international economic competition of the region at that time.

3.1.1 Geo-economic Pattern Evolution of ASEAN

In 1995, ASEAN's most important trading partners included Japan, the U.S., and Asia's emerging industrial countries (areas); traditional trading powers Germany and the U.K. also took a place. In general, Japan and the U.S. had the greatest influence on the international trade of ASEAN; ASEAN's import and export with Japan accounted for 24.85 and 14.38% of ASEAN's total import and export; and its import and export with the U.S. took up 14.11 and 18.92%. In addition, ASEAN's trade volumes with its neighboring countries and intraregional countries were also very significant. For example, the proportions of the Four Asian Tigers in ASEAN's import and export are as high as 18.21 and 22.20%. At that time, China just tanked among top 10 exporters to ASEAN, accounting for merely 3.08%.

In 2000, ASEAN trade pattern changed little, and its most important trading partners were still the U.S., Japan, intraregional countries and EU. Among them, Japan and the U.S. remained ASEAN's largest importers and exporters. Specifically, Japan occupied 19.59 and 13.57% in ASEAN's total import and export, while the U.S. accounted for 13.74 and 18.98% in ASEAN's total import and export; both of their influences slightly declined compared with those in 1995. During the same period, the Four Asian Tigers accounted for 19.41 and 22.02% in ASEAN's import and export, respectively, with little change in their influences. In addition, China took up 5.34 and 3.87% in ASEAN's import and export, indicating a rising influence.

By 2010, China had been ASEAN's largest trading partner for four years in a row, and competed fiercely with Japan and the U.S. in the region. China's import and export ratios accounted for 13.40 and 10.81% of total import and export of ASEAN countries, Japan's import and export ratios took up 12.21 and 9.84%, and the U.S.' import and export ratios occupied 8.68 and 9.58%, respectively. In addition, the proportions of the four dragons continued to decline, whereas Australia and India ranked among top 10 importers from ASEAN, accounting for 3.61 and 3.53%, respectively.

In 2016, China became the largest trading partner of ASEAN for 10 consecutive years, and further expanded its trade advantage over Japan and the U.S. China's import and export ratios rose to 20.52 and 12.69% respectively, Japan's import and export ratios declined to 9.61 and 8.40% respectively, while the U.S.'s import and export ratios maintained at 7.71 and 11.28%. Over the same period, the ratios of the Four Asian Tigers continued to decline, Australia fell out of top 10, and India's trade influence had no change (see Table 14).

3.1.2 Geo-economic Pattern Evolution of SAARC

In 1995, the U.S., Japan, EU and neighboring countries were SAARC's most important trading partners. Their import and export ratios to the U.S. were 9.40 and 20.83% in the total import and export of SAARC, their import and export ratios to Japan were 8.58 and 6.93%, their import and export ratios to Germany were 7.66 and 7.46%, and their import and export ratios to the U.K. were 5.73 and 7.12% respectively. In the year, China ranked 6th among SAARC's original countries of import, accounting for 4.12%, while India took the 10th place, accounting for 3.59%.

In 2000, the U.S. remained SAARC's most important trading partner, and the U.K., Germany and Italy also had high trade ratios. The import and export ratios of the U.S. were 6.42 and 26.18% in the total import and export of SAARC, and the import and export ratios of Japan decreased to 6.04 and 3.25%; meanwhile, China's import ratio was 4.40%, which had almost no change compared with that in 1995.

By 2010, China was already SAARC's largest trading partner, accounting for 11.20% of total trade, which was more than 9.05% of the U.S.; however, the U.S. remained SAARC's largest export target. In the regional trade pattern, China, the U.S. and UAE were the core countries, and EU countries also had a big influence, while Japan's trade status declined dramatically.

Table 14 Key trading partners of ASEAN in 1995–2016 (*Unit %*)

ASEAN's top 10 original countries of import and trade ratio								ASEAN's top 10 target countries of export and trade ratio							
Country 1995	Import ratio	Country 2000	Import ratio	Country 2010	Import ratio	Country 2016	Import ratio	Country 1995	Export ratio	Country 2000	Export ratio	Country 2010	Export ratio	Country 216	Export ratio
Japan	24.85	Japan	19.59	China	13.40	China	20.52	The U.S.	18.92	The U.S.	18.98	China	10.81	China	12.69
The U.S.	14.11	The U.S.	13.74	Japan	12.21	Japan	9.61	Japan	14.38	Japan	13.57	Japan	9.84	The U.S.	11.28
Malaysia	7.12	Malaysia	8.05	The U.S.	8.68	The U.S.	7.71	Singapore	9.11	Singapore	8.23	The U.S.	9.58	Japan	8.40
Singapore	5.92	Singapore	6.27	Singapore	6.68	Korea	7.33	Malaysia	8.14	Malaysia	7.43	Hong Kong, China	7.14	Hong Kong, China	6.84
Taiwan, China	4.87	China	5.34	Malaysia	6.41	Malaysia	5.64	Hong Kong, China	6.27	Hong Kong, China	5.31	Malaysia	6.25	Malaysia	4.97
Korea	4.74	Taiwan, China	5.29	Korea	6.05	Taiwan, China	5.56	Thailand	3.86	Taiwan, China	4.78	Singapore	5.66	Singapore	4.82
Germany	4.48	Korea	5.20	Taiwan, China	5.14	Singapore	5.40	Taiwan, China	3.61	China	3.87	Indonesia	4.64	Korea	3.98
Thailand	3.15	Thailand	3.77	Thailand	4.54	Thailand	4.55	Germany	3.29	Korea	3.70	Korea	4.28	Indonesia	3.97
China	3.08	Germany	2.98	Indonesia	3.85	Indonesia	3.37	Korea	3.21	Netherlands	3.68	Australia	3.61	Thailand	3.42
Hong Kong, China	2.68	Hong Kong, China	2.65	Germany	2.74	Germany	2.72	The U.K.	3.15	Thailand	2.99	India	3.53	India	3.28
Total	75.00	Total	72.88	Total	69.70	Total	72.41	Total	73.94	Total	72.54	Total	65.34	Total	63.65

Source Calculation and tabulation are based on UNCTAD Stat

In 2016, SAARC had almost no change in its foreign trade pattern, China, the U.S. and UAE remained the most important trading partners, and Europe also took a big share. While China further increased its export to SAARC, its influence on the regional import declined sharply. During the period, China's import and export ratios were 19.15 and 3.57% in SAARC's total import and export; the U.S.'s import and export ratios were 5.35 and 16.53%, and UAE's import and export ratios were 5.51 and 9.68% respectively. In addition, India's import ratio was 3.99%, and Japan's import ratio was only 3.01% (see Table 15).

3.1.3 Geo-economic Pattern Evolution of GCC

In 1995, GCC's main trading partners were Japan, the U.S., Europe and ASEAN countries. Among them, the U.S. was the largest original country of import, whereas Japan was the largest target country of export. The U.S.'s import and export ratios were 14.48 and 10.60% in the regional total import and export, while Japan's import and export ratios were 9.26 and 27.37% in the regional total import and export. In addition, India's import and export ratios were 3.34 and 5.34% respectively, while China's import ratio was only 3.26%.

In 2000, Japan's trade influence on GCC slipped a bit, but it remained the region's largest trading partner. Japan's import and export ratios in GCC were 9.48 and 24.71% in the total regional import and export, while the U.S.'s import and export ratios in GCC were 11.53 and 9.43%. Meanwhile, China's import and export ratios in the region were 4.67 and 5.73%, while India's import and export ratios were 4.47 and 3.65%.

In 2010, China, India, Japan, the U.S. and Europe had a fierce trade competition in GCC. Among them, China was the largest original country of import in the region, while Japan was the largest target country of export. Specifically, China's import and export ratios in the region were 11.17 and 8.83% in the total regional import and export, India's import and export ratios in the region were 10.43 and 11.57%, Japan's import and export ratios in the region were 6.68 and 15.94%, and the U.S.'s import and export ratios in the region were 9.58 and 5.71%.

In 2016, China, the U.S., Japan, India and Europe remained the most important trading partners of GCC. However, China had an increasing trade influence, and became the region's largest trading partner and largest original country of import. Specifically, China's import and export ratios in GCC were 12.92 and 10.37%, the U.S.'s import and export ratios were 11.58 and 4.98%, Japan's import and export ratios were 4.74 and 10.73%, and India's import and export ratios were 8.27 and 9.88% (see Table 16).

3.1.4 Geo-economic Pattern Evolution of COMESA

In 1995, EU countries (more than half of top 10 countries) had a significant trade influence on COMESA, and as did the U.S., Japan and South Africa. Specifically,

Table 15 Key trading partners of SAARC in 1995–2016 (*Unit %*)

SAARC's top 10 original countries of import and trade ratio								SAARC's top 10 target countries of export and trade ratio							
Country 1995	Import ratio	Country 2000	Import ratio	Country 2010	Import ratio	Country 2016	Import ratio	Country 1995	Export ratio	Country 2000	Export ratio	Country 2010	Export ratio	Country 2016	Export ratio
The U.S.	9.40	The U.S.	6.42	China	12.82	China	19.15	The U.S.	20.83	The U.S.	26.18	The U.S.	12.52	The U.S.	16.53
Japan	8.58	Saudi Arabia	6.35	UAE	8.19	UAE	5.51	Germany	7.46	The U.K.	6.66	UAE	11.03	UAE	9.68
Germany	7.66	The U.K.	6.06	The U.S.	5.30	The U.S.	5.35	The U.K.	7.12	Hong Kong, China	5.50	China	7.17	The U.K.	4.44
The U.K.	5.73	Japan	6.04	Saudi Arabia	5.11	Saudi Arabia	4.45	Japan	6.93	Germany	5.41	The U.K.	3.85	Hong Kong, China	4.24
Singapore	5.24	Singapore	5.48	Australia	3.52	India	3.99	Hong Kong, China	5.71	UAE	5.70	Hong Kong, China	3.85	Germany	4.22
China	4.12	Belgium	5.11	Singapore	3.47	Switzerland	3.34	UAE	4.00	Japan	3.25	Germany	3.77	China	3.57
Korea	4.04	China	4.40	Germany	3.29	Indonesia	3.18	Italy	3.24	Belgium	3.25	Singapore	3.51	Singapore	2.37
UAE	3.74	Germany	3.67	Korea	3.10	Korea	3.05	France	3.01	Italy	2.93	Netherlands	3.10	France	2.32
Malaysia	3.72	Malaysia	3.54	Switzerland	3.08	Japan	3.01	Netherlands	2.84	France	2.82	France	2.50	Belgium	2.25
India	3.59	Korea	3.50	Japan	2.88	Germany	2.91	Bangladesh	2.70	Netherlands	2.39	Belgium	2.42	Netherlands	2.19
Total	55.82	Total	50.57	Total	50.76	Total	53.94	Total	63.84	Total	64.09	Total	53.72	Total	51.81

Source Calculation and tabulation are based on UNCTAD Stat

Table 16 Key trading partners of GCC in 1995–2016 (*Unit %*)

GCC's top 10 original countries of import and trade ratio								GCC's top 10 target countries of export and trade ratio							
Country 1995	Import ratio	Country 2000	Import ratio	Country 2010	Import ratio	Country 2016	Import ratio	Country 1995	Export ratio	Country 2000	Export ratio	Country 2010	Export ratio	Country 2016	Export ratio
The U.S.	14.48	The U.S.	11.53	China	11.17	China	12.92	Japan	27.37	Japan	24.71	Japan	15.94	Japan	10.73
Japan	9.26	Japan	9.48	India	10.43	The U.S.	11.58	The U.S.	10.60	Korea	11.70	India	11.57	China	10.37
The U.K.	8.15	Germany	6.70	The U.S.	9.58	India	8.27	Korea	8.91	The U.S.	9.43	Korea	10.10	India	9.88
Germany	7.24	The U.K.	6.68	Japan	6.68	Germany	6.64	Singapore	6.42	Taiwan, China	5.42	China	8.83	Korea	7.79
France	5.85	Saudi Arabia	5.57	Germany	6.49	UAE	5.31	India	5.34	China	5.37	Taiwan, China	7.35	The U.S.	4.98
Italy	5.42	France	4.78	Saudi Arabia	3.90	Japan	4.74	Netherlands	3.19	Singapore	4.82	The U.S.	5.71	Singapore	4.00
Saudi Arabia	4.53	China	4.67	Korea	3.55	The U.K.	3.20	Taiwan, China	2.87	India	3.65	Singapore	4.25	Taiwan, China	3.85
Korea	3.60	India	4.47	The U.K.	3.8	Italy	3.13	France	2.64	Thailand	2.89	Iran	3.64	Switzerland	3.84
India	3.34	Korea	4.37	Italy	3.24	Korea	3.05	Thailand	2.05	Pakistan	2.18	Thailand	3.20	Iran	3.82
China	3.26	Italy	4.35	UAE	3.19	Saudi Arabia	2.93	Pakistan	1.99	Netherlands	1.89	UAE	2.28	Saudi Arabia	2.74
Total	65.12	Total	62.60	Total	62.03	Total	61.77	Total	71.38	Total	72.06	Total	72.87	Total	62.00

Source Calculation and tabulation are based on UNCTAD Stat

Italy's import and export ratios were 8.00 and 18.97% in the total regional import and export, Germany's import and export ratios were 8.51 and 10.37%, the U.S.'s import and export ratios were 9.82 and 6.00%, South Africa's import and export ratios were 8.51 and 2.56%, Japan's import and export ratios were 5.63 and 2.96%, and India's import ratio was only 2.37%.

In 2000, South Africa surpassed the U.S. as the largest original country of import, whereas Italy remained the region's largest target country of export. Specifically, Italy's import and export ratios were 6.98 and 23.12%, South Africa's import and export ratios were 10.44 and 2.92%, the U.S.'s import and export ratios were 8.85 and 5.41%, China's import ratio was 4.13%, and Japan's import ratio was 3.66%.

In 2010, the region's largest trading partner and original country of import became China, while its biggest target country of export remained Italy. China's import and export ratios were 11.47 and 15.26%, Italy's import and export ratios were 5.23 and 17.08%, and the U.S.'s import and export ratios were 6.22 and 4.49%. In addition, the trade status of EU countries and GCC countries remained relatively important, while Japan withdrew from the competition for top 10.

In 2016, China became the region's largest trading partner, original country of import and target country of export, while EU, the U.S., South Africa and GCC countries still had an important trade status. Among them, China's import and export ratios were 12.92 and 10.37% in the regional total import and export, the U.S.'s import and export ratios were 4.20 and 4.86%, and South Africa's import and export ratios were 6.01 and 4.51% (see Table 17).

3.2 Analysis on Influence of China, the U.S., Japan, Australia and India on the "Indo-Pacific" Geo-economic Pattern

Further exploration is made for the evolution of "Indo-Pacific" geo-economic pattern at the country level. With the "Indo-Pacific" strategy pushers the U.S., Japan, Australia and India as well as the strategy's balance object China as subjects, a comparative analysis is conducted on the geo-economic capabilities of the five countries in the "Indo-Pacific" region.

According to data, the U.S. is undoubtedly the world's largest economy with incomparable international economic capacity and geographical influence. In 2016, the U.S.'s GDP gross accounted for up to 24.76% of the global total, which was approximately equal to the sum of that of China (14.83%), Japan (6.53%), India (2.99%) and Australia (1.72%) (see Fig. 5). However, since China caught up with and surpassed Japan in 2010, its share in global GDP has risen rapidly, and China has become the most challengeable country to the U.S.'s current economic status. Meanwhile, China is still the greatest contributor to the average annual growth of global GDP. From 2010 to 2016, its average annual contribution rate was up to 28.85%, whereas those of the U.S., Japan, Australia and India were respectively

Table 17 Key trading partners of COMESA in 1995–2016 (*Unit %*)

COMESA's top 10 original countries of import and trade ratio								COMESA's top 10 target countries of export and trade ratio							
Country 1995	Import ratio	Country 2000	Import ratio	Country 2010	Import ratio	Country 2016	Import ratio	Country 1995	Export ratio	Country 2000	Export ratio	Country 2010	Export ratio	Country 2016	Export ratio
The U.S.	9.82	South Africa	10.44	China	11.47	China	17.31	Italy	18.97	Italy	23.12	Italy	17.08	China	10.21
South Africa	8.51	The U.S.	8.85	South Africa	6.71	South Africa	6.01	Germany	10.73	Germany	9.69	China	15.26	UAE	8.85
Germany	8.34	Italy	6.98	The U.S.	6.22	India	5.65	The U.K.	6.90	The U.K.	6.61	France	7.34	Italy	5.75
Italy	8.00	Germany	6.14	Italy	5.23	Germany	4.43	The U.S.	6.00	Spain	6.46	Spain	5.33	Switzerland	4.98
France	6.93	France	5.51	Germany	4.99	The U.S.	4.20	France	5.97	France	5.87	The U.S.	4.49	The U.S.	4.86
The U.K.	6.24	The U.K.	4.82	India	4.90	UAE	4.19	Spain	5.97	The U.S.	5.41	Germany	4.08	South Africa	4.51
Japan	5.63	Saudi Arabia	4.22	France	3.69	Italy	3.70	Belgium	2.99	China	3.14	UAE	3.52	The U.K.	3.73
Netherlands	2.66	China	4.13	UAE	3.65	Saudi Arabia	3.31	Japan	2.96	South Africa	2.92	The U.K.	3.25	Germany	3.37
Korea	2.40	Japan	3.66	Saudi Arabia	3.50	Turkey	3.16	South Africa	2.56	Turkey	2.91	Switzerland	2.45	Saudi Arabia	3.11
India	2.37	UAE	2.89	Turkey	3.28	France	2.93	Turkey	2.22	Belgium	2.66	South Africa	2.40	France	3.02
Total	60.90	Total	57.64	Total	53.64	Total	54.89	Total	65.27	Total	68.79	Total	65.20	Total	52.39

Source Calculation and tabulation are based on UNCTAD Stat

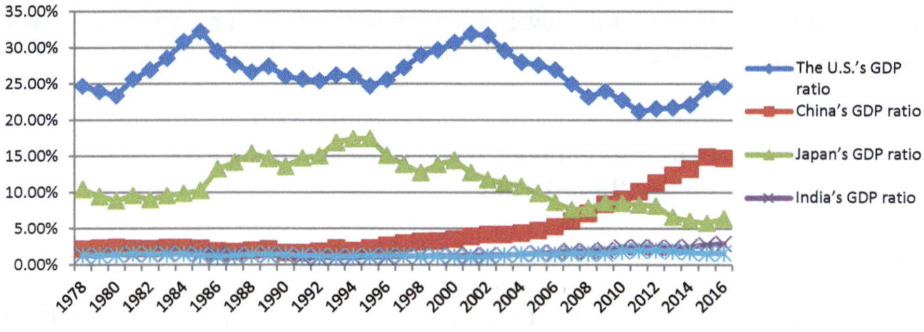

Fig. 5 Changes in shares of China, the U.S., Japan, Australia and India in global GDP. *Source* Calculation and charting are based on UNCTAD Stat

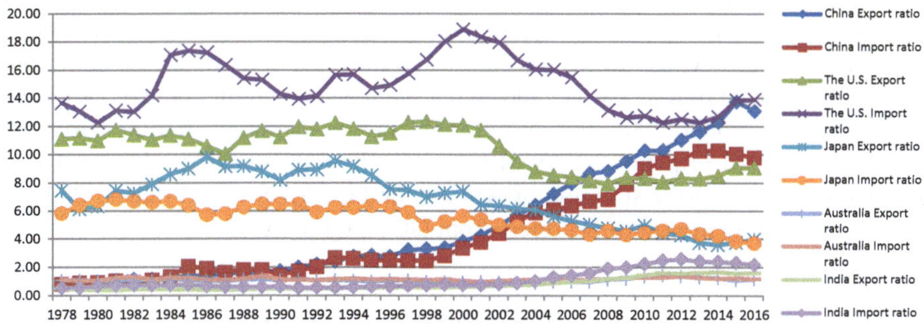

Fig. 6 Changes in shares of China, the U.S., Japan, Australia and India in global import and export. *Source* Calculation and charting are based on UNCTAD Stat

16.51, 3.87, 1.81 and 6.81%. In the field of international trade, China has become the world's largest cargo trading country and cargo exporter and the second largest cargo importer, and took up 9.83 and 13.12% of global import and export shares; meanwhile, the U.S. was the world's largest cargo importer, and occupied 13.94 and 9.10% of global import and export shares (see Fig. 6). In addition, according to data of *2017 World Investment Report*, at the end of 2016, among the world's major economies, the U.S. accounted for up to 24.40% of the global foreign investment stock, Japan took up 5.40%, China occupied 5.20%, and Australia accounted for 1.50%. In terms of FDI flow, China, the U.S. and Japan accounted for 20.60, 13.5 and 10.00% respectively. The U.S. was the world's largest FDI inflow and outflow country, and China was the world's third largest FDI inflow country and the second largest FDI outflow country. The U.S.'s FDI inflow and outflow volumes were respectively 2.92 times and 1.63 times of those of China.

Data analysis shows differences in economic strength and international economic capacity between China and the U.S. at the global level. In terms of size, both China and the United States are huge economies, while the comprehensive economic strength and international economic capacity of Japan, Australia and India were in the second tier. However, at the level of the "Indo-Pacific" alone, what about their geo-economics influence?

3.2.1 Comparison of International Trade Influence of the Five Countries on the "Indo-Pacific"

First, an analysis is made on the trade influence of the five countries on the "Indo-Pacific" areas, namely the proportions of bilateral trade volume between the five countries and ASEAN, SAARC, GCC (including Iran and Iraq) and COMESA in their total foreign trade volume. According to Table 18, from 1995 to 2016, China's trade influence on the "Indo-Pacific" areas has been continuously enhanced. Especially around 2010, China's international trade influence surpassed that of the U.S. and Japan in an all-round way; and its trade advantage has been continuously expanded in recent years. In fact, according to the UNCTAD data, China became the most important trading partner and an international economic force of the "Indo-Pacific" region around 2007. For instance, China was the largest trading partner as well as the largest original country of import in the four areas. In addition, China was the largest export destination of ASEAN and COMESA, and ranked 2nd and 6th respectively in the list of exporters from GCC and SAARC.

3.2.2 Comparison of Influence of the Five Countries Based on International Trade on GDP Growth of the "Indo-Pacific"

In addition to the analysis on the trade influence of the five countries on the "Indo-Pacific", it is also necessary to measure the foreign trade dependence of the regional economic growth on the five countries, or calculate the proportion of bilateral trade volume between the areas and the five countries in their regional GDP. As a matter of fact, due to the difference in the trade dependence among the "Indo-Pacific" areas, the trade volumes of these areas have different contributions to GDP. Among them, China accounts for the largest trade share, so it contributes the most to regional GDP, but with different contribution degrees. In addition, in recent years, the "Indo-Pacific" areas have begun reducing their foreign trade dependence. Therefore, even if the total foreign trade has been increasing, their contribution to GDP may also reduce. For example, from 2015 to 2016, as the foreign trade dependence of ASEAN, SAARC, GCC and COMESA decreased from respectively 88.31, 31.64, 83.55% and 31.00 to 82.87, 28.80, 79.20 and 30.40%, their contribution to regional GDP would also decline. For example, in 2015, China's contributions to the regional GDP of the above mentioned areas were respectively 19.28, 4.08, 9.79 and 5.84%, respectively, which fell to 17.70, 3.83, 8.37 and 5.34% in 2016 (see Table 19).

Table 18 Changes in trade influence of the five countries on the "Indo-Pacific" region

Country/year	1995 (%)	2000 (%)	2005 (%)	2010 (%)	2015 (%)	2016 (%)
Proportion of bilateral trade with the five countries in ASEAN's total foreign trade volume						
China	3.01	4.87	10.35	14.62	20.95	20.21
The U.S.	15.38	17.15	12.15	9.11	10.30	10.65
Japan	18.67	15.80	11.77	10.68	8.56	8.40
Australia	1.88	2.32	2.75	2.93	2.34	2.22
India	0.89	1.16	2.16	2.89	3.09	2.93
Proportion of bilateral trade with the five countries in SAARC's total foreign trade volume						
China	2.99	3.91	8.09	11.20	13.09	13.47
The U.S.	14.08	16.09	11.73	9.05	10.02	10.54
Japan	8.06	5.12	2.95	2.62	2.23	2.31
Australia	1.55	1.59	2.20	2.60	1.63	1.66
India[a]	4.74	4.54	8.56	9.30	10.66	9.98
Proportion of bilateral trade with the five countries in total foreign trade volume of GCC (Iraq and Iran)						
China	1.85	4.02	6.12	10.34	14.09	13.09
The U.S.	10.45	11.02	9.21	6.84	6.96	7.07
Japan	17.74	16.64	13.80	10.96	5.82	6.39
Australia	0.85	1.32	0.75	0.68	0.62	0.61
India	3.43	3.04	4.08	9.42	8.63	9.05
Proportion of bilateral trade with the five countries in COMESA'S total foreign trade volume						
China	1.74	3.98	7.40	13.36	18.13	17.72
The U.S.	9.26	9.38	8.08	6.21	5.24	4.58
Japan	4.63	3.43	3.14	2.01	1.64	1.49
Australia	0.34	0.90	0.54	0.53	0.34	0.28
India	1.92	1.98	2.47	3.72	5.51	5.21

Source Calculation and tabulation are based on UNCTAD Stat
[a]Only trades between India and 7 SAARC countries are calculated, which is different from India's proportion in SAARC's intraregional trade

3.2.3 Comparison of Investment Influence of the Five Countries on the "Indo-Pacific"

Globally, the U.S. is the largest FDI inflow and outflow country from the prospective of either stock or flow. China ranks respectively 3rd and 2nd in FDI inflow and outflow and 6th in investment stock, with big gaps from the U.S. Due to differences in regional investment statistics among countries, the comparison only covers a rough investment

Table 19 Foreign trade dependence of the "Indo-Pacific" areas on the five countries in 1995–2016

Country/year	1995 (%)	2000 (%)	2005 (%)	2010 (%)	2015 (%)	2016 (%)
Foreign trade dependence of ASEAN's GDP on the five countries						
China	2.90	6.34	13.62	14.81	19.28	17.70
The U.S.	14.80	22.30	15.99	9.23	9.48	9.33
Japan	17.97	20.54	15.48	10.82	7.88	7.36
Australia	1.81	3.02	3.61	2.97	2.15	1.94
India	0.86	1.51	2.84	2.92	2.84	2.56
Foreign trade dependence of SAARC's GDP on the five countries						
China	0.64	0.94	2.59	3.96	4.08	3.83
The U.S.	3.02	3.86	3.75	3.20	3.13	2.99
Japan	1.73	1.23	0.94	0.93	0.70	0.66
Australia	0.33	0.38	0.70	0.92	0.51	0.47
India[a]	1.41	1.53	3.39	3.47	3.42	3.12
Foreign trade dependence of GDP of GCC (Iraq and Iran) on the five countries						
China	1.01	2.68	4.72	7.53	9.79	8.37
The U.S.	5.72	7.33	7.10	4.98	4.83	4.52
Japan	9.71	11.07	10.64	7.98	4.04	4.09
Australia	0.47	0.88	0.58	0.49	0.43	0.39
India	1.88	2.03	3.15	6.86	6.00	5.79
Foreign trade dependence of COMESA's GDP on the five countries						
China	0.57	1.21	3.55	6.18	5.84	5.34
The U.S.	3.05	2.86	3.88	2.87	1.69	1.38
Japan	1.52	1.05	1.51	0.93	0.53	0.45
Australia	0.11	0.28	0.26	0.25	0.11	0.09
India	0.63	0.60	1.19	1.72	1.77	1.57

Source Calculation and tabulation are based on UNCTAD Stat

scope. In 2016, China's foreign investment stock totaled US$1.3573 trillion, and its investment in Asia, Africa and Oceania was about US$987.6 billion, accounting for 72.70% of the total foreign investment stock. Specifically, China invested US$905.8 billion in the four major areas of the "Indo-Pacific" and major East Asian countries (Japan, Korea, Hong Kong, Macao and Taiwan), accounting for 66.74% of its total foreign investment stock in the year. The U.S. invested US$950.1 billion in the "Asia-Pacific", the Middle East and Africa, taking up 17.82% of its total foreign investment stock. Japan invested US$385.5 billion in Asia, the Middle East and Africa, occupying 28.37% of its total foreign investment stock. Australia invested US$92.3 billion in top 20 largest investment destinations (71.60%), ASEAN and EU, accounting for 21.54%. India invested US$19.261 billion in the region between 2014 and 2017, taking up 48.70% of its total direct foreign investment during the period (see Table 20). According to the investment data, there is little difference in absolute value of investment stock in the "Indo-Pacific" areas between China and the U.S., both are close to 1 trillion dollars. However, because the U.S.'s investment statistics pointed to the "Indo-Pacific", it has lower investment value against the "Indo-Pacific". By ratio, the "Indo-Pacific" region is the most important investment destination of China, as well as the main target of India's foreign capital flow.

In general, the investment of China, the U.S., Japan, Australia and India in the "Indo-Pacific" region mainly focuses on East Asia or Singapore, with less direct investment in the four areas. ASEAN that has the largest investment from the five

Table 20 Distribution of direct foreign investment stock of China, the U.S., Japan, Australia and India by the end of 2016 (*Unit* US$100 million)

Investment flow target	Investment stock	Proportion (%)
Distribution of direct foreign investment stock of China		
Asia	9095	67.00
North America	754	5.60
Oceania	382	2.80
Africa	399	2.90
Europe	872	6.40
Latin America	2072	15.30
Distribution of direct foreign investment stock of the U.S.		
Canada	3639	6.82
Europe	31,749	59.54
Latin America and other western hemisphere countries	8434	15.82
Africa	575	1.08
The Middle East	459	0.86
The Asia-Pacific	8467	15.88
Distribution of direct foreign investment stock of Japan		
Asia (East Asia, Southeast Asia and South Asia)	3683	27.10
North America	4698	34.56
Latin America	899	6.62
Oceania	747	5.50
Europe	3393	24.96
The Middle East	72	0.53
Africa	99	0.74
Distribution of direct foreign investment stock of Australia		
The U.S.	918.38	21.43
The U.K.	565.40	13.19
New Zealand	514.42	12.00

(continued)

Table 20 (continued)

Investment flow target	Investment stock	Proportion (%)
Singapore	152.94	3.57
Papua New Guinea	122.04	2.85
China	102.73	2.40
Bermuda	62.56	1.46
Netherlands	62.56	1.46
Canada	58.70	1.37
India	13.90	0.32
Other ASEAN countries	139.03	3.24
Other EU countries	182.29	4.25
Other countries	1391.09	32.46
Distribution of direct foreign investment stock of India (FY2014–2017)		
Mauritius	80.36	20.32
Singapore	78.84	19.94
The U.S.	56.55	14.30
UAE	33.41	8.45
Netherlands	32.34	8.18
The U.K.	29.23	7.39
Switzerland	17.23	4.36
Russia	9.14	2.31
Jersey	4.84	1.23
British virgin islands	4.59	1.16
Other areas	48.95	12.64

Source China's data is sourced from *China Foreign Investment Bulletin 2016*; the U.S.'s data is sourced from U.S. Bureau of Economic Analysis; Japan's data is sourced from JETRO; Australia's data is sourced from Australia Bureau of Statistics; India's data is sourced from Reserve Bank of India

countries is taken for example. In ASEAN's total FDI inflow in 2012–2016, Japan's investment accounted for 12.90%, the U.S.'s investment took up 12.80%, China's investment occupied 6.00% (11.20% after adding Hong Kong's share), Australia's investment accounted for 2.80%, and India's investment took up 1.80%. At the same time, according to the proportion of the direct investment from the five countries to ASEAN in their total direct foreign investment, India's investment in ASEAN accounted for the highest proportion, which reached 21.70% and exceeded that of Japan (13.00%), Australia (6.81%), China (6.00%) and the U.S. (5.00%).[38]

[38]The ASEAN Secretariat, UNCTAD, ASEAN Investment Report 2017, http://asean.org/storage/2017/11/ASEAN-Investment-Report-2017.pdf.

4 Comparison on Trade Dependence of Five Countries in "Indo-Pacific" Region

Besides trade and investment contributions to the "Indo-Pacific" Region and efforts to promote the GDP growth of various regions, the geo-economic dependence of China, the US, Japan, Australia and India on "Indo-Pacific" Region is also worthy of being studied, because it can show for which countries the "Indo-Pacific" Region is more important in global economy.

In terms of imports, from 1995 to 2016, the dependence of the five countries on "Indo-Pacific" Region showed a tendency of ascending at first and descending at last. The dependence of China, Japan and India on "Indo-Pacific" Region picked up a little bit between 2015 and 2016. On the whole, India and Japan were more dependent on the trade in "Indo-Pacific" Region, with a share of 26.26 and 25.28% in 2016 respectively, followed by Australia and Japan, with a share of 19.88 and 17.30% respectively. Over years, there has been little change in the proportion of US's imports from "Indo-Pacific" Region to US' total imports, at 11.38% in 2016. By regional breakdown, the five countries were most dependent on ASEAN, then GCC and COMESA. They had almost no dependence on SAARC. Even the proportion of India's imports to SAARC was only 0.60% (see Table 21). In terms of exports, China and India became more and more dependent on "Indo-Pacific" Region, while there were small fluctuations and little change in the dependence of the US, Japan and Australia on this region. The dependence of five countries on export trade in "Indo-Pacific" Region were 35.48, 20.87, 20.20, 17.74 and 10.87% respectively (see Table 22). By regional breakdown, China, the US, Japan and Australia were most dependent on ASEAN in exports, while India was most dependent on GCC in exports. China and Australia is more dependent on COMESA than GCC in exports. On the whole, China and India were dependent on "Indo-Pacific" Region in exports more and imports less, while the US, Japan and Australia were depend on this region in imports more and exports less. From the perspective of the dependence on both imports and exports, the trade volume of China, Japan, Australia and India to "Indo-Pacific" Region exceeded one fifth of their respective trade volume, while the trade volume of the US to this region only accounted for around one ninth of its total trade volume.

5 Geo-economics Interpretation on the Origin and Pattern Evolution of "Indo-Pacific"

Through the analysis on above data and indicators, we can draw following conclusions:

First, the shift of world economic center is not evident. From the perspectives of land area, population, GDP, per capita GDP, FDI inflow and outflow, import and export trade and other key indicators, "Asia-Pacific" region is still the core region

Table 21 dependence of five countries on import trade in "Indo-Pacific" Region (*Unit %*)

Year	1995	2000	2005	2010	2011	2012	2013	2014	2015	2016
Proportion of China's imports from each region to China's total imports										
ASEAN	7.50	9.85	11.36	11.08	11.07	10.77	10.23	10.63	11.58	12.36
SAARC	0.16	0.48	0.69	1.29	1.16	0.92	0.69	0.58	0.52	0.46
GCC	1.05	2.86	3.03	4.05	4.98	5.54	5.42	5.44	4.10	3.53
COMESA	0.52	0.84	1.63	1.64	1.50	1.24	1.08	1.03	1.01	0.93
Total	**9.22**	**14.04**	**16.71**	**18.06**	**18.71**	**18.48**	**17.42**	**17.68**	**17.21**	**17.30**
Proportion of US' imports from each region to US' total imports										
ASEAN	8.36	7.29	5.97	5.69	5.41	5.45	5.65	5.88	6.79	7.26
SAARC	0.21	0.17	0.33	0.32	0.21	0.30	0.25	0.15	0.17	0.17
GCC	1.48	1.62	2.12	2.09	2.80	3.26	3.07	2.77	1.48	1.25
COMESA	1.32	1.49	1.65	2.08	2.16	2.29	2.38	2.46	2.59	2.69
Total	**11.37**	**10.56**	**10.07**	**10.18**	**10.57**	**11.30**	**11.36**	**11.27**	**11.03**	**11.38**
Proportion of Japan's imports from each region to Japan's total imports										
ASEAN	14.42	15.69	14.07	14.56	14.61	14.58	14.14	14.26	15.65	15.23
SAARC	0.24	0.26	0.47	0.29	0.41	0.25	0.24	0.11	0.12	0.09
GCC	8.07	11.10	14.62	14.77	16.66	17.76	17.86	17.14	8.12	8.90
COMESA	1.16	0.86	0.72	0.96	0.95	0.95	1.05	1.06	1.04	1.06
Total	**23.89**	**27.92**	**29.87**	**30.58**	**32.62**	**33.54**	**33.29**	**32.57**	**24.93**	**25.28**
Proportion of Australia's imports from each region to Australia's total imports										
ASEAN	8.70	14.08	17.97	19.20	18.33	18.76	18.37	19.05	16.56	16.37
SAARC	0.09	0.07	0.10	0.25	0.15	0.51	0.36	0.05	0.06	0.05
GCC	2.03	2.50	1.59	1.73	2.46	1.95	2.02	1.59	1.33	1.16
COMESA	0.97	0.93	0.98	1.16	1.22	1.36	1.32	1.60	2.29	2.29
Total	**11.79**	**17.59**	**20.63**	**22.35**	**22.15**	**22.59**	**22.07**	**22.29**	**20.25**	**19.88**
Proportion of India's imports from each region to India's total imports										
ASEAN	9.07	12.73	12.00	9.96	10.00	9.38	9.76	10.12	11.02	10.97
SAARC	0.87	0.70	0.60	0.82	0.82	0.90	0.90	0.76	0.61	0.60
GCC	11.42	10.82	11.54	18.57	19.53	21.10	20.54	18.47	13.53	13.90
COMESA	0.62	1.16	1.47	0.61	0.56	0.55	0.54	0.60	0.75	0.78
Total	**21.98**	**25.42**	**25.62**	**29.96**	**30.92**	**31.93**	**31.74**	**29.95**	**25.90**	**26.26**

Source UNCTAD Stat

Table 22 Dependence of five countries on export trade in "Indo-Pacific" Region

Year	1995	2000	2005	2010	2011	2012	2013	2014	2015	2016
Proportion of China's exports from each region to China's total exports										
ASEAN	7.04	6.96	7.27	8.76	8.96	9.97	11.05	11.61	12.20	12.20
SAARC	0.53	0.61	0.68	1.01	0.92	1.08	1.09	1.22	1.45	1.42
GCC	1.33	1.48	1.81	2.28	2.47	2.65	2.70	2.93	2.98	2.68
COMESA	1.69	1.52	2.09	3.65	3.76	3.44	3.41	3.66	4.15	4.57
Total	**10.59**	**10.57**	**11.85**	**15.70**	**16.10**	**17.14**	**18.25**	**19.42**	**20.78**	**20.87**
Proportion of US' exports from each region to US' total exports										
ASEAN	6.81	6.07	5.48	5.51	5.15	4.88	5.00	4.85	4.98	5.16
SAARC	0.63	0.52	0.54	0.74	0.59	0.58	0.53	0.69	0.55	0.39
GCC	1.75	1.30	2.12	2.46	2.57	3.22	3.39	3.25	3.55	3.53
COMESA	0.83	0.59	1.11	1.89	1.89	1.68	1.64	1.57	1.67	1.79
Total	**10.02**	**8.48**	**9.26**	**10.60**	**10.20**	**10.35**	**10.57**	**10.36**	**10.76**	**10.87**
Proportion of Japan's exports from each region to Japan's total exports										
ASEAN	17.59	14.29	12.70	14.66	14.95	16.20	15.52	15.16	15.20	14.82
SAARC	0.42	0.26	0.29	0.40	0.33	0.42	0.45	0.49	0.48	0.40
GCC	1.48	1.54	2.19	2.61	2.38	3.13	3.14	3.62	3.69	3.03
COMESA	1.06	0.87	1.01	1.58	1.82	1.74	1.62	1.73	1.99	1.95
Total	**20.55**	**16.96**	**16.19**	**19.26**	**19.48**	**21.48**	**20.73**	**20.99**	**21.36**	**20.20**
Proportion of Australia's exports from each region to Australia's total exports										
ASEAN	14.53	13.75	11.41	9.44	10.26	10.36	8.77	11.08	10.37	9.84
SAARC	0.28	0.85	0.55	0.40	0.39	0.42	0.41	0.37	0.35	0.26
GCC	1.02	2.97	2.95	2.23	2.06	2.18	1.76	2.77	2.97	2.76
COMESA	2.07	2.57	5.68	7.73	6.34	5.51	3.82	3.80	4.92	4.89
Total	**17.89**	**20.14**	**20.59**	**19.80**	**19.05**	**18.46**	**14.77**	**18.03**	**18.62**	**17.74**
Proportion of India's exports from each region to India's total exports										
ASEAN	8.61	6.30	10.25	10.42	11.44	11.15	11.25	9.86	10.00	10.13
SAARC	2.46	2.19	2.38	2.98	2.79	3.69	3.65	4.17	3.89	3.36
GCC	7.08	8.69	11.46	16.08	15.32	16.94	15.50	16.17	15.79	15.49
COMESA	5.47	4.06	5.38	5.04	4.29	4.74	5.02	6.25	6.53	6.50
Total	**23.63**	**21.23**	**29.48**	**34.52**	**33.84**	**36.53**	**35.43**	**36.44**	**36.21**	**35.48**

Source UNCTAD Stat

of geo-economics in a real sense. Even in terms of growth momentum, there is no clear evidence that the world economic center has shifted to "Indo-Pacific" Region. The FDI contribution growth rate of "Asia-Pacific" Region is still far above that of "Indo-Pacific" Region, even the global GDP and trade contribution of "Indo-Pacific" Region upgraded faster. Particularly nowadays, the two regions are striving to reduce their dependence on foreign trade and continue to increase the introduction of foreign capital at the same time. Such adjustments may cause the economic growth rate of "Indo-Pacific" Region with high dependence on foreign trade to slow down in a certain period.

Second, "Indo-Pacific" Region is not an economic cooperation entity, while the economic integration of each region is still at a low level. By comparison, we can see in "Asia-Pacific" Region that, its intra-regional economic tightness is very high; its intra-regional trade share is up to 69.00%; its intra-regional investment share is about 58.00%. "Asia-Pacific" Region is superior to EU in the foresaid aspects. Thus, in spite of loose institutions, APEC has formed the close economic cooperation. By contrast, "Indo-Pacific" Region hasn't formed close economic cooperation and is still at a low level in intra-regional trade and investment shares. Even the best performer ASEAN only enjoyed less than one third of APEC's intra-regional trade and investment shares, mainly because the four regions of "Indo-Pacific" Region lack of endogenous driving force and strong intra-regional global economic power.

Third, from the perspective of inter-regional trade connections, the economic dependence of "Indo-Pacific" region on "Asia-Pacific" region was far above that of "Asia-Pacific" region on "Indo-Pacific" region. However, in terms of energy, commodity transportation and added value, "Asia-Pacific" became more and more dependent on "Indo-Pacific" region. Moreover, no matter the primary products or industrial products enjoyed strong bilateral trade complementarities which continued to increase from whole. In future, there will be great potential for economic and trade cooperation. Therefore, the economic development of the two regions will depend on each other in different levels, and the dependence will keep on increasing.

Fourth, since 1990s, such geo-economic powers and the balance of geo-economic powers as affect the geo-economics of "Indo-Pacific" region have gradually changed. China has served as a key factor that affects the geo-economic pattern of "Indo-Pacific" region. We can say that China has become a maintainer of the geo-economics in "Indo-Pacific" region and the most important extraterritorial contributor of the regional economy, while the US, Japan, Europe and the "Indo-Pacific" Strategy participants Australia and India have become the challengers of existing geo-economic order in "Indo-pacific" region. In 1995, whether in ASEAN, SAARC, GCC, or COMESA, the traditional western economic powers such as the US, Japan, EU (mainly Germany, the UK, France, Italy and the Netherlands) have powerful international economic influence. Benefiting from the flying-geese model of Japan, the emerging industrial countries in Western Pacific Region (represented by "Four Asian Tigers") have also started to become the important trade partners of ASEAN, SAARC and even GCC. Even the most powerful countries in each region, for example, Singapore to ASEAN, India to SAARC, the UAE and Saudi Arabia to GCC, South Africa to the coastal countries of the Western

Indian Ocean, they are inferior to the western countries in regional economic influence. Till 2000, in the wake of Japan's long-term economic downturn, Japan saw a decline in its influence on various areas of the "Indo-Pacific" Region to a certain extent. The US and EU still maintained relatively great international economic advantage due to their sustained attention to this region. When emerging Asian industrial countries continued to make constant progress, India, the UAE, South Africa and other economic powers in this region started to strengthen their economic influence, and China also started to make its way into the top 10 in the foresaid four regions. Between 2006 and 2010, the geo-economic pattern in "Indo-Pacific" Region dramatically changed. China became the largest trading partner of ASEAN and SAARC as well as the largest export destination of ASEAN and the largest import source of the four regions. During that period, the influences of the US and Japan on the trade of each region continued to decline, while the influence of China and India, particularly that of China, increased steeply. Till 2016, China had been the largest trading partner of ASEAN for ten years in a row, the largest trading partner of SAARC and COMESA for 11 years in a row, and the largest trading partner of GCC (the EU as a whole served as the largest trading partner areas of GCC).

Fifth, in the "Indo-Pacific" region, China has become one of the most important international economic powers and also serves as one of the largest foreign contributors in regional economic growth in this region. On a global scale, the US is still superior to China in its global resource mobilization capacity and geo-economic influence. Yet, in the "Indo-Pacific" region, China has surpassed the US, Japan and Europe in global trade presence since 2007 and continued to expand its trade advantages in recently years, making important contributions to the GDP growth of the "Indo-Pacific" region, especially ASEAN and GCC. Moreover, by the end of 2016, China had shifted 66.74% of its foreign investment stock to the "Indo-Pacific" region including East Asia and continued to convey development power to this region.

Sixth, in term of geo-economics, the "Indo-Pacific" region is more important to China, Japan, Australia and India than to the US. Compared with Japan, Australia and India, China and the US make greater contributions to this region in volume of trade and investment. However, the US doesn't focus economically in the "Indo-Pacific" region but on the "Asia-Pacific" region and Europe, with the trade and investment dependency of 11.12 and 17.82% separately on the "Indo-Pacific" region. In comparison, the trade and investment dependency of China, Japan, Australia and India on the "Indo-Pacific" region is 66.74, 28.37, 21.54 and 48.70% respectively, a number exceeding 20.00%. Among them, the trade dependency of India on the "Indo-Pacific" region has hit around 30.00%.

According to the finding above, we can re-explore the two origins of "Indo-Pacific", namely "the transfer of world economic centers" and "counterbalancing China's increasing geo-presence", from the perspective of geo-economics. The analyses show that **there is no significant trend of the world economic center transfer, so the growing attention on "Indo-Pacific" more likely originates from the increasing energy dependence of the "Asia-Pacific" region, which serves as a world economic center, on the "Indo-Pacific" region and the dependence on**

the Indian Ocean, which serves as an important energy and goods transportation corridor. Furthermore, China continues to grow its economic presence in the "Indo-Pacific" region. Since 2007, China has become a leading force of international economy in this region and continued to dilute the geo-economic presence of the US, Japan and European countries. Because of a serious decline in its economic presence in the "Indo-Pacific" region, Japan initiated the "Quadrilateral Cooperation" in 2007 with an aim to contain China's geo-economic momentum. However, the other three parties, namely US, Australia and India, didn't pay much attention to China's geo-economic presence, so Japan failed to boost its plan. After years of efforts, China's presence in the "Indo-Pacific" region has started to break through the geo-economic level. As the controversial "China Case" continuously reaps success and repeatedly creates the development miracles amidst western fabrication of the China Collapse, a lot of imitators appear from the "Indo-Pacific" region, especially Southeast Asia, South Asia and Africa. In recent years, some imitators of "China Case" such as Vietnam, Cambodia, India and Ethiopia have made rapid progress, while Afghanistan, Iraq, Libya, Syria and the Arab Spring countries have failed collectively under the foreign policies of the US and the Europe. By contrast, more and more countries in this region have started to think positively of the "China Case". Furthermore, after China becomes the second largest foreign investor, the US is more worried that China will export the "China Case" in combination with its capital and political systems, oriental viewpoint of value and the government-led market-oriented economic mode, and thus poses a huge threat to western democracy and universal values and the implementation of a free-market economy in this region. Therefore, **"Indo-Pacific" originates from not only the geo-economics itself but also the realistic or perceptual threats posed by the communication of Chinese development mode driven by the success of geo-economy on the US, Japan and Australia**.

Except the origins of "Indo-Pacific" Strategy, many studies also focus on the possibilities and effects of its advancement. From the perspective of geo-economics, it is a historical normal that there are both competitions and cooperation between geo-economic rivals. If the competition between the maintainer and challenger is a healthy one, they will surely find the convergence of interests and develop cooperation, and thus advance the development of the regions on a win-win basis. However, if the bilateral competition is a cutthroat one, it only because that one party's geo-political and other demands far outweigh its geo-economic considerations and the party spares no expense to pay certain economic costs to hurt the other party. The economic involvement is measured by the percentages of other country's foreign trade volume and FDI volume to the total foreign trade volume and FDI volume of the home country respectively, while the economic cost is measured by the loss of economic involvement. According to the statistical analysis, China has the largest economic involvement as a whole in Indo-Pacific region, followed by India. The economic involvement of Japan and Australia also exceeds one-fifth of the total respectively. For such countries, especially China and India, the weight of geo-economy is definitely big. Yet, for the US, the economic cost is not high; especially under the Cold War mentality, the geo-economic growth can also be sacrificed. If the US, Australia and India repeatedly challenge and even publicly contain China in

Indo-Pacific region, it is bound to trigger and aggravate the geo-conflict in the region. If the Indo-Pacific countries have to choose between China and the US, the tearing of geopolitics and geo-economy will finally harm the long-term economic growth and regional integration of this region. Moreover, such “Indo-Pacific” Strategy that excludes China and may harm the regional economic growth will be not conducive to the realization of Australia’s ideal of a “Middle Power”, and will also impede the achievement of such ambitious goals as India’s “Made in India” and Japan’s “Building an Ocean of Prosperity and Freedom.

Different views on geo-economic weights, to some extent, can explain the different attitudes of different countries towards the “Indo-Pacific” strategy, and can also be considered as a favorable factor to protect the healthy competition and cooperative development in this region. China shall pay attention to the trend of “Indo-Pacific” strategy and endeavor to work with Japan, Australia and India together to seek common ground while reserving differences and defuse the unfavorable factors in the convergence of geo-economic interests. Meanwhile, we cannot place the hope on the disintegration of quadrilateral cooperation, but shall proactively work for a more open and inclusive geo-economic cooperation mode and continuously strengthen the cooperation with the “Indo-Pacific” countries and regions and the partners outside the Indo-Pacific region, especially the neighboring and surrounding regions, so as to build a sound development environment and supports for the sustainable growth of China in the post-globalization era.

References

Abe, Shinzo. 2007. “Confluence of the Two Seas”, Speech by Mr. H.E. Shinzo Abe, Prime Minister of Japan at the Parliament of the Republic of India, Ministry of External Affairs. http://www.mofa.go.jp/region/asia-paci/pmv0708/speech-2.html. Accessed 11 Mar 2018.

Chacko, Priya. 2016. “3 India and the Indo-Pacific from Singh to Modi.” In *New Regional Geopolitics in the Indo-Pacific: Drivers, Dynamics and Consequences*, vol. 57, p. 43.

Khurana, G.S. 2007. Security of Sea Lines: Prospects for India–Japan Cooperation. *Strategic Analysis* 31(1): 139–153.

Khurana, Gurpreet S. 2017. The ‘Indo-Pacific’ Concept: Retrospect and Prospect. http://maritimeindia.org/View%20Profile/636215922419657386.pdf.

Lin, Minwang. 2018. Construction of “Indo-Pacific” and Tension of Asian Geopolitics. *Foreign Affairs Review* (1):103–114.

Liu, Zongyi. 2014. Conflict or Cooperation?—Geopolitics of the “Indo-Pacific” and Geo-economics Selection. *Indian Ocean Economic and Political Review* (4): 4–20.

Medcalf, Rory. 2012. “A Term Whose Time Has Come: The Indo-Pacific”. http://thediplomat.com/flashpoints-blog/2012/12/04/a-term-whose-time-has-come-the-indo-pacific/.

Medcalf, Rory. 2015. Reimaging Asia: From Asia-Pacific to Indo-Pacific. The Asian Forum, 26 June 2015. http://www.theasanforum.org/reimagining-asia-from-asia-pacific-to-indo-pacific/.

Scott, D. 2012. “The ‘Indo-Pacific’: New Regional Formulations and New Maritime Frameworks for US-India Strategic Convergence”. *Asia-Pacific Review* 19(2): 88.

Scott, D. 2013. Australia’s Embrace of the ‘Indo-Pacific’: New Term, New Region, New Strategy?. *International Relations of the Asia-Pacific* 13(3): 425–448.

Weigert, H.W. 1942. Review: Haushofer and the Pacific. *Foreign Affairs* 20(4): 732–742.

Wu, Zhaoli. 2014. The "Indo-Pacific" Originates from Multinational Strategic Games. *Pacific Journal* 29–40.

Xia, Liping. 2015. U.S. "Indo-Pacific" Strategy from Dual Perspective of Geopolitics and Geoeconomics. *American Studies* (2): 32–51.

Zhu, Qingxiu. 2016. Can Japan's "Indo-Pacific" Strategy Succeed?. *Northeast Asia Forum* (3): 16–35.

The Challenge to ASEAN Centrality Under Indo-Pacific Strategy

Liu Wu

Abstract With the rapid economic development of the western Pacific and Indian Ocean region, especially China and India's rapid rise, the western Pacific and Indian Ocean are getting important in the position in world politics and world economy. Indo-Pacific strategy mainly proposed and promoted by the United States, Japan, India and Australia, India, is gradually taking shape. The proposal and implementation of the strategic concept of "Indo-pacific", it is the dividend that some countries pay to share the rapid economic development of the Indo-pacific region,but the main purpose of the strategy is to curb the rapid rise of China. ASEAN, which had played a central role in the Asia-pacific region, could be an important pillar of the Indo-Pacific strategy, but there is a contradiction between the aim of Indo-Pacific strategy to deter China and the purpose and the principles of the ASEAN, the Indo-Pacific group does not see ASEAN as an important pillar. But given the role of ASEAN in Indo-Pacific strategy, Indo-Pacific strategy group has embraced parts of Southeast Asia, considering the ASEAN region as an important part of the strategic vision of India. The Indo-Pacific strategy seeks to contain China beyond the "ASEAN Centrality" regional cooperation and dialogue mechanism: on the one hand, it is bound to aggravate regional tensions and weaken the "ASEAN Centrality" in the regional mechanism-construction, on the other hand, it will lead to differences within ASEAN and increase intra-ASEAN conflict.

Keywords Indo-Pacific strategy · The "central position" of ASEAN · Geopolitics · Internal divergence in ASEAN

1 Introduction

The Indo-Pacific strategy is initially a marine bio-geographic concept, and now has been developed into geopolitical, geo-strategic and geo-economic concepts over the recent years, with rising of the geopolitical status of the Indian Ocean and Pacific

L. Wu (✉)
Research Institute for Indian Ocean Economies (RIIO), Yunnan University of Finance and Economics, Kunming, China

C. Zhu (ed.), *Annual Report on the Development of the Indian Ocean Region (2018)*, Research Series on the Chinese Dream and China's Development Path, https://doi.org/10.1007/978-981-13-7693-1_9

Ocean region. Raising from an academic concept Track 2 discussion to the official formal discourse, the Indo-Pacific strategy gradually evolves to the practice of building regional power structure from debate. The Indo-Pacific concept also gradually evolves into Indo-Pacific strategy, by which, big powers hope to achieve their strategic objectives in the West Pacific Ocean and Indian Ocean region. During this process, the academic community conducts relatively in-depth analysis on the challenges and impacts that the Indo-Pacific strategy may cause on the regional situation and relevant countries, and strategies that relevant actors may adopt. While, presently, the studies about the challenges and impacts brought by this the Indo-Pacific strategy are usually limited to study about the impacts brought by the strategic plan on its main driving parties, i.e. the US, Japan, India and Australia, especially, analysis about the opportunities and challenges brought by the strategic plan to India and Australia, and analysis about the Indo-Pacific strategy impact on China, which is the target that the strategy is intended to contain and guard against.

Regarding the Indo-Pacific strategy impacts on relevant countries, scholars are generally of a view that, even as strong supporters of the Indo-Pacific strategy, India and Australia still may face some adverse challenges and impacts. Lin Minwang is of an opinion that despite that the US has raised India to a "backbone" status for its Asia strategy, but for India, the Indo-Pacific strategy is a "hot potato".[1] Manoj Joshi from India is of an opinion that, the Indo-Pacific strategy brings India the danger of being dragged into the Indo-Pacific military camp, but two most important regions of India, the Gulf of Persia and the Arabian Sea, are excluded out of the discussion of the Indo-Pacific strategy.[2] Although India's academic community of strategic study doubts whether the Indo-Pacific strategy and practice can bring actual benefits for India, they generally believe that, implementation of the Indo-Pacific strategy will raise India's status in the Indo-Pacific region. India will be a beneficiary of implementation of this regional bloc mechanism. India also hopes that it can cooperate with the US to contain China's development in the Indian Ocean through the Indo-Pacific strategy, and India seeks dominance in the wide area of the Indian Ocean that extends to the Gulf of Persia in the north, the Antarctica in the south, the Cape in the west, and the east coast of Africa and the Strait of Malacca and Indonesia in the east. Australia's motive in actively participating in the Indo-Pacific strategy is that Australia hopes to continuously maintain an alliance relationship with the US through the Indo-Pacific strategy, and gradually integrate into Asia economically.[3] Australia also wants to play the role of a "medium-sized big power" by virtue of the Indo-Pacific concept, hoping to address the "uncertainty of China's rising", and get benefit from its economic connection with China and India by developing a security relationship with the US, India and other countries.[4] "Australia also hopes to offset China's influence in the south part of the Indo-Pacific region, through strategic

---

[1]Lin (2018).

[2]Manoj Joshi, "Trump Got It Wrong Again. His Asia Tour Was No Success", http://www.orfonline.org/research/trump-got-it-wrong-again-his-asia-tour-was-no-success/.

[3]Chacko (2012).

[4]Liu (2014).

cooperation with the 4 countries in the Indo-Pacific region", so as to ensure its dominant position in the region.

Generally, the US and Japan have a greater motive to push forward the Indo-Pacific strategy. As the dominant country in the Indo-Pacific strategy, The US actively push forward the Indo-Pacific strategy, with the main purposes of hoping its allies and partners in the region to assume more responsibility on security through the Indo-Pacific strategy and attempting to continue to maintain its dominance and contain the rising China through some strategic balancing measures under the context that its comprehensive national power is experiencing a relative fall.[5] The US considers China a main rival that it should contain and guard against, and lists the constraint of China's rising as a main content of promoting this structure and implementing a rebalancing strategy in Asia Pacific.[6] The Indo-Pacific strategy landscape shaped by the US will exacerbate China's surrounding security environment, strengthen China's insecurity feeling and the strategic suspicion between China and the US, and increase variables and deepen suspicion for development of the China-India relations as well.[7] Japan is an important driving force for the Indo-Pacific strategy. Japanese Prime Minister Shinzo Abe put forward the "Bigger Asia" plan in 2007, and at the time, the US-Japan-Australia-India Quadrilateral Relationship contained the early form of the Indo-Pacific strategy. The future Indo-Pacific strategy may adopt the various-regions security cooperation mechanisms taking the US-India-Japan-Australia "quadrilateral relationship" as the core. The implementation effect of this plan is to achieve the "Greater Asia" plan, so-called objective of ensuring security in the ocean area of Asia Pacific and India.

Under the Indo-Pacific strategy, the Southeast Asian countries and ASEAN that serve as a bridge to link Asia, the Pacific Ocean and the Indian Ocean region are of high strategic importance. However, so far, only a few studies and relatively fragmented discussions have been conducted about the status and role of Southeast Asian countries and ASEAN in the Indo-Pacific strategy, and about the challenges and impacts brought by the Indo-Pacific strategy on Southeast Asian countries and ASEAN. Based on an analysis about ASEAN's geopolitical status in the Indo-Pacific strategy, this paper attempts to discuss about the Indo-Pacific strategy influences on ASEAN's "central position" in Asia Pacific, and the impacts probably caused on ASEAN's internal unity.

I. ASEAN's Status in the Indo-Pacific Strategy

(I) ASEAN's geopolitical status in the Indo-Pacific strategy

After the Indo-Pacific strategy enters into international politics, the academic community's description about the regions and the geographic scope covered by the Indo-Pacific strategy is not consistent. The scope of the Indo-Pacific strategy in a broad sense includes the countries and regions in Pacific Rim and the Indian Ocean

---

[5] [Australia] Brewster (2016).

[6] Zhang (2013).

[7] Wei (2013).

Rim: it includes the water areas of the Pacific Ocean and the Indian Ocean, as well as the land area of the Indian Ocean region and the Oceania bordering both of the Pacific Ocean and the Indian Ocean. While, the geographic scope of Indo-Pacific in a narrow sense refers to Northeast Asia, Southeast Asia, and relevant water areas and adjoining areas in the north of the Indian Ocean, namely, the main energy and commerce and trade passageways on the West Pacific Ocean and North Indian Ocean, and the areas where the big powers challenge each other fiercely. Viewed from the background of proposing the Indo-Pacific strategy, its implementation process, and its aim of guarding against and containing China's rising, the core area of this strategy actually is the geographic scope of the Indo-Pacific strategy in a narrow sense. Besides, during the specific implementation process of the Indo-Pacific strategy, the word "Indo" in the Indo-Pacific concept refers to both India and the Indian Ocean region that may play an important role in the Indo-Pacific strategy. While, the word "Indo" also refers to India in most cases, since India is a dominant country in the Indian Ocean Region, occupies an important geopolitical position in the Indian Ocean region, and also can serve a role in the Indo-Pacific strategy that is far more important than other countries in the Indian Ocean region.

Whether in the geographic scope referred to by the Indo-Pacific strategy in a broad sense, or in the geographic scope referred to by the Indo-Pacific concept in a narrow sense, the Southeast Asia region invariably enjoys an important geopolitical status. ASEAN's geopolitical importance in the Indo-Pacific strategy can be displayed in two aspects. On one side, many countries in the Indo-Pacific region, especially countries in the West Pacific Ocean, highly rely on Southeast Asia. The Southeast Asia region constitutes an "intersection" between Asia and Oceania, and between the Pacific Ocean and the Indian Ocean, as well as the heartland of the Indo-Pacific region. The main maritime commerce and trade sea routes that run from the west coast of the Pacific Ocean and East Asia, to East Africa, West Asia and South Asia, all must pass through the straits in the Southeast Asia. Among them, the Strait of Malacca is the most important. China, India and other East Asian countries import and export goods, and import energy resources and mineral resources mainly through the maritime sea routes that run through Southeast Asia. The energy and economy arteries of such East Asian countries as Japan and South Korea can be controlled by holding the maritime transportation line that runs through the Southeast Asia in the Indian Ocean and the West Pacific Ocean, therefore influencing energy import and economic development security of East Asian countries. On the other side, without participation of Southeast Asian countries, it will be difficult to achieve the main objective that the Indo-Pacific strategy is intended to achieve: to guard against and contain the rapidly rising China. The high geopolitical importance of the Southeast Asia region determines that implementation of the Indo-Pacific strategy cannot succeed without joining of ASEAN, or at least some countries of ASEAN.

Due to the geographic adjacency between Southeast Asia and China, and Southeast Asia's geopolitical importance for China, the US has always considered that using the countries in the Southeast Asia region to build a defense line for containing China an important strategy. During the early period of the cold war, in order to contain China's influence on Southeast Asian countries, President Dwight Eisenhower put forward the "Domino" theory, appealing to the US to guard the Southeast Asian region against threats from socialist countries by intervening in the situation in Southeast Asia In order to establish a strategic ring for encircling the newly founded socialist China, the US gathered some pro-US countries to establish the Southeast Asia Treaty Organization in 1955, of which, Thailand and Philippine are member countries, and South Vietnam, Cambodia and Laos are under military protection of the organization. The US also gave encouragement and support for any actions that can enhance the Southeast Asia region's power, or can contain China's influence. For example, during 1954–1967, the US supported in succession establishing the "Southeast Asian Buddhist Countries Bloc", Malaysia-Thailand-Philippine Southeast Asia Alliance, Philippine-Malaysia-Indonesia Trilateral Alliance, and the Association of South East Asian Nations (ASEAN) composed of the 5 countries in the Southeast Asia, and the Asia Development Bank (ADB) designed to provide development funds to Asian Countries including Southeast Asian Countries. In order to prevent the imagined communist power from spreading its power to the Southeast Asia, the US even got involved in the Vietnam War. After being defeated in the Vietnam War, the US, which had been conducting strategic contraction, put forward the "New Pacificism" regarding Southeast Asia again in 1975 through the president Gerald Rudolph Ford. He required the US to actively participate in the affairs in the Southeast Asia, and to vigorously develop economic connections with Southeast Asian countries.[8]

After the cold war, the US put forward the "returning to the Southeast Asia" policy, the "Rebalancing in the Asia Pacific" policy, and the Indo-Pacific strategic. One important common objective of them is to contain China's rising by using the Southeast Asia's position in the east part of Asia and west Pacific. In the current US-dominated Indo-Pacific strategy, the US is the core and the dominating country; while, India, Japan and Australia are three backbones of the strategic plan. Although ASEAN failed to become a backbone of the Indo-Pacific strategy, while, actually, in any strategic plan and regional cooperation in the Asia Pacific region, ASEAN's participation is indispensable. Currently, ASEAN is not considered a main backbone of the Indo-Pacific strategy, since on one side, this strategic plan is still in a starting stage, and ASEAN's status and role in the Indo-Pacific strategy has not yet been clearly realized; and on the other side, in the context that it may be difficult to get collective support of ASEAN for the strategic plan in a short term, the US had no choice but to go with the second best option: strive to get Indonesia, Singapore, Vietnam and Brunei and other maritime countries to support the Indo-Pacific strategy. From February 10–12, 2018, Japanese Foreign Minister Taro Kono visited Brunei and Singapore. Besides strengthening the two countries' relationship, this visit was also intended to show that ASEAN plays an important role in the Indo-Pacific strategy that was proposed by Japan. Before Taro Kono started his visit, Japanese Ministry of Foreign Affairs claimed that on one side, this visit showed the importance of its relationship with Brunei and Singapore; on the other side, it showed that Singapore and Brunei are very important for the free and open Indo-Pacific Strategy that Japan advocates, because the two countries lay high stress on the maritime order. Taro

[8]Zhang (2008).

Kono's visit to Singapore and Brunei shows that Japan has recognized the importance of Southeast Asian maritime countries in the Indo-Pacific strategic.[9]

(II) ASEAN's geo-economic status in the Indo-Pacific strategy

Besides its important geopolitical status in the Indo-Pacific strategy, ASEAN also enjoys an important geo-economic status. ASEAN is the third largest economy in Asia. With a total population of 614,000,000, and a total territory area of 4,478,100 km^2, ASEAN has a huge market. In 2016, ASEAN achieved a total GDP of 2.559 trillion dollars and a total volume of imports and exports of 1.72 trillion dollars, and used total foreign capital of 98 billion dollars. In 2016, ASEAN used 12.214 billion dollars, 11.535 billion dollars, 3.397 billion dollars and 1.046 billion dollars of foreign capital from the US, Japan, India and Australia respectively.[10] The total amount of foreign investment in ASEAN from the US, Japan, India and Australia was as high as 28.192 billion dollars, accounting for 28.77% in the total foreign investment on ASEAN. The foreign investments that ASEAN gets from the US, Japan, India and Australia accounted for 3.34, 7.94, 20.45 and 56.51% respectively in these countries' total foreign investments. In 2016, the total volumes of trade between ASEAN and the US, Japan, India and Australia were 211.801 billion dollars, 201.892 billion dollars, 58.449 billion dollars and 52.788 billion dollars respectively.[11] ASEAN was respectively the fifth, the third, the fourth and the third largest goods export market, and the fifth, the second, the third and the third source of imports of the US, Japan, India and Australia. With respect to economy and trade, ASEAN is of prominent importance for China, which the Indo-Pacific strategy is intended to contain and guard against. Thanks to strategic partnership between ASEAN and China over the past 15 years and the China-ASEAN free trade zone built in 2010, China has been ASEAN's largest trading partner consecutively for 9 years, and ASEAN is China's third largest trading partner, fourth largest export market and second largest source of imports. The trade volume between China and ASEAN increased to a new high in 2017, reaching 514.8 billion dollars, in which, China's total export volume to ASEAN reached 279.1 billion dollars, and China's total import volume from ASEAN reached 235.7 billion dollars.

Most regions of ASEAN are located in the junction area between the Asia Pacific strategic arc and the Indian Ocean strategic arc, being in a "central position" in the Indo-Pacific geopolitical scope, and bordering with China, which the Indo-Pacific strategy is intended to contain and guard against. Viewed from the narrow geopolitical perspective, the broad geopolitical perspective, or the geo-economic perspective of the Indo-Pacific strategy ASEAN invariably occupies an important strategic position in the plan. This importance determines that, to achieve the objective of containing China's rising, and achieve economic interest in the region, the Indo-Pacific strategy

[9]Prashanth Parameswaran, "ASEAN's Role in Japan's Indo-Pacific Strategy", February 13th, 2018, https://thediplomat.com/2018/02/aseans-role-in-japans-indo-pacific-strategy/.

[10]Sources of data: The statistics published by ASEAN based on relevant data, https://www.aseanstats.org/.

[11]Sources of data: The statistics published by ASEAN based on relevant data, https://www.aseanstats.org/.

bloc must draw ASEAN or some member countries of ASEAN to its side. While, if China wants to neutralize the Indo-Pacific strategy's influence of containing and encircling it, it must further develop its relationship with ASEAN or some member countries of ASEAN.

II. Establishing ASEAN's Central Position in Regional Cooperation in the Asia-Pacific Region

(1) ASEAN's contribution to regional cooperation in the Asia-Pacific region

After the World War II, big powers' confrontation in the Southeast Asia region became increasingly fiercer, which resulted in local wars in Southeast Asia. In order to maintain peace and security in the Southeast Asia region, and to ensure the security of countries in the region, the foreign ministers of Thailand, Philippine, Singapore and Indonesia, and Vice Prime Minister of Malaysia held a conference in Bangkok in 1967. They issued the Declaration on Establishment of the Association of Southeast Asian Countries, namely, the Bangkok Declaration, which formally announced the establishment of ASEAN. The initial motive of establishing ASEAN is not to solve political and security issues in the region, but to build a community of Southeast Asian countries by equal cooperation between them, and to achieve a regional alliance of independent countries. ASEAN actually plays an active role in solving disputes and conflicts between countries in the region, for example: ASEAN has come forward to mediate the territory dispute between Malaysia and Philippine, the territorial sea dispute between Malaysia and Indonesia, and helped achieve political solution of the Cambodia issue. ASEAN started with promoting friendly cooperation between sovereign countries in the region, and developed for more than 50 years. After completing building of the ASEAN Free Trade Area, ASEAN proposed in 2003 that it would build a community of economy, security and social culture by 2020. After the "ASEAN Charter" that was passed in 2007 became effective in 2008, ASEAN has become a regional community with legal status from a loose regional cooperation organization.

Besides building itself into a "community with political security", "an economic community", and "a social and cultural community", ASEAN also established various free trade zones and regional cooperation relationship with countries outside the region. Since China proposed to build a China-ASEAN Free Trade Zone with ASEAN in 2000, ASEAN has negotiated with Japan, South Korea, New Zealand, Australia and India about building free trade zones. On the basis of successful building of the "ASEAN 10+1" and "ASEAN 10+6" mechanisms, ASEAN reached a consensus with China, Japan, South Korea, India, New Zealand and Australia in 2012, launching the Regional Comprehensive Economic Partnership (RCEP). Different from the "10+1" free trade zone framework, the "Regional comprehensive economic partnership" means that ASEAN and other 6 countries are integrated into this free trade zone framework. This can help achieve economic integration between the ASEAN economic community and other countries, and lay the foundation for building an economic community in a wider area.[12]

---

[12]Zhang (2017a).

With rising of ASEAN's influence, ASEAN began to give a more active voice as a group in external relationship and regional security cooperation. It promoted the establishment of such security cooperation mechanisms as ASEAN Regional Forum (ARF) and East Asia Summit (EAS) with ASEAN at the core, striving to build a regional security and cooperation framework in Southeast Asia and surrounding regions. The ASEAN Regional Forum and East Asia Summit have become the most important platforms and mechanisms by which ASEAN promotes regional dialogue and cooperation in the East Asia and Asia-Pacific region. The mission and objective of the ASEAN Regional Forum, which was established in 1994, is to conduct constructive dialogue and contact with other countries regarding the political and security issues in the Asia-Pacific region, and to conduct cooperation in such fields as confidence building measures, peace maintaining, maritime security, nuclear non-proliferation, exchange of military intelligences and preventive diplomacy.[13] Currently, except the 10 member countries of ASEAN, the ASEAN Regional Forum includes another 4 countries in South Asia, namely, India, Pakistan, Bangladesh, and Sri Lanka, and another 27 countries, including the US, Japan, Australia and China. The forum has become the most important political and security dialogue and cooperation platform in the Asia-Pacific region. Based on dialogue, the platform is intended to gradually raise the level of regional cooperation. For this purpose, the forum develops a three-phase regional cooperation agenda, namely, promote building of mutual trust, promote preventive diplomacy; and discuss about solutions of regional conflicts.

In 2005, ASEAN advocated organizing the East Asia Summit, the aim of which is to promote the East Asia Integration Process, and to achieve an East Asia community. Member countries of East Asia community include the 10 member countries of ASEAN, and other 18 countries, including China, Japan, India, Australia and the US. The East Asia Summit covers all main countries in the region, and is explicitly authorized to promote dialogue and cooperation regarding key issues that affect this region. The ASEAN summit is also a regional cooperation mechanism that seeks to integrate the Pacific Ocean and the Indian Ocean at the leadership level. Actually, regarding promoting more extensive regional cooperation in the Indian Ocean and Pacific Ocean region, although the ASEAN summit has many shortcomings, it is undoubtedly a proper means in the current period to promote the ASEAN summit by centering around ASEAN.[14]

(2) Building the "central position" of ASEAN

While strengthening its integration, and promoting regional dialogue and cooperation in East Asia and the Asia-Pacific region, ASEAN also built a series of regional cooperation mechanisms and frameworks centering around ASEAN, which cover major big powers in the East Asia and Asia-Pacific region, play a "central role" in advocating the agenda and guiding concepts, and have become an important force in

[13]See Footnote 12.

[14]Chitriya (2015).

building the Asia-Pacific regional integration process and order.[15] In order to ensure ASEAN's "central position" in these cooperation mechanisms, the regional cooperation mechanisms advocated by ASEAN make requirements on the members' status, and strive to ensure that ASEAN dominates the meetings' procedures. It is required that those countries attending the ASEAN Summit must be ASEAN's comprehensive dialogue partner, and have joined in the Treaty of Amity and Cooperation in Southeast Asia (TAC), or maintain substantial political or economic relationship with the ASEAN organization.[16] For example, in order to dominate the ASEAN summit's agenda and direction, this mechanism also stipulates that the ASEAN's regional forum hold conference of foreign ministers in ASEAN's rotation presidency countries every year.

"Being ASEAN-centered" is considered the guiding principle for ASEAN to address external relationship, promote regional dialogue and cooperation, and build regional cooperation and mechanism. ASEAN Charter stipulates that, in any mechanism or arrangement that was initiated or proposed by ASEAN, ASEAN shall always be in a "central position", and its leading position should be recognized.[17] After over 50 years' exploration and development, now, internally, ASEAN focuses on promoting economic cooperation. It gradually develops from an area with preferential duties, to a free trade zone and then a community, and achieves building of a regional organization with a legal status; externally, ASEAN establishes many "ASEAN-centered" regional cooperation platforms and mechanisms, through which ASEAN conducts dialogue and promotes cooperation on important bilateral, regional and global issues, and strives to increase ASEAN's status and influence in regional affairs.[18] Considering the complicated relationship between ASEAN countries and countries outside the region, ASEAN is unlikely to implement a uniform foreign policy. In such a situation, ASEAN can only build a framework and mechanism of external dialogue and cooperation based on the regional organization's position and status, and always adhere to the "ASEAN-centered" principle in building the mechanism. Adopting an "ASEAN-centered" policy not only can maintain ASEAN's dominating role, but also can give a better play to the influence of "ASEAN means".[19]

The aim that ASEAN build a cooperation mechanism of multi-tiered external relations centering on ASEAN is to establish a balanced network for great powers in the Asia-Pacific region. Balancing and mutual restriction of external forces in the Asia-Pacific region can to some degree prevent certain one power, especially a great power, from dominating affairs in the Asia-Pacific region. Besides, regional cooperation agenda designed by ASEAN to promote regional cooperation can effectively guarantee ASEAN's interest. As a central force in promoting cooperation in the Asia-Pacific region, in the aspect of building a platform and mechanism for regional cooperation in the local region, ASEAN counters against the great powers through

[15] Caballero-Anthony (2014), Stubbs (2014).

[16] Wang (2013a).

[17] Hsu (2015).

[18] Zhang (2010).

[19] Zhang (2017b).

its soft power, not hard power. It means that ASEAN uses the power of regional organizations to deal with the great powers, and to get an initiative by balancing the strength of the big powers. ASEAN should give a high play to its guiding role, but should not stick to its own views; and as a core coordination force, it should listen to the opinions of all relevant parties, and make the best efforts to promote a consensus among them.[20]

But, the establishment and continuity of ASEAN's "central position" is conditional. It is not based on a supremacy that is built on ASEAN's strength; rather, it is a staged result of ASEAN's conducting balancing of strength between the big powers using a balanced diplomacy based on its special geopolitical landscape in the Asia-Pacific region. More importantly, it is a result of the big powers' compromise regarding regional affairs and ASEAN's central position. Under governing of ASEAN, that ASEAN occupies a "central position" in the region is not a stable state, and its "central position" in the Asia-Pacific region is based mainly on compromise between the big powers and their recognition of the strength of each other. If it is difficult to achieve a compromise between the great powers in the region regarding their fighting for interests, and their contradictions and conflicts are difficult to be solved, and ASEAN doesn't have the hard power to mediate a coordination and balance between them, the contradictions and conflicts between the great powers necessarily will bring significant impacts on the various security mechanisms that ASEAN strives to push forward in the region. The new power competition landscape among the big powers will replace the ASEAN-centered regional security landscape. In such a situation, a new strategic landscape will be formed in East Asia and the Asia-Pacific region. Currently, in the West Pacific Ocean and Indian Ocean region that surrounds the Southeast Asia region, the Indo-Pacific strategy bloc comprised of the US, Japan, India and Australia,, apparently forms a new strategic landscape with other powers in the region. It is actually a preventing and anti-preventing strategic landscape, with the US, Japan, India and Australia of the Indo-Pacific strategic bloc on one side, with China on the other side. For ASEAN, the forming and evolution of such a new strategic landscape is difficult to control, therefore, such a new strategic landscape certainly will threat ASEAN's "central position" in the Asia-Pacific region.

Meanwhile, the establishment and continuity of ASEAN's "central position" in the Asia-Pacific region also benefits from compromise reached between the great powers in the region. Regarding the great powers' mutual compromise with each other in the Asia-Pacific region, the most important is the compromise between western style democratic countries and China. Over the past a long period of time, although China's economy has been quickly growing, the US didn't think that the growth of China's national strength will pose a significant challenge to the strategic landscape in the Asia and Pacific region, or to the great powers' status and strategic interest in the Indo-Pacific region. In other words, it can be said that during this period, the US believed that China doesn't has an urgent need to challenge the US's supremacy in the region. The compromise between the great powers in the Asia-Pacific region facilitates to

[20]Wang (2013b).

establish ASEAN's "central position". But over the recent year, with China's national strength and military power rapidly growing and developing, especially with China becoming the world's second largest economy and the second strongest power in terms of military spending, the US is increasingly feeling a pressure from China. The US's strength falls relatively over the period. It believes that the change in the power structure in the Asia and Pacific region as a result of China's rising has threatened its supremacy in the region, and it feels China's challenge to its global supremacy. In order to address the challenge that the US imagines China's rising will pose to its supremacy in the region, the US encouraged those pro-American countries and non-China friendly countries in the Indian Ocean and Pacific Ocean region to form an Indo-Pacific strategy bloc, attempting to ally with these countries to encircle and contain China. Aggravation of the conflict between the great powers in the Asia-Pacific region surely will influence ASEAN's role and position in the region.

Another reason why the US recognized ASEAN's "central position" in building a regional mechanism in the past is that, ASEAN, as a neutral regional power, practices neutralism in the Asia-Pacific region and a diplomacy of pursuing balance between the great powers, and considers the US an important force to rely on for security in the Asia-Pacific region. Therefore, when the US's supremacy in the Asia and Pacific region is not threatened, and no country is rising to challenge its supremacy in the Asia and Pacific region, the US acknowledges that ASEAN occupies a "central position" and plays a "central role" in security affairs in the region.

On one side, establishment of ASEAN's "central position" is a result of ASEAN's unremitting efforts for pushing forward regional cooperation over the past dozens of years. On the other side, it shows the great powers' recognize ASEAN's peaceful force in regional affairs and a platform and mechanism provided by ASEAN for regional cooperation. It means that the great powers think that ASEAN is not harmful, and can provide a platform and mechanism for regional dialogue in the region. As China's neighbor, ASEAN constitutes a hinterland for China in terms of security and economy. A neutral and peaceful ASEAN is beneficial to China. The platform of ASEAN was required for the socialist China to change from being closed to implementing reform and opening up, from isolation to entering onto the world stage. Therefore, for a long time, China has always recognized ASEAN's central position in regional security dialogue. In the "One Belt and One Road" initiative, China also considers ASEAN an important cooperation partner, regarding ASEAN region as a hinterland and a pivotal area for implementation of the initiative. In order to conduct more in-depth cooperation with ASEAN, the "One Belt and One Road" initiative also plans to push forward and strengthen building of multilateral cooperation mechanisms in the ASEAN region, for example, the initiative plans to give a better play to the role of the multilateral cooperation mechanisms initiated by ASEAN and ASEAN countries, i.e. China-ASEAN "10+1", Asia Cooperation Dialogue (ACD), the Greater Mekong Sub-region (GMS) Economic Cooperation, Lancang-Mekong Cooperation (LMC), and ASEAN regional forum. So, that conduction of the "One Belt and One Road" initiative in the Indo-Pacific region consolidates rather than weakens ASEAN's "central position" in the regional cooperation and dialogue mechanism in the region.

The core aim of the Indo-Pacific strategy is that the US gathers other countries to contain China's rising. The antagonism nature inherent with the strategy and the strained situation it causes is not in line with the mission of "promoting peace and neutrality" stated by ASEAN since its founding, and also impacts ASEAN's "central position" that ASEAN has been working hard to establish in East Asia and Asia-Pacific region. Therefore, the proposition and implementation of the Indo-Pacific strategy necessarily will impact ASEAN's "central position", resulting in weakening of ASEAN's "central position" and differentiation of the forces in ASEAN.

2 The Challenge brought by the Indo-Pacific strategy to the central position of ASEAN

(I) The impact of Indo-Pacific strategy on ASEAN's "central position"

Since ASEAN began to promote East Asia integration in 1997, it continued to establish various regional cooperation mechanisms taking advantage of the contradictions between the great powers in East Asia. In this way, ASEAN gradually dominated the cooperation mechanism and agenda during the regional integration process in East Asia, and thus established its "central position" in the East Asia region. The series of mechanisms that ASEAN established and dominated, i.e. the ASEAN "10+3" mechanism, the East Asia summit, the ASEAN regional forum, and the "regional comprehensive economic partnership", all play an important role on establishing and maintaining ASEAN's "central position". While, ASEAN's a "central position" in the regional cooperation in the Asia Pacific is only a functional "central position", since it mainly serves the role of providing a cooperation mechanism and platform, rather than as a real center of power. Separation of the power center and functional center makes ASEAN's position in East Asia very special, resulting in that ASEAN must maintain its position of "functional center" by maintaining its platform role.[21]

Before the Indo-Pacific strategy was released, most of the great powers, including the US, India, Japan, Australia and China, all support ASEAN's "central position" in promoting regional cooperation. For example, the US has always held a relatively supportive attitude toward various regional mechanisms dominated by ASEAN and ASEAN's "central position". That is why the US proposed the Lower Mekong Initiative, signed the Treaty of Amity and Cooperation in Southeast Asia (TAC), and established a strategic partnership with ASEAN. India's "Look East" policy and "Act East" policy have always been promoting and supporting ASEAN's "central position" in regional cooperation in the Asia Pacific region. Strong ASEAN can ensure that the Southeast Asia region doesn't rely on a single great power. In the process of building a peaceful, stable, developing and prosperous regional coop-

---

[21] See Footnote 20, Qi (2011).

eration architecture, ASEAN's "central position" is of extremely high importance to India.[22] Japan also actively supports the ASEAN initiative, especially ASEAN's efforts on building a community of politics and security. Japan also actively participates in the multilateral forums that ASEAN promotes, i.e. "ASEAN+3", ASEAN regional forum, East Asia Summit, expanded ASEAN Defense Ministers Meeting, respecting ASEAN's "central position" in East Asia.[23] The Foreign Policy White Paper that Australia issued in 2017 stated that Australia's bilateral relationship in Southeast Asia is a "high priority"; especially in the security aspect. Southeast Asia constitutes Australia's north route, which is Australia's most important trade route. China recognizes ASEAN's active role in regional cooperation in the Asia Pacific, and supports ASEAN to promote various regional cooperation mechanisms. Because China regards ASEAN as the political and economic partner and the friend to rely on in foreign relations, politically, ASEAN is a friend that China can depend on and can get support from when needed; economically, ASEAN is an important trading partner and a huge market for China. Diplomatically, ASEAN is an important stage where China's foreign policies regarding its surrounding areas are implemented.[24] The China-ASEAN relationship develops from the China-ASEAN consultation partnership in 1992, to the China-ASEAN comprehensive dialogue partnership in 1996, and to the "21st century-oriented good neighborliness and mutual trust partnership" in 1997. In 2003, China joined in the Treaty of Amity and Cooperation in Southeast Asia (TAC), establishing a "peace and prosperity-oriented strategic partnership" with ASEAN. China also firmly supports ASEAN's stance and advocacies in regional affairs, for example, China supports ASEAN to establish a "nuclear free zone" in Southeast Asia, and China is the first nuclear power that agrees to sign the Southeast Asia Nuclear Weapon Free Zone (SEANWFZ) Treaty with ASEAN.

Although the great powers generally recognize ASEAN's "central position", with evolution of international relations in the region and change in the contradictions and conflicts between the great powers, ASEAN's "central position" in regional cooperation began to face a challenge. The first challenge comes from the "Trans-Pacific Partnership" (TPP) pact that the US vigorously promoted in 2009.[25] During that period of time, many ASEAN member countries, including Singapore, Brunei, Vietnam and Malaysia, all joined in the "Trans-Pacific Partnership Pact", and Thailand, Philippine and Indonesia also expressed an intention to join in. To address the possibility that the TPP pact may divide and harm ASEAN's "central position", ASEAN promptly proposed to establish a "regional comprehensive economic partnership" that is comprised of 16 economies including the ASEAN+China, Japan, South Korea, Singapore and India, which has obtained support of its partners. For the period of time since then, ASEAN has been dominating the negotiation, which

---

[22] [Australia] See Footnote 5.

[23] Ministry of Foreign Affairs of Japan (2015).

[24] Lu (2016).

[25] After the US announced its withdrawal out of the TPP, original 11 member countries of TPP signed a new free trade pact in November 2017, which was newly named "Comprehensive Progressive Trans-Pacific Partnership" (CPTP).

fully displays its influence of "central position". After Donald John Trump came to power and announced that the US would withdraw out of the TPP pact, the pact's impact on ASEAN's "central position" was reduced a little. Then, the challenge that TPP poses to ASEAN's "central position" gradually decreased, but currently, the Indo-Pacific strategy promoted by the US, Japan, India and Australia brings a bigger challenge to ASEAN's "central position".

Based on great powers' recognition on East Asia integration promoted by ASEAN but not ASEAN's dominant role and supremacy, ASEAN plays a "central role" in promoting integration of the East Asia region. The big powers' acknowledging about ASEAN's "central position" in regional cooperation in East Asia is based on two conditions: The first condition is that the big powers with many contradictions can reach a compromise with each other in regional cooperation in East Asia, the second condition is the big powers' approval of the series of regional cooperation mechanisms that were proposed by ASEAN, which follows a neutralism policy. With the trade-off between different powers in the East Asia region and deepening of the contradiction between the big powers, especially, with proposing of the Indo-Pacific strategy, the two conditions for establishing of ASEAN's "central position" is being gradually challenged.

The first condition for ASEAN's "central position" is gradually disappearing due to that the Indo-Pacific strategy is gradually taking shape. The Indo-Pacific strategy bloc adopts a China encircling and containing policy, which causes a strained situation in the Indian Ocean region and the Pacific Ocean region, results in a strategic standoff in the region, and harms the big powers' mutual compromise in the region. With China's rising, the opinion that China is the US's all-around political rival, global economic rival and regional military rival has been widely established and gradually strengthened among the US's elites. To implement a China containing policy to address China's rising naturally becomes a critical part of the US's foreign strategy.[26] That to contain the rapidly rising China, prevent China from becoming a dominant country in the Asia Pacific region, and eliminate the possibility of China's posing a serious challenge to the US's global dominance, has become a core objective of the Indo-Pacific strategy that the US advocates. The rapid growth of China's national strength has caused a change of the position and strength of China and Japan that is to the disadvantage of Japan, and Japan considers China a main strategic rival and threat. In order to mitigate the huge pressure from China, Japan chose to actively participate in and promote other countries to participate in the Indo-Pacific strategy bloc. When Shinzo Abe visited India in 2017, he said when delivering a speech at India's Congress: As the oceans of freedom and prosperity, the Pacific Ocean and the Indian Ocean are bringing dynamic links; and an "expanded" Asia that breaks the geographic boundary began to form.[27] The US-Japan-India-Australia bloc of the Indo-Pacific strategy was primarily formed with promoting by the Abe administration. India is also an active promoter of the Indo-Pacific strategy, since in the context that "India's strength is relatively weak and it is not able to balance against

[26] Wu (2014).

[27] Wu (2017).

China by itself, India hopes to cooperate with other big powers in East Asia, so as to address the external pressure from China's tough diplomacy jointly with these big powers".[28] Indian Prime Minister Narendra Modi who came to power in 2014 clearly stated that India shall promote the Indo-Pacific strategy, strengthen its relations with the US, Japan, and Australia, and strengthen its "Act East" policy for developing eastward, which was intended to replace previous "eastward" policy. Australia also expressed its desire to strengthen its relation with the US, and to promote the Indo-Pacific strategy in many occasions. The containing and anti-containing battle between China and the Indo-Pacific strategy bloc is difficult to compromise. ASEAN, which is in a "central position" in regional integration, doesn't have the required hard power and mechanism for reconciling the contradictions between the two parties. That building an Indo-Pacific strategy bloc by allying with countries in the Indo-Pacific region has become a strategic choice of the US, whose national strength is gradually declining, for containing China, and bypassing the regional security mechanism. Therefore, the conditions for ASEAN's being in a "central position" in security and cooperation in the East Asia region are facing an increasingly bigger challenge.

The second condition for ASEAN's being in a "central position" in integration of the region is also facing a challenge. Change of the strategic landscape in the Asia Pacific region that appears since start of the 21st century is adverse to the US, which gets the US to lodge complaints about that the various ASEAN-centered regional cooperation mechanisms and security mechanisms cannot achieve their strategic objectives. The US has criticized for many times the ASEAN-advocated series of mechanisms of being just ineffective "hall of empty talk", and during the George Walker Bush administration, the US's State Secretary was absent from the ASEAN regional forum for two times. Hillary Clinton once claimed that, "the establishing and operating of regional organizations" that are represented by the ASEAN regional forum, should be pushed forward with specific and actual considerations. Compared with establishing new organizations, what's more important is to get these organizations produce good results.[29] The US's allies—Japan and Australia, are also much dissatisfied with the fact that ASEAN stands in a "central position" in the regional landscape, and that its decision-making mechanism cannot make decisions that are favorable to them. That former Japanese Prime Ministers Junichiro Koizumi and Yukio Hatoyama vigorously promoted the "East Asia Community" idea during their administrations reflects their dissatisfaction with the ASEAN regional forum. Ron Huisken, a former official from Australian Department of Defense gives a more direct criticism. He is of an opinion that, in order for the ASEAN regional forum to play its role, ASEAN should give up its central position in the region, and let big powers to go to the front to serve as the leader.[30] Then, Australian Prime Minister Kevin Michael Rudd once criticized that, the series of regional mechanisms that

[28]Sun (2017), Prakash (2016).

[29]Shi (2016), Hillary (2010).

[30]Huisken (2002).

ASEAN established cannot sufficiently effectively and comprehensively address the challenge in the region, so it advocates building an "Asia Pacific community".[31]

Viewed from the perspective of geographic scope, the scope covered by the Indo-Pacific strategy falls in between the scope covered by the ASEAN Summit and that covered by the ASEAN Regional Forum, specifically, the geographic scope that the Indo-Pacific strategy covers is a little bigger than the scope the ASEAN summit covers, but smaller than the scope the ASEAN Regional Forum covers. Viewed from the perspective of the political and security objectives that these plans are intended to achieve, presently, no specific contents have been determined for the Indo-Pacific strategy yet, but we may get a glimpse into its main contents and core objectives through the two quadrilateral meetings that the US, Japan, India and Australia held. The US, Japan, Australia and India held the first quadrilateral meeting and the second quadrilateral meeting in May 2017 and November 2017 respectively, and the published main subjects discussed at these two meetings are: Asia needs: a rules-based order, sea travel freedom and the freedom of flying over, respect for international law, improved connectivity, maritime safety, the threat from South Korea and nuclear non-proliferation, and terrorism.[32] Actually, these contents all can be included into the agenda of the ASEAN-dominated ASEAN summit and ASEAN Regional Forum, since both of the ASEAN summit and the ASEAN regional forum are open forums and cooperation mechanisms, and can conduct dialogue and cooperation in the field of cooperation, integration and political security in the region. Therefore, the proposing and pushing forward of the Indo-Pacific strategy by the US, Japan, Australia and India actually means that these countries do not recognize ASEAN's "central role" in pushing forward the series of regional cooperation mechanisms in East Asia any more.

(II) The impacts that the Indo-Pacific strategy may bring on ASEAN's unity

The Southeast Asia region not only is an important geographic unit of the Indo-Pacific strategy, but it is also located in the central part of the Indian Ocean and the Pacific Ocean region. Besides, it is a junction part that connects the Asia continent and Australia continent, and guards the main maritime passageways between the Pacific Ocean and the Indian Ocean. In such a context, the design and implementation of the Indo-Pacific strategy cannot be achieved without participation of Southeast Asian countries. However, the Indo-Pacific strategy's action of encircling and guarding against China and exacerbating regional situation is not in line with the mission and objective that ASEAN is established for. The contents of the quadrilateral meetings that are published by the 4 key member countries of the Indo-Pacific strategy have some things in common with the work pushed forward by ASEAN's series of regional cooperation mechanisms. But to achieve the objection of containing and guarding against China in the Indo-Pacific region through the Indo-Pacific strategy, it necessarily will exacerbate regional conflict and contradiction in the region. Therefore, this is not in line with ASEAN's mission and objective that are stated in its some guideline

[31] See Footnote 29.

[32] Ankit (2017).

documents, like the Treaty of Amity and Cooperation in Southeast Asia (TAC) and the Bangkok Declaration. ASEAN's mission and objective is to, with the principle of equality and cooperation, jointly promote economic growth, social progress and cultural development in the region, and lay a foundation for building a prosperous and peaceful community of countries in Southeast Asia.[33] So, it is very difficult for ASEAN, which is established to promote peace and stability in the region, to, as a whole, conduct strategic cooperation with the Indo-Pacific strategy bloc that is provoking conflicts and contradictions in the region.

Meanwhile, ASEAN sticks to the "ASEAN ways", namely, the actions that ASEAN takes all must get unanimous consent of all members of ASEAN, and ASEAN is required not to interfere in the internal politics of its member countries and settle disputes by interfering means. This restricts ASEAN's ability to implement a uniform policy regarding the Indo-Pacific strategy, but doesn't restrict the right of ASEAN's member countries to develop relations with countries participating in the "strategy".

ASEAN declares to build an ASEAN community by 2020 that is supported by "ASEAN political and security community", "ASEAN economic community", and "ASEAN social and cultural community", but ASEAN has always adhered to the policy of non-interference of internal politics and national sovereignty of its member countries. This fact determines that even ASEAN successfully builds an ASEAN community, "ASEAN security community will continue to recognize its member countries' national sovereignty in pursuing their own foreign policy, and defense arrangement", as stipulated in the "Declaration of Bali Concord II".[34] ASEAN's various documents and diplomacy practices also show that ASEAN doesn't pursue the objective of establishing a common security policy and military alliance system in the region. It only advocates multilateral security cooperation, and "the key reason why ASEAN advocates multilateral security cooperation, while, doesn't exclude unilateralism on security at the same time, lies in that ASEAN countries do not want to sacrifice their sovereignty and right to independently take actions to form a supra-national body".[35] In such a situation, the members of ASEAN mainly adopt a self-service approach on security issues to realize their interests. Although many members of ASEAN support ASEAN to play its role on regional security at the ASEAN Regional Forum, they worry about that ASEAN is not capable of ensuring their national security. Some countries, mainly maritime countries in Southeast Asia, maintain its security by forming ally or establishing partnership with great powers to strengthen military security connection with military powers from inside and outside of the region.

With the Indo-Pacific strategy pushing forward, a standoff is appearing in the Indo-Pacific region, with the rapidly rising China on one side, and the powers of the Indo-Pacific strategy led by the US on the other side. ASEAN adheres to its mission and objectives and follows a neutralism policy. As a whole, ASEAN is unlikely to lean

---

[33]Wang (2014).

[34]Wei (2015).

[35]See Footnote 34.

toward either side, but some of its members have made tendentious choices. Except Vietnam, most continental countries in Southeast Asia are inclined to view China's rising and role in regional security positively. Except Philippine being hostile to the US, and Malaysia being still vacillating, most maritime countries in Southeast Asia are inclined to embrace the Indo-Pacific strategy bloc. Among ASEAN's member countries, Indonesia, Vietnam and Singapore have explicitly expressed their support for the Indo-Pacific strategy. Those countries are gradually accepting the Indo-Pacific strategy concept, externally expressing their support for the Indo-Pacific strategy, or more actively developing their relations with the Indo-Pacific strategy bloc.

To promote the Indo-Pacific strategy to some Southeast Asian countries and strengthen defense cooperation with these countries, many US officials, including the US President and defense secretary, have strengthened diplomatic offensive toward some Southeast Asian countries over the recent year. During Trump's visit to Vietnam in November 2017, the US and Vietnam issued a joint statement. According to the statement, the two countries shall strengthen bilateral cooperation on defense, security and intelligence, including that one US aircraft carrier shall be assigned to visit the former US navy base at the Cam Ranh Bay, realizing the first visit like this since the end of the Vietnam War. Trump also explained the free and open Indo-Pacific framework during his visit to Vietnam.[36] Vietnam has become a cooperation partner of the US to maintain the current rules-based free and open order in the Indo-Pacific region. To strengthen defense arrangement with Southeast Asian countries that are inclined to the Indo-Pacific strategy, and to encircle and guard against China from the South China Sea direction, the US strengthened defense cooperation and arrangement with such countries like Vietnam, Indonesia and Singapore. Singapore is an important node in the Indo-Pacific strategy, while the Changi base in Singapore is the US army's only foothold in Southeast Asia. Singapore is located at the entrance and the exit to the Strait of Malacca that links the Indian Ocean and the Pacific Ocean, so it certainly doesn't want to miss this opportunity of raising its status with the help of the Indo-Pacific concept.[37]

Among Southeast Asian countries, Indonesia is the country that most strongly hopes to raise its geopolitical importance and statehood by participating in the Indo-Pacific strategy. In the changing geopolitical landscape, Indonesia very much hopes to strengthen its cooperation with the Indo-Pacific strategy bloc based on its geopolitical importance in the Indo-Pacific strategic arc, so as to ensure its peace and security. As a coastal country bordering with both of the Indian Ocean and the Pacific Ocean, Indonesia becomes a power that all parties compete to draw to their sides in the context of the "Indo-Pacific" strategy. At the ASEAN-India summit in January 2018, Joko Widodo stated, the Indo-Pacific region is a stable, peaceful and prosperous land. Indonesia hopes that the architecture of the Indo-Pacific region can be built based on the principles of "openness, transparency and inclusiveness". Indonesia also said ASEAN and India are backbones of the maritime cooperation, and the mechanisms led by ASEAN, like the East Asia Summit, and the Treaty of Amity

[36] Storey (2017).

[37] See Footnote 27.

and Cooperation in Southeast Asia (TAC), can well fit with the Indian Ocean Rim Association, and facilitate communication and integration between the whole Indian and Pacific Ocean Region. In her 2018 annual speech about foreign policy, Indonesian Foreign Minister Retno Marsudi mentioned the importance of the Indian Ocean Rim Association (IORA), and the ASEAN-India and East Asia Summit. She also believes that, in some aspects, the Indo-Pacific strategy is similar to the peaceful, stable and prosperous regional cooperation mechanism that ASEAN attempts to build.[38] In January 2018, Retno Marsudi said, a preferred option in Indonesia's foreign policy in 2018 is to strengthen ASEAN's unity, and to seek to expand ASEAN's presence in the Indo-Pacific region.[39]

To attract more Southeast Asian countries to join in the Indo-Pacific strategy bloc, the US also continues to strengthen defense and security cooperation with Southeast Asian countries. At the 53rd Munich Security Conference in Bonn, Germany, on February 19, 2017, the US Defense Secretary James Mattis, discussed about defense issues with Singapore Defense Secretary NG Eng Hen. At the beginning of April, the two parties discussed about development of geopolitics and defense issues again in the US. In June 2017, James Mattis attended the Asia Security Conference (Shangri-La dialogue) in Singapore, explicitly stating the US's attitude of continuing to actively participate in affairs in the Asia Pacific region. In August 2017, Vietnam Defense Secretary visited the US, discussing about US-Vietnam defense relationship, regional security issues, and navy cooperation. From January 22 to 24, 2018, Mattis visited Indonesia, discussing with Indonesian leaders about defense cooperation and maritime security cooperation. Mattis said that, he shall try to get Indonesia to play a "central role" on maritime security in the Asia Pacific region, and to become an offshore pivot of the Indo-Pacific strategy. From January 24 to 25, 2018, Mattis visited Vietnam. From March 6 to 10, 2018, Carl Vinson aircraft carrier formation visited Vietnam for the first time, which is the first time that a major US warship visited Vietnam during the 43 years since the end of the Vietnam War in 1975.

The reason why China recognizes ASEAN's "central position" is disputes and contradictions between the great powers in the East Asia region, Southeast Asia's role of an important market for China's economic opening, and neutrality of Southeast Asia in regional security. Once ASEAN or some ASEAN countries give up their neutrality, China may adjust its policy regarding ASEAN and ASEAN countries, strengthening its diplomacy with some ASEAN countries, especially diplomacy with some ASEAN countries that neighbor China. This diplomatic strategy surely will result in division of ASEAN into two parts: on one side is the part of ASEAN that is inclined toward the Indo-Pacific strategy bloc, on the other side is the part of ASEAN that is inclined toward China. A divided ASEAN certainly will affect ASEAN's role in regional security, and weaken ASEAN's "central position".

---

[38]Evan (2018).

[39]Bishop (2018).

3 Conclusion

The geographic scope of the Indo-Pacific strategy covers a wide ocean and land area that the Pacific Ocean and the Indian Ocean reach, including the Indian Ocean rim and Pacific Ocean rim countries and regions. The core area of the Indo-Pacific strategy is the arc-shaped area that extends from Northeast Asia, through Southeast Asia, to the North of the Indian Ocean. The main objective of the Indo-Pacific strategy is to contain and guard against the influence of China's rising on the global and regional landscape by uniting with the 4 key countries in the Indo-Pacific region, namely, the US, Japan, India and Australia. The forming of the Indo-Pacific strategy bloc and the strained situation accordingly caused in the Indo-Pacific region have brought a serious challenge to and a great impact on ASEAN's "central position" and its internal unity. The ASEAN-centered Asia-Pacific regional dialogue and cooperation mechanism has made big contributions to the peace, stability and regional cooperation in the Asia Pacific region. But such an ASEAN-centered regional cooperation model must rely on the support and coordination of the great powers, which is the greatest disadvantage. It means that security objectives can be achieved only through compromise and cooperation between the great powers. The Indo-Pacific strategy is mainly aimed to contain and guard against China. It is a competition or even confrontation strategy that the US, India, Japan and Australia put forward to address China's rising. Therefore, the regional "cooperation and security" model that ASEAN advocates and promotes contradicts with the competitive confrontation model. ASEAN's "central position" in regional cooperation is also under impact from the Indo-Pacific strategy, even causing ASEAN to lose its "central role" in promoting regional cooperation in the Asia Pacific. Due to the loss of ASEAN's "central position", the platform on which contact is conducted through ASEAN's series of mechanisms probably loses effect, the Asia-Pacific countries may lose a platform by which they conduct in-depth contact, and that ASEAN may lose a channel by which it mediates among the great powers and affects the relations between the great powers. Under impact of the Indo-Pacific strategy, ASEAN may lose its "central position" in regional cooperation, and some of its member countries even may choose to join in the Indo-Pacific strategy bloc, which may aggravate the divergence and contradiction between ASEAN's member countries on major security issues, and further impact ASEAN's unity.

References

Ankit, Panda. 2017. "U.S. Japan, India, and Australia Hold Working—Level Quadrilateral Meeting on Regional Cooperation". *The Diplomat*, 13 November 2017. https://thediplomat.com/2017/11/us-japan-india-and-australia-hold-working-level-quadrilateral-meeting-on-regionalcooperation/.

Bishop, Hon Julie. 2018. "Minister for Foreign Affairs, ASEAN: The Nexus of the Indo-Pacific". Asia Society Speech, New York, 8 March 2018. https://foreignminister.gov.au/speeches/Pages/2018/jb_sp_180308.aspx.

Brewster, David. 2016. *India's Ocean: The Story of India's Bid for Regional Leadership*. Trans. Du Youkang, and Mao Yue, China Social Sciences Press, pp. 228–252.

Caballero-Anthony, Mely. 2014. "Understanding ASEAN's Centrality: Bases and Prospects in an Evolving Region-al Architecture". *The Pacific Review, 27*(4), 563–584.

Chacko, Priya. 2012. "Priya Three Countries, on Centre of Gravity". *The Hindu*, 12 December 2012. http://www.thehindu.com/opinion/op-ed/three-countries-one-centre-of-gravity/article4188788.ece.

Chitriya, Pinthong. 2015. "The Evolving Regional Architecture for the Asia-Pacific: Toward an Indo-Pacific Idea". *RJSH, 2*(1), 20.

Evan, Laksmana. 2018. "An Indo-Pacific Construct with 'Indonesian Characteristics'", 6 February 2018. https://www.aspistrategist.org.au/indo-pacific-construct-indonesian-characteristics/.

Hillary, Clinton. 2010. "Remarks on Regional Architecture in Asia: Principles and Priorities". Hawaii, 12 January 2010. http://www.state.gov/secretary/20092013clinton/rm/2010/01/135090.htm.

Hsu, Kristy. 2015. "ASEAN Centrality: A Quest for Leadership Role in East Asian Economic Integration". *Asian Leadership in Policy and Governance*, 69–105, 28 August 2015. http://doi.org/10.1108/S2053-769720150000024004.

Huisken, Ron. 2002. Civilizing the Anarchical Society: Multilateral Security Processes in the Asia-Pacific. *Contemporary Southeast Asia, 24*(2), 187–202.

Lin, Minwang. 2018. "The Construction of 'Indo-Pacific' and the Tension in the Geopolitics in Asia". *Foreign Affairs Review* (1).

Liu, Zongyi. 2014. Conflict or Cooperation: The Geo-political and Geo-economic Options in the Indo-Pacific Region. *Indian Ocean Economic and Political Review* (4):6.

Lu, Jianren. 2016. "On ASEAN's Important Strategic Position in the Asia Pacific Region". *Frontiers* (10).

Ministry of Foreign Affairs of Japan. 2015. "Japan-ASEAN Friendship and Cooperation: Shared Vision, Shared Identity, Shared Future", p. 5. 2 April 2015. http://www.asean.emb-japan.go.jp/documents/20150402%20pamphlet.pdf.

Prakash, Panneerselvam. 2016. "Advancing India's Relationship with Japan and South Korea: Quest for Middle Power Cooperation". IPCS Issue Brief 262, August 2016.

Qi, Huaigao. 2011. "Some Ideas about the Leadership Model for Regional Cooperation in the East Asia: The Leadership Model of the China-US-Japan Cooperation under the ASEAN Mechanism". *Southeast Asian Studies* (4):55–59.

Shi, Tianyi. 2016. "Regional Risks and the Offsetting Strategy of ASEAN Countries", *World Economics and Politics* (5).

Storey, Ian, and Malcolm Cook. 2017. "The Trump Administration and Southeast Asia: Enhanced Engagement". Yusof Ishak Institute, No. 87.

Stubbs, Richard. 2014. "ASEAN's Leadership in East Asian Region-Building: Strength in Weakness. *The Pacific Review, 27*(4), 523–541.

Sun, Xianpu. 2017. "India-Japan Defense Cooperation in the Indo-Pacific Context", *Theoretical Horizon* (3).

Wang, Mingguo. 2013a. "The Complexity of International Regimes and East Asia Integration Process". *The Journal of Contemporary Asia-Pacific Studies* (1).

Wang, Yuzhu. 2013b. "The RCEP Initiative and ASEAN's 'Central Position'". *International Studies* (5):53.

Wang, Mingguo. 2014. "Validity Assessment of the Governance Mechanism in East Asia Region and Future Development", *The Journal of Contemporary Asia-Pacific Studies* (4).

Wei, Zongyou. 2013. The US's Strategic Adjustment in the Indo-Pacific Region and the Impact of Its Geopolitical Strategy. *World Economics and Politics* (10):154.

Wei, Hong. 2015. "ASEAN's Security View and Security Cooperation Mechanism in Southeast Asia Region". *The Journal of Central China Normal University* (*Humanities and Social Sciences Edition*) (6).

Wu, Zhaoli. 2014. "Origin of the Indo-Pacific Strategy and Multi-nation Strategic Playing". *Pacific Journal* (1).

Wu, Minwen. 2017. "What about the Prospect of Trump's 'Indo-Pacific Strategy'", *China Youth Daily,* p. 11. 16 November 2017.

Zhang, Yanjie. 2008. "*An Attempted Study about the Big Power Factor in the US's Policy Regarding Southeast Asia since the World War II*". 2008 Master Thesis of Jinan University, p. 18.

Zhang, Bowei. 2010. "Wen Qiping: Historical Transition of ASEAN's Status: A Study from the Perspective of Regional Economic Integration". *Asia-pacific Economic Review* (5):9.

Zhang, Li. 2013. The 'Indo-Pacific' Strategic Plan's Impact on the Multilateral Landscape in the Asia-Pacific Region. *South Asian Studies Quarterly* (4):7.

Zhang, Yunling. 2017a. "The 50 Years' History of ASEAN: Exploration and Advancing in Marching Forward". *World Economics and Politics* (7):27.

Zhang, Yunling. 2017b. "The 50 Years' History of ASEAN: Exploration and Advancing in Marching Forward". *World Economics and Politics* (7):32.

New Trend in the Construction of "Indo-Pacific" and Its Impact on South Asia

ChuanLu Feng

Abstract In 2017, the concept of "Indo-Pacific" continues to develop further. The latest sign indicates that the construction of the concept may go beyond "hype" and enter the strategic level, and even to the specific deployment. At the same time, a series of regional effects and chain reactions brought about by the strategic adjustment of great powers and the reshaping of international relations have gradually emerged under the construction of the "Indo-Pacific" concept. For example, Trump hypes the concept of "Indo-Pacific" and the "Indo-Pacific strategy" of the US surfaces gradually. The relations between the US and India continue to develop further with bilateral defense co-operations on the rise in both frequency and quality. The Sino-Indian relations have declined significantly, and the flattening trend of the strategic triangle among China, the US and India has become more prominent. Japan and India have accelerated their strategies cooperation, and the security dialogue among the four countries is re-launched. Small and medium-sized countries in the relevant regions have actively engaged in strategic speculation and power rent-seeking. All of these events have exerted pressure on China's geopolitical security and rise. As far as the influence of the "Indo-Pacific" construction on South Asia is concerned, it has not only enhanced the strategic position of South Asia in global geopolitics, but also deepened the imbalance of power structure here. It has strengthened the strategic role of India, but increased the rift in international relations in South Asia. It has greatly raised the strategic importance of Sri Lanka and the Maldives in the Indian Ocean, but almost completely ignored the inland areas of Bhutan, Nepal and Bangladesh. It has not only made different South Asian countries enjoy different environment in international strategies, but also restricts the formation of regional cooperation and regionalism in South Asia. The New South Asia Strategy of the Trump Administration, in particular, may further tear South Asia from the security strategy, while the increasingly tough South Asian Policy of India in the Modi era may further deteriorate the international isolation of regional countries to Pakistan, and may even exclude and hinder China's efforts to promote economic integration and regional stability in South Asia.

C. L. Feng (✉)
Institute for Research Institute for Indian Ocean Economies (RIIO),
Yunnan University of Finance and Economics, Kunming, China

C. Zhu (ed.), *Annual Report on the Development of the Indian Ocean Region (2018)*, Research Series on the Chinese Dream and China's Development Path, https://doi.org/10.1007/978-981-13-7693-1_10

Keywords "Indo-Pacific" · "Indo-Pacific Strategy" · Regional effects · New South Asia Strategy of the US · South Asia Pattern

The concept of "Indo-Pacific" is not a new term today, so it is meaningless to just research some views and literatures that everyone knows. However, the regional effects and many chain reactions brought about by the construction of "Indo-Pacific" are gradually emerging, and these contents are no doubt more important and more complex than those side issues, such as clarifying the original source of the "Indo-Pacific" concept, the specific geographical boundaries or who use it under what circumstances. Then, in the subsequent research, it is necessary to follow up the regional effects of the concept construction and the impact of relevant events on China. Meanwhile, it is also necessary to study the concept from the macro level to the mid and even micro-level.

1 The Basic Connotation and Research Status of the "Indo-Pacific" Construction

The "construction" used in social science research is a term borrowed from architecture, originally referring to the constructing a structure. In this paper, the meaning of "construction" is not limited to the cultivation of the common ideas of constructivism, but also includes the connotations of realist alliance activities and geostrategic design; and the construction of "Indo-Pacific" here corresponds to the concept construction of "Indo-Pacific" by the US, Japan, India and Australia and the game arrangement taking China as a competitor in the overall strategic space of the concept.

In the past few years, it is an indisputable fact that the concept of "Indo-Pacific" has been transformed from a marine biogeographic concept[1] into a geostrategic concept and continues to be developed further. The term is not only frequently seen in the official texts and government speeches of some important strategic bodies in the world such as the US, India, Japan and Australia, but also in international media reports and related pages of serious academic journals. Up to now, although opinions vary on the specific geographical boundaries of the "Indo-Pacific", the academic community has at least no major differences on its general scope and core areas. In a broad sense, the Indo-Pacific region covers the Indian Ocean and the Pacific Ocean, as well as the coastal countries to which they are adjacent,[2] and for the region in the narrow sense, the core area includes at least the sea area adjacent to the intersection of the Western Pacific and the East Indian Ocean and the lands around them. According

[1] "Indo-Pacific" originally described a biogeographic region of the global ocean, specifically including the tropical waters of the Indian Ocean, the western and central Pacific Oceans, and the Indonesian waters connecting the above-mentioned waters, excluding the temperate and polar regions of the Pacific and Indian Oceans, and the tropical region of the East Pacific Ocean and the Pacific coast of the Americas. See Zhao (2013a).

[2] Wei (2013).

to above consensus, in the strategic space defined by the concept of "Indo-Pacific", there are emerging powers with the strongest rising momentum and growth pole that is the most dynamic in the global economy (for example, the weighting of China's economic growth in global has been up to 30% in recent years); there are the world's busiest marine lifeline, essential strategic stronghold like the Holmow Strait, the Straits of Malacca, and the world's most abundant oil and gas resources and the disputes brought about by these, as well as terrorism that has caused global uneasiness and long-standing piracy; meanwhile, what is more decisive is that some of the most important strategic bodies, such as the US, China, Japan, and India, have their major strategic interests and concerns here with complex relations between each other, and related geographical neighbors still have some territorial or waters disputes.

In view of the above, the current great powers have adjusted their global strategies (or regional strategies) based on a new strategic perspective and view of time and space. Correspondingly, the international relations within the "Indo-Pacific" region have also begun to show a new round of complex evolution. After observing the current strategic situation of the "Indo-Pacific region, it's easy to find out that, with the hype of the concept, the "Indo-Pacific strategy" of the Trump administration has gradually surfaced, and the "Act East" policy of India is actively promoted, as well as the "free and open Indo-Pacific strategy" of Japan, the security dialogue among the US, Japan, India and Australia was re-launched, the "strategic triangle" of China, the US and India was in flattening trend, and the relevant small and medium-sized countries (such as Vietnam, Myanmar, Singapore, etc.) are actively seeking strategic speculation and power rent-seeking—and so on. All of these have made the "Indo-Pacific" security pattern and the geopolitical order potentially instable and uncertain, thus exerting pressure on China's geo-security and rise. In short, "Indo-Pacific" has become a new geostrategic concept based on the reality. It makes the current Asia-Pacific region and the Indian Ocean region as a global strategic space, which constitutes the central stage for the world's important strategic bodies.

As for the domestic research, the academia's concern about the concept of "Indo-Pacific" and the discussion on the situation of "Indo-Pacific" (Asia-Pacific) have kept on developing since it first being a hot issue a few years ago, and now a new round of concerns emerges. In these discussions, there are many outstanding achievements from scholars, such as Zhao Qinghai, Xia Liping, Liu Zongyi, Wei Zongyou, Wu Zhaoli, Lin Minwang, Wu Minwen, Chen Jimin, Wu Huaizhong, which have provided many academic enlightenments for the study of this issue. However, most of the domestic interpretations on "Indo-Pacific" are geopolitical based on the overall perspective up to now, such as the following papers, *The Concept of "Indo-Pacific" and Its Implications for China,*[3] *The Origin of "Indo-Pacific" and the Multinational Strategy Game,*[4] *Conflict or Cooperation?—Geopolitical and Geoeconomic Choices in the "Indo-Pacific" Region",*[5] *The Impact of the "Indo-Pacific" Concept on the*

[3]Zhao (2013b).

[4]Wu (2014).

[5]Liu (2014).

Multilateral Pattern of the Asia-Pacific Region,[6] *The Strategic Adjustment of the US in the Indo-Pacific Region and Its Geostrategic Impact*,[7] *The Development, Limitations and China's Response to the Indo-Pacific Strategy*.[8] Certainly, some scholars have recently noticed the "construction" meaning of the regionalism inherent in "Indo-Pacific". For example, *The Construction of "Indo-Pacific" and the Tension of Asian Geopolitics* by Lin Minwang analyzes the construction of "region" in international politics in detail, pointing out the process and outcome of conceptual construction in shaping the power game. It believes that the Indo-Pacific concept is obviously not a simple copy of the Asia-Pacific concept, and further explores the inner tension of Asian geopolitics reflected by the "Indo-Pacific".[9]

The above researches have provided some insight for follow-up research, and also leaves room for improvement. First, with booming development, many new trends have emerged in the current construction process of "Indo-Pacific" to be followed up. Second, the construction of "Indo-Pacific" has brought about complex regional effects and chain reactions, but the research in this area is comparatively scarce. Third, although the macro-view based on overall perspective has certain analytical advantages, the research perspective of "Indo-Pacific" should be more diversified and rich, such as regional perspective and the microscopic unit perspective.[10]

On the one hand, given that the geographical connotation of the "Indo-Pacific" concept is to strengthen India's strategic role and highlight the strategic position of the Indian Ocean, this paper believes that the strategic appeal of "Indo-Pacific" is to build "Asian NATO" and "Indo-Pacific Strategic Arc" targeting China in the overall strategic space of this region to hinder the rise of China and the spread of its influence; On the other hand, under the vision of "Indo-Pacific", India is exactly the primary power in South Asia, and South Asia is exactly the largest geographic plate for people to explore the Indian Ocean from coast to the center, and it is also place where the Flagship Project of China-Pakistan Economic Corridor in China's "Belt and Road" Initiative located, as well as the Bangladesh-China-India-Myanmar Economic Corridor. It's also the first stop of China's "Westward Advance" and the land corridor of China to the Indian Ocean. Therefore, the research on the impact of the "Indo-Pacific" construction on South Asia is undoubtedly an excellent regional case for exploring the regional effects brought about by it, the chain reaction of various strategic bodies, and China's response strategies. It is also an effective research perspective.

Based on new developments in the construction of Indo-Pacific and combining with the development of situation in South Asia in 2017, this paper will conduct

[6]Zhang (2013).

[7]Wei (2013).

[8]Wu (2018c).

[9]Lin (2018).

[10]Recently, the first 2018 *Modern International Relations* published a series of theme papers of "Indo-Pacific Strategy" based on country studies, such as Wu (2018a), Xia and Qi (2018), Zhou and Wan (2018), Li (2018), Yang and Wang (2018), Chen (2018), all these results have reflected that the research perspective at the unit level has begun to be valued by the academia.

a case study on the impact of the construction of the Indo-Pacific on the South Asia pattern, summarize the emerging and potential regional effects, and further make some framework discussions on China's due vision of Indo-Pacific and the geostrategy in South Asia.

2 New Trends in the Construction of "Indo-Pacific" since 2017

This part will review and summarize the new trends in the construction of "Indo-Pacific" since 2017, and outline the new geopolitical blueprint of the "Indo-Pacific" region. The following aspects shall be attached great importance among many new trends emerged in 2017. First, Trump hyped the concept of "Indo-Pacific" to make the "Indo-Pacific strategy" of the US gradually surface. Second, the US-India relations continued to be further developed with the bilateral defense cooperation "speeding up and improving". Third, the Sino-India relations has been clearly on a downward slide, and the Sino-India interactions on "Boundary Issues" and the Belt and Road became international hotspots; Fourth, Japan and India accelerated their strategy cooperation, and security dialogue among the four countries taken up again; Fifth, under the above background, small and medium-sized countries in the relevant regions actively engaged in strategic speculation and rent-seeking for geopolitical power.

(1) **Trump hyped the concept of "Indo-Pacific" to make the "Indo-Pacific strategy" of the US gradually surface.**

On January 21, 2017, the Trump Era was officially opened since Trump swore in as the President of the US. For more than one year in power, Trump has in fact continued the strategic vision of the "Indo-Pacific" started from Obama's "Asia-Pacific Rebalancing" and the strategic thinking regarding India as an important increment in the strategic resources for "Indo-Pacific" to create "Asia's NATO", under the cover of the seemingly messy diplomatic style. Trump's "Indo-Pacific Strategy" of has gradually surfaced at the end of 2017 when he received and hyped the concept of "Indo-Pacific".

In fact, the Obama administration had already put forward the concept of "Indo-Pacific" in the official text *Asia-Pacific Maritime Security Strategy*[11] in 2015; during the talks with Indian Prime Minister Modi who visited the US on June 26, 2017 for the first time, Trump first used the concept officially in a diplomatic occasion. At that time, Trump proposed that the US and India would deepen strategic partnership to jointly promote the fight against threat from the terrorism, thus promoting the stability of the Indo-Pacific region, strengthening free and fair trade and cooperation

[11]U.S. Department of Defense, "Asia-Pacific Maritime", Strategy https://www.defense.gov/Portals/1/Documents/pubs/NDAA%20A-P_Maritime_SecuritY_Strategy-08142015-1300-FINALFORMAT.PDF.

goals in energy relations, etc.[12] Then, Trump tried to further hype the concept of "Indo-Pacific" to advocate the vision during his first visit to Asia.[13] On November 5, Trump flew to the Yokota military base of the US in Tokyo, Japan. In his speech, he clearly stated that "we will cooperate with friends and allies to seek a free and open Indo-Pacific". This can be seen as the high-profile response of Trump to the "Indo-Pacific strategy" proposed by Abe at the African Development Conference on August 27, 2016. Then the two parties discussed the concept and reached agreement on strengthening cooperation to achieve the "free and open Indo-Pacific" in talks with Abe on November 11.[14]

After Trump advocated the vision of the "Indo-Pacific" during his travel to Asia and during the end of 2017 and the beginning of 2018, Trump administration issued the first global strategic document, the *National Security Strategy Report*,[15] followed by the new *National Defense Strategy Report*[16] and the *Nuclear Situation Review Report*[17] *of* the US Department of Defense. The core meaning of the "Indo-Pacific" part in these documents is to emphasize that China has not only become a major strategic competitor bringing power challenges to the US, but also constitutes a revisionist factor threatening peace, stability and economic order in the Indo-Pacific region. The US needs to unite its allies and new partners to cope with this threat. Through power counterbalancing and institutional constraints, the US shall regulate China's rise under the security order led by the US and within the international mechanism and institutional framework led by the US, so as to maintain and expand the geopolitical and geo-economic interests, and protect its global hegemony.

A series of actions have been adopted with these strategic cognitions. For example, in the context of the sluggish domestic economy in 2017, the US Senate still passed the defense budget of up to 700 billion US dollars for 2018, with an increase of more than 10% over the previous year[18]; In 2017, the US repeatedly dispatched aircraft carriers to the southern island reef area of China and even China's territorial waters within 12 nautical miles to proclaim the so-called freedom of navigation; The US completed the deployment of the Terminal High Altitude Area Defense (THAAD) on the Korean peninsula in 2017; The Trump administration has recently launched

[12]The White House, Office of the Press Secretary, "Remarks by President Trump and Prime Minister Modi of India in Joint Press Statement," June 26, 2017, https://www.whitehouse.gov/the-pressoffice/2017/06/26/remarks-president-trump-andprime-minister-modi-india-joint-press.

[13]Whitehouse, "Remarks by President Trump at APEC CEO Summit: Da Nang, Vietnam", Nov. 10, 2017, https://www.whitehouse.gov/briefings-statements/remarks-president-trump-apec-ceo-summit-da-nang-vietnam.

[14]Wu (2018b).

[15]White House, "National Security Strategy of the United States of America", December 2017, http://www.informationclearinghouse.info/article2320.htm.

[16]U.S. Department of Defense, "National Defense Strategy", https://www.defense.gov/Portals/1/Documents/pubs/2018-National-Defense-Strategy-Summary.pdf.

[17]U.S. Department of Defense, "The Nuclear Posture Review Report", https://www.defense.gov/Portals/1/features/defenseReviews/NPR/2010_Nuclear_Posture_Review_Report.pdf.

[18]Associated Press, "Senate approves $700B defense bill", September 19, 2017, https://nypost.com/2017/09/19/senate-approves-700b-defense-bill/.

a series of joint strategies, such as issuing the New South Asia policy of re-entering Afghanistan, supporting India and hindering Pakistan; signing the *Taiwan Exchange Act* to disrupt the situation in the Taiwan Strait, thereby activating Taiwan as an assistant; launching an unprecedented scale of trade war against China, with the attempt of forcing China to substantially reduce its trade surplus by raising tariffs. It's obvious that the Trump administration showed a comprehensive safety, political, and economic cards and significantly strengthened and accelerated actions on these aspects.

However, compared with the above-mentioned aspects, the thing with far more profound impacts is that the Trump administration has basically completed the key elements of strategy with the release of important documents such as the *National Security Strategy Report*, the *National Defense Strategy Report*, and the *Nuclear Situation Review Report* at the end of 2017 and the beginning of 2018. These key elements include redefining core national interests, reassessing the strategic environment, redefining strategic opponents, re-establishing strategic goals, proposing new ideas for alliance governance, and clarifying US military reform-related plans, etc. Therefore, the overall framework and main connotations of the "Indo-Pacific Strategy" of the Trump administration have basically been clarified.

The first *National Security Strategy Report* submitted by Trump on December 18, 2017, is mainly about the core issues of security, prosperity and world status, which defined the "four core national interests" of the US: protecting the people and homeland security of the US, promoting national prosperity, seeking peace with strength, and increasing national influence; The report regarded China and Russia, Iraq and North Korea and the international terrorism as the three major challenges facing the US, which claimed that China and Russia are the main strategic competitors, Iran and North Korea are "rogue regimes", and the above two aspects and the international terrorism organizations attempting to attack the US constitute the three major sources of threat to US security.[19]

The US Department of Defense subsequently issued a new version of the *Defense Strategy Report*[20] on January 19, 2018. The content disclosed in this report is divided into five parts: introduction, strategic environment, objectives of the Department of Defense, strategic initiatives and conclusions, with a total of 11 pages, accounting for about one-fifth of the non-public version.[21] In the introduction, the report clearly points out the current strategic competitor of the US and that the "strategic competition is now the primary issue of national security, not terrorism". It also specifically mentions that "China, as a strategic opponent, coerced its neighbors with predatory economic activities and implemented the militarization of the islands in the South China Sea at the same time; Russia bullied the borders of neighboring countries and pursued a veto on the economic, diplomatic and security decisions of neighbor-

---

[19]"National Security Strategy of the United States of America", December 2017, http://nssarchive.us/wp-content/uploads/2017/12/2017.pdf.

[20]U.S. Department of Defense, "National Defense Strategy", https://www.defense.gov/Portals/1/Documents/pubs/2018-National-Defense-Strategy-Summary.pdf.

[21]"National Defense Strategy", p. 1.

ing countries. At the end, it emphasizes that "in general, our strength posture, the structure of allies and partner countries, and the modernization of the Department of Defense will provide the capabilities and flexibility required in winning the struggle and maintaining peace through strength."[22]

In the second part for the strategic environment assessment, the report argues that "the main challenge for US prosperity and security is the re-emergence of long-term strategic competition", "Another change in the global security environment is that US military advantage is challenged", and "New business technology will change society and eventually change the form of war." The report clearly defines the so-called "4 + 1" threat judgment, namely, four national actors of China, Russia, North Korea and Iran, as well as non-state actors such as the terrorist organization "Islamic State". The report points out that competitors are increasingly strengthening formal and informal forces, combining different strategies, and taking actions with concealed forms, ambiguous property, flexible means, and less cost to achieve their goals. It also points out that the rapid development and diffusion of technology will provide competitors with a lower access threshold.[23]

In the third part, the report clearly lists 11 strategic objectives of the Department of Defense. The objectives include: defending the US from attack; maintaining the military superiority of the joint forces in the world and key areas; deterring the opponents from infringing the key interests of the US; enabling the US's cross-sector partners to promote the influence and interests of the US; maintaining a favorable regional power balance in Indo-Pacific, Europe, the Middle East and the Western Hemisphere; protecting allies from military aggression, supporting partners from coercion, and fairly sharing the common defense responsibility; discouraging, preventing or deterring the rival countries and non-state actors from acquiring and diffusing or using weapons of mass destruction; preventing terrorists from directly acting as or supporting other actors to launch attacks on the US and citizens, allies and overseas partners; ensuring the openness and freedom of the international commons; changing the thinking, culture and management system of the Department of Defense to improve the speed and effectiveness of creating performance; establishing the "21st National Security Innovation Foundation" to effectively support the operation of the Department of Defense, maintain security and solvency.[24]

In the fourth part, the report elaborates on the strategic path for the US to win: first, strengthen armaments and build a joint force with stronger lethality; second, strengthen alliances partnership and attract new partners; third, reform management of the Department of Defense to improve effectiveness and economy.[25]

Based on the paper, in terms of strategic thinking, the national defense report is full of the mentality of cold war and "zero-sum" game concept, which deliberately distorts China's national defense and foreign policy, hypes strategic competition against China and Russia, and also fully embodies the strategic thinking of "seeking

[22]"National Defense Strategy", p. 1.

[23]"National Defense Strategy", pp. 2–3.

[24]"National Defense Strategy", p. 4.

[25]"National Defense Strategy", pp. 5–10.

peace through strength" and "military priority" by Trump administration. In terms of strategic measures, the report proposes to optimize armaments and build joint forces with stronger lethality, emphasizing absolute military superiority and building regional deterrence; the report proposes to expand the network of alliances and make "Indo-Pacific" as a key point of national defense strategy, which intends to promote the form of the "Asian NATO" among the US, Japan, Australia and India so as to contain China in the "Indo-Pacific" region; and the report also proposes to optimize the organizational structure and management model of the Department of Defense to improve the efficiency of national defense management and reduce economic costs.

Generally, Trump has sublated the diplomatic legacy of Obama, but he maintained a comparatively stable trend in strategic concerns about the Indo-Pacific region, basic standpoint on China's affairs, the basic setting of India's strategic role, inheritance of the strategic tradition of "offshore balancing hands", as well as the emphasis on partnership management and security responsibility sharing.

Up to now, there are still many analysts who believe that the "Indo-Pacific strategy" of the US is nothing more than a concept hype. In this regard, this paper holds different opinions and believes that the "Indo-Pacific strategy" is not groundless, but has substantial content. The "Indo-Pacific strategy" of the Trump administration is not just an empty shell, but obviously highlights the competition and containment. Therefore, China has no reason to take it lightly. In particular, the "Indo-Pacific Strategy" of Trump emphasizes the absolute superiority of military power and the effectiveness of enhancing strategic deterrence. In fact, it is stimulating armament races and manufacturing security dilemma among major powers; and the US is not forging a free and open "Indo-Pacific" but constructing a disrupt and opposed one through strengthening the alliance system and internal reform of the Department of Defense.

(2) **The US-India relations continued to be further developed with the bilateral defense cooperation "speeding up and improving".**

For the Trump administration, the increasingly close relations with India and the gradually deepened defense cooperation are the few and important diplomatic legacy of the previous government. During the Obama era, the US and India signed the new *Defense Cooperation Framework Agreement* in 2015, regarding India as the main defense partner of "non-NATO allies". Then the two counties signed the *Logistics Exchange Memorandum Agreement* in 2016. All these actions reflected that the US-India relation between the Obama Government and Modi Government was unprecedentedly closer, with a historic breakthrough in defense cooperation. On the last day of the Obama administration, namely, the day before Trump swearing in as the 45th president of the US, the US Federal Department of Commerce announced to loosen the Indo-specific defense export control norms, and the Bureau of Industry and Security (BIS) revised the *Export Administration Regulations* (EAR), established general licensing policies for licenses for export or re-export to India and modified provisions about the Verified End User (VEU) of the US's exports and corresponding authorization provisions. According to the new BIS policy, those goods exported from the US and authorized by the VEU in India can finally be used for civilian or military, including materials used in nuclear, missile, chemical or biological weapons. The actions of Obama administration on the day before Trump swearing in as president of the US were thought to have resolved some of the major problems for India to import the most advanced defense technology and military equipment from the US.[26] Trump, as the US president, continued to operate bilateral relations with the Modi government to further promote the defense cooperation between the two countries to "speeding up and improving" on the basis of Obama administration; in terms of development trend in the next few years, the US-India relations will probably continue to be further developed, and d defense cooperation will be deepened.

In fact, in the 20 years before Trump took office, the US-India relations was always on the rise, the defense cooperation between the two countries grew by leaps and bounds especially after the Asia-Pacific Rebalancing strategy of the US. The US-India relations started from the low point brought about by India's nuclear test in 1998, and moderated after the 911 in 2001, then became better; then it continued to be developed further after the Asia-Pacific Rebalancing strategy implemented by Obama administration, and reached an all-time high. During the Bush era, as India actively supported the anti-terrorism, the US not only ended the severe sanctions imposed on India for development of nuclear weapons, but also spared no effort to upgrade India's status as a major force out of the war on terrorism; the US and India formally signed the first *Defense Framework Agreement* for ten years in 2005, which in fact established a basic framework for the US-India defense cooperation. In the Obama era, the strategic focus of the US shifted from anti-terrorism to coping with competition from major powers, especially the strategic competition brought about by the rise of China; For India, the domestic economy had experienced rapid growth during this period, leading the international status to rise constantly. In particular, Modi, a political strongman, stepped on the central stage of state power, and ambitiously upgraded India's "Toward East" strategy to "Act East" Strategy. In view of that the rise of India might balance the rise of China, and the "Act East" Strategy objectively had offset China's influence, which drove the US to redefine India's strategic role and enhance US-India relations. India regarded the US as a powerful tool for enhancing its status as a major power and closely maintaining relations with countries in the Asia-Pacific region, catering to the US exultingly. During the Obama's visit in February 2015, the US President participated in the celebration of the Republic of India as the guest of honor for the first time. And it became a "sign" for the Modi government to open its arms to the US. During the period, the two sides also issued the J*oint Strategic Vision of the US and India in the Asia-Pacific and Indian Ocean Regions*. The document emphasizes that "the closer partnership between the US and India is indispensable for promoting peace, prosperity and stability in the Asia-Pacific and Indian Ocean regions"[27]; they also decided to extend the

[26]PTI, "US sees India as key nation in Asia Pacific region: Pentagon", April 13, 2017, http://indianexpress.com/article/world/us-sees-india-as-key-nation-in-asia-pacific-region-pentagon-4611618/.

[27]"US—India Joint Strategic Vision for the Asia—Pacific and Indian Ocean Region", January 25, 2015. http://www.mea.gov.in/bilateral-documents.htm?dtl/24728/USIndia_Joint_Strategic_Vision_for_the_AsiaPacific_and_Indian_Ocean_Region.

Defense Framework Agreement signed in 2005 for 10 years, and formally signed the *Defense Cooperation Framework Agreement* in June 2015. In this new document, the two countries break new grounds related to defense cooperation, simplify the relevant transfer procedures of defense technology, and determine to strengthen the joint development cooperation of relevant military and industry; this new defense cooperation framework has promoted greatly the security cooperation. In June 2016, during Modi's fourth visit to the US, the two countries jointly issued a statement named *US and India: Global Enduring Partnership for the 21st Century*, in which the US declared publicly that India is an "important defense partner" and it is necessary to further promote India as the "major defense partner" of the US, and to rise the defense cooperation with India to the level corresponding to closest partner relations between the US and India.[28] As for specific measures, the US announced to support military technology and joint armament production cooperation under the *Defense Technology and Trade Initiative* (DTTI); the two parties signed a military procurement agreement up to $1.1 billion, which includes that the US would sell advanced P-8I Maritime Patrol Aircraft to India.[29] What's more, they officially signed the *Logistics Agreement Memorandum Agreement* on August 29, 2016, ending negotiations about logistics conducted continuously for 12 years; according to the agreement, the military forces of US and India can then share military base of each other to carry out logistics operations, which will bring the defense cooperation to a new level.

On January 20, 2017, Trump officially took office as the US president, and the US-India relations entered into a new historical stage. Trump criticized the failures of both domestic and foreign policies of the previous government on different occasions weakened the economic strength, strategic capabilities and international appeal of the US, then he proposed to "make the US strong again" and adjust the domestic and foreign strategies with "American priority" as the principles; However, in terms of the role recognition and strategic guidance to India, the Trump administration has basically inherited Obama's diplomatic legacy and been committed to integrating India into its strategic track. Of course, based on his characteristics of "businessman", Trump did not forget to criticize the large trade surplus of India to the US and demanded India to further open its domestic market.

Trump attached great importance to India in many aspects. In his first telephone conversation with Indian Prime Minister Modi shortly after his election on January 24, 2017, Trump emphasized that the US regarded India as a true friend and partner in solving many of the world's challenges, and must strengthen cooperation with India in economic, defense and the global fight against terrorism.[30] On June 26, 2017, Modi visited the US and issued a joint statement with Trump to expand and deepen

---

[28]The White House, Office of the Press Secretary, "The US and India: Enduring Global Partners in the 21st Century," June 07, 2016, https://obamawhitehouse.archives.gov/the-press-office/2016/06/07/joint-statement-united-states-and-india-enduring-global-partners-21st.

[29]Kronstadt and Akhtar (2017, p. 15).

[30]The White House, Office of the Press Secretary, "Readout of the President's Call With Prime Minister Narendra Modi of India," January 24, 2017, https://www.whitehouse.gov/the-pressoffice/2017/01/24/readout-presidents-call-primeminister-narendra-modi-india.

the strategic partnership between the two countries and to achieve the common goal: coping with the threat of terrorism, promoting the stability in Indo-Pacific region, enhancing freedom and fair trade, and strengthening energy links.[31] During this visit to the US, Modi and Trump also discussed the establishment of a "2 + 2" bilateral dialogue mechanism between the US and India at the diplomatic and national defense level - this mechanism is similar to the "2 + 2" bilateral dialogue mode between the US and Japan, which can be used to replace the form that was restricted to the two foreign secretaries and the commerce secretaries during the Obama era. On August 21, 2017, the Trump administration announced to implement a new Afghan and South Asia policy, in which India became an important partner; however, Trump did not forget the economic interests of the US, so he pointed out that India had made tens of billions of dollars in trade with the US, and hoped that India can contribute more to Afghanistan in economic assistance and domestic reconstruction.[32]

On September 26, 2017, James Mattis, US Secretary of Defense, visited India and met with Nirmala Sitharaman, the female Defense Minister, and Ajit Doval, National Security Adviser of India in New Delhi. Mattis's visit to India includes two major agendas, of which the first one is to strengthen US-India cooperation in defense equipment and technology, and to promote arms sales agreements between the two countries on drones, and the second one is to implement Trump's new Afghanistan and South Asia policy, conducting consultations on providing more help for peace and stability in Afghanistan[33]; the fundamental purpose is to seek to establish a new institutional mechanism with India to enhance the defense relations between the US and India and the level of cooperation on regional issues.

On October 18, 2017, the day before visiting India, Tillerson,[34] US Secretary of State, gave a speech under the title of *Defining Our Relations With India for the Next Century*[35] in Center for Strategic and International Studies (CSIS), in which he unavoidably pointed out that the convergence of strategic interests between the US and India is the motivation for the Trump administration to substantially deepen the US-India strategic partnership. "The US must cooperate with India to ensure that the Indo-Pacific region is increasingly becoming a place of peace, stability and prosperity, but not a region of chaos, conflict and predatory economy."Tillerson stressed that the

---

[31] The White House, Office of the Press Secretary, "Remarks by President Trump and Prime Minister Modi of India in Joint Press Statement," June 26, 2017, https://www.whitehouse.gov/the-pressoffice/2017/06/26/remarks-president-trump-andprime-minister-modi-india-joint-press.

https://www.whitehouse.gov/the-press-office/2017/08/21/remarks-presidenttrump-strategy-afghanistan-and-south-asia.

[32] The White House, Office of the Press Secretary, "Remarks by President Trump on the Strategy in Afghanistan and South Asia," Arlington, Virginia, June 26, 2017.

[33] News Transcript, "Secretary Mattis Joint Press Conference with Minister of Defense of Nirmala Sitharaman," Press Operations, Sept. 26, 2017, https://www.defense.gov/News/Transcripts/TranscriptView/Article/1325283/secretary-mattis-joint-pressconference-with-minister-of-defence-nirmala-sithar/.

[34] Trump, US President, suddenly announced on March 13, 2018 that the Director of the Central Intelligence Agency (CIA) Pompeo succeeded Tillerson as the new US Secretary of State.

[35] "Remarks on 'Defining Our Relationship With India for the Next Century'", October 18, 2017, https://www.state.gov/secretary/remarks/2017/10/274913.htm.

US and India had been committed to developing friendly relations based on similar values in the past few decades, but still needed to establish a higher level of relations. Furthermore, Tillerson did not use the traditional "Asia-Pacific" geography concept in his speech, but instead used "Indo-Pacific" to define the geopolitical region from the Western Pacific to the Indian Ocean in the US Asian Strategic Framework. Tillerson also made insinuations that foreign activities conducted by China in the surrounding area were predatory economies.

(3) **The Sino-India relations slide obviously, "Boundary Issues" and the interactions on the Belt and Road become international hot topics.**

In 2017, the US-India relations continued to warm up, but India took an extremely tough stance on the diplomatic attitude to China at the same time. India boycotted Beijing Belt and Road Forum for International Cooperation at first, and then confronted China in Docklam, which cast a shadow over Sino-India relations, and made the relations slide quickly.

China and India are close neighbors in Asia. The relations between the two countries contain both historical issues and the shadows they have produced. It also includes the so-called two-power strategic competition brought about by the simultaneous rise of the two countries and the contradictions derived from the competition. From the perspective of geography and history, there are, so far, thousands of kilometers of undecided borderline and the war memory left due to border disputes, as well as geopolitical shadows such as the South Tibet issue, issues Tibetan Government in Exile, and even China-Pakistan relations and cross-border water resources and the growing influence of China in the Indian Ocean, all of these have continued to generate complex effects in the relations between the two countries. Of course, the decline in Sino-India relations is affected by bilateral issues, as well as third-party factors.

If the Sino-India relations are observed under the background of the "Indo-Pacific" construction, they are obviously influenced by the US. If the context of the "Asia-Pacific" rise many years ago included the regional economic cooperation with China, in the concept of "Indo-Pacific" which is popular in recent years, the main connotation is to reject China and conduct geopolitical confrontation with it as an "imaginary enemy". The reason of this confrontation lies in that the strong rise of China is increasingly changing the world power structure. At the same time, the rapid development of India, its national dimension and geographical location have made India have the potential to hinder China's influence. As the global hegemon, the US will inevitably judge the situation and formulate its strategy based on its own interests, playing the role of offshore balancer to maintain global hegemony by selecting China as the enemy and India as the friend. On April 13, 2017, Jeff Davis, the Pentagon spokesman, emphasized to the Indian Public Technology Institute (PTI) that India is a pivotal nation ensuring the safety of the Indo-Pacific region and a major defense partner of the US.[36] In his visit to India on October 25, 2017, Tillerson, US Secretary

[36]PTI, "US sees India as key nation in Asia Pacific region: Pentagon", April 13, 2017, http://indianexpress.com/article/world/us-sees-india-as-key-nation-in-asia-pacific-region-pentagon-4611618/.

of State, declared that India and the US were natural allies and looked forward to discussing the trade of F16 and F18 fighters with India; in the joint statement of Tillerson and Indian Foreign Minister Swaraj, Tillerson claimed that "the US supports India's rise as a dominant force and will continue to help India improve its ability to secure the region. We are willing to provide the best technology for India's modern military."[37] It is in this context that US-India relations have continued to develop further, and Sino-India relations have declined rapidly. At the same time, on many practical issues, China is now facing the pressure from the US and India. For example, India and the US hold the same attitude toward the South China Sea issue, the US supported India's accession to the Nuclear Suppliers Group (NSG), supported India to add the leader of the armed group "Muhammad Army" Masood in sanctions list of the UN Security Council, and also supported India to become a permanent member of UN Security Council, etc.. Under the different developments of the strategic relations between China and the US, China and India and the US and India, confrontations in the strategic interaction between China and the US and China and India have tended to increase. And it has shown a flattening trend for the strategic triangle relations among the three countries.

Real inter-country relations most often are not reflected in passionate or exquisite diplomatic statements, but in cold and serious political realities. The current interactions between India and China have many unique characteristics which also reflect the complexity of Sino-India relations. First, the current strategic interaction between the two countries is carried out simultaneously in both land and sea, and involves in bilateral, regional and international systems. Second, Sino-India interaction is under asymmetric power relations, asymmetric system status, asymmetric mutual cognition, and asymmetric mutual demand; Third, confrontational games, strategic competition, compromise coordination, and reserved cooperation and other complex content exist in real Sino-India relations. Fourth, the process of interaction between China and India on different issues may bring several different interactive results. International relations constructivists believe that "identity determines interests".[38] China and India share common identities. On the one hand, these common identities make the two countries have broad common interests and a win-win outcome on the interests of certain issues, bringing opportunities for development of relations; However, on the other hand, the common identities have also brought about competition or disagreement on the strategic interests of both parties and a "zero-sum" outcome on the interests of certain issues; of course, there is still an interaction result between "win-win" and "zero-sum", namely a state of power and interest distribution that neither satisfies the two parties nor makes them very depressed; However, in case of a vicious interaction between China and India, a possible situation of "lose-lose" probably appears. As far as the status quo is concerned, China and India have a

[37] *US Secretary of State Visits India: Supporting India as a Leading Force to Rise and Provide Armaments*, China.com, October 26, 2017, http://military.china.com/important/11132797/20171026/31606163_2.html.

[38] [US] Alexander Winter: *Social Theory of International Politics*, Peking University Press, 2005 edition, p. 143.

certain tacit understanding of avoiding this kind of situation, with the peaceful end of the Docklam incident as a proof. In short, there are several possible outcomes of Sino-India interaction, such as a win-win situation (with difference in profit), a unilateral profit, but not too much loss or profit for other party (no significant impact on the status quo of the other party's interests), zero sum (one party gains what the other party losses) and lose-lose (with difference in loss).

The status quo and future prospects of Sino-India relations are all most directly reflected in the interactions of China and India on the "boundary issues" and the Belt and Road. Therefore, it is necessary to have "calmthinking" on these two "hot issues".

First, the "calmthinking" about the "boundary issues".

First of all, Docklam Confrontation ended peacefully, but the discussion on it hasn't quieted down immediately. Up to now, the discussion about the win-loss of China and India is full of rising national sentiment, the irritated remarks and even fling abuses without limits on the Internet. From the domestic perspective, some netizens' logic of venting their emotions not only show contempt for India, but also contains either overt or covert allegory of China's weakness. However, thinking back, the theory of winning or losing has no meaning to the confrontation. The quick quarrel has no value in solving the Sino-India border issue. The only function may be to stimulate domestic nationalism in India and to have increasingly strong anti-Chinese sentiment, which will only have potential negative effects on the future development of Sino-India relations.

Therefore, it's beneficial that the discussion on the win or loss of Docklam Confrontation should be promptly quieted down, with less angry voices, but more calm thinking.

Secondly, there should be a pre-judgment on the "boundary issue" and the future of Sino-India relations. For this, we must first make it clear why the Docklam Confrontation can be peacefully ended. In fact, it seems that the confrontation over two months is abruptly ended peacefully, but it is not without traces. At the same time, careful analysis of the inherent development of the sea power logic will be slightly helpful in judging the future direction of China-India relations.

First of all, there is no bloodshed in the confrontation, so the situation could basically be controllable. The two countries wage a tit-for-tat struggle in diplomatic rhetoric, but they are still more restrained in their actions, which leaves room for change in the subsequent policy. Second, India's manipulation of the border issue has made it a jetton for the game with China and a political tool for coping with domestic issues. However, India also has a bottom-line thinking and fears that the situation will be out of control. The hype on the border issue has become a jetton for the game with China, and the strategic cost paid by India has been small up to now, but the strategic benefits of close relations with the US and Japan are more obvious. This can partly explain why India is never bored with making troubles on the border issue. At the same time, the hype on the border issue has become a political tool for the Indian government to deal with domestic issues, such as transferring domestic pressure and winning public support. When China emerged as an external threat signal, this could at least partially shift people's attention, and nationalism in India clearly overwhelmed regional separatism. Therefore, for the Indian government, it obviously can provoke China on the border issue in a timely and appropriate manner. Of course, the border issue is a historical issue, which involves in national sentiment, so it is easy to use but hard to control; then, the Indian government needs to end on a good note with it as a policy tool. In other words, India needs to have bottom-line thinking on the manipulation of the border issue, so as to prevent the situation from being out of control. This inherently stipulates a foreseeable result, that is, to a large extent, the longer the Sino-India confrontation lasts, the less likely it will spark a conflict accidentally. Third, for the current overall strategy of both countries, the strategic appeal to solve the border issue is not the most urgent. In other words, China and India have always maintained strategic restraint or highlighted the strength of their respective powers, because the border issue itself is not the core issue in Sino-India relations, or that the border issue is not a fundamental factor determining the development of Sino-India relations. That is why China is not in a hurry when conditions for solving the boundary issue are not mature. Fourth, the bilateral boundary issue is beyond the bilateral level, and the structural contradictions between major powers can be seen through boundary issues; For India, the border issue is complicatedly intertwined with other issues, such as national sentiment, domestic interest groups, military enterprises, and military status. Therefore, the border issue is not easy to solve and will not make great progress in the short term. Fifth, the prospect of solving the boundary issue is likely to happen when the international system has obvious structural changes again and relations among the major powers have new realignment and regrouping. Sixth, after the confrontation, the Sino-India relations are bound to enter a period in which the main features are no war and no peace.

Second, the "calm thinking" about the role of Indian in the Belt and Road.

There are too many similarities between China and India, which both are located in Asia, have larger population in the world, stay among the BRICS countries and are the two major economies in emerging markets. However, the relations between the two countries are very complicated and tortuous. As mentioned above, India recently first confronted and contradicted the Belt and Road Summit, and later unreasonably obstructed and confronted China in Docklam, which cast a strong shadow on Sino-India relations. Therefore, it is also very necessary to have some "calm thinking" about the role of India in the Belt and Road in the future.

Undoubtedly, India, as an important country along the Belt and Road, has its influence and strategic capabilities. As long as India is willing to give support, it will contribute more to the construction of the Belt and Road than other countries. If India secretly resists it, it will also place more hindrance to the construction of the Belt and Road than other countries. Unfortunately, it seems that relevant actions taken by India in reality tend more to hinder but not give support.

Despite the ups and downs, China still hopes that India can play an active role in the Belt and Road and positions India as a potential partner rather than a competitor. For example, at the Astana Heads Summit in June 2017, the Shanghai Cooperation Organization led by China, accepted India as a new member of the SCO regardless of unpleasantness.

However, in author's opinion, the identity of India, as the geopolitical strong neighbor of China, should not be artificially underestimated in any way. There are two problems worthy of China's vigilance in particular: First, in the international system, India tends to play the role of counterbalancing China. Second, in the bilateral interaction between China and India, India tends to take tough behavioral pattern to China.

First of all, India tends to play the role of counterbalancing China. In South Asia, the Belt and Road Initiative proposed by China shall be promoted to the Persian Gulf of the Western Indian Ocean through the China-Pakistan Economic Corridor, and to the Bay of Bengal in the East Indian Ocean through Bangladesh, China, India and Myanmar. From the potential prospects of the geo-economics, in theory, if China and India, the two largest Asian countries, can take the Belt and Road Initiative as an opportunity, there will be a broad stage for their cooperation; if India can recognize the historical trend, cast aside old geopolitical thinking, and accept international concepts like "harmonious world", "Asian common security" from China, as well as participate in global governance with China, and jointly shape the new international political and economic order, then the vision of the "harmonious world" will not be a mirage from the geopolitical point of view, at least a "harmonious Asia" is worth looking forward to.

However, the promotion of the China-Pakistan Corridor is regarded by India as a major part of China's Indian Ocean Strategy, with the intention of targeting and even deterring India, and India is very vigilant that the construction of the corridor may involve in part of Kashmir.[39] On the practical level, although India gave some vocal support to the Belt and Road, it provides no substantive cooperation. On the contrary, the "Monsoon Plan" and "Free Corridor" have shown that India intends to upgrade the cooperation with countries within the Indian Ocean and great powers outside of this region, in order to balance and damage the impact of the Belt and Road. In terms of the geostrategic preferences, India wants to have strategic autonomy and flexibility. Even from the perspective of geo-economics, India also expects to obtain the investment and capital dividends from China. However, many strategic scholars in India believe that creating a "Monsoon Plan" through strategic independence to promote the Interconnectivity with Central Asia and Southeast Asia is to lead the cooperation process by India itself, which is naturally preferable compared with following the Belt and Road of China. In general, the appeal for win-win cooperation of China cannot eliminate India's doubts about China, and India is also willing to play a strategic role of "counterweight" in the international community to gain strategic autonomy and geopolitical speculation.

Second, India tends to be tough to China. From the perspective of behavioral patterns or strategic attitudes, it's easy to understand India being mighty or pretending to be mighty; Based on the early action inertia and path dependence, such as the stern style of the Indian authorities, the current "beneficial" international situation (at least India believes it is beneficial) and China's tolerance posture, the author believes that India may continue to be tough to China in the "Belt and Road" in the future.

---

[39]Zhao (2016).

Apart from the stern style of the current Indian authorities, India is currently in an international environment that is unprecedentedly favorable with the concept of "Indo-Pacific" rising suddenly, and this favorable situation will not change for some time. As Chinese scholar Zhu Cuiping pointed out that compared with the "contact + containment" of the US policy toward China, the US is adopting "roping in and utilizing" policy for India to incite and even support India to a certain extent, so as to benefit from the tussle between India and China as the third party.[40] For this purpose, the US not only gives some lip services to India in terms of big power and strategic role, but also some practical interests to cater to India's pleasure, thereby enhancing India's strategic confidence and the toughness of its policy to China. In fact, the current international environment has different strategic implications for Indian and Chinese diplomacy, which is good for India as a whole. Indian diplomacy needn't consider the containment and counter-measure of the systemic hegemonic state and its affiliated alliances at the global and regional levels like China diplomacy. And it also needn't worry about "China threat theory" or "China expansion theory". India bears no excessive external pressure from the international system on India.

Moreover, India is deeply aware of that China's peaceful rise requires a peaceful and stable external environment. In addition, China won't adopt stern measures toward India for the principle of "keeping a low profile" obeyed for years. Based on past experience, if India provokes and even angers China within the controllable range, such as interviewing the Dalai Lama who has attempted to split China, accommodating Tibetan separatists, and provoking small incidents on the Sino-Pakistani border, China basically will leave it unsettled. Therefore, these stern actions against China do not have to pay too much strategic cost, but can win the acclaim of international anti-China forces and raise India's status for them.

(4) **Japan and India accelerated their strategy cooperation, security dialogue among the four countries taken up again**.

Under the background of "Indo-Pacific" construction, Abe first proposed the "free and open Indo-Pacific strategy" at the TICAD held in August 2016, and Modi proposed an upgraded version of "Act East" in 2015; in 2017, the two countries actively promoted strategic cooperation and action coordination of the "free and open Indo-Pacific strategy" and the "Act East". When the China-Pakistan Economic Corridor steadily advanced and under the background of the renewed friction between China and India and the continuous tension between China and Japan due to the Diaoyu Islands dispute, India and Japan have responded to each other tacitly at the east and west of China. The two countries have accelerated comprehensive strategic docking of politics, economy and security, which has become a compelling international phenomenon.

1. **Japan and India accelerate strategic approaching**.

Since India and Japan are both close neighbors of China and have land and sea disputes respectively with China, and at the same time they have a close strategic

[40] Zhu (2015).

relations with the US, with the so-called common democratic state attribute, top government leaders of Japan and India have interacted frequently in 2017 and reached a consensus on the docking of the "Indo-Pacific strategy" and the "Act East"; they have made a lot of progress in economic and trade relations, energy cooperation, infrastructure construction and security.

However, traditionally, the relations between India and Japan are relatively loose. During the Sino-India War and the India-Pakistan War, Japan stayed neutral. During the Cold War, they also belonged to different groups, therefore forming indifferent relations. After the Cold War, since India had a strong expectation on improving relations with the US, and proposed an "Act East" policy based on India's status as a major power and economic interests, it actively promoted economic and trade contacts with East and Southeast Asian countries. Under this background, the relations between India and Japan rapidly improved. After India and Pakistan successfully completed the atomic bomb test successively in 1998, Japan followed the US to take tough stance to India on the issue of nuclear non-proliferation. Japan not only actively criticized India on relevant international occasions, such as the G8, but also took the initiative to stop the political interaction with India, interrupt relevant economic assistance to India, and cooperate with the US to take sanctions against India, which directly led to the record low relations between the two countries. After entering the 21st century, the relations between Japan and India has also improved with the improvement of US-India relations, with the repositioning of India's strategic role by the US. In particular, with the visit of former Japanese Prime Minister Yoshiro Mori to India in 2000, Japan and India reached a consensus on establishing "a global partnership facing the 21st century" which lay a favorable foundation for the future development of their relations. But it was after Shinzo Abe took office in 2006 that their relations really began to be close. Japanese Prime Minister Shinzo Abe and Foreign Minister Taro Aso who both took office in 2006, advocated the establishment of the so-called "Arc of Freedom and Prosperity"[41] in diplomacy and launched diplomatic lobbying for this purpose. In 2007, Abe visited India and gave a speech named "Confluence of the Two Seas" at the Indian Parliament, in which he vigorously hyped the concept of "Indo-Pacific" and emphasized that a strong Japan and a strong India were in line with the strategic interests of both countries. It can be seen from this that the "Indo-Pacific Strategy" of Japan had been roughly formed ten years ago. Since then, under the active promotion of the Abe administration, there was the first security dialogue among the US, Japan, India and Australia, as well as the first "Malabar" military exercise jointly held by the four countries and Singapore in 2007.

However, then Japanese state leaders changed and Abe left office, which made the Japan-India relations stagnated and the security dialogue among the four countries interrupted. Abe bobbed up in 2012 and proposed a strategy to balance China's

---

[41] Ministry of Foreign Affairs of Japan, "Speech by Mr. TaroAso, inister for Foreign Affairs on the Occasion of the Japan Institute of International Affairs Seminar 'Arc of Freedom and Prosperity: Japans Expanding Diplomatic Horizons'", November 30, 2006, http://www.mofa.go.jp/announce/fm/aso/Speech0611.html.

"Democracy and Security Diamond" Initiative in an attempt to curb China with the US, India and Australia by building a strategic arc across the Indian Ocean and the Pacific Ocean. Under this background, the revitalization of India-Japan relations became an important issue. At the beginning of 2014, Abe was invited by India to participate in the celebration of "Republic Day" in India as a guest. In September of the same year, Modi paid a return visit to Japan, during which Abe and Modi established a "Special Strategic Global Partnership", which boosted the relations between India and Japan to quickly develop again. In December 2015, India and Japan issued the *Joint Statement on the 2025 Vision of India and Japan* during Abe's visit to India, indicating that the two countries would carry out all-round cooperation in the "Indo-Pacific" region.[42] In November 2016, during Modi's visit to Japan, he expressed appreciation for Abe's "Indo-Pacific Strategy" and pointed out the great cooperation potential between "Act East" of India and "Indo-Pacific Strategy" of Japan.[43]

For Japan, its status as an East Asian power and its strength are relatively shrinking and weakened due to rapid rise of China. According to the report of the International Monetary Fund (IMF) in April 2017, up to 2016, the GDP of Japan for the whole year had been already less than half of China since China's GDP exceeded Japan in 2010[44]; Moreover, as is well-known that the Sino-Japanese relations are complex, the two countries have been in a stalemate due to Diaoyu Islands in recent years. Under this circumstance, Japan is eager to reverse the competitive disadvantage to China. In 2017, Abe proposed the so-called "free and open Indo-Pacific strategy" for Japan, under which, Japan will probably have geo-economic gains by wooing India. For responding to the geopolitical pressure brought by China, the alliance with the US, India and Australia has become the preferred solution for Abe.

Abe vigorously promoted his "Indo-Pacific Strategy" and made an appeal of "hoping to manage the world together with the ASEAN facing the Indian Ocean and the Pacific Ocean" when he attended the ASEAN Summit and the East Asia Cooperation Leaders Series Meeting in September 2017. During the Japan-India Summit held on September 14, Abe specifically explained the "Indo-Pacific strategy" to Indian Prime Minister Modi, claimed that "India is the most important country connecting Asia and Africa" and hoped that "Japan and India would work together to concretize this concept."[45] Abe also stressed that Japan and India should be "a strong India for Japan and a strong Japan for India", complete the docking of India's "Act East" and Japan's "free and open Indo-Pacific strategy", and then form specific cooperation proposals covering from Southeast Asia to Africa. Modi expressed support for this and declared

---

[42]First post, "Full text: Joint Statement on India and Japan Vision 2025", https://www.firstpost.com/politics/full-text-joint-statement-on-india-and-japan-vision-2025-2543222.html.

[43]Ministry of External Affairs, Government of India, "India–Japan Joint Statement during the visit of Prime Minister to Japan", November 11, 2016. http://www.mea.gov.in/bilateral-documents.htm?dtl/27599/IndiaJapan_Joint_Statement_during_the_visit_of_Prime_Minister_to_Japan.

[44]IMF, "World Economic Outlook, April 2017: Gaining Momentum?", http://www.imf.org/en/Publications/WEO/Issues/2017/04/04/world-economic-outlook-april-2017.

[45]Mei (2017).

that the ASEAN countries expected that the cooperation between India and Japan could provide a model for regional development. During a meeting with Modi in Manila, Philippines on November 11, 2017, Abe said: I hope to achieve a free and open Indo-Pacific based on the rule of law and develop bilateral relations"; Considering the active marine activities of China, the two countries once again reached a high consensus on promoting Abe's "free and open Indo-Pacific strategy" and said that Japan-India cooperation should go deep into the security field. On December 7, 2017, the Kyodo News Agency of Japan reported that the "free and open Indo-Pacific strategy" would officially be listed in the new *National Security Strategy* of Japan, which indicated that Japan would work with the US, Australia and India to promote extensive security cooperation in the Western Pacific and Indian Ocean; "This action is intended to counterbalance China which strengthens marine activities."[46]

On December 11, 2017, the first ASEAN-India Communication Summit (AICS) was held in New Delhi, India. Although the summit is for India and ASEAN, India invited Japan as the only extraterritorial country to participate in the Summit; the *Times of India* claimed that this was another new initiative of India to unite Japan and ASEAN countries against China's the Belt and Road Initiative.[47] The *Economic Times* of India quoted the words of the Japanese ambassador to India, Mr. HiraMatsushii, to evidence that Japan participated in the Summit to achieve the docking of the "free and open Indo-Pacific strategy" and the "Act East" and improve the cooperation with India in the northeast region.

The rapid development of Japan-India relations is embodied not only in reaching strategic consensus, but also in multiple specific cooperation areas. In the economic field, Japan not only actively invested in projects in India in 2017, but also cooperated with India on relevant cross-regional projects. For example, in April 2017, Japan and India signed an agreement that the Japan International Cooperation Agency (JICA) would invest 670 billion yen (about 610 million US dollars) in India for the construction of the NH54 road in Mizoram and the NH51 road in Meghalaya.[48] In May 2017, India refused to attend the 2017 Belt and Road International Cooperation Summit, but at the same time reached a vision document for the establishment of the Asia-Africa Growth Corridor Program (AAGC) with Japan with jointly initial investment of 40 billion dollars in this Program. With the development of cooperative projects, the construction of quality infrastructure and institutional linkages, the building of capacity and skills, and partnerships among people as four pillars,[49] the Asia-Africa Growth Corridor seeks to open up a new marine corridor, connecting the African continent with India, South Asia and Southeast Asian countries to create

[46] Wang Dingjie: *The Decade for Indo-Pacific Strategy (b): the Deepening Anti-China Alliance of Japan and India*, http://mp.weixin.qq.com/s/NhFJanOHVWuiuGql_U0bfQ.

[47] Li (2017).

[48] Lin (2017).

[49] Wang (2017).

a "free and open Indian Ocean and Pacific Ocean".[50] It's no doubt that an important consideration for Japan and India to propose the Asia-Africa Growth Corridor is to hinder the impact of China's the Belt and Road Initiative. In fact, during the Docklam confrontation between China and India in July and August 2017, Japan was the only power which supported India in secret. On August 3, 2017, the Japanese Embassy in India and the Ministry of Development of Northeast India jointly held the "India-Japan Coordination Forum for the Development of the Northeast Region". In the speech, the Japanese Ambassador to India stated that the development of Northeast India has interests in both strategy and economy. Except for assistance to the domestic development in India, Japan also actively worked with India to build cross-regional cooperation projects. As for nuclear energy cooperation, the *Japan-India Nuclear Energy Agreement* was approved by the Japanese House of Representatives in April 2017, and entered into force since July 20, which cleared the way for nuclear technology cooperation between Japan and India. The defense relations between Japan and India are also constantly strengthening. On September 13, 2017, Shinzo Abe visited India. In the meeting with Indian Prime Minister Modi, they not only had dialogue on cooperation in the fields of high-speed rail, trade and cultural exchanges, but also discussed the military co-operations including Japan providing US-2 seaplanes for India.

2. **The security dialogue among the US, Japan, India, and Australia was restarted.**

Under the complex international backgrounds, such as the "free and open Indo-Pacific strategy" proposed by Abe, the "Act East" upgraded by Modi, clearly defining China as a strategic competitor in the *National Security Strategy* of Trump and the *Defense Strategy Report* of US Defense Department, and high Chinese exclusion voices in Australia for a period of time, security dialogue among the US, Japan, India and Australia restarted in 2017, which further revealed the fact that the "Indo-Pacific" strategy is booming into the reality but not just a concept.

On August 7, 2017, Taro Kono, the Japanese Foreign Minister, Tillerson, the US Secretary of State and Bissau, the Australian Foreign Minister held talks in Manila, the Philippines. They exchanged views on the US-Japan-Australian strategic dialogue and discussed on cooperation intentions. On September 19, 2017, the three foreign ministers of the US, Japan and India met in New York and agreed to work together to increase investment in strategic ports and other infrastructure in the Indo-Pacific region, and reached consensus on trilateral maritime security cooperation.[51] On October 25, 2017, Japanese Foreign Minister Taro Kono revealed in an exclusive interview of the Nihon Keizai Shimbun that Japan hoped to establish a summit-level strategic dialogue with the US, Australia and India, and promote free trade and cooperation in defense with the South China Sea-Indian Ocean-Africa as the axis.

[50]MG Asher, M Ganapathy, "India and Japan's Strategic Opportunity in Africa: The Asia Africa Growth Corridor (AAGC) Initiative", https://www.researchgate.net/publication/322419387_India_and_Japan's_Strategic_Opportunity_in_Africa_The_Asia_Africa_Growth_Corridor_AAGC_Initiative.

[51]Chen (2017).

Wozwells, the US Assistant Secretary of State told the press on October 27, 2017 that Japan, the US, India and Australia would hold high-level negotiations on strategic cooperation in maritime security and infrastructure investment of four countries to cope with the rise of China in Asia.

On November 12, 2017, Foreign Affairs Bureau officials of the US, India, Japan and Australia held a four-nation meeting during the informal meeting of APEC leaders in Vietnam to discuss the issue of "the common interests in the Indo-Pacific region"; a decade later, the Security Dialogue was restarted, which means that the concept of "Indo-Pacific" has been officially confirmed, and also reflects a new trend of emerging geopolitics in Asia in recent years. On December 12, 2017, Tillerson proposed to further promote the US-Japan-India-Australia cooperation in the speech to the Atlantic Council of the US. He pointed out: "Japan, Australia and the US had established trilateral relations in the Indo-Pacific region long time ago. Now we are working hard to promote quadrilateral relations that can include India, because of the growing economic importance of India and the common national security concerns I think we share with India."[52] On December 18, 2017, Trump clearly stated in his first *National Security Strategy Report* that: "We will seek to enhance cooperation with Japan, Australia and India."[53] On January 18, 2018, the senior officials from the US, Japan, India and Australia further discussed the construction of the "Indo-Pacific Strategy" framework and its strategic implications and cooperation ideas in the "Raisina Dialogue" held in India.

(5) **Under the above background, small and medium-sized countries in the relevant regions actively engaged in strategic speculation and rent-seeking for geopolitical power**.

Under the construction of the Indo-Pacific, Vietnam, Indonesia, Singapore and even the entire ASEAN have been seeking strategic speculation in the game of the "Indo-Pacific" among the great powers to different extents, and using their geographical location or special attributes to carry out geopolitical power rent-seeking.

Taking Vietnam as an example, it is a core country in the Indo-China Peninsula and a country with a long coastline in the South China Sea. At the same time, it still has many disputes with China on the ownership of related islands and reefs and the development of oil and gas resources; therefore, under the construction of the Indo-Pacific, it has become a target actively wooed by India, Japan and the US; In order to make full use of its superior marine geographical location and the strategic expectations of the US, Japan and India and other countries to Vietnam to obtain military technology, resources development and the jetton in the game with China, it has formed the foreign strategy with the "three priorities" of "priority to great power, priority to neighboring countries and priority to the traditional friendly countries"[54]

---

[52]See Footnote 51.

[53]White House, "National Security Strategy of the United States of America", December 2017, p. 46. http://www.informationclearinghouse.info/article2320.htm.

[54]Wu (2016).

to accelerate the bilateral and multilateral strategies closeness to the US, Japan and India.

Under the Indo-Pacific vision, the development of bilateral relations between India and Vietnam has attracted much attention. During the visit of Nguyen PhuTrong, the General Secretary of the Communist Party of Vietnam, to India in November 2013, India granted a $100 million loan to Vietnam to purchase four high-speed patrol boats made in India and signed a "mutual protection information exchange agreement". During the meeting with Vietnamese Prime Minister Nguyen Tan Dung in October 2014, Modi said that India would help Vietnam achieve defense modernization. In May 2015, India and Vietnam signed the *2015–2020 Common Vision Statement of India-Vietnam Defense Cooperation* and agreed to expand maritime security cooperation and military training activities.[55] In September 2016, Nguyen XuanPhuc, the Vietnamese Prime Minister invited Modi to visit Vietnam. During this visit, he and Modi promoted the relations between the two countries to a "comprehensive strategic partnership" and signed several bilateral cooperation agreements in various fields such as national defense, cybersecurity, UN peacekeeping, and maritime information sharing; Modi announced that India would provide 500 million U.S. dollars in credit to Vietnam to purchase military equipment from India, and 5 million U.S. dollars for the establishment of the Army Software Park at the University of NhaTrang. In 2014, India had provided $100 million in defense credit to Vietnam. On March 2, 2018, Tran Dai Quang, Vietnamese President visited India to commemorate the 45th anniversary of the establishment of diplomatic relations between the two countries. Before the visit, Tran Dai Quang emphasized the importance of the development of defense and security cooperation between India and Vietnam, calling it efficient strategic field cooperation and praising the support of India for personnel training, capacity building, defense technology transfer and national defense credit, etc. According to reports, during the visit of Tran Dai Quang to India, the two countries would reach a civilian nuclear energy agreement and planned to jointly develop a port project with a throughput of 5 million tons in the province of Nghe An, Vietnam. In addition, they also expected to reach some agreements on the establishment of a coal terminal project worth more than 50 million US dollars.[56]

The distribution of Vietnam's land is beneficial to the monitoring of the South China Sea and is an important link of the "Indo-Pacific Strategy" of the US. Therefore, the US is working hard to improve relations with Vietnam. In May 2017, the US decided to donate the "Morgenthau", the "Hamilton" long-range law enforcement ship retired from the US Coast Guard to Vietnam. On January 25, 2018, Matisse visited Hanoi, Vietnam. They agreed that the US aircraft carrier would visit Vietnam in March 2018. That would be the first time that the US aircraft carrier visits Vietnam since the end of the Vietnam War in 1975. Considering that Vietnam has similar maritime disputes and complex historical grievances with China, Japan has also actively developed strategic cooperation with Vietnam. On November 7, 2017, Japanese Foreign Minister Taro Nono visited Da Nang in central Vietnam and expressed his hope

[55] Mu (2016).

[56] Zhang (2018).

to strengthen cooperation in the field of marine safety with Vietnam, including providing new patrol boats to Vietnam; During the talks with Kono, Pham Binh Minh, the Foreign Minister of Vietnam, positively affirmed the "free and open Indo-Pacific strategy" advocated by Shinzo Abe, and expressed his expectation of realizing it and obtaining new developments of Japan-Vietnam relations in this process.

Furthermore, other countries, like Indonesia, Singapore, Malaysia, and Sri Lanka, are also valued by the strategic systems of great powers. For example, Indonesia is located close to the so-called "Indo-Pacific strategic arc", controls several straits such as the Makassar Strait, Lombok Strait and the Sunda Strait, and monitors several important sea passages communicating the Indian Ocean and Pacific Ocean. Therefore, it has also become a target wooed by relevant countries[57]; similar situations also exist in Singapore, Malaysia and Sri Lanka. These countries have different relations with China and different distances from China. However, they all have chosen a balanced diplomacy among great powers. Although these countries have relatively weak national strength, their standpoints may also affect the trend of the entire "Indo-Pacific" pattern based on geographical location or other attributes.

In fact, in the construction of "Indo-Pacific", the island and peninsula countries with special strategic positions in the Indian Ocean and the Pacific Ocean have become the countries with the most obviously improved international status and the most direct benefits in geopolitical economy.

3 2017 Regional Situation and Strategic Pattern Change of South Asia under the Construction of the "Indo-Pacific"

This part will focus on the case study on the influence of the "Indo-Pacific" construction on South Asia to deepen the understanding of it. The concept is booming and is driven by the geopolitical game of great powers, which reflects the return of geopolitical strength; at the same time, "Indo-Pacific" has been widely popular because it is doned the cloak of promoting the development of economic globalization. However, in any case, "Indo-Taiwan" is not so much a new concept of economic geography as a new geopolitical concept. Of course, a "free, open, prosperous Indo-Pacific"—this concept regards the two traditionally independent regions, Asia-Pacific and India Ocean, as a whole space, at least give people an imaginary space–that the construction of the "Indo-Pacific" will facilitate the flow of production factors and promote the regional economic integration. This will enhance the legitimacy and rationality of the concept, which in turn further contributes to the international spread of this concept; In fact, the connectivity of geospatial space will not change because of the concept of "Indo-Pacific". The integration degree of geo-economics may not be enhanced by the slogan of "freedom, openness and prosperity"; On the contrary, booming situation

[57] Wu (2017).

of the concept has promoted the profound adjustment of the geopolitical strategy by the great powers, and the new adjustment and evolution of the relations among countries has also emerged.

South Asia is an important geographic sector in the Indo-Pacific region. In the construction of this "Indo-Pacific", many issues have been redefined by different countries, such as the strategic function and security significance of India by the US and Japan, the regional role of Pakistan and its connection with international terrorism by the US and India, China's strategic motives on promoting the China-Pakistan Economic Corridor and its far-reaching influences by India, the US, Japan, etc.. Accordingly the strategic importance of South Asia has been reassessed, the relations between China and South Asia have been re-examined, and the power pattern has been reshaped.

Under the construction of "Indo-Pacific", the characteristic that "India is the Center" in the power structure of South Asia in 2017 tends to be strengthened, and the imbalance of regional strategic power is intensified, or it can be said that the dominant position of India in South Asia is further expanded; in the foreign relations and strategic situation of South Asian countries, the strategic role of India has been repositioned by the US and Japan with relatively favorable international strategic environment. But Pakistan is largely abandoned by the US in strategy with unfavorable strategic situation. At the same time, island countries in the Indian Ocean such as Sri Lanka, Maldives, are increasingly valued by the great powers, and Sri Lanka is also actively carrying out balanced diplomacy among the US, India and China; the strategic relations of Bangladesh, Nepal, Bhutan with China have has been developed further; in terms of the security situation in South Asia, the Afghanistan issue, the India-Pakistan Kashmir conflict and intra-regional terrorism are three major observation indicators,[58] but in 2017, each of the three indicators revealed that the security problem in South Asia did not improved. Worse still, to a large extent, the construction of "Indo-Pacific" has contributed to the regional expansionism, adventurism and tough stance of India, increasing the risk and security dilemma of the arms race in South Asia at the same time.

1. **The construction of "Indo-Pacific" has enhanced the strategic position of South Asia in global geopolitics**.

The construction of "Indo-Pacific" has great impact on the strategic position of South Asia, enhancing the strategic position of South Asia in global geopolitics.

First of all, the "Indo-Pacific" concept is a product of geographical integration, which emphasizes the connectivity between the Asia-Pacific region and the Indian Ocean region, as well as the connectivity between the Western Pacific and the East Indian Ocean; under such background, South Asia is increasingly important because of its geographical location.

Observed from the perspective of "Indo-Pacific", South Asia links the Indo-China Peninsula, the Southwest China, the Central Asia and the West Asia on the land from the east to the west, and connects the surrounding oceans of the Persian Gulf, the

[58]Feng (2017, p. 3).

Arabian Sea, the Bay of Bengal, Amanda Sea and the Straits of Malacca from the west to the east. This geographical connectivity makes South Asia have close geographical relations with the extraterritorial regions. In geopolitics, the geographical factors are essential to influence and even determine the political behavior of a country; geography is one of the foundations of international politics and is the chessboard of the "great chess game". Under the vision of "Indo-Pacific", South Asia is located in the middle of the crescent-shaped zone on the periphery of Eurasia. It holds the vital waterways of Asia and Oceania to Europe and Africa, close to the oil production area in Persian Gulf, overlooking the important oil channel for the west and the east. Therefore, its important strategic position cannot be ignored.[59]

Secondly, the first geographical connotation in the construction of the "Indo-Pacific" is to strengthen the strategic role of India. With India as precisely the primary power in South Asia, it became even more important as India's strategic role has been highlighted in the construction of "Indo-Pacific". India and China are geographical neighbors. From the perspective of national size and strategic capabilities, only Japan and India can form effective constraints on the expansion of China's influence from the east and west of China in "Indo-Pacific". For the US and Japan, the key to success, failure, gain and loss of the South Asia policy lies mainly in India; the importance of India is partly the same with the importance of South Asia.

Thirdly, another significant geographical connotation in the construction of the "Indo-Pacific" concept is to highlight the strategic position of the Indian Ocean; however, South Asia is precisely the largest geographic plate that penetrates the Indian Ocean from the Indian Ocean coast, then South Asia will become more important no matter from the strategic perspective of "land-based sea" or "sea-based land" under the background of highlighting the strategic importance of the Indian Ocean. Geographically, as part of the southern extension of the Asian continent, the South Asian subcontinent is inserted into the Indian Ocean for thousands of kilometers in a wedge shape from the north to the south, forming a natural geographical advantage that clamps the Indian Ocean; In terms of geographical relations, South Asia is the edge zone of Asian continent on the northern shore of the Indian Ocean—"the godfather of the containment policy" Nicholas Spykman believes that the "edge zone" is the key area for the expansion of the land powers and the sea power countries to the heart of the mainland, the importance of which has transcended the "heart zone" defined by Mackinder.[60] Relying on the South Asian subcontinent, the sea powers can take South Asia as a step from south to north, and drive straight into Central Asia, the "heart zone" of the Eurasian continent, thereby affecting East Asia, West Asia and even Europe; From the top down, the land powers (such as the former Soviet Union) or the coastal countries like India can rely on the South Asian subcontinent as a springboard to enter the Indian Ocean.[61] While the concept of "Indo-Pacific" promotes the strategic position of the Indian Ocean, South Asia will inevitably become more important accordingly.

---

[59]Dai and Qin (2010).

[60](US) Spicman: *Peace Geography*, translated by Liu Yuzhi, The Commercial Press, 1965, p. 78.

[61]Feng (2017, p. 4).

Finally, the core goal of the "Indo-Pacific" construction is to build "Asian NATO" and "Indo-Pacific strategic arc" against China in the overall strategic space of "Indo-Pacific". Under the background of highlighting the prevention of China's influence expanding overseas in the construction of "Indo-Pacific", South Asia is the first stop of China's "Westward Advance", the site for the flagship project of China-Pakistan Economic Corridor in the Belt and Road Initiative and the Bangladesh-China-India-Myanmar Economic Corridor, the important passage for China to the Indian Ocean. Pakistan, the only global all-weather partner in China, is also situated in South Asia. Therefore, for the US and India, the South Asia is also an important position to prevent the spread of China's influence. Based on the strategic perspective of balancing China's influence, the importance of South Asia is different from the past.

2. **Influence of the construction of "Indo-Pacific" on the power structure in South Asia**.

The power structure in South Asia is fundamentally determined by the strength contrast and nature of relations of the countries in the region. However, as a major environmental factor, the construction of "Indo-Pacific" has an important impact on it. Looking back at the development of the situation in South Asia in 2017, first of all, under the construction of "Indo-Pacific", the "asymmetry" of regional strategic forces intensified, the "Centrality of India" in the regional power structure was strengthened as well; secondly, in sharp contrast to the fact that the dominant position of India in South Asia is further expanded, the international and security situations of Pakistan are becoming more and more serious; moreover, Sri Lanka has become the target of great powers.

(1) In 2017, the dominant position of India in South Asia becomes increasingly prominent.

As everyone knows, India now occupies the main part of the South Asian subcontinent, which has the seventh largest land area in the world and is 2.5 times the total land area of the rest countries of South Asia; India has the second largest population in the world, the sum of the population of other neighboring countries is still less than its 30%; The GDP of India is the fifth in the world with high-speed growth rate, the sum of GDP of other neighboring countries is also less than its 30%; Today, the number of armed forces in India's sea, land and air ranks fourth in the world. With the growing defense expenditure, the armed forces of India also far outclass the sum of its neighbors. In 2017, benefiting from the good momentum of domestic economic development and the increasingly favorable political ecology of the ruling party, this has enhanced the strategic capabilities of the Indian government. Meanwhile, the external environment has also brought India good relations with other countries. The strategic position of India in "Indo-Pacific" space has also been deliberately elevated by the US, Japan and other countries.

In terms of the economic development in India, in the first half of 2017, although the economy continued to be affected by the "waste money" movement and the new tax reform, causing GDP growth rate in the second quarter to fall to 5.7% and become the single-season lowest in the past three years, the economic growth rate rebounded significantly in the second half of the year. According to forecast report of Indian financial institutions, the GDP growth rate of India will reach 6.8% in FY2017/2018. Goldman Sachs predicts that its growth rate will reach 8% and 8.3% in 2018 and 2019 respectively.[62] As for attracting foreign investment, in the first half of 2017, India attracted foreign bond investment of 23 billion US dollars, a year-on-year increase of 19 times, and foreign direct investment also achieved a high growth rate of nearly 30%. In November 2017, Moody, the international rating agency, upgraded the sovereign credit rating of India from Baa3 to Baa2, with the rating outlook raised from positive to stable. In the latest *Global Business Environment Report*, the World Bank also raised India by 30 slots to 100, which is the biggest rise for India in recent years.

From the domestic political situation in India, the Modi government continued to vigorously promote domestic reforms in 2017, with ability to control the situation further enhanced. In particular, Modi rendered to the public that the "golden age" for India is coming, constantly improving their political prestige; meanwhile, in the party competition in 2017, the dominant position of the BharatiyaJanata Party was established and further expanded. Since the BharatiyaJanata Party won the presidential and vice presidential elections in the parliamentary federal elections, the impact of the Party's political rise has directly removed the dominant right of the Congress Party lasted for 65-year in the Federal Court. Thus, the key seats, such as Prime Minister, the President, Vice President, Chief Ministers of the major states are all occupied by the BharatiyaJanata Party, which never happened during the administration of the Congress Party and is also the first time in Indian history. Up to now, the centralization trend of the BharatiyaJanata Party is very clear; BharatiyaJanata Party has taken over the traditional sphere influenced by the Congress Party in two local state elections respectively held in March and December 2017 and seized Uttar Pradesh known as the "parliamentary ticket bunker" with a population of up to 200 million. It can be seen that the effective control of BharatiyaJanata Party has further broken through the "Heart of the Hinduism" and basically covers the whole country. Recently, the Modi government has also begun to make a show of power for the 2019 general election. He proposed the grand goal of bringing 200 million people in India out of poverty and building a "new India" by 2022.

In terms of the foreign relations, in 2017, while isolating Pakistan, India focused on promoting diplomatic interaction and interconnectivy with small countries in South Asian. While continuing to be indifferent to the Belt and Road Initiative of China, it further deepened the strategic relations and security cooperation with the US and Japan; in order to shape great power status and international influence, it participated more actively in international organizations and regional mechanisms, and organized a number of related forums and international conferences. In 2017, India successfully joined the Shanghai Cooperation Organization, which could possibly enhance India's cooperation with Central Asian countries; it successfully obtained the Phase

[62]Goldman Sachs, 2018 global economic outlook As Good As It Gets, November 15, 2017, p. 5. http://www.goldmansachs.com/our-thinking/pages/macroeconomic-insights-folder/2018-globaleconomic-outlook-as-good-as-it-gets/report.pdf.

1 management of the Chabahar Port of Iran and opened up the strategic channel into Central Asia. For India, the geostrategic significance of managing the Chabahar Port is very important, which is a strategic hedging or monitoring of the China-Pakistan Economic Corridor and Pakistani maritime forces. In addition, in response to Pakistan's security threats, India expects to improve relations and expand cooperation with Afghanistan. In November 2017, Modi invited the Afghan President to visit India, and they signed cooperation documents on building air cargo corridors and strengthening the training of police officers.[63] During the first India-ASEAN Interconnectivity Summit held in India in December 2017, the Foreign Minister Singh said in his speech that India was committed to working with other countries in ASEAN and the Indo-Pacific region to enhance the Interconnectivity between India and ASEAN countries.

For India, the increasingly close strategic relations with the US and its allies can be seen as a huge diplomatic achievement in 2017 and a strategic resource for standing in the international arena. On August 21, 2017, Trump highlighted the important role of India in stabilizing the situation in Afghanistan in his speech about South Asia policy, and indicated that strengthening strategic partnership with India was a vital part of the New South Asia policy. On December 18, 2017, Trump released the first US *National Security Strategy Report* during his term of office. According to the Report, the US expected India to become a new partner and a stronger security force and would support India to further influence the region and strengthen the cooperation with India, Japan and Australia. In the new *Defense Strategy Report* on January 19, 2018, the Ministry of National Defense clearly stated that the US should strengthen its alliance and attract new partners, emphasizing the need to optimize the network construction and security cooperation with strategic partnership in the "Indo-Pacific" region. "It's a priority to have a long-lasting alliance and long-term security partnership strengthened by the alliance security network and supported by the basic alliance",[64] which fully reflects the shift of the US geostrategic focus to the East and the basic strategic thinking of operating "Indo-Pacific" strategy. The reason that Trump launched the "Indo-Pacific Strategy" is to integrate the Indian Ocean and the Pacific region from a geostrategic perspective, deepen the strategic security relations with important countries in the region, and emphasize that the relations between the US and India is one of the most important strategic relations in the 21st century, highlighting that India is a supporting point on one side of the Indian Ocean to constitute the "Indo-Pacific strategy". The South Asia strategy newly launched by the US also emphasized the special role of India.

In general, the US supports India to become a "security provider", and vigorously develops defense cooperation with India, docking with the development strategy and diplomatic layout of India. Meanwhile, Japan increases investment and project cooperation with India. And Australia also actively interacts with India. They all con-

[63]Zhong (2018).

[64]U.S. Department of Defense, "National Defense Strategy", p. 1. https://www.defense.gov/Portals/1/Documents/pubs/2018-National-Defense-Strategy-Summary.pdf.

tributed to the expansion of regional power advantages of India in capital, technology, market, military capabilities and security cooperation.

(2) The political ecology and security situation in Pakistan tend to beserious.

In 2017, although Pakistan remained a good momentum in domestic economy, it faced the trend of severe international and security situations. Then it stepped up its implementation of the "2025 Vision" plan, gradually rolling out the domestic infrastructure construction; the national economic growth showed good performance due to the transformation and upgrading of the national power grid and the substantial progress in the construction of key projects such as power stations and highways. From the economic index, the GDP growth rate of Pakistan reached 5.28% in the FY2016/2017, hitting a record high in the past decade. However, judging from the domestic political situation, Pakistan fluctuated greatly in 2017, as Prime Minister Sharif was forced to step down because of concealing overseas assets. The difficulties and challenges faced by Sharif's Muslim League in the administration are increasing. The domestic political transformation is struggling in Pakistan, due to not only the political and economic turmoil brought about by domestic political parties and warlord games, but also the anti-terrorism situation. From the perspective of the domestic security situation, terrorist activities are still raging in Pakistan in 2017. Many places, such as Lahore, Sekhwan have repeatedly suffered major terrorist attacks. At the end of the year, a large-scale protest march was held in religious parties in Pakistan. All of these have reflected the resurgence of extremism, and current state of violent culture in Pakistan in 2017, which also revealed that the domestic security situation had not yet substantially improved.

In terms of the foreign relations, Pakistan faces severe strategic situation due to the adjustment of the US to strategy on South Asia. On August 21, 2017, Trump delivered a speech on South Asia policy. On the one hand, he announced that the US could not rush to withdraw troops from Afghanistan, but should increase the number of troops stationed in Afghanistan to prevent the situation in Afghanistan from getting out of control and terrorism staging a comeback. On the other hand, Trump particularly emphasized the important role of India in stabilizing the situation in Afghanistan, pointing out that strengthening strategic partnership with India is a vital part of new South Asia policy made by the US. What is even more remarkable was that Trump fully criticized Pakistan in his speech about South Asia policy at the US Fort Myers military base. He claimed that Pakistan has provided shelter to "chaos, violence and terrorist forces" and has become a land of terrorism such as the Taliban. He even declared that Pakistan posed a threat to Afghanistan and regional stability, and should be directly responsible for the deterioration of current situation and regional security in Afghanistan[65]; He demanded Pakistan to "stop asylum" for extremist armed groups, and expressed to use drones to expand the attacks on terrorist organizations in Pakistan. He also proposed to change the policy of US to Pakistan, such as suspending large sums of aid to Pakistan and lowering expectations for Pakistan as an anti-terrorist ally, on the grounds that Pakistan has "deception" and

---

[65]Zhang (2017).

"perfunctory" on the US in the fight against terrorism. Shortly after Trump's speech, the US Congress approved the suspension of the anti-terrorist military assistance originally provided to Pakistan.

(3) Sri Lanka has become the target of great powers with rising strategic position.

Known as the pearl of the Indian Ocean, Sri Lanka has a coastline of 1200 kilometers. It is located on the maritime traffic route connecting Africa, Europe, the Middle East and the western Pacific, northwest facing India across the Pak Strait, and 10 nautical miles south to the gateway to the Indian Ocean. It's an important partner in China's initiative to build the 21st Century Maritime Silk Road; however, in recent years, not only has the US strengthened its relations with the Sri Lanka, but Japan and India have also joined forces to promote infrastructure construction and related security cooperation in Sri Lanka. Australia also continuously enhanced its cooperation with Sri Lanka and expanded their economic ties in the past two years. It's not by fits and snatches that the US, India, Japan, Australia and other countries all coincidentally intensified their strategic attention to Sri Lanka and sought to carry out relevant project cooperation with Sri Lanka, but for deep strategic considerations. The construction of "Indo-Pacific" has obviously enhanced the strategic position of Sri Lanka, and the competition among great powers for Sri Lanka will be more complicated and fierce.

Judging from the relations between the US and Sri Lanka, it has continuously been improved by the active promotion of the US. In January 2015, after the new government of Sri Lankan came to power, the two countries changed its previous "frozen" relations. Then Kerry visited Sri Lanka in May 2015, which was the first visit of the US Secretary of State to Sri Lanka for 43 years; In February 2016, the US established a partnership dialogue mechanism with Sri Lanka; then the navies of the two countries held the first fathomless naval exercise in October 2017. The second partnership dialogue was held on November 6, 2017, during which the two countries expressed the wish to build a free and open Indo-Pacific region and promote the establishment of a rule-based order.[66]

Sri Lanka also keeps close relations with India and Japan. India is eager to promote relations with Sri Lanka, mainly because that the deepening economic cooperation and potential strategic relations between China and Sri Lanka may even bring military advantages and therefore attracted much attention of India.[67] In his visit to Sri Lanka in January this year, Japanese Foreign Minister Taro Kono publicly stated that Sri Lanka is the "core country" in the "free and open Indo-Pacific strategy" of Japan, showing his high attention to the geopolitical position of Sri Lanka. India has taken active diplomatic action to deal with the situation that the traditional influence of India on Sri Lanka is being strongly impacted by China. After Sirisena was elected as the President of Sri Lanka in January 2015, Modi visited Sri Lanka in March, rewriting the history that the Indian Prime Minister never visited Sri Lanka in the past 20 years. Modi claimed to leave a "golden chapter" in the history of relations

[66]Lin (2018).

[67]Zhou (2017).

between India and Sri Lanka[68]; and in order to make up for its disadvantages in terms of capital and technology compared with China, India showed a strategic attitude of welcoming and seeking cooperation toward Japan's economic diplomacy in Sri Lanka. For example, on March 8, 2018, India, Japan and Sri Lanka signed a tripartite memorandum (MOU), agreeing to establish a joint venture to build integrated facility of LNG import, storage and power generation near Colombo. In this joint venture, the Petronet LNG of India accounted for 47.5% of the shares, the Mitsubishi Corporation and Shuangri Club of Japan accounted for 37.5%, the Sri Lanka government accounted for 15%. This is the first LNG power generation project in Sri Lanka and is expected to be completed in 2021.

The current government of Sri Lanka is currently faced with a series of economic problems such as increased debt pressure, serious trade deficit and rapid price increase, so that foreign investment is urgently needed to stimulate economic growth; accordingly, when great powers offer olive branches, the current government implements its balanced diplomacy to achieve success. In April 2017, the Prime Minister of Sri Lankan VikramMahinha started another visit to India on the 10th after the visit Japan to discuss issues such as investment and infrastructure cooperation. On March 10–16, 2018, the President Sirisena visited India and Japan successively and was cordially received by Modi and Shinzo Abe. It can be seen that Sri Lanka has not only framed its partners as China. It also shows an undisputed fact that Japan and India have tried to expand their influence in Sri Lanka in the past two years. In recent years, the cooperation of Japan and India in Sri Lanka has mainly focused on infrastructure cooperation and marine security. The fastest growing in infrastructure cooperation is the liquefied natural gas (LNG) power generation project in Colombo. Apart from the project, Japan and India also plan to strengthen cooperation in the development of the TingkomariPort and the new container terminal in Colombo Port. In terms of maritime security, their cooperation is mainly embodied in strengthening the naval links among the three countries, inviting Sri Lanka to participate in the Japanese-Indian sea training and exercises, and tying the naval officers of the three countries up closely through training.

3. **The construction of "Indo-Pacific" has deepened the crack of international relations in South Asia**.

Judging from the international relations in South Asia, the construction of "Indo-Pacific" directly shapes the international relations between the outside powers and the South Asian countries, and indirectly affects the internal international relations among South Asian countries, leading to major changes in the regional strategic situation in turn. Under the construction of "Indo-Pacific", it may be arbitrary to say that the strategic pattern for South Asia, the US and India working together to tackling the cooperation between China and Pakistan is a foregone conclusion. However, in 2017, it's unquestionable to show the polarization that the US cooperated with India

[68]*China's Access to Sri Lanka's Port Management Rights Will Curb the US and India? Expert: Think too much*, Refer to News Network, August 16, 2017, http://www.cankaoxiaoxi.com/world/20170816/2220851.shtml.

to cope with the ally of China and Pakistan under the basic pattern of India-Pakistan opposition in the international relations pattern of South Asia.

(1) The basic pattern of India-Pakistan opposition.

First of all, from the perspective of relations within South Asia, India-Pakistan relations remain tense in 2017, with frequent frictions happening in Kashmir. It's normal for the Modi government to be tough to Pakistan. The Kashmir issue has always been the crux of the two countries. Since July, 2017, they have frequently fought in the real control line of Kashmir. According to statistics, the number of fights between India and Pakistan has exceeded 105 times from July 2017 to November 2017 and 12,000 times since 2002, resulting in the death of about 144 people.[69] As early as in 2003, in order to avoid more bloody conflicts, the two countries had signed a ceasefire agreement in the real control line of Kashmir. However, the ceasefire agreement was repeatedly broken and gradually lost its binding force on both sides. Up to now, the sovereignty disputes and ethnic conflicts between the two countries in Kashmir have failed to find an effective solution. The frequent armed conflicts have made many efforts to improve India-Pakistan relations in vain. On July 8, 2017, the Indian and Pakistani troops had a fierce fighting in the Kashmir region. Both sides accused each other of firing and causing casualties. On the evening of July 21, they fought again near the actual control line. On the morning of October 2, the two armies violently fired near Heverly County; on October 3, the border security forces of India were attacked by suicide bombings; on October 14, two Pakistani children died and three children injured in the fighting; on November 2, a 25-year-old Indian border guard soldier died in a fight in the Samba area.

The continuous conflicts in the Kashmir region have strained relations between the two countries and have also closed some possible dialogue. As a sign of continued tension in relations between the two countries, India did not attend the Asian Multilateral Maritime Security Conference in 2017–a conference held in Pakistan on October 24–25. The Asian Multilateral Maritime Security Conference, as one of the few very important international conferences held in Pakistan in 2017, could have provided a dialogue platform for easing India-Pakistan relations and reducing maritime risks, but India was still absent from this meeting. Considering that India is the largest country along the Indian Ocean, the security situation in the Indian Ocean is closely related to India. India refused to participate in the meeting held in Pakistan, reflecting the deep-rooted rigidity in India-Pakistan relations and the isolated policy of India toward Pakistan.

For a long time, the foreign policy of India toward Pakistan has been trying to label Pakistan as a "terrorist supporter" and isolating Pakistan in the international community. There is precedent that India boycotts an international conference in Pakistan. In 2016, India led some countries like Bangladesh, Bhutan, and Afghanistan to refuse to participate in the 19th South Asian Association for Regional Cooperation (SAARC) summit in Pakistan, resulting in the failure of the summit. The above cases

[69] *The 105th in the year! India and Pakistan Kashmir fight again, with 1 Indian soldier died*, overseas network, Nov. 2, 2017, http://news.haiwainet.cn/n/2017/1102/c3541093-31166860.html.

reflect the complexity and some internal changes in relations among South Asian countries, and the general trend is that Pakistan will be further weakened and easier to suffer collective isolation in South Asia with the further expansion of India's regional advantages. Beyond that, Pakistan is also facing a pressure from the US and a strategic abandonment.

(2) The polarization between the US-India and the Sino-Pakistan.

As for the external relations of the South Asia, great powers have obvious impacts on South Asia. The US and China are key external variables that promote the pattern change in South Asia; from the diplomatic interaction between the great powers and South Asia in 2017, there are two opposites situations. On the one hand, US-India relations continued to heat up, while US-Pakistan relations hit bottom; on the other hand, China-Pakistan relations strengthened steadily, while Sino-India relations fell rapidly.

In 2017, the adjustment of the US South Asia policy undoubtedly led to the most significant change in the pattern of South Asia. Trump has changed the previous balanced diplomatic route to India and Pakistan, tending to "supporting India but abandoning Pakistan". At present, with the deepening defense cooperation between the US and India, this situation is likely to further increase the security anxiety of Pakistan. In the future, a new round of arms race between Pakistan and India may be further upgraded. On August 22, 2017, the US Huffington Post website published *Trump Marks out the Geopolitical Front in South Asia* written by James Dorsey, a senior researcher at the Rajaratnam School of International Studies in Singapore. The article said that the front marked out by Trump in South Asia has intensified its efforts against the Taliban in Afghanistan. Trump also adopted a tougher attitude toward Pakistan, and has cooperated more closely with India, which is likely to have a chain reaction in Eurasia. The most direct result of this chain reaction is to bring about a further reverse change in the relations between the US and India and the US-Pakistan relations. The US's adjustment for South Asia policy is bound to affect the geopolitical pattern of South Asia, and will further highlight the dominant position of India in the South Asian region, while Pakistan will face more severe strategic situation.

To a large extent, the construction of "Indo-Pacific" has given India a favorable international environment and dominant position, which did not positively contributed to the security issues and regional cooperation in South Asia; on the contrary, these factors contributed to the regional expansionism, adventurism and tough attitude to China in India, and further increased the strategic dilemma of Pakistan as well as the risk of arms race, regional rift and security dilemma in South Asia. In terms of the security situation in South Asia, the Afghan issue, the conflict between India and Pakistan, and the terrorist activities in the region are the three major observation indicators of the regional security situation. However, in 2017, any indicator of the three revealed that the security issue of South Asia has not improved. The US's adjustment for South Asia policy in 2017 will further deepen mutual hatred between India and Pakistan and expand the rift between the two countries.

In fact, Pakistan's current judgment on US's adjustment for its policy on South Asia is that the US has begun to make India a regional police force to weaken Pakistan's regional role, regarding India as an anti-terrorist ally, but Pakistan as a stumbling block to counter-terrorism; Washington supports India's participation in the Nuclear Suppliers Group (NSG), but regards Pakistan as one of the threats of nuclear proliferation. Meanwhile, Pakistan believes that India has been trying to weaken its strength. And the deep cooperation between India and Afghanistan will impair strategic interests of Pakistan in Afghanistan; the port cooperation between India and Iran poses a threat and challenge to the security and economic benefits of Gwadar Port.

Moreover, China has increasingly become an important factor affecting the geopolitical economy of South Asia. But the geopolitical contradictions between India and Pakistan are deeply rooted, which become the biggest problem for China's geopolitical operation in South Asia.

In 2017, US-Pakistan relations hit bottom, but China-Pakistan relations continued to be strengthened, with the China-Pakistan Economic Corridor entering a further advanced stage. In the past year, China-Pakistan Economic Corridor has progressed in an orderly manner, making breakthroughs in the construction of Gwadar Port, energy and transportation infrastructure, and the coal-fired power stations in Sahiwal and Kassim Port have been put into operation. China has also negotiated with Pakistan on the upgraded free trade zone, but the process has been frustrated due to different opinions. On the whole, the investment and economic support from China will contribute to the economic development and people's livelihood in Pakistan, as well as the domestic political stability; the security cooperation and military technology exchanges between China and Pakistan will also help to strengthen Pakistan's defense forces and ease the strategic dilemma. China-Pakistan relations are as solid as ever, and China has become the indispensable strategic support factor for Pakistan in the "Indo-Pacific" region.

Bilateral relations are essentially related to the specific process and objective results of the interaction between two countries, as well as their subjective perceptions. China-India relations are no exception. In 2017, US-India relations continued to heat up, while Sino-India relations fell significantly, even hitting bottom after the Docklam Confrontation. For the current Sino-India relations, China needs to think more, especially from the perspective of India rather than China. It's a great goal of contemporary China to achieve the rise of a great power and national rejuvenation, so does India. It needs a stable and prosperous environment in "Indo-Pacific" to gain development opportunities and realize the rise of the country. Therefore, India's foreign strategy is aimed at providing a stable and prosperous external environment for the development of India with various diplomatic efforts. Then the key factor of the question is: Does India think that it is more conducive to its rise to take the initiative to adapt to the "Indo-Pacific" regional order led by the US and cooperate with the US to contain China, or to help China share the rising pressure and jointly fight against US hegemony?

As for the current stage, it is clear that India believes that "Indo-Pacific" regional order led by the US and cooperation with the US to constrain the influence of China are more conducive to its rise. Then India will not help China share the rising pressure and challenge US global hegemony. To a large extent, it is the rise of China that has enabled the US and India to find a strategic point that is more important than ever.

India needs a stable and prosperous environment in "Indo-Pacific", which is not dominated by China; India believes that a strong China around it will most likely restrict India's development opportunities and rising momentum directly. India needs to strengthen its defense strength and improve its technical equipment, but the military procurement and technology sources cannot and should not be obtained from China, and the military technology also cannot be jointly developed with China. India also attaches importance to its close relations with the Asia-Pacific economy and has its own Interconnectivity plans within and outside the region. However, these plans include too many considerations to prevent or hedge the spread of China's influence, but not seeking strategic docking with China. India needs anti-terrorism, but it believes that Pakistan is an ally of China, and China favors Pakistan on the issue of terrorism related to Pakistan (India believes that Pakistan has implicit support for terrorists within the country).

In short, because India judges that the Indo-Pacific regional order led by the US is more conducive to its national interests and the rise as a great power. Meanwhile, India and China have deep strategic mutual doubts. Then in terms of strategic preferences, India certainly seeks for strategic speculation to the US in an active way, but guard against China, roughly choosing the route of the "befriending the far and attacking the near". Before then, the main partner of Indian military procurement and technology has always been Russia; but now it seems that the US has replaced Russia as the first arms sales and technology source; furthermore, India has shown a wavering attitude toward its "non-alignment policy", which, in fact, as a foreign policy, is not absolutely static, but always subject to national interests.

In any case, the hidden trend of the strategic pattern in South Asia has been brought by the decline of Sino-India relations, the development of China-Pakistan relations, the rise of US-India relations and the decline of US-Pakistan relations, that is, the polarization of US-India side and the Sino-Pakistan side on the basis of the India-Pakistan opposition. As mentioned above, the construction of "Indo-Pacific" is the concept shaping and game arrangement in this region with the US, Japan, Australia and India regarding China as a competitor; and the South Asia strategic situation can be regarded as a miniature version of it. The US New South Asia strategy of the Trump era, which gradually surfaced recently, may further tear South Asia artificially from the security strategy, while the fact that Modi administration has adopted increasingly tough South Asia policy is likely to further contribute to the international isolation of South Asian countries to Pakistan, and may also further exclude and hinder China's efforts to promote economic integration and regional stability in South Asia.

4 Conclusion

Discussion on the significant influence of the construction of "Indo-Pacific" on the situation and strategic pattern in South Asia will help deepen the understanding of the regional effects about this concept. With regard to the influence on the South Asia pattern, construction of "Indo-Pacific" has enhanced the strategic position of South Asia in geography and geopolitical relations, but deepened the asymmetry of power structure in South Asia; it has strengthened the strategic role of India, but increased the regional crack in South Asia; it has greatly enhanced the strategic importance of Sri Lanka and Maldives in the Indian Ocean, but almost completely ignored the inland areas of Bhutan, Nepal and Bangladesh; it has not only made the strategic situation of different South Asian countries change differently, which has increased the crack between the countries in the region and has also restricted the development of regional cooperation and regionalism in South Asia.

For China, "Indo-Pacific" is actually a concept for large periphery. In this region, China borders 14 countries on land and faces six countries across the sea; 6 (India, Indonesia, Russia, Japan, Pakistan, Bangladesh)of 10 countries with the largest population in the world around China; 8 of the top 25 countries with strongest military power in the world; 4 of the 8 countries with nuclear weapons (India, Pakistan, North Korea, Russia); 4 of the world top 5 potential hotspot conflict areas (Persian Gulf, Central Asia, South Asian subcontinent, Taiwan Strait, Korean Peninsula); the world major strategic forces, except the EU, the US, Russia, Japan and India are all around China.[70] Therefore, the international strategic planning of China also needs to be quickly switched and adapt to the "Indo-Pacific" vision. As for the current research on the concept of "Indo-Pacific", or the research requirements of researchers, the study of US-India relations, Sino-India relations, US-Sino relations, or the relations among China, the US and India must also be investigated in the strategic space of Indo-Pacific, especially in mutual cognition and strategic preferences, and the interaction process and results.

Currently, peripheral diplomacy has been elevated to a new height in China's overall diplomacy. Under the booming situation of the "Indo-Pacific" concept, the peripheral relations and even global partnerships of China have both the possibility of degradation and opportunities for improvement, the key of which is how to operate the geopolitics and geo-economics of China. According to this paper, economic diplomacy is an important means of bridging partnerships. However, supply security products and development of defense cooperation are indispensable for optimizing partnerships, which is an urgent need for breakthroughs in the China's layout for "Indo-Pacific".

[70] Cao (2015).

References

Cao, Yibing. 2015. Research on Geographical Visual Analysis Technology of Land Borders. Ph.D Thesis of PLA Information Engineering University, p. 8.

Chen, Jimin. 2017. The "Indo-Pacific" Strategy of the Trump Administration is Still Unclear. *China Defense News*, December 22.

Chen, Jimin. 2018. Trump Administration "Indo-Pacific Strategy": Policies and Limits. *Peace and Development* (1): 26–42.

Dai, Yonghong, and Yonghong, Qin. 2010. The Geopolitical Strategic Considerations in Energy Cooperation between China and South Asia. *Journal of Sichuan University* (Philosophy and Social Sciences) (2): 79.

Feng, Chuanlu. 2017. A Survey of Geopolitical Patterns and Regional Situations in South Asia from the Perspective of the Belt and Road Initiative. *South Asian Studies* (3): 3, 4.

Kronstadt, KA, and SI Akhtar. 2017. "India-U.S. Relations: Issues for Congress". Congressional Research Service Report, 19 June 2017, 15. http://www.hsdl.org/?abstract&did=801952.

Li, Yiqing. 2017. To Fight Against The Belt and Road, ASEAN-India Communication Summit Held and Japan Invited. The paper. cn, 11 December 2017. http://www.thepaper.cn/newsDetail_forward_1900313.

Li, Li. 2018. India's "Act East" Strategy and Indian Diplomacy. *Modern International Relations* (1): 37–45.

Lin, Minwang. 2017. India–Japan Relations Entering the "Honeymoon Period"? *Contemporary World* (10): 27.

Lin, Minwang. 2018. The Construction of "Indo-Pacific" and the Tension of Asian Geopolitics. *Diplomatic Review* (1): 16–35, 28.

Liu, Zongyi. 2014. Conflict or Cooperation?—Geopolitical and Geoeconomic Choices in the "Indo-Pacific" Region". *Indian Ocean Economies* (4).

Mei, Xiuting. 2017. "Indo-Pacific Strategy": The Essence of Abe's new Diplomatic Strategy. *Learning Times*, 20 February 2017.

Mu, Xiaoming. 2016. India–Vietnam Defense Cooperation Continues to Heat up but Has Limited Impact on Regional Patter. *China Youth Daily*, 1 October 2016.

Wang, Daozheng. 2017. The Construction and Prospects of the Asia–Africa Growth Corridor by India and Japan. *Research on the Indian Ocean Economies* (5): 125.

Wei, Zongyou. 2013. The Strategic Adjustment of the US in the Indo-Pacific Region and Its Geostrategic Impact. *World Economics and Politics* (10): 141.

Wu, Zhaoli. 2014. The Origin of "Indo-Pacific" and Multinational Strategic Game. *Journal of the Pacific* (1).

Wu, Zhaoli. 2016. India's "Toward East" and Vietnam "Toward West": The Driving Force behind Strategic Interactions. *World Knowledge* (3): 34.

Wu, Minwen. 2017. Trump's Indo-Pacific Strategy Intended to Prevent China. *China Youth Daily*, 22 December 2017.

Wu, Huaizhong. 2018a. Abe Government's Indo-Pacific Strategy and China's Response. *Modern International Relations* (1): 13–21.

Wu, Huaizhong. 2018b. The Indo-Pacific Strategy of Abe Government and China's response. *Modern International Relations* (1).

Wu, Zhaoli. 2018c. Development, Limitations and China's Response to the Indo-Pacific Strategy. *Journal of Xinjiang Normal University (Philosophy and Social Sciences)* 39: 1–9.

Xia, Liping, and Zhong Qi. 2018. Analysis of "Indian Strategic Concept" Under the Trump Administration. *Modern International Relations* (1): 22–28.

Yang, Rui, and Shida Wang. 2018. India and "Indo-Pacific Strategic Conception": Positioning, Intervention and Limitations. *Modern International Relations* (1): 46–52.

Zhang, Li. 2013. The Impact of the "Indo-Pacific" Concept on the Multilateral Pattern of the Asia-Pacific Region. *South Asian Research Quarterly* (4).

Zhang, Li. 2017. Tillerson's Trip to India and Pakistan: Accurate Delivery of the Policy of the US to South Asia. *World Knowledge* (22): 80.

Zhang, Hualong. 2018. Vietnamese President Chen Daguang Visited India, the India–Vietnam Defense Cooperation has been the Focus under the "Indo-Pacific" strategy. *Wen Wei Po*, 2 March 2018.

Zhao, Qinghai. 2013a. The Concept of "Indo-Pacific" and Its Implications for China. *Modern International Relations* (7): 14.

Zhao, Qinghai. 2013b. The Concept of "Indo-Taiwan" and Its Implications for China. *Modern International Relations* (7).

Zhao, Gancheng. 2016. China's Challenges and Responses in the Surroundings of South Asia. *International Relations Research* (1): 36.

Zhong, Lin. 2018. Accelerated Evolution of the Order in Area with Strong Economic Growth—A Summary of the Situation in South Asia. *Contemporary World* (2): 59.

Zhou, Liangchen. 2017. Modi's Visit to Sri Lanka to Consolidate India's influence for Not Tending to China. *Global Times*, 12 May 2017.

Zhou, Fangyin, and Wan, Wang. 2018. Indian Strategy from the Perspective of Australia and China's Response. *Modern International Relatio*ns (1): 29–36.

Zhu, Cuiping. 2015. The Dilemma and Strategic Choice of the Indian Modi Government's Policy to China. *South Asian Studies* (3): 12.

MIX
Papier aus verantwortungsvollen Quellen
Paper from responsible sources
FSC® C105338

If you have any concerns about our products,
you can contact us on
ProductSafety@springernature.com

In case Publisher is established outside the EU,
the EU authorized representative is:
Springer Nature Customer Service Center GmbH
Europaplatz 3, 69115 Heidelberg, Germany

Printed by Libri Plureos GmbH
in Hamburg, Germany